The Children's and Young Adult Literature Handbook

Recent Titles in the
Children's and Young Adult Literature Reference Series
Catherine Barr, Series Editor

Best Books for Middle School and Junior High Readers, Grades 6-9
John T. Gillespie and Catherine Barr

Best Books for High School Readers, Grades 9-12
John T. Gillespie and Catherine Barr

Popular Series Fiction for K-6 Readers: A Reading and Selection Guide
Rebecca L. Thomas and Catherine Barr

Popular Series Fiction for Middle School and Teen Readers: A Reading and Selection
Guide
Rebecca L. Thomas and Catherine Barr

Fantasy Literature for Children and Young Adults: A Comprehensive Guide, Fifth Edition
Ruth Nadelman Lynn

The Children's and Young Adult Literature Handbook

A Research and Reference Guide

John T. Gillespie

Children's and Young Adult Literature Reference Series
Catherine Barr, Series Editor

LIBRARIES
UNLIMITED
A Member of the Greenwood Publishing Group

Westport, Connecticut • London

British Library Cataloguing in Publication Data is available.

Library of Congress Control Number: 2005927740
ISBN: 1-56308-949-1

First published in 2005

Libraries Unlimited, 88 Post Road West, Westport, CT 06881
A Member of the Greenwood Publishing Group, Inc.
www.lu.com

Printed in the United States of America

The paper used in this book complies with the
Permanent Paper Standard issued by the National
Information Standards Organization (Z39.48-1984).

10   9   8   7   6   5   4   3   2   1

CONTENTS

◆

Note: A detailed analysis is provided at the beginning of each chapter.

PREFACE

When the editors at Libraries Unlimited asked if I would be interested in revising the esteemed work by Margaret W. Denman-West titled *Children's Literature: A Guide to Information Sources* (1998), I readily accepted. However, when I began planning for the revision, my thoughts about the new work gradually evolved into a radically different book than first imagined. The result is this handbook, which is much broader in scope and coverage than the original guide. Not only does it include coverage of other English-speaking countries, but it also explores many subjects and areas untouched in the Denman-West volume.

The book is intended as a selection guide and collection development aid for libraries, and as a navigation tool for researchers and children's literature scholars. It will also be a useful reference for educators seeking particular types of information about children's literature or authors and illustrators. It describes and evaluates more than 1,000 publications covering the complete spectrum of information sources in the field—from general reference and bibliographies to review sources, awards, manuals, biographies, and professional organizations.

It has taken a vast amount of time to compile this handbook. (It was almost two years in the writing, during which I did take time off for other projects, such as working on a new set of Best Books bibliographies.) The research was fascinating and involved many sources. Whenever possible, the items listed were examined firsthand; when this was not possible, I used reliable secondary sources. In addition to conducting innumerable searches on the Internet, I spent weeks in libraries around the globe. The principal library collections examined and used in the United States were the New York Public Library (often the Central Children's Room at the Donnell Library) and the library at C. W. Post College of Long Island University. In Canada, the Vancouver Public Library and the library at the University of British Columbia were very helpful, and in London, England, I used the collections at the Book Trust, at the University of Roehampton, and at the British Library. I also visited many of the historic collections discussed in Chapter 10, and other libraries, public and academic, were also tapped.

The book is organized into 11 chapters. In the first chapter, American general guides and reference sources are listed and annotated, followed by general reference sources that deal with other English-speaking countries, a lengthy list of important monographs and critical studies, and a bibliography of salient periodicals in the field, again broken down by country. Chapter 2 deals with retrospective bibliographies. General bibliographies from various countries are followed by more specialized ones originating in the United States. Here there are subdivisions by age group, by specific audience (for example, gifted readers and the physically disabled) and by genre and format (historical fiction, pop-up books, and so forth). Chapter 3 covers current American sources including book reviewing periodicals, annuals, and children's magazines. Bibliographies on curriculum-related subjects such as science, mathematics, and social studies are found in Chapter 4, and Chapter 5 lists and annotates bibliographies relating to multicultural topics, with separate sections on different ethnic groups. Chapter 6 deals with literary awards and prizes, giving material on individual prizes, followed by a directory of international and national awards and a lengthy section on regional American awards. The focus shifts in Chapter 7 to the patron. This chapter covers the promotion, use, and enjoyment of books and other media, looking at such areas as booktalking, program planning, and storytelling, along with guides to writing and publishing children's books. Chapter 8 discusses aids to finding biographical information about authors and illustrators, and Chapter 9 is a directory of important professional organizations, agencies, publishers, and booksellers. Chapter 10 describes outstanding historical collections of children's books both in this country and internationally. Internet resources are integrated whenever possible throughout this work, but the last chapter gives a rundown of the most important Internet sites and other non-print resources including audiobooks. The contents page offers general organizational guidance; further detail is provided at the beginning of each chapter.

There are three indexes. The Name Index covers authors, awards and prizes, library collections, organizations and other agencies, publishers, and book dealers. The Title Index provides access to titles of books, annuals, periodicals, and Web sites. Lastly, there is a Subject Index.

To amass and organize this vast amount of material, I have had many, usually willing, helpers. First there are the many librarians at the institutions where I worked who gave so generously of their time and knowledge. Also, Henry Rasof, who initiated this project; my dear friend and antiquarian book collector Doug Bower; the knowledgeable Edgardo Zaghini from the Book Trust in London; Judith Saltman, library school professor at the University of British Columbia; and Barbara Ittner, Libraries Unlimited acquisitions editor, who was the soul of patience. Most of all, I wish to thank and recognize my editor (and collaborator in many other projects), Catherine Barr. I can truthfully say that without her help this book would never have been completed. Thank you all. I hope our combined efforts will prove to be of value.

—John T. Gillespie

The Children's and Young Adult Literature Handbook

CHAPTER 1

GENERAL BACKGROUND SOURCES AND HISTORIES

A. BOOKS

1. American and General Reference Sources

1   Allen, Marjorie N. *100 Years of Children's Books in America, Decade by Decade.* Facts on File. 1996, $38.50 (0-8160-3044-8).

This is a chronological survey, arranged by decade, of the best and most important children's books published in the United States from the 1890s through 1995. As well as annotated bibliographies, there are profiles of such authors and illustrators as Dr. Seuss, Maurice Sendak, Beverly Cleary, and Cynthia Voigt. Coverage includes books written for preschoolers through young adults. Appendixes on important collections of juvenile books and on award-winning titles are followed by a list of books mentioned, arranged by age level, and author and title indexes.

2   Ang, Susan. *The Widening World of Children's Literature.* St. Martin's, 2000, $59.95 (0-3122-2668-3).

This history traces the changing shape of children's literature from the 18th through the 20th centuries. The author notes the evolution from didactic origins, through the more-liberated Romantic views of childhood, to the freedom of content now seen in contemporary works. She maintains that the development of children's literature has been essentially a struggle between enclosure and exposure, control and freedom, restriction and openness. There are examples from many important writers (chiefly British), such as Lewis Carroll, Louisa M. Alcott, and Rudyard Kipling. Her comments on bibliotherapy and on the current bleakness in young adult literature are especially interesting.

3   Arnold, Arnold, ed. *Pictures and Stories from Forgotten Children's Books.* Dover, 1969, pap., $11.95, o.p.

From his vast collection of antique children's books, the editor has chosen about 500 illustrations from 75 books published from 1750 to 1850. The works are arranged into groups that cover the manners, literary style, and graphic fashions of the time. Chapters cover morals and manners, nursery rhymes, street cries, fairy tales, humor and riddles, plus books on sports, games, and pastimes. A lengthy introduction covers a general history of printing during this period. Part of the publisher's paperback Pictorial Archives series.

4   Avery, Gillian. *Behold the Child: American Children and Their Books, 1621–1922.* Johns Hopkins University, 1995, $43, o.p.

The renowned British children's author has written a useful and thoroughly engaging interpretive history of American children's literature from colonial times through the early 20th century. With a generous use of illustrations and a succinct text, this book supplies a basic historical survey complete with valid, always fascinating critical comments. Of particular interest is the last section, "Behold the Child," in which the author contrasts American themes with those of British children's books and highlights geographical and cultural differences. For example, she claims that American books emphasize energy, optimism, and self-fulfillment, whereas British literature explores class distinctions and creates realms of imaginary freedom.

5   Axel-Lute, Melanie. *Quotation Index to Children's Literature.* Libraries Unlimited, 2001, pap., $40 (1-56308-809-6).

This index identifies and locates quotations and phrases found in various important works of children's literature, including poetry, folktales and fairy tales, and award-winning books. About half of the book consists of quotations arranged alphabetically by author's last name, plus a short section that lists quotations from such traditional sources as fairy tales and the Arabian Nights. There follows a lengthy keyword index, an essential tool for locating a specific quotation by topic or subject. A title index and a general bibliography complete this volume.

6   Bader, Barbara. *Picture Books from Noah's Ark to the Beast Within.* Macmillan, 1976, o.p.

The purpose of this book, which traces the history of American picture books from the late 1800s through 1975, is to "identify all the picture books published, to examine as many as possible, and . . . to learn the circumstances of their publication." Full-color or black-and-white illustrations appear on nearly every page. This clearly written, comprehensive account also examines influences and practices relating to the development of this genre and assesses the importance of significant authors and illustrators. The biographical and bibliographical information is especially valuable to researchers of both individuals and specific books. An extensive subject bibliography is also included. This groundbreaking book is out of print but available through secondhand book sources.

7   Barrett, Frank. *Where Was Wonderland? A Traveller's Guide to the Settings of Classic Children's Books.* Hamlyn, 1997, £6.99 (0-600-59345-2).

This unique reference book highlights important authors, the settings of their books, and the inspiration behind each locale. Although the emphasis is on British children's literature, there is some coverage of foreign writers and the places they used in their works. In addition to including a plot outline and a biographical note about the author, this book explains the setting, suggests a tour, and supplies a map.

8   *Beacham's Guide to Literature for Young Adults.* Beacham/Gale (various editors, dates, prices, and ISBNs).

This multivolume set, begun in 1989, now numbers about 20 volumes and is priced between $90 and $120 per volume. Each volume contains about 200 analytic essays on fiction and biographical works written for young adults. Occasionally, books of short stories and general nonfiction works are also analyzed. A typical entry covers the author's life; the book's contents, setting, themes, and characters; and literary qualities; plus topics for discussion, ideas for reports, related titles, and a bibliography. This set is particularly well suited for young readers doing research projects on particular books.

9   Bingham, Jane, and Grayce Scholt. *Fifteen Centuries of Children's Literature: An Annotated Chronology of British and American Works in Historical Context.* Greenwood, 1980, $75 (0-313-22164-2).

The authors' stated purpose for this volume is "to provide a single annotated chronological listing of significant or representative books written for or used with or appropriated by British and American children from the 6th century to 1945." Divided into six time segments (for example, 1900–1945), the book supplies information on both historical and literary developments, provides details on contemporary social attitudes for each period, and gives data on the books judged by the authors to be of great importance. There is a bibliography of sources consulted, a chronology of children's periodicals, material on rare-book collections, and a list of facsimile and reprint editions. There are numerous indexes, including one listing printers and publishers (John Newbery, for example). This is a work of meticulous scholarship and painstaking research.

10   Blanck, Jacob. *Peter Parley to Penrod: A Bibliographical Description of the Best-Loved American Juvenile Books.* Bowker, 1956, o.p.

This is the latest reprint of the bibliographic classic originally published in 1938. With publication dates of the books included ranging from 1827 to 1926, this is a highly selective list of "books which have withstood the years of change in reading taste and are favorites still." More than 100 titles receive full treatment, including a title-page transcription, a thorough physical description, and details on publication. An additional 50 books receive less-detailed listings. The arrangement is chronological, and suitable indexes are provided.

11   Carpenter, Humphrey, and Mari Prichard. *Oxford Companion to Children's Literature.* Oxford, 1984, o.p.

Though now out of print and dated in its coverage, this single-volume work contains valuable background information on children's literature in the United Kingdom, the United States, Canada, Australia, and New Zealand. Coverage ends at May 1983. Almost half of the nearly 2,000 entries are short biographies of authors, illustrators, and others concerned with children's books. Other entries contain country and period surveys, plus material on genres, literary prizes, important books and characters, and major children's magazines. There are about 100 small, functional, black-and-white illustrations. This source is particularly strong on British children's literature. The articles are well written and the coverage is noteworthy.

12   Carruth, Gorton. *The Young Reader's Companion.* Bowker, 1993, o.p.

Now out of date, this single-volume literary encyclopedia still contains enough accurate historical information on literature for both children and young adults that it will continue to be useful for grades 5 through high school. There are about 2,000 entries dealing with books (800 entries), authors (750), historical persons (280), and mythological and legendary characters (200). Many adult books and adult authors suitable for young adults are discussed. Entries are about 200 words in length and the title entries contain summaries, bibliographic information, and an indication of reading and interest level. A unique aspect of this book is its subject index, which lists books covered under such topics as African Americans, Family Life, Fantasy, and Historical Fiction. There are a few black-and-white illustrations.

13   Cart, Michael. *From Romance to Realism: 50 Years of Growth and Change in Young Adult Literature.* HarperCollins, 1996, $24.95 (0-06-024289-2).

This volume is an informal discussion of young adult literature from its beginnings in the 1950s to the mid-1990s. The first half of the book deals, in a chatty fashion, with developments to 1990, with mention of important authors, their works, changing subjects and attitudes, and noteworthy resource studies and background articles. The second half discusses the 1990s from a topical point of view, with material on how current young adult writers handle such topics as social problems, family situations, sex, AIDS, and suicide. A final chapter, on why people read, focuses on ways that young adult literature can meet the needs of different readers. There are excellent appended bibliographies. This thoughtful, brief survey of the genre is both wise and entertaining.

14   Cart, Michael. *What's So Funny? Wit and Humor in American Children's Literature.* HarperCollins, 1995, $25 (0-06-024453-4).

After an overview of theories concerning the nature of humor as found in the writings of such authorities as Aristotle and Schopenhauer, the author examines humor in the works of a select number of prominent American writers of children's books. Most attention is paid to his favorites, such as Walter R. Brooks and Hugh Lofting, but other writers highlighted include Beverly Cleary, Arnold Lobel, Robert McCloskey, and Sid Fleischman. Many amusing examples are from their books, and personal reactions are cited in this delightful, thoughtful book that will both entertain and edify.

15   *The Children's Book Handbook, 2001.* Book Trust, 2001, o.p.

First published as *The Children's Book Handbook* in 1997, this one-volume paperback supplies a multitude of basic information about children's books and their publishers, principally in the United Kingdom. There are, for example, sections on organizations, clubs, publishers, dealers, book prizes, writing competitions, courses, best-selling children's books, and book fairs. The "International Section" includes material on international organizations, magazines and journals, book prizes, and key events in many countries, with an emphasis on the United States and Commonwealth countries. The preface describes the purpose and activities of the children's division of Book Trust, which is the U.K. equivalent of the Children's Book Council. Its services include an examination center of current children's books, a Beatrix Potter Study Room, and a number of publications. Address inquiries to Book Trust, 45 East Hill, London SW18 2QZ, England.

16   *Children's Literature Review: Excerpts from Reviews, Criticism, and Commentary on Books for Children.* Gale (various editors, dates, prices, and ISBNs).

This extensive and expensive set, begun in 1976, now numbers more than 100 volumes, with prices fixed at $185 per volume. The number of volumes published each year varies; in 2005 six volumes were added (volume 107 appeared at the end of the year). Each volume contains collective criticism of about a dozen authors and illustrators. A typical entry is in four parts: a list of major works by the subject; a critical introduction that comments on the historical, literary, and artistic merits of the person's output; a commentary by the author/illustrator on the nature and evolution of his or her works; and lengthy excerpts from significant reviews and articles about individual books. More than 600 authors and illustrators are now covered in this set. Each volume contains a cumulative author index and there is a title index published separately. Access to the first 90 volumes became easy in 2003 through the publication of *Children's Literature Review Cumulative Index* (Gale, 2003, $217.75 [0-7876-7134-7]). This is a scholarly but highly readable critical compendium of information on major contributors to the field of children's literature.

17   Chin, Beverly Ann. *The Dictionary of Characters in Children's Literature.* Grolier/Watts, 2002, $34 (0-531-11984-X).

The entries in this children's dictionary are arranged alphabetically by book title. After basic bibliographic information, there is a brief plot summary and a list of major characters, each with an accompanying sketch. The titles chosen for analysis are among the most popular read and taught in the upper elementary and middle school grades—*Black Beauty, The Wonderful Wizard of Oz, Wayside School Is Falling Down,* and *The Giver,* for example. Sidebars include material on similar works or other works by the author, data on the author, excerpts from the stories, and quotes from critics. There are indexes by author, title, and characters.

18   Cullinan, Bernice E., and Diane G. Person. *The Continuum Encyclopedia of Children's Literature.* Continuum, 2001, $150 (0-8264-1271-8).

Five years in the making, this amazing resource by two American scholars is currently the most complete, up-to-date, single-volume reference source on children's literature. It covers 150 years of children's literature in many English-speaking countries (there is excellent balance between British and American topics) plus salient subjects relating to continental Europe, Africa, and Asia. There are 1,200 biographical entries for authors and illustrators of both children's and young adult books. Each contains a biography, a succinct critical analysis, and a bibliography of books by and about the subject. There are also topical entries on such subjects as African literature, censorship, professional organizations, important collections, genres, awards, series, characters, presses, and important Web sites. The book is generously illustrated with black-and-white portraits of authors and color illustrations from outstanding picture books. Internal cross references using capital letters within entries make the book self-indexing. This is an excellent resource that is a fine starting point for quick reference or beginning research. In 2003, a less expensive edition was published (Continuum, $59.95 [0-8264-1516-4]).

19   Cullinan, Bernice E., and S. Lee Galda. *Literature and the Child,* 5th ed. Wadsworth, 2001, $86.95 (0-5342-4683-4).

This comprehensive textbook is a practical handbook that will be especially useful to classroom teachers of reading. It focuses on children—on how and why they read and how they respond to books. Instead of presenting long lists of recommended books, the authors stress how to evaluate children's books. There are, however, several highly selective book lists that are useful in directing children to high-quality titles. The text is filled with author and illustrator profiles and many teaching tips and ideas. Part I contains individual chapters on genres (such as folklore and historical fiction) and Part II deals with pedagogical issues (literature-based instruction and so forth). Part II also contains material on planning a literature curriculum. This new edition includes a CD-ROM that gives access to a database of particular topics, Web links, and many bibliographies, including lists of prize winners. Another important book by Bernice E. Cullinan is *More Children's Literature in the Reading Program* (International Reading Association, 1999, pap., $21.95 [0-87207-371-8]), a continuation of the out-of-print 1989 title from the International Reading Association, *Children's Literature in the Reading Program*.

20   Cummings, Pat. *Talking with Artists, Vol. 3.* Houghton Mifflin, 1999, $20 (0-39-589132-9).

In this book intended for elementary school children, 13 important children's book illustrators talk about themselves in a series of interviews. The questions asked explore the artist's personal and professional life, with material on their childhoods, their families, how they became illustrators of children's books, how they spend their days, and the advice they would give to budding artists. Readers will enjoy seeing photographs of each artist's studio, portraits of the artists, and color examples of their works. Some of the artists included in this volume are G. Brian Karas, Betsy Lewin, Anna Rich, Peter Sís, and Paul O. Zelinsky. The two earlier volumes are *Talking with Artists, Vol. 1* (Simon & Schuster, 1992, $22.95 [0-02-724245-5]) and *Talking with Artists, Vol. 2* (Atheneum, 1997, o.p.).

21   Cummins, Julie, ed. *Children's Book Illustration and Design, Vol. 2.* PBC International, 1998, $55 (0-86636-393-9).

In this sumptuous, oversize volume, 56 book illustrators are presented, each with one or two double-page spreads that highlight one or two major books. Following a sidebar that contains a photograph of the artist and some biographical information, the book or books are introduced with two full-color illustrations from each and a brief paragraph about each work by the artist. The illustrators are arranged alphabetically beginning with Tedd Arnold and ending with Dirk Zimmer, with such luminaries as Leo and Diane Dillon, Emily Arnold McCully, and Matt Novak in between. This book not only documents the current scene in book illustration but also gives the reader an opportunity to compare and contrast different artistic styles. There are indexes by author/illustrator and title. The first volume in this set was published in 1992 by PBC International, but is now out of print.

22   Cummins, Julie. *Wings of an Artist: Children's Book Illustrators Talk About Their Work.* Abrams, 1999, $17.95 (0-8109-4552-5).

In this lovely, colorful volume, 20 children's book artists describes, each in a single oversize page full of pictures and words, how they became artists and what art means to them. Among the artists are Graeme Base, Susan Jeffries, William Joyce, and Maurice Sendak. Page after page is filled with different art styles, techniques, media, and interpretations that allow children from grades 4 and up to view the diversity of current children's book illustration. Appended is an activity guide by Barbara Kiefer intended for elementary school students.

23   Dalby, Richard. *The Golden Age of Children's Book Illustration.* Book Sales, 2001, $34.50 (0-7858-1427-2); DIANA, 2002, $29.95 (0-7567-5654-5).

This is a wonderful collection of classic children's book illustrations from the 1860s to the 1930s. There are biographies of more than 50 of the artists who created this Golden Age and more than 150 faithfully reproduced black-and-white and color illustrations. This valuable historical document includes illustrations by many of the artists and illustrators who are not covered in sparsely illustrated general histories of the period.

24   Darling, Harold. *From Mother Goose to Dr. Seuss: Children's Book Covers 1860–1960.* Chronicle Books, 1999, pap., $22.95 (0-8118-1898-5).

Harold Darling, a noted collector of children's books and a distinguished writer on the subject, has assembled about 300 full-color book covers that represent the art and design found in 100 years of children's books. A decade-by-decade arrangement allows one to trace the evolution of graphic styles and subjects. Following this overview, there are special chapters on such topics as Mother Goose, series books, annuals, back covers, and different covers that illustrate the same story, About 150 artists are represented, including such historical figures as Kate Greenaway, Walter Crane, and Palmer Cox. The brief text only identifies the cover and its artist. The pictures speak for themselves. There are title and illustrator indexes.

25   Donelson, Kenneth L., and Alleen Pace Nilsen. *Literature for Today's Young Adults*, 6th ed. Pearson, 2000, $92 (0-321-03788-X).

This is an update of the basic, most-used, and most-trusted text on young adult literature. It is noted for its completeness and integrity as well as the way it reflects young adults, their psychology, and their current interests and needs. The book is divided into three parts. The first, on understanding young adults and books, gives solid information about young adults, stages in their development and literary appreciation, a history of young adult literature from 1800 on, and information on pop culture and mass media, with material on their roles in the lives of young adults. The second and longest part discusses the many types of young adult literature—such as realistic family stories, novels about personal problems, and genre fiction (including science fiction and historical stories)—and presents a lengthy section on nonfiction. The third part gives material on evaluating, promoting, and using young adult literature in both the library and classroom. Booktalking, writing reviews, reading guidance, displays, and censorship are a few of the topics covered. Valuable appendixes complete this cornucopia of facts, suggestions, and sound opinions about literature for teenagers.

26   Egoff, Sheila, et al. *Only Connect: Readings on Children's Literature*, 3rd ed. Oxford, 1976, pap., $19.95 (0-19-541024-6).

This volume contains more than 40 stimulating essays by distinguished scholars, each of which explores a different aspect of literature for children. It is divided into nine parts. The first presents an overview of the subject followed by sections on myth and folklore, fantasy, science fiction, picture books, poetry, gender relations, young adult literature, and recent trends. The authors include Peter Hunt, Joan Aiken, Perry Nodelman (three essays), and John Rowe Townsend. In short, this excellent anthology provides a basic introduction to the world of children's literature and how to appreciate it, as seen through the eyes of various authors and critics. The material does not duplicate any of the essays in the first edition (Oxford, 1969, o.p.) or its revision, the second edition (Oxford, 1980, o.p.), both of which remain valuable as reference sources. Sheila Egoff is also the author of *Thursday's Child: Trends and Patterns in Contemporary Children's Literature* (American Library Association, 1981, o.p.), a thoughtful work that examines and assesses children's literature published from approximately 1955 through 1980.

27   Gerhardt, Lillian N., et al. *School Library Journal's Best: A Reader for Children's, Young Adult, and School Librarians*. Neal-Schuman, 1997, $75 (1-55570-203-1).

One hundred seminal articles from past issues of *School Library Journal* are included in this volume, along with 32 provocative editorials by former editor Lillian Gerhardt. Topics include censorship, the Internet, literacy, multicultural services, new technology, children's and young adult literature, copyright issues, and funding for programs. This anthology brings together some of the best and most lasting writings that appeared in this periodical over a period of 40 years.

28   Gillespie, John T., and Corinne J. Naden. *Characters in Young Adult Literature.* Gale, 1997, $80 (0-7876-0401-1).

The purpose of this work is "to survey the entire field of young adult literature by outlining the plots and delineating the important characters in a representative group of novels that are significant in the development of literature suitable for young adults." The result is a book that presents more than 2,000 characters from 232 novels by 148 authors. Half the books are young adult novels, a quarter are for adults, and a quarter are literary classics. After the plot summary, important characters are introduced with details about their traits, appearance, and importance in the novel. Entries are arranged alphabetically by author from Douglas Adams to Paul Zindel, and each entry also contains a bibliography of sources about the book and author. There are numerous black-and-white illustrations and a 57-page character and title index.

29   Griswold, Jerry. *Audacious Kids: Coming of Age in America's Classic Children's Books.* Oxford, 1992, $29.95, o.p.

This entertaining, readable, but nevertheless scholarly work explores American culture and national identity through an examination and analysis of 12 children's books published during the "Golden Age" of 1865 to 1914. Among the books examined are *Tom Sawyer, Little Women, Hans Brinker, The Prince and the Pauper, Huckleberry Finn, Little Lord Fauntleroy,* and *Pollyanna.* The book ends with *Tarzan of the Apes.* The author maintains that the narrative patterns enjoyed by young readers are repeated, as are many of the themes (orphan narratives and poverty, for example). An interesting book that links children's literature to our history. Another stimulating book by this author is *The Classic American Children's Stories: Novels of the Golden Age* (Penguin, 1996, o.p.).

30   Hearn, Michael Patrick, et al. *Myth, Magic, and Mystery: One Hundred Years of American Children's Book Illustration.* Robert Rinehart, 1996, $50 (1-57098-080-2); pap., $29.95 (1-57098-079-9).

Based on an exhibition on children's book illustration that toured the United States during 1996 and 1997, this handsome, coffee-table book contains more than 200 illustrations that trace a century of book art. Most major illustrators are included, from Beatrix Potter (though not an American), Howard Pyle, and N. C. Wyeth to Maurice Sendak and Edward Gorey. The curators have contributed informative essays that explore four major categories of books: alphabet and nursery rhymes; myths, fables, and fairy tales; stories for young readers; and adolescent adventures and mysteries. This impressive, beautifully illustrated volume is a fine overview of the history, theory, and techniques used in book illustration.

31   Hearne, Betsy, and Deborah Stevenson. *Choosing Books for Children: A Common Sense Guide*, 3rd ed. University of Illinois, 1999, $29.95 (0-2520-2516-4); pap., 2000 (0-2520-6928-5).

Two well-known children's literature specialists offer wise, witty, and sound advice on choosing books for children. Aimed primarily at parents, this guide begins with a general introduction that outlines basic considerations in choosing books for various ages and interests. There follows a series of chapters that survey various genres, such as picture books, pop-up books, classics, poetry, folktales, young adult titles, books for beginning readers, and factual books. Each chapter ends with an annotated list of recommended titles. There is also a section on holiday books and one on controversial books that includes coverage of such topics as the Holocaust, AIDS, slavery, and child abuse. A delight to read, this book reflects the impeccable taste of its authors.

32   Helbig, Alethea K. *Dictionary of American Children's Fiction 1859–1959: Books of Recognized Merit.* Greenwood, 1985, $105 (0-313-22590-7).

This is the first in a series of volumes that trace the history of children's book publishing in America by highlighting superior works that are often prize winners. In the first volume, 420 books are discussed and analyzed by title and subject in 1,266 entries. The main entry, under title, gives bibliographic data; information on genre, setting, plot, main characters, and significant motifs; and a brief critical evaluation. There are also brief entries for authors that contain biographical and evaluative information, plus entries for outstanding characters and settings. A second volume, *Dictionary of American Children's Fiction 1960–1984: Recent Books of Recognized Merit* (Greenwood, 1986, $105 [0-313-25233-5]) continues the coverage for the next 24 years and contains 1,550 entries based on 489 books. Each of these works contains extensive indexes by setting, period, first-person narrative, subject, theme, illustrator, and genre. Since the publication of these two volumes, three supplements, each covering five years, have been published. They contain comparable coverage and average about 200 titles. An appendix in each lists the books by the awards and there are also the same extensive indexes. The supplements are:

> Helbig, Alethea K., and Agnes Regan Perkins. *Dictionary of American Children's Fiction 1985–1989: Books of Recognized Merit.* Greenwood, 1993, $72.95 (0-313-27719-2).

Helbig, Alethea K., and Agnes Regan Perkins. *Dictionary of American Children's Fiction 1990–1994: Books of Recognized Merit.* Greenwood, 1996, $97.95 (0-313-28763-5).

Helbig, Alethea K., and Agnes Regan Perkins. *Dictionary of American Children's Fiction 1995–1999: Books of Recognized Merit.* Greenwood, 2001, $99.95 (0-313-30389-4).

33   Helbig, Alethea K., and Agnes Regan Perkins. *Dictionary of American Young Adult Fiction, 1997–2001: Books of Recognized Merit.* Greenwood, 2004, $75 (0-313-32430-1).

The authors, both professors of English language and literature, have supplemented their previous publications on children's and young adult books of merit with this excellent dictionary. Nearly 300 books for young adults, written by more than 240 authors, are covered. It contains approximately 750 alphabetically arranged entries for individual works, authors, characters, and settings. Many of the books were written for adults but appeal to young adults. They all received major awards. Plot summaries and critical assessments are given in the entries for works. Biographical entries highlight aspects of interest to young people. There is a list of books by awards.

34   Helbig, Alethea K., and Agnes Regan Perkins. *Dictionary of Children's Fiction from Australia, Canada, India, New Zealand, and Selected African Countries.* Greenwood, 1992, $109.95 (0-313-26126-1).

This book is one of the best reference sources on children's literature in the English language from an international perspective. It offers comprehensive coverage of 260 works of fiction by 162 authors from Canada, Australia, New Zealand, India, and some African countries. The 726 entries provide plot summaries, biographical and bibliographical material on authors, details of important settings and characters, and critical assessments. The books selected for coverage have both historical and current importance; many of them are prize winners.

35   Horning, Kathleen. *Cover to Cover: Evaluating and Reviewing Children's Books.* HarperCollins, 1997, $24.95 (0-06-024519-0).

Horning has produced a thoughtful, practical guide to evaluating children's books, aimed at the novice book reviewer. The first chapter, which supplies an overview of children's publishing and the elements of a book, is followed by six chapters that discuss the characteristics of various genres and criteria for evaluation. Included are books of information, poetry, easy readers, traditional literature, picture books, and fiction. Examples from young adult literature are included when appropriate. The last chapter, "Writing a Review," gives a detailed explanation of how to plan and write an effective book review. A sensible, useful volume on the subject.

36   Huck, Charlotte S., et al. ***Children's Literature in the Elementary School,*** 7th ed. McGraw Hill, 2003, $87.75 (0-0728-7841-X).

This highly respected text on children's literature gives an excellent survey of the kinds of children's literature and ways of making them central to a school's curriculum. First published in 1961, the book covers such topics as learning about children and their literature, understanding children's responses to literature, and a history of their literature, and provides lengthy introductions to various genres, including beginning books, picture books, fairy tales, myths and legends, poetry, fantasy, family stories, historical fiction, biography, and other nonfiction. Each chapter contains valuable bibliographies of books and materials about children's literature and lists of quality titles. Hundreds of books are cited. The last section, on planning and developing a literature program, gives many practical suggestions and lists of suggested classroom activities. A companion CD-ROM expands the book's coverage into the world of the Internet.

37   Hunt, Peter. ***Children's Literature.*** Blackwell, 2001, pap., $26.95 (0-6312-1141-1).

Part of the Blackwell Guides to Literature series, this is an introduction to English-language children's literature written by one of Britain's foremost scholars in the field. The first sections are on general concepts involving children's literature. Under such headings as "Cultural Context" and "Themes and Topics," theoretical viewpoints and changing cultural attitudes are discussed. The two largest sections are on authors and key texts. The former looks at 40 prominent authors, from Janet Ahlberg to Patricia Wrightson, with coverage of a few Americans (such as Maurice Sendak), some historical figures (Robert Louis Stevenson, for example), and many contemporaries (Philip Pullman, Margaret Mahy, and J. K. Rowling, to name just three). Each author receives three to five pages of text, with critical comment. The key texts section includes an analysis of more than 30 important books alphabetically arranged from *Anne of Green Gables* to *The Wizard of Oz.* A final section contains short essays on 13 topics—including censorship, picture books, school stories, and other genres. This is a useful, intelligent introduction to children's literature, but it is not for quick reference.

38   Hunt, Peter, ed. ***Children's Literature: An Illustrated History.*** Oxford, 1995, o.p.

Unfortunately now out of print, this is an extremely attractive one-volume history of children's literature in English-speaking countries from the 16th century to the end of the 20th. The 12 chronologically arranged chapters are all written by specialists including Peter Hunt (the editor), Gillian Avery, Julia Briggs, and Zena Sutherland. Two of the chapters deal exclusively with a history of American children's literature and a third, on contemporary children's literature, also contains good U.S. coverage. The last chapter supplies historical information on developments in Australia, Canada, and New Zealand. The book contains more than 200 black-and-white and color illustrations, a chronology, an excellent bibliography for further reading, and a single index that includes both authors and subjects.

39 Hunt, Peter, ed. *International Companion Encyclopedia of Children's Literature.* Routledge, 1996, $185 (0-415-08856-9).

This work offers 86 scholarly essays on children's literature grouped under four main headings: "Theory and Critical Approaches," "Types and Genres," "The Context of Children's Literature," and "The World of Children's Literature." The first offers 10 essays on such theoretical aspects as psychoanalytic criticism and reader-response criticism; the second has 26 entries on genres including family stories and historical fiction; the third contains 18 essays on such topics as censorship, prizes, and bibliotherapy; and the last has 31 chapters on children's literature in individual countries. Many essays reveal individual biases and the emphasis is decidedly British, but individuals with an academic interest in children's literature and book publishing around the world will find this an informative, thought-provoking compilation. Thirteen of the most basic and provocative essays from this encyclopedia have been collected in *Understanding Children's Literature: Key Essays from the International Companion Encyclopedia of Children's Literature* (Routledge, 2000, pap., $28.95 [0-415-129546-2]). Two other works of criticism by Peter Hunt are *Criticism Theory and Children's Literature* (Blackwell, 1991, o.p.) and *Literature for Children: Contemporary Criticism* (Routledge, 1993, o.p.).

40 Hurlimann, Bettina. *Three Centuries of Children's Books in Europe.* Trans. by Brian W. Alderson. World, 1968, o.p.

Written by one of the leading editors and publishers of children's books in post-World War II Europe, this is a fascinating survey of the development of children's literature in Europe, with coverage of the literary and sociological backgrounds in various countries. Though roughly organized in chronological order, there are separate chapters on such notables as Hans Christian Andersen and Jean de Brunhoff. The book contains many beautiful reproductions of illustrations, some in color, and photographs of many noted authors. This important general introduction is considered a classic in the field. Another key work by Hurlimann, also unfortunately out of print, is her copiously illustrated critical survey of picture books for children from 24 countries, *Picture-Book World* (World, 1969, o.p.).

41   Jarvis, Janie, and Richard Jarvis. *The Magic Bookshelf: A Parent's Guide to Showing Growing Minds the Path to the Best Children's Literature.* Lorica, 1999, $12.95 (0-9665-1110-7).

A readable, accessible handbook that will help parents create a reading environment in their homes. It gives advice on becoming involved in children's reading, and supplies information on choosing the right books at various levels and interests. Some of the chapters are "Nurturing the Reading Habit, Naturally," "Good Taste Is Learned," "Luring the Non-interested Reader," and "Mixing Books with Other Media." This book is easy to use and contains many excellent bibliographies of recommended works.

42   Jones, Raymond E. *Characters in Children's Literature.* Gale, 1997, $80 (0-7876-0400-3).

The 230 works of fiction analyzed in this excellent reference are from the 19th and 20th centuries and represent publications not only from the United States and Great Britain but also from Australia and Canada. The titles were chosen by the author in consultation with a board of advisers. Arranged alphabetically from Joan Aiken (*The Wolves of Willoughby Chase*) to Jane Yolen (*Commander Toad in Space*), each entry begins with the author's name and bibliographical information, followed by a brief plot summary, an examination of themes, and a detailed analysis of characters and the roles they play in the novel. A total of 1,700 characters are delineated. Many of the entries include black-and-white illustrations. Each entry concludes with a list of reference works about the author and the book. An extensive character and title index combines references to both this volume and *Characters in Young Adult Literature* by Gillespie and Naden (see entry above).

43   Kelly, Patricia P., and Robert C. Small, Jr. *Two Decades of the ALAN Review.* National Council of Teachers of English, 1999, $31.95 (0-8141-5544-8).

This collection of articles from 20 years of *The ALAN Review* (see entry under "Professional Periodicals About Children's Literature" later in this chapter) helps trace the development of young adult literature from a mediocre offshoot of children's literature to a legitimate literary form. In addition, there are interviews with eight important young adult authors, including Sandy Asher, Sue Ellen Bridgers, Robert Cormier, Virginia Hamilton, and Paul Zindel.

44 Latrobe, Kathy H., et al. *The Children's Literature Dictionary: Definitions, Resources, and Learning Activities.* Neal-Schuman, 2002, $45 (1-55570-424-7).

The authors present 325 basic terms in this informative dictionary. Areas covered include literary devices, genres, poetic concepts, literary awards, parts of a book, literary styles and movements, and media and artistic techniques used in picture books. A typical entry includes a clear definition, examples from children's literature, and classroom activities that demonstrate the concept. About a third of the book is devoted to indexes: a title index—using a chart format, all of the titles cited in the text are listed in an index together with the literary term represented—and author and subject indexes, plus bibliographies of background professional materials.

45 Leeming, David Adams. *The Dictionary of Folklore.* Grolier/Watts, 2002, $34 (0-531-11985-8).

Myths, superstitions, nursery rhymes, folk songs, legends, fairy tales, tall tales, fables, and riddles are covered here, plus works of such writers as Charlotte Brontë and Mark Twain. The emphasis is on American folklore emanating from such North American groups as Native Americans, European Americans, African Americans, and Asian Americans. A useful overview that will be used principally by children.

46 Lukens, Rebecca R. *A Critical Handbook of Children's Literature*, 7th ed. Pearson, 2002, $51 (0-2053-6013-0).

First published in 1955, this textbook for students of children's literature aims to develop critical thinking, increase understanding regarding children's literature, and promote discriminating readership. Chapters are devoted to various elements found in fictional books (for example, plot, character, theme, setting, and point of view) and how they are used effectively and differently by various authors. Other chapters develop criteria for evaluating various genres, such as poetry, biography, and information books. There are lists of recommended titles at the end of each chapter and a separate section on prizes and prize winners. Lukens is also the author of *A Critical Handbook of Literature for Young Adults*, 5th ed. (Pearson, 1995, o.p.).

47 Lundin, Anne, and Carol W. Cubberley. *Teaching Children's Literature: A Resource Guide with a Directory of Courses.* McFarland, 1995, $45 (0-89950-990-8).

Now out of date, this useful work is divided into three parts. The first is an annotated bibliography of reference books, journals, children's literature textbooks, and journal articles on teaching children's literature, both to college students and to children and adolescents. The second part presents eight representative college syllabi, from English departments as well as from schools of education and library science, on how to teach children's literature. The third part is a directory of courses in children's literature given at colleges in the United States.

48   Lundin, Anne, and Wayne A. Wiegand. *Defining Print Culture for Youth: The Cultural Work of Children's Literature.* Libraries Unlimited, 2003, $45 (0-313-32177-9).

Sponsored by the Center for the History of Print Culture in Modern America, this volume features a lengthy introduction followed by ten papers delivered at the center's second national convention. The papers are written by scholars in the field; each centers on children's literature and its place in print culture.

49   Lynch-Brown, Carol, and Carl M. Tomlinson. *Essentials of Children's Literature*, 4th ed. Pearson, 2001, $46 (0-2053-3593-4).

This concise college text is useful in beginning survey courses in children's literature. Part 1 discusses current trends and basic material useful in selecting, reading, and evaluating children's books. Part 2 introduces specific genres and important examples from each, and Part 3 presents curriculum and teaching strategies. This edition also includes a bibliography of bilingual books, a discussion of censorship, lists of suitable read-alouds, a catalog of more than 2,000 recommended books, a chapter on multicultural literature, and extensive coverage of various prizes and prize winners in a number of English-speaking countries.

50   Lystad, Mary H. *From Dr. Mather to Dr. Seuss: 200 Years of American Books for Children.* Hall, 1980, o.p.

In writing this historical account of American children's literature from its beginnings to 1975, the author examined and analyzed more than 1,000 rare books from the Library of Congress. As well as linking this literature to theories on the nature of children and their place in society, individual chapters focusing on broad chronological periods supply a basic history. Two additional chapters comment on social values and views regarding the socialization of children, and a table presents the changes in presentation of gender and race in children's books. There are many quotes from individual authors and 50 well-chosen illustrations. A useful source that should be updated.

51 McClure, Amy A., and Janice V. Kristo. *Books that Invite, Talk, Wonder, and Play.* National Council of Teachers of English, 1996, $19.95 (0-8141-0370-7).

In a series of nearly 40 essays, many well-known authors who write children's literature share their thoughts and discuss how they plan plot twists, create atmosphere, and bring their characters to life. Among the writers are Jerry Spinelli, Gary Paulsen, Jane Yolen, Katherine Paterson, and Avi. A variety of genres is represented, including historical fiction, folklore, fantasy, nonfiction, poetry, and picture books.

52 Mahmoud, Lisa V., ed. *Books Remembered: Nurturing the Budding Writer.* Children's Book Council, 1997, pap., $14.85 (0-9336-3304-1).

This charming slim book features entries by and about several prominent authors of children's books. The authors list the books they enjoyed as children, give comments on the contents of the books, and explain their influence on their lives and writing. Three of the authors included are Joan Aiken, Roald Dahl, and Katherine Paterson.

53 Marantz, Kenneth A., and Sylvia S. Marantz. *Creating Picturebooks: Interviews with Editors, Art Directors, Reviewers, Booksellers, Professors, Librarians and Showcasers.* McFarland, 1997, $35 (0-7864-0415-9).

This is a behind-the-scenes look at the commercial world of the children's picture book. The authors explore viewpoints of those responsible for making, publishing, reviewing, selling, and using these books. Decisions such as what books will be published and how many copies will be printed are covered, and there are interesting chapters on important book houses, reviewing journals, and selling techniques. Indexes are by title, people mentioned, and subject. An update would be useful.

54 Marantz, Sylvia, and Kenneth A. Marantz. *The Art of Children's Picture Books: A Selective Reference Guide*, 2nd ed. Garland, 1995, $53, o.p.

This bibliography of sources emphasizes children's books as an art form and, therefore, references to picture books predominate. The body of this book is an amazing reference work that includes articles, books, films, and videos about the history and production of picture books and about individual artists and their work. Chapters are organized by subject (for example, history, criticism, important collections). The alphabetically arranged entries within each chapter are annotated, the length varying with the material's importance. This second edition contains all the material from the first edition plus coverage from 1986 through the first half of 1993. One would welcome a third edition of this scholarly reference.

55   Meigs, Cornelia, et al. *A Critical History of Children's Literature: A Survey of Children's Books in English from Earliest Times to the Present, Prepared in Four Parts.* Macmillan, 1969, o.p.

This book is as close as we have come to a definitive history of children's literature in this country. Originally published in 1953, this revised edition carries the coverage to 1967 and corrects many of the errors that plagued the original edition. Totaling a lengthy 700 or so pages, it is divided into four parts, each written by a specialist in the area. The first part, from colonial times to 1840, gives excellent coverage on the British writers who influenced our early children's books. The second, entitled "Widening Horizons," covers 1840 to 1890, and the third continues the history to 1920. The last and longest part, "Golden Years and Time of Tumult, 1920–1967," was written by Ruth Hill Viguers, long associated with *Horn Book.* It discusses the development of many different genres during this period, covers important authors, and describes outstanding books. There are no illustrations, but this remains an invaluable reference for all concerned with children's literature.

56   Moon, Brian. *Literary Terms: A Practical Glossary.* National Council of Teachers of English, 1999, pap., $19.95 (0-8141-30089).

Useful for teachers and for high school students, this work defines both traditional literary terms—*style* and *theme,* for instance—and terms associated with new theories. The definitions are up to date, with examples from classic literary sources and from popular books, films, and television shows. These explanations and examples are often reinforced by puzzles, problems, and other activities.

57   Murray, Gail Schmunk. *American Children's Literature and the Construction of Childhood.* Twayne, 1998, $33 (0-8057-4107-0).

Part of Twayne's History of American Childhood series, this volume attempts to "understand the critical connection between the creative work of fiction and the cultural and social reality of which the author is a part." Told in chronological order, it begins with a study of colonial childhood and children's texts, followed by books published in the new nation by such pioneers as Noah Webster and William McGuffey. The book ends with an epilogue, "Into the Twenty-First Century." This is a fascinating history of childhood in America and its relation to developments and changes in children's literature. The final bibliographic essay will be helpful to scholars.

58　Norton, Donna E., and Saundra Norton. *Through the Eyes of a Child: An Introduction to Children's Literature*, 6th ed. Prentice Hall, 2002, $88 (0-1304-2207-X).

Through the years, this work has become a highly respected source for beginning students of children's literature. The comprehensive text includes chapters on history, evaluation, artists and illustrations, and multicultural literature. Genres are covered in two parts: the first part discusses the genre and the second gives tips on introducing and teaching the genre. Current approaches to education are emphasized, and an explanation of literature-based instruction is included. Other highlights are tips on writing and publishing children's literature, a wealth of color illustrations, and a CD-ROM to help teachers and librarians identify books on a variety of subjects.

59　O'Malley, Andrew, and Jack Zipes. *The Making of the Modern Child: Children's Literature in the Late Eighteenth Century*. Routledge, 2003, $85 (0-4159-4299-3).

Our current concept of the nature of childhood is a phenomenon that emerged in the late 18th century along with such social and economic developments as capitalism and the growth of the middle class. This book explores how this concept was constructed through the children's literature of the day as well as through pedagogical and medical ideas and texts. Many examples from the period's authors and their writings are quoted in this book that examines the link between our beliefs about childhood and the early history of children's literature.

60　Opie, Iona, and Peter Opie. *The Oxford Dictionary of Nursery Rhymes*, 2nd ed. Oxford, 1998, $55 (0-19-860088-7).

This anthology of traditional nursery rhymes is included here because it is also a meticulous work of scholarship that traces the history of more than 500 British and American rhymes. Included are rhymes like "Jack and Jill" and "Yankee Doodle Came to Town," plus important songs, nonsense jingles, and lullabies. Each entry contains a history of the rhyme, when it was first published, how it originated, changes that have occurred over time, and parallels in other languages. There are more than 100 illustrations that, in themselves, chronicle the changes in children's book illustration over the years. The excellent introduction supplies details on early collections of these rhymes, and explores such topics as the identity of Mother Goose. A highly recommended source on this subject.

61   Pavonetti, Linda M. *Children's Literature Remembered: Issues, Trends, and Favorite Books.* Libraries Unlimited, 2003, $49.50 (0-313-32077-2).

The Children's Literature Assembly of the National Council of Teachers of English held an important workshop following the 1999 fall conference. From these meetings comes this stimulating collection of speeches and other contributions, all of which give rare insights into the development of children's literature in America during the 20th century. Contributors include such authors as Julius Lester and Lois Lowry and such children's literature authorities as Terry Lesene and Barbara Elleman.

62   Perrin, Noel. *A Child's Delight.* Dartmouth College, 2003, pap., $15.95 (1-5846-5352-3).

The author has written a series of short, delightful essays in which he highlights 30 works of children's fiction that he feels have been unduly neglected. Both picture and chapter books are included, most of which were published in the 20th century. For each book, he supplies plot summaries and thorough comments about the work and its merits. Some of the titles included are *The Story of Dr. Dolittle*, *The Borrowers*, and Ursula Le Guin's *A Wizard of Earthsea*. This is an appealing read for children's literature enthusiasts.

63   Reed, Arthea J. S. *Comics to Classics: A Guide to Books for Teens and Preteens.* International Reading Association, 1988, $5.95 (0-8720-7798-5).

This well-organized guide defines the characteristics and needs of teens and preteens, explains the stages in reading development, and relates all of this material to these age groups' reading habits and taste. For each stage there are excellent annotated reading lists that are organized for teen appeal. Individual genres are also discussed—biographies, historical fiction, puzzle books, and science fiction, for example. Tips are given on how to encourage teens to read and how television and movies can help promote reading. There is an annotated bibliography of 500 books. An updating of this useful handbook would be welcome.

64   Robinson, Richard D. *Historical Sources in U.S. Reading Education 1900–1970: An Annotated Bibliography.* International Reading Association, 2000, $17.95 (0-87207-271-1).

The author has selected the most useful and relevant sources on reading and reading instruction from the first 70 years of the 20th century and organized this material into 15 sections, each dealing with a major topic. All entries are annotated. Readers will realize that many of the issues and problems facing modern classroom teachers are, with variations, the same as those faced by their predecessors even though teaching methods and materials have changed. A valuable work for anyone doing research on reading.

65   Russell, David L. *Literature for Children: A Short Introduction*, 4th ed. Allyn & Bacon, 2000, $53 (0-8013-3086-6).

This introductory text, a concise but comprehensive guide to children's literature, focuses on genres rather than on individual authors. This edition gives an expanded history of children's literature as well as a unique overview of critical theories on the subject. There are separate sections on such topics as picture books, folk literature, poetry, fantasy, realism, and nonfiction. Current issues and trends are discussed, but there are no lengthy bibliographies.

66   Short, Kathy G. *Research and Professional Resources in Children's Literature: Piecing a Patchwork Quilt.* International Reading Association, 1995, o.p.

This out-of-print title supplies an excellent annotated guide to important research and professional materials on children's literature through grade 8 that appeared between 1985 and 1993. It is divided into three sections: major research studies as reported in journals; the names of journals that have included research topics; and a select bibliography of professional books. These sections are organized by major topics. There are also author and subject indexes. This is an excellent resource for researchers and educators interested in tracing developments in specific areas. Its coverage is now out of date and a continuation would be helpful.

67   Silvey, Anita, ed. *Children's Books and Their Creators.* Houghton Mifflin, 1995, $40, o.p.

Using contributions from approximately 200 critics, artists, and writers, the editor has compiled a weighty, oversize book of almost 800 entries on outstanding and best-loved authors and illustrators of books for children. From Aesop to Zindel, each entry gives some biographical material but focuses on the subject's important contributions. Not all publications are listed but major ones are discussed. Many entries feature sidebars, called "Voices of the Creators," which contain personal statements from the artists and writers. The volume emphasizes 20th-century works, particularly those of the last half of the century. There are also a number of overview articles on various genres, countries, minority groups, topics related to book design, and controversial subjects. Scattered throughout the book are about 175 black-and-white and color illustrations. This excellent basic reference also contains a massive general index and a basic bibliography of the best in children's books.

68   Silvey, Anita. *The Essential Guide to Children's Books and Their Creators.* Houghton Mifflin, 2002, $28 (0-618-19083-X); pap., $18 (0-618-19082-1).

This work is both an abridgement and an updating of the title discussed above. There are a total of 475 entries, 375 of which have appeared before but in many cases are now updated (for example, the entry on Philip Pullman covers the entire His Dark Materials trilogy). The 100 new entries are chiefly on authors and illustrators who have gained recent prominence, such as Randy Powell, J. K. Rowling, and Lemony Snicket. As in the previous volume, there are general articles on genres, historical topics, and multicultural literature, as well as 30 autobiographical entries called "Voices of the Creators." The basic book list is reprinted from the original edition and there is an excellent index. This is an affordable, highly recommended reference work. Owners of the earlier volume should retain it for its additional coverage.

69   Sloan, Glenna Davis. *The Child as Critic: Developing Literacy Through Literature, K–8*, 4th ed. Teachers College, 2003, $24.95 (0-8077-4340-2).

This is a new edition of the standard text in the Language and Literary series. It outlines how reading can be taught in all elementary school grades through the use of high-quality children's literature. While giving guidance in developing a sound reading program, the author discusses a number of important works of children's literature and explains how they can be used effectively in the classroom. Of particular value to teachers of language arts, this is a good professional tool.

70   Smith, Michael W., and Jeffrey D. Wilhelm. *"Reading Don't Fix No Chevys": Literacy in the Lives of Young Men.* Heinemann, 2002, pap., $23 (0-86709-509-1).

In a clear, easy-to-follow text, the authors report on a study that examined the attitudes toward literacy and the reading habits of 49 boys of various socioeconomic levels, races, ages, and educational histories. Many interesting tendencies and opinions are revealed and some logical conclusions are suggested. The authors concede that these results could also apply to girls. The findings can point the way to more effective methods of teaching and reading guidance.

71   Stewig, John Warren. *Looking at Picture Books.* Highsmith, 1995, o.p.

This is an introduction to the evaluation and understanding of art in picture books. It is aimed at people who have little or no background in the visual arts and includes a discussion of the pictorial and compositional elements of illustrations, material on the components of book design, and a study of influences on children's book illustration from major art movements. There is an annotated bibliography of art books. A fine book for the novice adult picture book reader.

72 Styles, Morag. *From the Garden to the Street: An Introduction to 300 Years of Poetry for Children.* Cassell, 1997, pap., $39.95 (0-3043-3222-4).

Divided by time periods and genres, this important history of poetry for children is a wonderful source of information and evaluative comment. Beginning with the Puritan verse of such writers as John Bunyan and Isaac Watts, the text covers many poets and their work as it traces the path from idealism to reality. It covers a wide range of topics—nature poets, nursery rhymes, and poetry of the street, for example. Important poets are given good coverage—whole chapters are devoted to Christina Rossetti and Robert Louis Stevenson. Coverage of the Romantics and of women poets is particularly good. Although British poets and developments are emphasized, American writers are mentioned. One critic called the thought-provoking study "a masterly piece of scholarship"; another said it is "a necessary addition to the scant existing scholarship on the history of poetry for children."

73 Sutherland, Zena. *Children and Books*, 9th ed. Addison Wesley, 1997, $97 (0-673-99733-2).

This work has become a standard text on children's literature, and rightly so because it gives a thorough and tasteful introduction to all aspects of this subject. It was first published in 1947 under the authorship of May Hill Arbuthnot; Zena Sutherland became the principal author with the fourth edition in 1969. It is presently organized into four broad areas: "Knowing Children and Books," "Exploring the Types of Literature," "Bringing Children and Books Together," and "Areas and Issues." The essays in the last section were written by Peggy Sullivan and are all new to this edition. All parts, particularly the second, contain helpful, basic bibliographies. Readers will also find material on selection aids, recommended readings on special topics, and a variety of attractive illustrations, some in color. Appendixes include a directory of publishers and material on children's book awards. There are author, title, illustrator, and subject indexes. This is a basic book on the subject.

74 Temple, Charles, et al. *Children's Books in Children's Hands: An Introduction to Their Literature (with Children's Literature Database CD-ROM, Version 2.0)*, 2nd ed. Allyn and Bacon, 2001, $86 (0-2053-6081-5).

This comprehensive approach to teaching children's literature gives an in-depth look at how literature elicits various responses from young children. It also provides a genre-by-genre approach, with many examples from important children's books. The first chapters deal with child development and supply a history of children's literature. The main section introduces various genres, covers the criteria for evaluation, and supplies many examples from the literature. Also included are several essays written by prominent children's authors about their profession. Throughout the book are many thoughtful and practical suggestions for sharing and exploring literature with children, as well as a number of full-color illustrations from outstanding children's books. This is a good, workable introduction.

75   Townsend, John Rowe. *Written for Children: An Outline of English-Language Children's Literature*, 6th ed. Scarecrow, 2003, $43 (0-8108-3117-1).

Originally published in 1965, this work has undergone many revisions and updates. The current witty, wise, and highly readable account covers the history of children's and young adult literature from its beginnings to the mid-1990s and includes a 2003 postscript with material on such important new authors as J. K. Rowling and Philip Pullman. The book is divided into four chronological periods: pre-1840, 1840 to 1915, 1915 to 1945, and 1945 to the present (1995). The author is highly selective in the examples and authors chosen for review, but the choices are judicious and the comments insightful and discerning. There is a fair balance between British and American coverage, and the last chapter quickly covers children's literature in other English-speaking countries, including Canada, Ireland, and Jamaica. There are some black-and-white illustrations and a good index. This is a basic history that is also fun to read.

76   Watson, Victor, et al. *The Cambridge Guide to Children's Books in English*. Cambridge, 2001, $50 (0-521-55064-5).

With an emphasis on British and American topics, this is an alphabetically arranged, critical overview of books written in English for children from pre-Norman times to the present. It is a hefty volume—more than 800 pages. Entries are basically of four types: authors, titles, topics, and technical terms (lithography and crosshatching, for example). Topical entries include titles of children's magazines, critical journals, major library and research centers, themes, literary figures, and biographies of important publishers, librarians, and editors. There are also entries on genres and formats, and articles on related topics such as blind readers, gay and lesbian literature, television, comics, media texts, and superheroes. All articles are signed and there is a six-page list of contributors. Some special features: tables of winners of 21 of the most prestigious literary prizes, excellent cross referencing, and strong coverage of contemporary authors and illustrators. There are some inconsistencies, and sometimes an imbalance in coverage, but considering the vast amount of material included, this is a wonderful reference tool that is also great for browsing.

77 Weiss, Jaqueline Shachter. *Profiles in Children's Literature: Discussions with Authors, Artists, and Editors.* Scarecrow, 2001, $55 (0-8108-3787-0).

In 1969, the author began inviting authors, illustrators, and editors involved in children's literature to her classes at Temple University. These talks and interviews were recorded on videotapes. From these and from additional background sources comes this collection of intriguing material on various aspects of the world of children's literature. Among the subjects are Arna Bontemps, Lorenz Graham, Marguerite de Angeli, Eleanor Estes, and Margaret McElderry. This book is illustrated with photographs taken from the tapes.

78 West, Mark I. *Everyone's Guide to Children's Literature.* Highsmith, 1997, o.p.

Sadly now out of print, this work was intended by the author "to provide (users) with a convenient, low-cost, up-to-date source of information about virtually every important aspect of literature for youth." The author succeeded admirably with individual chapters on such topics as key reference sources, journals and periodicals, organizations, Internet sites, special collections and libraries, major awards, and important books about children's literature. The books cited cover a wide range of subjects, including using books in literature programs, African American literature, and fairy tales and folklore. This easy-to-use source book still contains a great deal of helpful, pertinent information.

79 Zipes, Jack, ed. *The Oxford Companion to Fairy Tales.* Oxford, 2000, $49.95 (0-19-860115-8).

Focusing on fairy tales from Europe and North America, this work contains more than 800 entries on separate tales, authors, and illustrators, plus a wide array of general topics—such as motifs and how they have been used by adult writers and composers, and how they have been found in films, television programs, and other media. The longest entries are for countries and geographical areas (France, for example, gets 14 pages). There is also a useful introduction that describes the genre and supplies a brief history. Major entries contain bibliographies, and interesting appendixes list fairy tale studies, important collections, and specialized journals. About 70 black-and-white illustrations are included, many of them full-page. A useful, well-organized reference source.

2. General Reference Sources on Other Countries

A. AUSTRALIA

80   Lees, Stella, and Pam Macintyre. *The Oxford Companion to Australian Children's Literature.* Oxford, 1993, o.p.

The 1,600 entries in this volume provide easy access to information about Australian children's literature from 1841 to the early 1990s. Most of the entries are for authors or for significant books, such as award winners or groundbreaking novels. There are also entries on publishers, illustrators, famous characters, institutions, awards, genres (fairy tales, for example), and key events and figures that have inspired authors. There is coverage of important nursery rhymes and Aboriginal sources. The entries are short, but the author entries include a brief biography and a critical comment on main works. This is still a fine basic reference on Australian children's literature, but it needs an update.

81   Saxby, Henry Maurice. *Books in the Life of a Child: Bridges to Literature and Learning.* Macmillan Education Australia, 1998, pap., $39.95 (0-7329-4520-8).

There are many wise observations on the nature and value of children's literature in this volume, but its importance lies in the author's thorough study of the history and development of children's literature in Australia. Some material on New Zealand is also included. Covering early literature through the classic work of such contemporaries as Ruth Park and Margaret Mahy, this is a masterful history.

82   Saxby, Henry Maurice. *The Proof of the Puddin': Australian Children's Literature 1970–1990.* Ashton Scholastic (Sydney), 1992, o.p.

This is the third and last volume in Mr. Saxby's comprehensive, detailed history of Australia's children's books. The narrative is divided into 15 chapters. The first deals with general directions, trends, and changes in style; the rest cover 20 years of publishing history, by age groups and genres. Some sample chapter headings: "Books Before School," "The Picture Book," "Junior Books" (which contains sections on some important authors and then on such topics as the family), "Animals," "Multicultural Australia," and "The Young Adult." There are some reproductions of book illustrations. The two earlier volumes were originally published in 1969 and 1970, but have been recently been reissued in revised, retitled editions. They are:

> *Offered to Children: A History of Australian Children's Literature, 1841–1941.* Ashton Scholastic (Sydney), 1998 (price and ISBN not available).

> *Images of Australia: A History of Australian Children's Literature 1941–1970.* Ashton Scholastic (Sydney), 2002 (1-86504-277-3).

B. CANADA

83 Egoff, Sheila A. *Canadian Children's Books, 1799–1939, in the Special Collections and University Archives of the University of British Columbia Library: A Bibliographic Catalogue.* University of British Columbia Library, 1992, o.p.

This is a fascinating catalog of 850 items, arranged chronologically and then by author, that traces the history of Canadian children's literature. As the preface states, this book "helps establish early Canadian children's literature as a viable area for research and scholarship." Full bibliographic information is given for each item, plus a plot annotation and extensive background notes on both the book and its contents. Books in both French and English were included if their subject matter was Canada or a Canadian. Although the National Library of Canada (now Library and Archives Canada) in Ottawa and the Toronto Public Library have larger historical collections, neither has a comparable printed catalog. There is an author/title index. Another work edited by Sheila Egoff along with Ronald Hughes, *Books that Shaped Our Minds* (University of British Columbia, 1998, $95 [0-888652-13-5]), highlights 364 important historical items from the 3,000 children's books donated to the university by Rose and Stanley Arkley in 1976.

84 Egoff, Sheila, and Judith Saltman. *The New Republic of Childhood: A Critical Guide to Canadian Children's Literature in English.* Oxford, 1990, $20 (0-19-540576-5).

Following a general survey of Canadian children's literature and how it grew, this work contains ten chapters on different genres. Examples include "Realistic Fiction" (subdivided into survival stories, family life, mystery and detective stories, and so forth), "Historical Fiction," " Picture and Picture-Storybooks," and " Folk and Fairy Tales." Each chapter describes the genre, gives characteristics, and tells how it has developed and changed. Examples are cited in chronological order with material on plots, authors, and literary strengths and weaknesses. The last chapter traces a history of children's publishing in Canada. A 40-page appendix lists the works cited in the text under the same genre headings; there is a comprehensive index.

85 Waterson, Elizabeth. *Children's Literature in Canada.* Twayne, 1992, $25 (0-8057-8264-8).

Part of Twayne's World Authors Series, this is a brief survey of the full range of Canadian literature for children. After an overview chapter that highlights other important studies in the area and contains a discussion of the rewards children receive from reading, the author devotes the rest of the book to short chapters on important genres. These include cover-

age of folklore and fairy tales, easy-to-read books, animal stories, historical fiction, fiction dealing with social problems, and books for the young
adult. All of the books mentioned are listed in an appendix of primary
sources. There are also reference notes for each chapter, a bibliography of
secondary sources, and a short index.

C. IRELAND

86   *What's the Story: The Reading Choices of Young People in Ireland.*
Children's Books Ireland, 2002, 10 euros for members/29 euros for
nonmembers (1-8729171-0-0).

A total of 2,200 children in Ireland (and Northern Ireland) were sur-
veyed concerning their reading habits and preferences. Sixty-two schools
participated, representing youngsters from ages 7 through 16. Students
were asked about reading habits, favorite books and authors, and how
and why they enjoyed reading. It was found that younger children read
and enjoyed reading more than teenagers and that the amount of reading
declined not only by age but also by gender (girls read more than boys).
Even primary-age girls read more than primary-age boys. Reading of
magazines increased with age but was popular at all levels. Harry Potter
dominated reading preferences, but humor was the most popular overall
genre, followed by horror and adventure stories. The report is available
from Children's Books Ireland, First Floor, 17 Lower Camden St.,
Dublin 2, Ireland.

D. SOUTH AFRICA

87   Jenkins, Elwyn. *South Africa in English-Language Children's Literature,
1814–1912.* McFarland, 2002, $49.95 (0-7864-1105-8).

Beginning with the first books published in South Africa about 100
years ago, this work not only gives a history of original English-language
children's books from South Africa but also discusses the treatment of
South Africa in other books in English of the period. Included in the
later coverage are such adventure writers as G. A. Henty, M. Ballantyne,
and H. Rider Haggard. This is a fascinating story of a developing country and the children's literature it has produced.

E. UNITED KINGDOM

88   Blake, Quentin, ed. *Magic Pencil: Children's Book Illustration Today.*
British Council/British Library, 2002, £15.95 (0-7123-4770-4).

This well-researched and carefully edited book is actually an exhibition catalog of a show that originated in the Ling Art Galley in Newcastle upon Tyne and continued until March 2003 at the British Library in London. The 13 chosen illustrators represent an eclectic sampling of the best of contemporary British book illustration in the field of children's literature. The book begins with a 20-page, richly illustrated, brief history by Joanna Carey of children's book illustration in Britain. For each artist covered, there is a color photograph, an autobiographical statement about how and why each is a creative artist, and four pages of full-color examples of his or her work. Among the artists represented are Angela Barrett, Quentin Blake, John Burningham, Raymond Briggs, and Tony Ross. This handsome volume shows the diversity of styles in today's British book illustration.

89   Carpenter, Humphrey. *Secret Gardens: The Golden Age of Children's Literature.* Houghton, 1985, o.p.

Wonderfully wise and witty, this history has the further subtitle *From Alice's Adventures in Wonderland to Winnie-the-Pooh.* After a brief early history of children's literature, the first chapter deals with Charles Kingsley's *The Water Babies* and the second moves onto Lewis Carroll and the Alice book published in 1865. Other chapters cover such writers as George MacDonald, Mrs. Molesworth, Mrs. Ewing, Kenneth Grahame, E. Nesbit, James M. Barrie, and A. A. Milne. The only American given full treatment is Louisa May Alcott. An epilogue, "The Garden Revisited," discusses a few more contemporary writers, including J. R. R. Tolkien, Alan Garner, and Philippa Pearce, author of *Tom's Midnight Garden.* As one reviewer said, the author "permits us to see in a fresh light the interaction between cultural history and literature."

90   *Collecting Children's Books.* Book and Magazine Collector, 2001, £19.95 (0-95326-01-27).

Aimed primarily at collectors and dealers, this catalog contains 335 entries arranged alphabetically by author or illustrator surname. After a few identifying lines, the individual's books are listed in chronological order, each with publisher's name, a description, and full market value.

Prices are for books in "very good" condition. British prices are given, but many American writers are listed (Maurice Sendak, for example). Both British and American editions are given. There are hundreds of black-and-white illustrations of book jackets. This is a catalog for book collectors, but it contains a lot of interesting material for anyone involved in children's literature.

91   Collins, Fiona M., and Judith Graham. *Historical Fiction for Children: Capturing the Past.* David Fulton Publishers, 2001, pap., £15 (1-85346-768-5).

This collection of papers explores the world of historical fiction written for children in Britain. It is divided into three sections: the material of such fiction, the craft of writing it, and teaching with historical novels as working texts. Topics covered include emigration, children at work in various centuries, Peter Dickinson's exploration of prehistory, and time-slips. Chapters in which various writers of historical fiction comment on their craft and techniques are especially valuable.

92   Darton, F. J. Harvey. *Children's Books in England: Five Centuries of Social Life*, 3rd ed. British Library/Oak Knoll Press, 1999, $50 (1-8847-1888-4).

Since its first appearance in 1932, this work has been considered the classic, one-volume history of English children's literature. It was the first to emphasize the interrelationship between children's books and social history. This edition, which corrects and updates the first two editions, was edited by Brian Anderson who continues the coverage through the early 20th century (Victorian and Edwardian periods). The chapter arrangement is chronological with subdivisions by genre. Darton begins with two chapters on the Middle Ages and discusses first fables and then romances and books of manners. The bulk of the narrative deals with the 18th and 19th centuries. There are some black-and-white illustrations and several appendixes discuss Darton's many contributions to the field. This humane work remains a monument to scholarship.

93   Eccleshare, Julia. *Beatrix Potter to Harry Potter: Portraits of Children's Writers.* National Portrait Galley (London), 2002, £15 (1-85514-342-9).

This catalog, which accompanied a 2002 exhibition at the National Portrait Gallery in London, contains biographical and bibliographical information about 58 British children's writers and illustrators. It is divided into five sections each covering 20 years, beginning with 1900–1920 and ending with 1980–1999. Each profile includes a portrait, many examples from the individual's works, and material on his or her life, inspirations, influences, and creative ideas. Because the catalog is so selective, it can be considered only a valuable introduction to the world of British children's literature; it is nevertheless a handsome book that offers a great deal of interesting information.

94   Helbig, Alethea K., and Agnes Regan Perkins. *Dictionary of British Children's Fiction: Books of Recognized Merit.* 2 vols., Greenwood, 1989, $150 (0-313-22591-5).

The 1,626 entries in this work analyze 387 prize-winning books published from 1687 to 1985. Only works of 5,000 words or more were considered; therefore, picture books are excluded. There are entries for authors, titles, and major characters. The title entries are the most extensive, with information on both British and American editions, a plot summary, and a critical comment. Author entries supply biographical entries and a mention of important titles. The character entries simply give basic material for identification. There is a lengthy index, which includes subject and thematic references and a listing of books by time period and setting. This is a valuable historical reference on British children's literature.

95   Hunt, Peter. *An Introduction to Children's Literature.* Oxford, 1996, pap., $24.95 (0-19-289243-6).

This volume presents a concise history of British children's literature, with a focus on the past 130 years. The author balances nicely the relationship between history and social issues and covers both admirably. There is a particularly fine chapter on the development of picture books. As well as tracing the evolution of children's literature, the author explains the difference between adult literature and literature for children. The last chapter, "Stalking the Perfect Children's Books," recapitulates the author's selection criteria and gives a glimpse into the future. Also included are a chronology, a short bibliography, and a comprehensive index.

96   Lundin, Anne. *Victorian Horizons: The Reception of the Picture Books of Walter Crane, Randolph Caldecott, and Kate Greenaway.* Scarecrow, 2001, $60 (0-8108-3739-0).

This is an exploration of contemporary responses to the picture books of three pioneering Victorian illustrators of children's books. The author also discusses the way their picture books were read and reviewed in their time, the criticism they received, and the change in attitude toward them in the past 100 years. She positions these three artists in relation to each other and examines how and why each has become so prominent in the history of children's book illustration.

97   Manlove, Colin. *The Fantasy Literature of England.* St. Martin's, 1999, $59 (0-3122-1987-3).

This is Manlove's ninth book-length study of fantasy. Although the entire field of British fantasy writing is covered, the concentration on children's literature makes it important in this survey of sources. After a brief discussion of classic English fairy tales, the author covers fantasy in such classics as *The Tempest, Pilgrim's Progress,* and *Gulliver's Travels* and then devotes six chapters to major trends in fantasy literature of the past 200 years. In a separate chapter on children's fantasy, he examines the work of writers including E. Nesbit (whom he considers pivotal), Kenneth Grahame, Alan Garner, Robert Westall, Diana Wynne Jones, and Philip Pullman. This is a scholarly work that examines fantasy from various points of view and contexts.

98   Martin, Douglas. *The Telling Line: Essays on Fifteen Contemporary Book Illustrators.* Delacorte, 1990, o.p.

The lives and works of 15 contemporary British illustrators are highlighted in this oversize volume. Each illustrator is allotted about 20 well-illustrated pages, ending with a chronologically arranged list of the books illustrated (ending at 1989). The text covers biographical details, background material, influences, and techniques. Among the artists included are Anthony Browne, Janet and Allan Ahlberg, Quentin Blake, Raymond Briggs, John Burningham, Helen Oxenbury, Brian Wildsmith, and Charles Keeping. This is an interesting introduction to these artists.

99   Phinn, Gervase, ed. *The Address Book of Children's Authors and Illustrators.* LDA, 2002, pap., £15.95 (1-85503-355-0).

An entertaining book for children, this introduces 100 favorite British authors and illustrators. It is informal, with clever layouts and plenty of illustrations in color and in black and white. There is a photograph of each author/illustrator plus an autobiographical entry, and such additional material as a book extract and a "favorites" section where the subject's favorite books, food, words, and so on are noted. An American counterpart would be welcome.

100   Reynolds, Kimberley, and Nicholas Tucker. *Children's Book Publishing in Britain Since 1945.* Gower, 1998, $84.95 (1-8592-8236-9).

This collection of essays by specialists in their fields covers various aspects of the publishing, printing, and distribution of children's books in Britain since World War II. Separate chapters cover such topics as literary prizes, picture books, graphic novels, and movable books. Each chapter has a bibliography. This work covers a wider spectrum of topics than the title would suggest.

101   Thwaite, Mary F. *From Primer to Pleasure in Reading: An Introduction to the History of Children's Books in England from the Invention of Printing to 1914, with an Outline of Some Developments in Other Countries,* 2nd ed. Library Association (London)/Horn Book, 1972, o.p.

Although not as lengthy or detailed as the Darton book discussed above, this work is nevertheless considered another classic history of British children's literature. Thwaite gives greater coverage to the Victorian and Edwardian periods than Darton but also deals with the origins of children's literature, beginning with the invention of printing. From the beginning of the 19th century, the coverage is organized more by theme and genre rather than by a strict chronological approach. Coverage ends with 1914. The final chapter, "Children's Books Abroad," contains three sections, one on the United States, another on Australia, and a third on western Europe. Appendixes include a basic chronology and several bibliographies of general and specialized sources. Black-and-white illustrations are scattered throughout the text. Another pioneering history on the subject, also unfortunately out of print, is Percy H. Muir's *English Children's Books: 1600–1900* (Batsford, England, 1954, o.p.).

102   West, Mark I. *A Children's Literature Tour of Great Britain (On the Road with Mr. Toad, 1).* Scarecrow, 2003, pap., $29.95 (0-8108-4878-3).

Forty-nine sites in Great Britain that have a strong connection to children's literature are highlighted in this unusual literary guidebook. Each site is associated with a specific author (or in the cases of King Arthur and Robin Hood, a character). Each chapter supplies background information on the subject, including comments on the writings, biographical information, memorials, landscapes, visitor information, and even gift shops. Both children and adults will profit both from reading this book and from visiting these historic places.

103   White, Donna R. *A Century of Welsh Myth in Children's Literature.* Greenwood, 1998, $85 (0-313-30570-6).

This important study discusses the nature and place of fantasy in children's literature as well as its relationship specifically to Welsh lore. The author concentrates on the Welsh legends collectively known as the Mabinogion and supplies information on how these legends have been used as a source of inspiration for writers in the past 150 years. The author analyzes in depth the works of British writer Alan Garner and American Lloyd Alexander and more briefly discusses the novels of others. In passing, she studies the different perceptions of fantasy on both sides of the Atlantic. This is a highly readable volume on a specialized but interesting topic.

3. Important Monographs and Critical Studies

104   Agnew, Kate, and Geoff Fox. *Children at War: From the First World War to the Gulf.* Continuum, 2001, $85.95 (0-8264-4848-8).

Two English scholars wrote this overview of children's and young adult literature that deals with 20th-century wars. After an introductory overview, chapters each cover a different war. Two chapters are devoted to World War II: the first on the United Kingdom and North America and the second on mainland Europe. Each chapter is subdivided into specific topics, and individual books are discussed within each subdivision. The authors use an interesting narrative style and good critical judgment. Both old titles (for example, *The 39 Steps*) and new are covered, with an emphasis on young adult literature and books with a British focus.

105   Allen, Marjorie N. *What Are Little Girls Made Of? A Guide to Female Role Models in Children's Books.* Facts on File, 1999, $31.50 (0-8160-3673-X).

A fascinating book that traces the history and development of female characters in children's literature and notes the changes, trends, and developments that have been important. Allen also studies and enumerates the ways in which these characters have served and will serve as role models for female readers.

106   Anatol, Giselle Liza. *Reading Harry Potter: Critical Essays.* Praeger, 2003, $39.95 (0-313-32067-5).

The essays in this collection explore various aspects of the novels about Harry Potter, the boy-wizard with magical powers. The range of interests of the contributors allows for a variety of approaches and interpretations as they explore the meanings and attitudes toward such topics as justice, education, race, foreign cultures, class structure, and gender as revealed in these novels.

107   Anderson, Brian. *Sing a Song of Sixpence.* Cambridge, 1987, o.p.

To celebrate the 1986–87 exhibition at the British Library that was a homage to Randolph Caldecott and his work, Anderson wrote this elegant essay. It describes the history of picture books and production techniques from illustrated manuscripts to today's product, with an emphasis on Caldecott. Anderson gives an appraisal of those who influenced Caldecott and details the effect he had on those who followed him. A richly illustrated book.

108 *The Arbuthnot Lectures, 1980–1989.* American Library Association/ Association of Library Services for Children, 1991, $12, o.p.

May Hill Arbuthnot (1884–1968) was a distinguished professor and writer on children's literature. The annual prize, named in her honor, recognizes an important contributor to the field. Many viewpoints are represented in these speeches by individuals including Dorothy Butler, a reading specialist from Australia; Fritz Eichenberg, an expatriate German illustrator; Aidan Chambers, a British scholar; and Leland B. Jacobs, an American educator. A previous volume was *The Arbuthnot Lectures, 1970–1979* (ALA/ALSC, 1981, o.p.).

109 Arizpe, Evelyn, and Morag Styles. *Children Reading Pictures: Interpreting Visual Texts.* Routledge-Falmer, 2003, $129.95 (0-415-27577-6).

These two well-known children's literature scholars report on a British two-year study of children's responses to contemporary picture books. Primary school children from different backgrounds read and discussed books by two British authors/illustrators, Anthony Browne and Satochi Kitamura. The children were also encouraged to create their own drawings inspired by these books. The authors found that children are more sophisticated readers than suspected and can make sense of complex images on different levels. They are able to understand different viewpoints, moods, and messages. Although this book is intellectual in treatment of the data, the work is fascinating and accessible. Morag Styles, along with Victor Watson, also edited another excellent examination of picture books, *Talking Pictures: Pictorial Text and Young Readers* (Hodder and Stoughton, 1996, o.p.). Another perspective on picture books is found in David Lewis's *Reading Contemporary Picturebooks: Picturing Text* (see entry below).

110 Aronson, Marc. *Beyond the Pale: New Essays for a New Era.* Scarecrow, 2003, $42.50 (0-8108-4638-1).

Part of the Scarecrow Studies in Young Adult Literature series, this is a new collection of provocative and informative essays, many of which were delivered as speeches during 2001 and 2002. Many subjects are covered, including the controversial topic of culturally specific book awards. Others essays deal with the impact of September 11, 2001, on art, history, and young people, and the process and difficulties of writing and publishing for a young adult audience. Aronson also discusses the problems in reaching a male audience. A final essay recapitulates many of the ideas explored earlier. One reviewer said this book should be required reading for anyone involved with young adults and their reading.

111   Aronson, Marc. *Exploding the Myths: The Truth About Teens and Reading.* Scarecrow, 2001, $27.50 ((0-8108-3904-0).

Aronson, an award-winning writer of books for teenagers, has written a series of provocative essays that explore the nature and potential of young adult literature, the problems that surround reading guidance for teenagers, the prejudices adults have about this group and their reading, and possible solutions to working with this new generation of readers.

112   Avery, Gillian, and Julia Briggs, eds. *Children and Their Books: A Celebration of the Work of Iona and Peter Opie.* Oxford, 1989, o.p.

This collection of 20 essays was assembled as a tribute to the children's literature scholars and writers Iona and Peter Opie. Many diverse topics are covered, including book collecting, children's diaries, and Puritan literature. About half of the essays deal with individual authors—J. R. R. Tolkien, Lewis Carroll, Henry James, and Beatrix Potter, for example.

113   Bang, Molly Garrett. *Picture This: How Pictures Work.* SeaStar Books, 2000, pap., $12.95 (1-5871-7030-2).

In this new edition of a book first published in 1991, the noted illustrator again uses drawings and text to explore the basic design ideas and the elements of composition that are found in children's picture books. Using the story of *Little Red Riding Hood* as an example, she discusses the characteristics of line, color, shape, and so forth, with explanations of their function in art. A fine beginning introduction to the elements of art, explained simply and clearly.

114   Beetz, Kirk H. *Exploring C. S. Lewis' The Chronicles of Narnia.* Beacham, 2001, pap., $24.95 (0-933833-58-X).

This guide to the seven Narnia novels is disappointing because of the repetitious, and often confusing, text. Nevertheless, it has some positive values. The introductory biography of Lewis is good and there is a map for each book, a chapter-by-chapter summary, explanations of references in the text, and discussion questions. Two additional guides are available from used-book dealers: *Journeys into Narnia* (Hope Publishing House, 1976, o.p.) by Kathryn Lindskoog and *Companion to Narnia* (Collier, 1980, o.p.) by Paul F. Ford.

115   Bettelheim, Bruno. *The Uses of Enchantment: The Meaning and Importance of Fairy Tales.* Vintage, 1989, pap., $19.95 (0-679-72393-5).

Written by the late, well-known analyst, this is an exploration of fairy tales from the psychoanalytical point of view. He discusses their hidden meanings, appropriateness at different ages, and value in the development of children. Chapters discuss different fairy tales under such headings as "Transformations" and "Oedipal Conflicts and Resolutions." Another psychological study on the subject is *The Interpretation of Fairy Tales* (Shambhala, 1996, pap., $14.95 [0-8777-3526-3]), by Marie-Louise von Franz and Kendra Crossen.

116   Bott, C. J. *The Bully in the Book and in the Classroom.* Scarecrow, 2004, $30 (08108-5048-6).

The opening chapter of this resource describes the bully and his or her victims. Subsequent chapters provide appropriate titles for K–12 students. Each chapter highlights eight to ten books, giving suggested activities, discussion topics, and up-to-date sources.

117   Brooks, Walter R. *The Art of Freddy.* Overlook, 2003, $35 (1-58567-351-3).

Many children in the 1930s through the 1950s enjoyed the exploits of Freddy the Pig and his friends from Bean Farm. This 75th anniversary volume is a collection of 200 text fragments and illustrations by Kurt Wiese that represent a cross-section of publications from 1928 through 1958. The arrangement is by topics and the editing is done in a masterful fashion by Michael Cart. There is a separate 24-page color section that showcases the cover art of each title. Some of these books are back in print and this volume will highlight their place in the history of children's literature.

118   Brown, Joanne, and Nancy St. Clair. *Declarations of Independence: Empowered Girls in Young Adult Literature, 1990–2001.* Scarecrow, 2002, $32.50 (0-8108-4290-4).

In this readable work, the authors first supply background historical material on the representation of female protagonists in early books for young adults (for example, the works of Louisa May Alcott and Maureen Daly). They then focus on the new "empowered" girls found in recent titles. Arranged by genre (for example, historical novels and fantasy), contemporary writers including Karen Hesse, Robin McKinley, and Virginia Euwer Wolff are discussed. This is a good introduction to the feminist approach in viewing young adult literature.

119   Butts, Dennis, ed. *Stories and Society: Children's Literature in Its Social Context.* Macmillan (London), 1992, o.p.

This important collection of essays by such writers as Gillian Avery, Perry Nodelman, and Peter Hunt explores children's literature from the standpoint of the social forces that have influenced its history and development in Britain and America. Most of the essays are arranged under such genres as the school story, the home story, the adventure story, and fantasy, but there are two essays on individual authors, Louisa May Alcott and A. A. Milne. The coverage is primarily British, but some American authors and developments are covered.

120   Carlsen, G. Robert. *Literature Is . . . Collected Essays by G. Robert Carlsen.* Auburn University, 1998, $12, o.p.

This compendium of significant essays by and about the noted scholar and advocate of adolescent literature was edited by Anne Sherrill and Terry C. Ley. It consists of 35 previously published articles by Carlsen about young adults and their reading, three chapters from his landmark *Books and the Teenage Reader*, now out of print, and three original essays by former students of Carlsen, including Ken Donelson.

121   Chambers, Aidan. *Reading Talk.* Thimble Press, 2001, pap., £10 (0-903355-50-7).

Chambers is one of the foremost British supporters of children's literature as well as a prize-winning writer of young adult novels. This collection of speeches and papers deals with such topics as the author's reading as a child, the problems and pleasures of translating foreign children's books into English, and foreign novels of note. Two other excellent books by Chambers are *Tell Me: Children, Reading, and Talk* (Stenhouse, 1995, $12.50 [1-571-10030-X]) and *The Reading Environment: How Adults Help Children Enjoy Books* (Stenhouse, 1995, $12.95 [1-571-110029-6]).

122   Clark, Beverley Lyon, and Margaret Higonnet. *Girls, Boys, Books, Toys: Gender in Children's Literature and Culture.* Johns Hopkins University, 1999, $45 (0-801-86053-9); pap., $21.95 (0-8018-6526-3).

After a splendid introduction by Clark on the history of feminist literary theory and children's literature criticism, this book, written by 22 scholars, examines facets of the intersection of feminism, children's literature, and culture. Topics discussed include Mary Poppins, Robert Louis Stevenson, 19th-century adventure stories, gender symbolism, and dinosaurs. This evocative collection of essays criticizes outmoded feminist thinking and proposes new ways of thinking about gender and children's literature.

123   Cooper, Susan. *Dreams and Wishes: Essays on Writing for Children.* McElderry, 1996, $18 (0-689-80736-8).

In an informal manner, the author discusses her personal sources of creativity in an introductory essay, 14 speeches that cover a 20-year span, and an interview. The reader learns about Cooper's ideas about life in her exploration of such topics as war, fear, education, and family. The noted writer of fantasy fiction also explores her beliefs about writing and reading and their importance in today's world.

124   Crew, Hilary S. *Is It Really "Mommie Dearest"? Mother-Daughter Narratives in Young Adult Fiction.* Scarecrow, 2002, $48 (0-8108-3692-0).

The author discusses mother-daughter relationships as portrayed in more than 100 young adult novels and short stories published between 1965 and 1998. While interweaving literary criticism with connections to adolescent psychology and sociology, she examines topics including various types of conflicts, sexual identity, cross-cultural communication, grandmother-granddaughter relations, independence, separation, and African American mother-daughter narratives. A fascinating look at an interesting topic.

125   Dresang, Eliza T. *Radical Change: Books for Youth in a Digital Age.* Wilson, 1999, $60 (0-8242-0953-2).

In this innovative work, the author discusses more than 200 groundbreaking books, ranging from picture books to young adult novels and including some nonfiction and poetry. Some titles are challenging in structure and subject matter, others break boundaries in format and style, and still others present different points of view and resolutions. All are intended to stimulate and enrich the reader. An evaluation guide and extensive annotated bibliography are included. As one reviewer said, this is a "valuable overview of the recent evolution of children's literature."

126   Eccleshare, Julia. *A Guide to the Harry Potter Novels.* Continuum, 2002, pap., $25.95.

This is a lively and enthusiastic analysis of the first four Harry Potter books. In addition to providing good plot summaries and fine character analyses, the author discusses the books' origins, influences, and place in children's literature. She supplies good background information but is not sufficiently critical in her evaluation of the books. There are several books on the Potter phenomenon. One aimed at the classroom teacher is *Beacham's Sourcebook for Teaching Young Adult Fiction: Exploring Harry Potter* (Beacham, 2000, $24.95 [0-9338-3357-1]) by Elizabeth D. Schafer and Elizabeth D. Sullivan. See also the entry under Lana A. Whited below.

127   Edwards, Margaret A. *The Fair Garden and the Swarm of Beasts: The Library and the Young Adult.* American Library Association, 2002, $20 (0-8389-3533-8).

To celebrate the 100th anniversary of Margaret Edwards's birth, this new edition of her 1969 book has been reissued with an introduction by Betty Carter, who puts the wise and wonderful thoughts penned by Edwards concerning her commitment to young adults and their readings into a 21st-century context. Some other inspirational classics about young people and their reading are:

Duff, Annis. *Bequest of Wings: A Family's Pleasure with Books.* Viking, 1944, o.p.

Duff, Annis. *Longer Flight: A Family Grows Up with Books.* Viking, 1955, o.p.

Hazard, Paul. *Books, Children, and Men.* Horn Book, 1947, o.p.

Smith, Lillian H. *The Unreluctant Years.* American Library Association, 1953, o.p.

Viguers, Ruth Hill. *Margin for Surprise: About Books, Children, and Librarians.* Little, Brown, 1964, o.p.

128   Evans, Janet, ed. *What's in the Picture? Responding to Illustrations in Picture Books.* Paul Chapman, 1998, $24.95 (1-85396-378-9).

In this British import, the contributors explore many issues involved in using picture books to promote emotional and intellectual development in children. The importance of using illustrations as clues to print understanding is emphasized. The fact that learning from picture books depends on such factors as race, gender, and class is explored in several essays. The use of picture books as a learning resource and as an aid for fostering both aesthetic development and reading skills is also covered in this interesting monograph.

129   Fox, Dana L., and Kathy G. Short, eds. *Stories Matter: The Complexity of Cultural Authenticity in Children's Literature.* National Council of Teachers of English, 2003, $35.95 (0-8141-4744-5).

This collection of essays discusses current debates, new questions and critiques, and historical events involved in authentically portraying different cultures in children's literature. Contributors include authors, illustrators, editors, publishers, educators, teachers, and librarians. Topics explored involve the social responsibility of authors, the role of imagination in writing for children, cultural sensitivity, authenticity of images, artistic freedom, and the role of multicultural literature in education.

130 Gavin, Adrianne E., and Christopher Routledge, eds. *Mystery in Children's Literature: From the Rational to the Supernatural.* Palgrave Macmillan, 2001, $75 (0-333-91881-9).

Several internationally recognized scholars contributed to this collection of 13 essays that explore the many facets of mystery writing for children, from the conventional detective story to supernatural and horror mysteries. Though British in emphasis, the authors and books discussed are from many English-speaking countries and represent a wide definition of the term "mystery." The authors covered include Enid Blyton, Philippa Pierce, and Margaret Mahy.

131 Greenway, Betty. *A Stranger Shore: A Critical Introduction to the Work of Mollie Hunter.* Scarecrow, 1998, $44 (0-8108-3469-3).

This is the first full-length study of the works of this distinguished British novelist. Although known primarily for her historical novels and her intriguing fantasies, Hunter is also the author of realistic novels set in contemporary times as well as a body of nonfiction essays on writing for children. All of these genres are examined in this revealing critical study.

132 Guroian, Vigen. *Tending the Heart of Virtue: How Classic Stories Awaken a Child's Moral Imagination.* Oxford, 1998, $22 (0-19-511787-5).

The purpose of this book, written by a conservative and a member of the religious right, is to help parents and others form moral character in their youngsters by leading them to stories that are rich in virtuous messages and Christian teachings. Many of the recommended authors and titles are from the 19th and early 20th centuries, when children's literature was more didactic and moralistic. Among the highlighted authors are Hans Christian Andersen, C. S. Lewis, and George MacDonald.

133 Hearne, Betsy, ed. *Story: From Fireplace to Cyberspace.* University of Illinois, 1998, $21.95 (0-87845-105-6).

This collection of ten papers presented at the Allerton Park Institute in 1997, explores "story" in four different contexts: first, as practice, in which a lengthy unit for second-graders on folklore is presented; second, as theory, which matches story and audiences; third, as literature, where story is used as a bridge to different cultures; and, finally, as institutional culture, in which publishing and libraries are discussed.

134 Hearne, Betsy, ed. *The Zena Sutherland Lectures, 1983–1992.* Clarion, 1993, $25 (0-395-64504-2).

In these lectures presented at the University of Chicago, ten authors discuss the creative process, influences that shaped their lives and writing, and their thoughts on childhood and growing up. Among the authors included are Maurice Sendak, Lloyd Alexander, Virginia Hamilton, Paula Fox, Jean Fritz, Betsy Byers, and Robert Cormier. A related collection also honoring this important advocate of children's literature is *Celebrating Children's Books: Essays on Children's Literature in Honor of Zena Sutherland* (Morrow, 1986, o.p.).

135   Hollindale, Peter. *Signs of Childness in Children's Books.* Thimble Press, 1997, £8.95, o.p.

This important British theorist on children's literature presents a provocative poststructuralist view on approaching children's literature. He proposes a new, refreshing way of studying books for children and reaching a definition of childhood. He also discusses the meaning of the term "youth" and of young adult literature. Another interesting viewpoint on picture books from Thimble Press is *Looking at Pictures in Picture Books* by Jane Doonan (Thimble Press, 1993, £8.50 (0-903355-40-X).

136   Howard, Vivian. *Hot, Hotter, Hottest: The Best of the YA Hotline.* Scarecrow, 2002, pap., $32.50 (0-8108-4240-8).

A collection of articles pertaining to young adult literature that appeared in *YA Hotline*, a newsletter written by graduate students in the Young Adult Literature and Media Interests class in the School of Library and Information Studies at Dalhousie University in Canada.

137   Hunt, Peter, ed. *Children's Literature: The Development of Criticism.* Routledge, 1990, $25 (0-415-02994-5).

This is a stimulating collection of essays that explore, from many facets, the nature of children's literature and how a body of valid criticism has been amassed. Some essays are historical in nature (for example, contributions by Dickens and Ruskin), but most deal with contemporary ideas on the subject by such writers as Hugo Crago, Lissa Paul, J. R. R. Tolkien, and John Rowe Townsend. Hunt's own book *Criticism, Theory and Children's Literature* (Blackwell, 1991, o.p.) is a probing study that questions basic assumptions about children's literature.

138   Jones, Gerard. *Killing Monsters: Why Children Need Fantasy, Super Heroes, and Make-Believe Violence.* Basic Books, 2002, $25 (0-465-03695-3).

The author maintains that violence in popular culture, particularly in high-quality books written for children, can often serve a useful purpose by objectifying the violent emotions youngsters feel and by giving an imaginary sense of power to the helpless child. In 13 chapters, the author explores these themes, with examples from research and from various media popular with young people. A stimulating, effective defense.

139   Kiefer, Barbara Z. *The Potential of Picture Books: From Visual Literacy to Aesthetic Understanding.* Prentice Hall, 1995, o.p.

This unique look at picture books combines material from art education, research on how children learn, and the author's background as a practicing artist. It examines theories about verbal and visual literacy and artistic response. There are also practical suggestions for teachers on using picture books in the curriculum to promote literacy and to involve children in the study of picture books.

140   Konigsburg, E. L. *Talk Talk: A Children's Book Author Speaks to Grown-Ups.* Atheneum, 1995, $29.95 (0-689-31993-2).

This collection of essays by the prize-winning juvenile author consists of acceptance speeches for various awards received between 1960 and 1990. The ten speeches reproduced here cover such topics as the creative spirit, the art of writing, the nature and importance of literature, and the young reader. She writes in a clear, interesting, and often humorous fashion.

141   Krashen, Stephen. *The Power of Reading: Insights from the Research*, 2nd ed. Libraries Unlimited, 2004, $25 (1-59158-169-9).

This new, updated, and welcomed second edition covers new research done in the last ten years and reviews older research, all pointing to the fact that reading is a prime factor in children and adults achieving success in their pursuits. The author again maintains that free voluntary reading (FVR) is an important tool in increasing a child's ability to read, write, spell, and comprehend. The collected data originate in studies made in a number of countries.

142   Lehr, Susan. *Battling Dragons: Issues and Controversy in Children's Literature.* Heinemann, 1995, $28 (0-4350-8828-9).

The 20 essays in this work emphasize the political and social dimensions of children's literature. Seven essays are by practicing authors such as Brian Jacques and Beverly Naidoo; the rest are by critics including John Milne and Barbara Keifer. Among the subjects covered are stereotypes, censorship, depiction of minorities, dragons in Eastern and Western literature, political correctness, and violence in picture books. This is an intriguing and valuable exploration of different points of view.

143   Lewis, David. *Reading Contemporary Picturebooks: Picturing Text.*
Routledge, 2001, $25.95 (0-4152-0887-4).

The author presents a philosophical approach to the study of children's
picture books. In a series of interconnected essays, he uses winners of the
United Kingdom's Emil Award (see Chapter 6) to analyze the role of picture books in reading instruction and to explore how children make
meanings from pictures. He also examines the interrelationship of text
and pictures and, applying ecological terms, sees each picture book as a
miniature ecosystem.

144   Lurie, Alison. *Boys and Girls Forever: Children's Classics from
Cinderella to Harry Potter.* Penguin, 2003, pap., $15 (0-14-200252-6).

In this collection of essays by the Pulitzer Prize author, Lurie explores the
premise that "the most gifted authors of books for children are not like
other writers: instead, in some essential way, they are children themselves." She examines works by Hans Christian Andersen, Louisa May
Alcott, L. Frank Baum, Walter de la Mare, Tove Jansson, John Masefield,
Dr. Seuss, and J. K. Rowling, and connects their private lives and struggles to their books for young readers. This is an engaging, effective exploration of an interesting idea.

145   Lurie, Alison. *Don't Tell the Grown-Ups: The Subversive Power of
Children's Literature.* Warner, 1998, $16.99 (0-3162-4625-5).

In this collection of pieces previously published in various journals, the
author discusses children's books that challenge adult authority and
mores. With a dry wit and entertaining writing style, Lurie analyzes the
works of writers including E. Nesbit, A. A. Milne, J. R. R. Tolkien, T. H.
White, Richard Adams, and William Mayne. Other areas considered
include folktales, street rhymes, and jokes and riddles. This excellent
overview shows how, in subtle ways, many classic authors embedded
social criticism within their stories.

146   McGillis, Roderick. *Children's Literature and the Fin de Siècle.* Praeger,
2002, $59.95 (0-313-32120-5).

Using an international approach, the essays in this anthology examine
the end-of-century conditions and tensions in 19th- and 20th-century
children's literature. Topics discussed include the breakdown of language,
social engineering, the Holocaust, fear in contemporary fantasy, and
evolving ideas of masculinity. The reader also gets a glimpse of what the
future might hold for children's literature.

147 McGillis, Roderick. *For the Childlike: George MacDonald's Fantasies for Children.* Scarecrow, 1992, $35 (0-8108-2459-0).

George MacDonald (1824–1905) was perhaps the most important of the Victorian fantasists, with such titles as *At the Back of the North Wind* and his *Fairy Tales* continuing in print through today. This is a collection of 16 essays edited by McGillis that explore various aspects of MacDonald as an important pioneer in British children's literature. Five of the essays are reprints and 11 are original to this anthology.

148 McGillis, Roderick. *The Nimble Reader: Literary Theory and Children's Literature.* Twayne, 1996, o.p.

The author, now a distinguished professor of English in Calgary, Alberta, shows how different literary theories can be applied when reading children's literature and how they can be used to produce insightful, imaginative, and creative readers. Each chapter deals with a different critical theory—formalism, new criticism, and poststructuralism, for example. In one fascinating section, several contexts are used to bring out different meanings in "Jack Be Nimble." Particularly noteworthy is how the author makes modern critical theory accessible and understandable.

149 McGillis, Roderick. *Voices of the Other: Children's Literature in the Postcolonial Context.* Garland, 2000, $75 (0-8153-3284-X).

The 18 essays in this collection by a variety of authors demonstrate a variety of approaches to children's literature from a postcolonial, international perspective. Topics discussed include culture, race theory, pedagogy, and multiculturalism. Divided into three sections, this book first presents theoretical considerations, followed by a discussion of postcolonial culture and literature for children from the 19th century on, and concludes with a lengthy section on contemporary texts that deal with colonialism.

150 Mackey, Margaret, ed. *Beatrix Potter's Peter Rabbit: A Children's Classic at 100.* Scarecrow, 2002, $37.50 (0-8108-4197-5).

An enjoyable, insightful collection of essays that celebrate one of the most endearing rabbits in all literature. The book is in four parts. In the first part, Lawrence R. Sipes reviews children's responses to this classic and Carole Scott applies semiotic theory to its words and pictures. The second part gives historical background, and the third part contains six essays that explore the popularity of the book. The concluding section gives details of the adaptations, changes, and translations of the text that have occurred during its 100-year history.

151   MacLeod, Anne Scott. *American Childhood: Essays in Children's Literature of the Nineteenth and Twentieth Centuries.* University of Georgia, 1994, o.p.

The 14 essays in this stimulating collection trace the changes in American concepts of childhood over a period of 200 years by examining the children's literature (particularly the domestic novel) of these times. Topics covered include censorship and the changing portrayal of parents and the family. Another study by this author on American society and its mirror in children's literature is *A Moral Tale: Children's Fiction and American Culture, 1820–1860* (Archon, 1975, o.p.).

152   Mallan, Kerry, and Sharyn Pearce, eds. *Youth Cultures: Texts, Images, and Identities.* Praeger, 2003, $64 (0-275-97409-X).

By examining youth and its culture as reflected in literature, magazines, computer games, films, television programs, popular music, and fashion, this volume of essays applies critical ideas and theories to the controversies that surround these media. The editors are both Australian scholars and the material covered has an international point of view.

153   Marantz, Sylvia S. *Picture Books for Looking and Learning: Awakening Visual Perceptions Through the Art of Children's Books.* Oryx, 1992, $24.95 (0-89774-716-X).

Through a detailed analysis of the picture book, this work fosters a greater understanding and appreciation of that art form. Focusing on 43 well-chosen books, the author discusses, in about four pages per book, all aspects of each book, especially design techniques such as shape, color, media, and design. She also looks at the illustrator, dust jacket, end papers, and title page, and gives a page-by-page analysis.

154   Marcus, Leonard S. *Ways of Telling: Conversations in the Art of the Picture Book.* Dutton, 2002, $29.99 (0-525-46490-5).

In conversations that took place from 1988 to 1999 with 14 picture book creators, the author illuminates the relationship between words and art and the dialogue that exists between the creator and his or her audience. Among those interviewed are Maurice Sendak, Robert McCloskey, Eric Carle, Mitsumasa Anno, Charlotte Zolotow, and James Marshall. Each artist describes influences and how the picture book is perceived. This is a highly readable glimpse into the creative process from various points of view.

155   May, Jill P. *Children's Literature and Critical Theory.* Oxford, 1995, $28.95 (0-19-509584-7).

This controversial work (Peter Hunt, the noted critic, calls it about the worst book ever on children's literature) has as its purpose "to encourage sensitivity to critical theory and to shape real readers into critical readers." It begins with an overview of different schools of literary criticism and then presents material on applying reader response theory to many different children's books. Such topics as criticism of myths, racist depictions in old texts and historical fiction, and how to help children find different levels of meaning are discussed.

156 Meek, Margaret, ed. *Children's Literature and National Identity.* Trentham Books, 2001, $65 (1-85856-204-X).

The question of national identity and its relation to children's literature is explored in this group of papers that were presented at a conference in 1998 by European writers. The papers explore various facets of what is considered "ourselves" and what is considered "others" in children's literature. After a general introduction on the international use of children's picture books, various contributors explore aspects of national identity in books from such countries as Hungary, the United Kingdom, France, Germany, Italy, and Ireland.

157 Meltzer, Milton. *Nonfiction for the Classroom: Milton Meltzer on Writing, History, and Social Responsibility.* International Reading Association and Teachers College Press, 1994, pap., $18.95 (0-8077-3378-4).

This is a collection of previously published speeches, articles, and essays by the famous nonfiction writer Milton Meltzer. Some of the issues addressed are racism, a writer's social responsibility, the importance of the study of history, and how to get youngsters to think critically. In short, this is a stimulating read for people interested in the writing and utilization of nonfiction for young readers.

158 Moore, John Noell. *Interpreting Young Adult Literature: Literary Theory in the Secondary Classroom.* Heinemann, 1997, pap., $27.50 (0-86709-414-1).

In separate chapters, the author discusses various contemporary literary theories—structuralism, archetypal theory, formalism, feminism, cultural studies, and deconstruction, for example—and applies them to specific adolescent novels including *M. C. Higgins, the Great* and *Moves Make the Man.* The text is abstract and scholarly, but this work is unique in that it brings contemporary literary thinking into the world of the young adult novel.

159 Nikolajeva, Maria. *Children's Literature Comes of Age: Toward a New Aesthetic.* Garland, 1996, $85 (0-8153-1556-2).

Part of Jack Zipes's Children's Literature and Culture Series, this highly abstract volume applies such current literary theories as semiotics, intertextuality, and metafictionality to children's literature. The opening chapters describe world literature versus children's literature, and the differences between children's and adult literature (the author maintains they contain two different "codes"). Later chapters trace the evolution of children's literature, again from a theoretical point of view. The author stresses the ways in which children's literature continues to evolve. Final chapters analyze the work of such writers as Lloyd Alexander, Natalie Babbitt, J. M. Barrie, L. Frank Baum, Cynthia Voigt, and Madeleine L'Engle.

160   Nikolajeva, Maria. *The Rhetoric of Character in Children's Literature.* Scarecrow, 2002, $55 (0-8108-4250-5).

In a series of thought-provoking chapters, the author explores the nature of character development in children's literature. The opening chapters explore ways in which characters come alive in fiction, methods of creating character, and approaches to understanding character. The second part of the book discusses the techniques of learning about characters. Examples are drawn from both classic and contemporary sources, from Christopher Robin and the Wizard of Oz to Harry Potter. In an earlier book, *From Myth to Linear* (Scarecrow, 2000, pap., $39.50 [0-808-4952-6]), the author discusses the concept of time in children's literature.

161   Nikolajeva, Maria, and Carole Scott. *How Picturebooks Work.* Garland, 2001, $95 (0-8153-3486-9).

The authors present an interesting thesis about picture books: that words and pictures serve different functions (the text speeds the action, and the pictures slow it down). When words and pictures complement one another and fill the gap between action and a comment on the action, then all is in harmony. This harmony is necessary to produce a satisfactory picture book. Many examples and black-and-white illustrations from British, American, Australian, and Swedish children's literature are included. This is an interesting application of contemporary literary criticism to the world of the picture book.

162   Nodelman, Perry. *Touchstones.* 3 vols. Scarecrow, 1989, $75 (0-8108-2564-3).

The three volumes in this set contain scholarly, analytical essays by prominent writers in the field of children's literature on individual books for children. Volume 1 focuses on well-known novels such as *Alice's Adventures in Wonderland, The Hobbit,* and *Harriet the Spy;* Volume 2 deals with collections of fairy tales, myths, legends, and poetry; and Volume 3 concentrates on picture books by such artists as Beatrix Potter,

Maurice Sendak, Ezra Jack Keats, and Leo Lionni. Each of these important critical works is also available separately:

Touchstones: Volume One: Reflections on the Best in Children's Literature. 1985, $39 (0-8108-2561-9).

Touchstones: Volume Two: Fairy Tales, Fables, Myths, Legends, and Poetry: Reflections on the Best in Children's Literature. 1987, $32 (0-8108-2562-7).

Touchstones: Volume Three: Picture Books: Reflections on the Best in Children's Literature. 1989, $32.50 (0-8108-2563-5).

163 Nodelman, Perry. *Words About Pictures: The Narrative Art of Children's Picture Books.* University of Georgia, 1988, $35 (0-8203-1271-1).

This important critical overview of picture books raises key issues and applies theories of art, literary criticism, and philosophy to a discussion of picture books, a genre that the author considers a serious art form. He explores the elements of text and pictures, discusses their separate natures, and points out how they work together. Using many examples from well-known artists, Nodelman shows how children can be encouraged to develop critical attitudes and perspectives. This is a scholarly, witty, and informative book by one of Canada's leading literary critics.

164 Nodelman, Perry, and Mavis Reimer. *The Pleasures of Children's Literature*, 3rd ed. Pearson, Allyn and Bacon, 2002, $57 (0-8013-3248-6).

The authors use recent research and literary theories to fulfill two goals. The first is to provide adults with the "contexts and strategies" to understand and enjoy children's literature and the second is to show that children "can be taught—and would benefit from—these contexts and strategies." The opening chapters are on the history of attitudes toward children and an exploration of the traditional ideas we have about children's literature. There follows an explanation of contemporary literary theory, plus an exploration of the influences of popular culture on literary appreciation. This is a thought-provoking scholarly volume. (See also Chapter 11 for an online bibliography related to this work.)

165 Oberstein, Karin Lesnik. *Children's Literature: Criticism and the Fictional Child.* Oxford, 1994, $87 (0-19-811998-4).

This book is a study of the "child" as presented in the field of criticism of children's literature. The author contends that the realm of childhood has been constructed by the adult reader, and she wants literary theory to be tempered by current thinking about childhood in psychology and psychotherapy.

166 Paterson, Katherine. *The Invisible Child: On Reading and Writing Books for Children.* Dutton, 2001, $24.99 (0-525-46482-4).

Some of the 22 essays and speeches found in this collection appeared previously in the author's *Gates of Excellence* (Elsevier/Nelson, 1981, o.p.), *The Spying Heart* (Dutton, 1988, o.p.), and *A Sense of Wonder* (Plume, 1995, o.p.). In addition to discussing her own writing, Paterson candidly discusses book publishing and marketing, the reading interests of children, and how characters are created on the printed page. Her acceptance speeches for two Newbery Awards and two National Book Awards are included. This is a refreshing, wise, and thoughtful treasure trove.

167 Paul, Lissa. *Reading Otherways.* Boynton/Cook, 1998, o.p.

As well as being an important work in feminist criticism, this volume points the way to new ways of teaching reading. The author stresses the need for familiarity with the text one teaches, which can be achieved through intense reading and rereading. She explains how several critical theories have evolved and shows how a good teacher can bring out different interpretations through questioning the reader. A behind-the-scenes look at publishing can be found in the author's recent *The Children's Book Business* (Routledge, 2003, $85 [0-4159-3789-2]).

168 Rahn, Suzanne. *L. Frank Baum's World of Oz: A Classic Series at 100.* Scarecrow, 2003, $39.95 (0-8108-4380-3).

After an introductory historical survey of the entire field of Oz, this book of collected essays is organized into three sections. In the first section, the essays explore the origins of Oz, with material on Baum himself; in the second, on the "World of Oz," Baum's world is explored, with material on concepts of home and family, his sense of humor, and his relationship to his readers. The third section discusses the various motion pictures that have been made of the Oz books.

169 Rahn, Suzanne. *Rediscoveries in Children's Literature.* Garland, 1995, $30 (0-8153-0930-9).

Rahn discusses the works of a number of writers she feels have been unjustly neglected. Among the authors highlighted are Frank Stockton (who created American children's fantasy), Florence Crannell Means, Maud Hart Lovelace and her Betsy-Tacy books, Dorothy Canfield, Diana Wynne Jones, and Beverly Cleary. Rahn argues for satisfying readers with tastes outside the mainstream, and suggests that librarians reach out to introduce a wider variety of good books. This book is attractively illustrated.

170   Reimer, Mavis. *Such a Simple Little Tale: Critical Responses to L. M. Montgomery's Anne of Green Gables.* Scarecrow, 1992, pap., $29.95 (0-8108-3985-7).

Lucy Maud Montgomery's enduring tale about Anne Shirley and her childhood on Prince Edward Island first appeared in 1908 and was followed by several sequels. Here is a compilation of the best critical essays on this beloved classic. There is also a comprehensive bibliographic guide to the research and criticism of this book, from the earliest reviews to the early 1990s.

171   Rollin, Lucy, and Mark I. West. *Psychoanalytic Responses to Children's Literature.* McFarland, 1999, $34.50 (0-7864-0674-7).

Drawing on the psychoanalytic thoughts and ideas of such authorities as Freud and Jacques Lacan, the author explores the psychological subtexts of a number of important children's books. In the book's 16 chapters such works are discussed as *Pinocchio, James and the Giant Peach, The Wind in the Willows, Harriet the Spy, The Prince and the Pauper,* and *Charlotte's Web.* Some chapters also focus on a single author, such as Beatrix Potter. Another important book by Mark I. West, now unfortunately out of print, is *Children, Culture, and Controversy* (Scarecrow, 1988), in which he examines some of the major controversies in the history of American children's literature.

172   Rose, Jacqueline. *The Case of Peter Pan or The Impossibility of Children's Fiction.* University of Pennsylvania Press, 1993, pap., $15.95 (0-8122-1435-8).

This is a reprint of the original 1984 edition, with a new introduction. In such chapters as "Peter Pan and Freud," "Peter Pan and Literature and the Child," and "Peter Pan and the Commercialization of the Child," the author explores the meanings of Peter Pan and what these meanings reveal about our conception of childhood. She uses the publication of *Peter Pan* as a springboard to go back through the history of children's fiction and to look at the evolution of today's criticism of children's literature. Along the way, she comments on some of the important contemporary writers of children's books. Although some reviewers hailed this as a landmark study, others disagree and find the author's arguments exaggerated.

173   Sadler, Glenn Edward, ed. *Teaching Children's Literature: Issues, Pedagogy, Resources.* Modern Language Association, 1992, $37.50, o.p.

This work treats children's literature as a serious subject for literary study and gives an overview of resources in the area. Some of the top specialists in the field of children's literature have contributed to this volume, including Jon Stott, Francelia Butler, Mark West, and Alethea Helbig.

The work is divided into four parts. The first part, which is the longest and best, covers such topics as a definition of the field, the nature of content, genre issues, the role of theory, and feminist issues. The second part gives course descriptions, and the third describes advanced programs and collections in children's literature. The last part contains a short list of resources—books, periodicals, annuals, and so forth. An update would increase this book's value.

174   Schwarcz, Joseph H., and Chava Schwarcz. ***Childhood Through the Art of Illustration.*** American Library Association, 1991, o.p.

As one reviewer stated, this book "develops levels of interpretation and response rarely accorded picture book art." In discussing the possibilities of picture book analysis, the authors look at topics including psychological dimensions of story and images, descriptions of emotional states, and the exploration of stress, love, and anxiety. Many examples are cited and more than 80 illustrators are discussed. Noteworthy are the analyses of Anthony Browne, Maurice Sendak, and Ezra Jack Keats. There are numerous illustrations, but they are all in black and white.

175   Sebesta, Sam Lector, and Ken Donelson. ***Inspiring Literacy: Literature for Children and Young Adults.*** Transaction, 1993, $24.95 (1-56000-668-4).

This collection of essays, by such specialists as Robert Probst, Bernice Cullinan, and Barbara Keifer, examines what children read and what motivates them to read. Topics addressed include trends in publishing, recent changes in teaching reading, and the status of multicultural literature.

176   Shulevitz, Uri. ***Writing with Pictures: How to Write and Illustrate Children's Books.*** Watson-Guptill, 1985, $29.95 (0-8230-5935-9).

After distinguishing between picture books and storybooks with pictures, the author discusses technical concerns and how they affect a book's physical structure, the various purposes of illustrations, and the art of drawing. He offers practical advice on creating storyboards, preparing pages for the printer, and making sketches. The emphasis is on drawing rather than on writing, but this is a fine, well-illustrated, and inspiring guide for the novice.

177   Smedman, M. Sarah, and Joel D. Chaston. ***Bridges for the Young: The Fiction of Katherine Paterson.*** Scarecrow, 2003, $39.50 (0-8108-4499-0).

This is a collection of essays by various literary critics on the novels of Katherine Paterson. As well as examining literary style, influences, themes, attitudes, and impact, these pieces often focus on individual titles. The books most frequently discussed are *Jacob Have I Loved*, *The Great Gilly Hopkins*, and *Bridge to Terabithia*.

178   Spitz, Ellen Handler. ***Inside Picture Books***. Yale University, 1999, pap., $13.95 (0-3000-8476-5).

Written in an informal, personal style, this book is intended for educated parents and practitioners rather than scholars. The work is in four parts. The first part explores books about bedtime and such topics as fear of separation through sleep. The second part discusses books about separation and loss, and the third looks at books about anger and aggression—*Where the Wild Things Are*, for example. The fourth part covers books about physical potential and evolving identity. The author illuminates some general psychoanalytic concepts and gives some fresh ideas about familiar books. Although criticized for being middle class and superficial, this book has also received praise from artists including Quentin Blake.

179   Spufford, Francis. ***The Child that Books Built: A Life in Reading***. Metropolitan/Holt, 2002, $23 (0-8050-7215-2).

In this imaginative and powerful memoir, Spufford looks at the books that led him through his childhood and adolescence. The first chapter tells how reading became an integral part of his life. In subsequent chapters titled "The Forest," "The Island," "The Town," and "The Hole," he discusses specific books and their relationship to his intellectual and emotional growth. This thoughtful, erudite, and entertaining reflection tells how literature "builds and stretches the chambers of our imagination." A great testament to the power and importance of reading in a child's life, this book explores the reasons why people love reading, and how the power of children's literature affects both children and adults.

180   Stephens, John. ***Language and Ideology in Children's Fiction***. Addison Wesley, 1995, o.p.

Stephens maintains that, although this may not be immediately apparent, children's books subconsciously confirm and sustain many specific societal and cultural presuppositions. He notes, for example, that many books outwardly preach individualism but actually manipulate readers into espousing socially acceptable ideas. He refers to selfhood as "negotiated separateness" and claims that, to achieve it, we negotiate privately between what we are and what society wants us to be. He explores these elements in literature and shows how language is used to express different ideologies. This is a fascinating book that questions basic assumptions about children's literature.

181   Thacker, Deborah Cogan, et al. ***Introducing Children's Literature: From Romanticism to Postmodernism.*** Routledge, 2002, $80 (0-415-20410-0).

This guide connects important children's books to general literary history. Major literary movements from romanticism to postmodernism are introduced, along with their characteristics, concerns, and attitudes. Each of these movements is then related to selected titles both for adults and for children, among them *Little Women*, *The Wizard of Oz*, *Alice in Wonderland*, *Mary Poppins*, *Charlotte's Web*, and Philip Pullman's *Clockwork*.

182   Trites, Roberta Seelinger. ***Disturbing the Universe: Power and Repression.*** University of Iowa, 2000, $29.95 (0-87745-732-8).

Using the theories of poststructuralists, such as Jacques Lacan and Michel Foucault, as an intellectual center, the author deconstructs a number of well-known novels by such writers as Francesca Lia Block, Chris Crutcher, Virginia Hamilton, S. E. Hinton, M. E. Kerr, and Paul Zindel. Viewing young adult literature as basically about power, she explores how elements such as sex, death, money, schools, religion, and family play their parts in achieving or repressing power. This is a groundbreaking study that applies rigorous criticism to young adult literature. The book is intellectually stimulating, but at times difficult to follow.

183   Trites, Roberta Seelinger. ***Waking Sleeping Beauty.*** University of Iowa, 1997, $24.95 (0-87745-590-2).

This is a well-documented study of feminism in children's and young adult titles. The author discusses many authors and their works, with an emphasis on their treatment of friendships and community, two elements that she finds are important in feminist children's novels. For the reader already familiar with the books discussed, this is a useful critical study on how feminism and literature for youth intersect.

184   Tunnell, Michael O. ***The Prydain Companion: A Reference Guide to Lloyd Alexander's Prydain Chronicles.*** Holt, 2003. pap., $19.95 (0-8050-7271-3).

This reference book contains entries on characters, groups of people, fantastic beings, animals, place names, concepts including good and evil, and magical objects that appear in the Prydain books. In addition to the five novels that make up the *Prydain Chronicles*, the author includes references to the other five books about Prydain, such as the picture book *Coll and His White Pig*. This is a rich treasury of information on the fantasy land that many young readers revere.

185 Vandergrift, Kay E., ed. *Mosaics of Meaning: Enhancing the Intellectual Life of Young Adults Through Story.* Scarecrow, 1996, $45 (0-8108-3110-4).

This companion volume to *Ways of Knowing* (see entry below) shows how young adults bring meaning into their lives through literature. The key article in this collection of essays was written by Vandergrift; it gives a theoretical framework for examining the feminist ideas and approaches that are found in later chapters. Although there is an emphasis on issues of feminism and gender, many essays explore other topics—showing how fear, hate, and violence can be confronted and fought through books, for example, and how teenagers can find purpose and direction through reading. One essay, "Coming of Rage," is on being young, black, and female in America.

186 Vandergrift, Kay E., ed. *Ways of Knowing: Literature and the Intellectual Life of Children.* Scarecrow, 1996, $45 (0-8108-3087-6).

The 15 essays in this collection deal with how literature can help develop the multiple intelligences of children. For example, one essay discusses the role of dance in a child's life and how books can increase this appreciation; another tells how books should fit into the art curriculum. There are essays on concept books, on feminism in picture books, on the importance of computers and technology as a factor in children's literature, and on gender and cultural biases. This is a stimulating study of the power of literature in the intellectual development of children. See also the companion volume *Mosaics of Meaning* (above).

187 Warner, Marina. *From the Beast to the Blonde: On Fairy Tales and Their Tellers.* Noonday, 1996, $22 (0-3745-2487-4).

This study of fairy tales and their relationship to historical contexts, and to today's values and cultures, emphasizes the role of women in this genre. The author, a noted English novelist and historian, maintains that most of the narrators and leading characters in fairy tales are women. In two sections, "The Tellers" and "The Tales," she highlights the roles of women in fairy tales from old crones to blushing brides, and, in a final section, she explores the associations of blondness with purity and desirability in these stories. This is an original and insightful study.

188 Warner, Marina. *No Go the Bogeyman.* Farrar, Straus, 1999, $35 (0-374-22301-7).

One critic called this study of fear in children's books "an exhilarating work of scholarship." From early children's tales to the works of such modern authors as R. L. Stine, the author studies bogeymen, ogres, child killers, pedophiles, cannibals, giants, witches, and other objects of evil in children's books. The book is divided into three sections: "Scaring," on books that terrorize; "Lulling," on books that soothe and assuage fears; and "Making Mock," which highlights books of dark humor that produce laughter. Some important books, such as *Where the Wild Things Are*, get separate chapters. In this compendium of fact, folklore, history, and art, the author examines the relationship of the books to our present culture.

189   Whited, Lana A., ed. *The Ivory Tower and Harry Potter: Perspectives on a Literary Phenomenon.* University of Missouri, 2003, $34.95 (0-8262-1443-6).

In this, another volume that explores the phenomenon of Harry Potter, 16 critics explore various facets of publishing's recent wunderkind. Topics covered include Harry as an archetypal hero, the books as a variation on English school stories, moral development in these novels, stages of boyhood represented, literary antecedents of Harry, and the nature and quality of the many translations now available. There is lots of material for Potter buffs.

190   Zipes, Jack. *Sticks and Stones: The Troublesome Success of Children's Literature from Slovenly Peter to Harry Potter.* Routledge, 2000, $25 (0-415-92811-7).

In this series of essays, many based on speeches given by the author-scholar at various functions, Zipes discusses a number of works and their appeal to children. Included are the fairy tales retold by Wanda Gag, the folktales collected by the Grimm brothers, and the controversial Struwwelpeter. Zipes also discusses the place of children's literature in our present culture with its emphasis on commercialism. A final essay explores the phenomenon of Harry Potter and its relationship to modern society.

B. GENERAL PERIODICALS

Foreign book reviewing journals are included in this chapter. Current U.S. book review sources and annual bibliographies are found in Chapter 3 under "Current American Reviewing Tools and Annual Bibliographies." See also the professional organizations listed in Chapter 10, which include information on publications. When available, the foundation date of the periodical is given immediately after the title along with frequency, price, and the address of the publication.

1. International

191   *The White Ravens.* Internationale Jugendbibliothek/International Youth
       Library (Schloss Blutenberg, D-81247 Munich, Germany).

       This invaluable annotated bibliography of the most noteworthy chil-
       dren's books published throughout the world comes out annually. Drawn
       from books sent to the International Youth Library by their publishers,
       the list usually contains more than 200 titles in approximately 30 lan-
       guages from more than 40 countries. The annotations are in English
       although many of the books may not be currently available in the United
       States. An excellent guide for those seeking to learn about the best in for-
       eign children's books.

2. United States

192   *The ALAN Review.* 1972, 3/yr., $15 (free for members). Assembly on
       Literature for Adolescents, National Council of Teachers of English,
       1111 Kenyon Rd., Urbana, IL 61801; (217) 328-3870; www.ncte.org;
       www.alan-ya.org.

       This periodical is devoted to an examination of literature for young
       adults and its place in America's schools. Issues occasionally are devoted
       to a single topic; more frequently they contain articles on a variety of
       subjects. There are many profiles of authors and their works, plus a
       removable center section of reviews of both hardcover and paperback
       titles suitable for junior and senior high school readers.

193   *American Teacher.* 8/yr. American Federation of Teachers, 555 New
       Jersey Ave. N.W., Washington, DC 20001; (202) 879-4431.

       This is the official publication of this national organization. Although
       not directly related to children's or young adult literature, the articles
       often pertain to the status of reading and literature in American schools.

194   *Book Links: Connecting Books, Libraries and Classrooms.* 1991, 6/yr.,
       $28.95. American Library Association, 50 E. Huron St., Chicago, IL
       60611-2795; (800) 545-2433; www.ala.org/booklinks.

       Each issue of this attractive magazine has articles and annotated lists of
       books on various subjects, places, events, or people, plus profiles of indi-
       vidual authors. There are also essays that link books on similar themes
       and occasionally issues devoted to a single subject (multiculturalism, for
       example). Issues average 60 pages and are intended for librarians and
       teachers working with children from preschool through 8th grade.

195   *Book Mark: Children's Literature in Review with Related Activities for Pre-Schoolers Through Young Adults.* 1977, 2/yr., $10. c/o Jane Bingham, Oakland University, School of Human Educational Services, Rochester, MI 48063; (313) 370-3005.

A "small" magazine that features good reviews and practical activities for young readers.

196   *Bookbird: A Journal of International Children's Literature.* 1962, 4/yr., $40. Bookbird Subscriptions, c/o University of Toronto Press, 5201 Dufferin St., North York, ON M3H 5T8.

This quarterly journal of the International Board on Books for Young People (IBBY) was founded by Jella Lepman and Dr. Richard Bamberger, who edited the first issues. Published in English, this prestigious periodical covers the international book scene, reports on books and authors from various countries, makes recommendations for book translations, and supplies information about prize-winning books. It gives a fascinating worldwide view of children's literature. *A Bridge of Children's Books* (O'Brien Press, 2002, $16.95 [0-86278-783-1]) is the inspiring autobiography of the remarkable Jella Lepman. Inquiries in the United States can be addressed to IBBY headquarters at the International Reading Association; (302) 731-1600.

197   *CBC Features: Containing News of the Children's Book World.* 1963, 2/yr., $60 (lifetime subscription). Children's Book Council, 12 W. 37th St., 2nd floor, New York, NY 10018-7480; (212) 966-1990; www.cbcbooks.org.

This newsletter of the Children's Book Council (formerly called "Calendar") contains information about council activities (including materials for the council-sponsored Children's Book Week) and information on publishers, authors, current books, prizes, and special events relating to children's literature, plus details of how to obtain free or inexpensive material from publishers including posters, bookmarks, author profiles, etc. Send a stamped self-addressed envelope for a free copy.

198   *Childhood Education: Infancy Through Early Adolescence.* 1924, 6/yr., $64 (free to members). Association for Childhood Education International, 17904 Georgia Ave., Suite 215, Olney, MD 20832-2277; (800) 423-3563; www.acei.org.

The official journal of the Association for Childhood Education International, this contains general articles relating to teaching children, many of them relating to reading and books. In five of the six yearly issues, there is an annotated list of about 25 recommended books for children.

Each issue also contains reviews of audiovisual materials, computer software, and professional books.

199 *Children and Libraries: The Journal of the Association for Library Service to Children.* 2003, 3 /yr, $40 (free to members). American Library Association/Association for Library Service to Children, 50 E. Huron St., Chicago, IL 60611; (800) 545-2433, ext. 2163; www.ala.org/alsc.

Children and Libraries, the official journal of ALSC, contains news items about the organization, conferences, current research, and so forth, plus timely articles about current trends and practices in library service to children. This periodical was previously known as *JOYS.*

200 *Children's Folklore Review.* 1979, 2/yr., $10. East Carolina University, Department of English, Greenville, NC 27858-4353; (252) 757-6672.

The journal of the Children's Folklore section of the American Folklore Society, this covers all aspects of children's literature relating to folklore, folktales, and the study of storytelling activities and techniques.

201 *Children's Literature.* 1972, annual, $20. Modern Language Association and Children's Literature Association, John Hopkins University Press, 2715 N. Charles St., Baltimore, MD 21218-4363; (410) 516-6988; www.press.jhu.edu/journals/childrens_literature/index.html.

The first issue of this publication stated that its purpose was "to stimulate the writing, teaching and study of children's literature by humanists." Now considered the most prestigious of children's literature journals, this annual is sponsored jointly by the Children's Literature Association and the Modern Language Association Division of Children's Literature. Each issue contains eight to ten lengthy, scholarly articles about various facets of children's literature, such as reexamination of classics, critical analyses of important authors, and specific issues in the areas of literary and cultural studies. Articles are well researched and expected to make important contributions to the field. Volume 27 (1999) contains an index by author, title, and subject for Volumes 1 to 25. Before Volume 31 (2003), this journal was published by Yale University Press, PO Box 209040, New Haven, CT 06520-9040. Contact Yale for back issues.

202 *Children's Literature Abstracts.*

This useful tool ceased publication in December 1997. It was issued quarterly and contained one-paragraph (from one sentence to several) abstracts of important articles and books about children's literature.

203   *Children's Literature Association Quarterly.* 1976, 4/yr, $75 (free to members). PO Box 138, Battle Creek, MI 49016; (269) 965-8180; http://ebbs.english.vt.edu/chla/index.html.

The official publication of the Children's Literature Association, this quarterly is devoted to the study of children's literature, particularly in literary and cultural contexts. Issues frequently focus on a particular topic—"mothers and daughters in children's literature," "ecology and the child," and "critical theory and adolescence literature," for example. In addition to scholarly articles, each issue contains reviews of books about children's literature, information about important dissertations, and association news.

204   *Children's Literature in Education: An International Quarterly.* 1970, 4/yr., $48. Springer Science+Business Media B.V., 233 Spring St., New York, NY 10013-1578; (212) 620-8000; www.springerlink.com.

Each issue of this international publication (which has both American and British editorial offices) contains about five lengthy, scholarly articles written by academics, librarians, teachers, or professional children's authors. Each article contains an abstract, a biographical note about the author, and extensive "notes" and "references," the latter being a bibliography of sources. Articles may explore the uses of children's literature in the classroom, chronicle children's responses to literature, or examine critically a single author's work. There are some black-and-white illustrations but no book reviews.

205   *Curriculum Review.* 1960, 6/yr., $108. PaperClip Communications, 125 Paterson Ave., Little Falls, NJ 07424; (973) 256-1333; www.curriculumreview.com.

Each issue begins with several feature articles on a timely curriculum topic for teachers of grades K–12. Some of these articles also contain useful retrospective bibliographies. There are columns devoted to new resources and materials for schools and libraries. These columns often highlight materials that can be of value in developing library collections, but this periodical is primarily a news magazine covering current trends and developments in schools. There are usually substantial reviews of texts, supplementary materials, books, multimedia kits, and software.

206   *Dragon Lode.* 2/yr. (free to members). International Reading Association. 800 Barksdale Rd., PO Box 8139, Newark, DE 19714-8139; (302) 731-1600; www.reading.org/association/about/sigs_childrens.html.

Children's Literature and Reading, a special interest group of the International Reading Association, publishes this journal that is intended primarily for classroom teachers. Each issue explores areas of concern for those involved in children's literature at the elementary school level and includes book reviews, information about authors, and, frequently, annotated bibliographies of children's books on a particular subject or theme.

207 *English Journal.* 1912, 8/yr., $75 (free to members). National Council of Teachers of English, 1111 W. Kenyon Rd., Urbana, IL 61801-1096; (877) 369-6283; www.ncte.org.

This professional journal from NCTE discusses issues, trends, and practices in the teaching of English in junior and senior high schools. Articles range from descriptions of classroom practices to outlines of units using specific young adult books and materials. There are sections that regularly review professional books, media, and computer software and frequent bibliographic articles survey young adult literature and related subjects. One regular column, "Young Adult Literature," publishes an annual list of honor books and regular lists of new or overlooked young adult books.

208 *The Five Owls: A Publication for Readers Personally and Professionally Involved in Children's Literature.* 1986, 4/yr., $35. PO Box 235, Marathon, TX 79842; (432) 386-4257; www.fiveowls.com.

Described as "a lively mixture of book reviews, articles about books and reading, and interviews with leading authors, illustrators, and others who are shaping the future of children's books," this periodical highlights a particular theme or subject each issue. A committee of librarians reviews children's books of unusual merit. The reviews (about 15 per issue) are lengthy and include a picture of the dust jacket. In addition to being a selection tool, this journal (according to the editors) is "a source of creative new ideas for your school or library, and an enjoyable way to stay in touch with what is happening in children's books."

209 *Journal of Adolescent and Adult Literacy.* 1957, 8/yr., $61 (free to members). 800 Barksdale Rd., PO Box 8139, Newark, DE 19714-8139; (302) 731-1600; www.reading.org.

Formerly known as *Journal of Reading,* this companion to *The Reading Teacher* is a journal for professionals working with adolescents and adult learners. In addition to information on concerns in this area and teaching strategies, the journal supplies reviews of instructional materials, professional books, books for young adults, tests, and software. There are also sections on current research and on reading supervisors and their interests.

210 *Journal of Children's Literature: A Journal of the Children's Literature Assembly of the NCTE.* 1994, 2/yr., $20 (free to members). National Council of Teachers of English, 1111 W. Kenyon Rd., Urbana, IL

61801-1096; (877) 369-6283; www.ncte.org; www.childrensliterature assembly.org.

Formerly called *The CLA Bulletin*, this journal focuses on the children's literature used in teaching from elementary school through college. Most issues revolve around themes such as audience responses, global perspectives, and feminist approaches. Some of the seven or eight articles per issue are on or by well-known authors and illustrators. Occasionally there are extended reviews of a single children's book or a professional publication. Each year the publication chooses the "Notable Trade Books in the Language Arts."

211   *Knowledge Quest.* 1997, 5/yr., $40 (free to members). American Association of School Librarians, 50 E. Huron St., Chicago, IL 60611; (800) 545-2433 ext. 4382; www.ala.org/aasl.

Subtitled *The Journal of the American Association of School Librarians*, this periodical (formerly called *School Library Media Quarterly*) appears bimonthly during the school year and contains articles about school library media centers and their design, management, programs, and educational impact. It also contains information about the association, its meetings, and its activities. Articles address the practice of school librarianship, new education theories, practical tips to assist building-level librarians, and other professional concerns.

212   *Language Arts.* 1924, 8/yr., $40 (free to members). National Council of Teachers of English, 1111 W. Kenyon Rd., Urbana, IL 61801-1096; (877) 369-6283; www.ncte.org.

This authoritative periodical deals with topics relating to the teaching of English in preschool through middle school settings. The articles deal with composition skills, language, and literature. In the latter area there are frequent articles on themes, subjects, and authors involved in children's literature. The October issue contains the annual "Notable Children's Books in the Language Arts." To be eligible, the book must deal with language, demonstrate unique use of language, or be particularly inviting to children.

213   *The Lion and the Unicorn: A Critical Journal of Children's Literature.* 1977, 3/yr., $29. Johns Hopkins University Press, Journals Division, 2715 N. Charles St., Baltimore, MD 21218-4319; (410) 516-6900; www.press.jhu.edu/journals/lion_and_the_unicorn.

This genre- and theme-oriented journal (each year there is one theme-oriented issue and two general ones) presents critical essays across the full spectrum of children's literature, with an emphasis on social and cultural issues. Recent thematic issues have covered Irish children's literature, violence in children's literature, and French children's literature. Each issue contains six to eight articles plus lengthy reviews of recent critical works. Special issues often highlight forgotten classics that "deserve renewed attention." This journal merits the international praise it receives as a scholarly but vital journal of children's literature and culture.

214 *The Mailbox Bookbag: Literacy Ideas for Teachers.* 1994, 6/yr., $39.95. The Mailbox Bookbag, 3515 W. Market St., Greensboro, NC 27455; (800) 334-0298; www.themailboxbookbag.com.

Aimed at librarians and teachers working with children in kindergarten through the 6th grade, this colorful publication includes original stories and articles, plus short reviews of recent children's books, recommendations for using children's literature, author information, and practical ready-to-use activities that integrate classics, award winners, and newer books into the curriculum. There are also often annotated bibliographies of books on a particularly subject that are ideal for use in theme-related literature units.

215 *Martha's KidLit Newsletter.* 1988, 8/yr., $30. Martha Rasmussen, PO Box 1488, Ames, IA 50014; (800) 292-9309.

This eight-page newsletter was started by Martha Rasmussen to search for children's books she wanted to add to her own collection. It has expanded and now also contains informal short essays by different collectors of children's books.

216 *Marvels and Tales: Journal of Fairy-Tale Studies.* 1987, 2/yr., $25. Wayne State University Press, Leonard N. Simons Bldg., 4809 Woodward Ave., Detroit, MI 48201-1309; www.langlab.wayne.edu/ MarvelsHome/Marvels_Tales.html.

This is a serious journal that explores scholarly studies of the world of fairy tales and other traditional forms of literature. Sometimes an issue is devoted to a single theme or individual, such as The Arabian Nights or Charles Perrault.

217 *Media and Methods: Educational Products, Technologies and Programs for Schools and Universities.* 1964, 6/yr., $39. American Society of Educators, 1429 Walnut St., Philadelphia, PA 19102; (800) 555-5657; www.media-methods.com.

Media and Methods concentrates on nonprint media and their use in education. Each issue has five or six articles on media projects and products and their management in the classroom or library. The review section in each issue includes material on videocassettes, filmstrips, books, databases, software, and videodiscs. There are also lists of catalogs to send for, directories of equipment manufacturers, and an annual listing of the year's best educational media.

218   *The New Advocate.* 1998, 4/yr., $40. Christopher-Gordon Publishers, 480 Washington St., Norwood, MA 02062; (781) 762-5577; www.christopher-gordon.com.

Articles written by authors, illustrators, scholars, and educators are divided into three sections: "The Creative Process," "Concepts and Themes," and "Practical Reflections." A fourth section, "Children's Voices: Responding to Literature," publishes children's writings on their reactions to books and reading. Also in each issue there are reviews of new children's books, professional resources, and selected nonprint media. This publication is a strong advocate of literature-based teaching.

219   *Parabola.* 1976, 4/yr., $24. Society for the Study of Myth and Tradition, 135 East 15th St., New York, NY 10003; (800) 560-6984; www.parabola.org.

This is a scholarly publication that deals with mythology, folklore, and the recurring folk motifs in today's world. Though not directly related to children's literature, the periodical often deals with themes and subjects found in children's folklore collections.

220   *Para*doxa.* 1995. 3/yr. $56. Delta Productions, PO Box 2237, Vashon Island, WA 98070; (206) 567-4373; www.paradoxa.com.

This unusual publication devotes single issues to a particular literary genre. The issues devoted to children's literature have been probing and stimulating.

221   *Reading Horizons.* 1960, 4/yr., $60. Western Michigan University, College of Education, 1903 W. Michigan Ave., Kalamazoo, MI 49008; (269) 387-3470; www.wmich.edu/tll/reading/readhorizons.htm.

A scholarly publication dealing with current research on reading at all levels of instruction.

222   *Reading Research and Instruction.* 1961, 4/yr., $50. College Reading Association, Department of Education, Mount Saint Mary College, Emmitsberg, MD 21727; (301) 447-5371.

Reading Research and Instruction reports on studies and research on reading, particularly at the young adult and adult levels.

223   *Reading Research Quarterly.* 1950. 4/yr. $61. International Reading Association, 800 Barksdale Rd., PO Box 8139, Newark, DE 19714-8139; (302) 731-1600; www.reading.org.

This important resource focuses on original and innovative research in reading. There are usually only four articles in each issue. Topics range from reading interests and instructional practices to reviews of research in a particular area. It covers literacy among learners of all ages. The major audience for this journal is at the university level or among independent researchers.

224   *The Reading Teacher.* 1947, 8/yr., $61 (free to members). International Reading Association, 800 Barksdale Rd., PO Box 8139, Newark, DE 19714-8139; (800) 336-7323; www.reading.org.

The Reading Teacher deals with various aspects of reading instruction at the elementary school level. Many of the articles deal with trends and issues affecting the teaching of reading, but others focus on children's literature and on a particular theme or genre. These articles often contain good bibliographies. A regular feature is "Children's Books," usually on a connecting theme that cites, with annotations, about 30 to 40 current books. The October issue features the winners of the "Children's Choices" award, an annual bibliography of books chosen by children as their favorites, and the November issue contains the "Teacher's Choices," books rated as exceptional for curriculum use (see Chapter 3).

225   *Reading Today.* 1950, 6/yr., $63 (free to members). International Reading Association, 800 Barksdale Rd., PO Box 8139, Newark, DE 19714-8139; (800) 336-7323; www.reading.org.

This is a bimonthly newspaper that is received with membership in IRA. It contains news and features about trends that influence literacy education and coverage of current developments in reading instruction. It uses many colorful photographs and graphics in a newsletter format.

226   *Research in the Teaching of English.* 1967, 4/yr., $45 (free to members). National Council of Teachers of English, 1111 W. Kenyon Rd., Urbana, IL 61801-1096; (877) 369-6283; www.ncte.org.

Multidisciplinary in nature, this journal explores the relationships between language teaching and learning at all levels from preschool through adult level. There are articles on teaching methods, issues of pedagogical concern, and such topics as evaluation, process, and content.

227 *School Library Media Activities Monthly.* 1984, 10/yr., $49. Libraries Unlimited, 88 Post Rd. West, Westport, CT 06881; (888) 371-0152; www.schoollibrarymedia.com.

This periodical focuses on teaching media skills in school libraries. It provides many creative ideas and activities for promoting books and reading with children. New books, computer software, and other media formats are reviewed regularly and librarians are encouraged to share their ideas and activities with others through the pages of this helpful magazine.

228 *School Library Media Quarterly.*

Ceased publication in summer 1997.

229 *Science and Children.* 1963, 8/yr., $62 (free to members). National Science Teachers Association, 1840 Wilson Blvd., Arlington, VA 22201; (703) 243-7100; www.nsta.org.

The teaching of science in elementary schools is the focus here, with some coverage of junior high schools (see also *Science Teacher* below). Articles deal with concerns and problems in science classrooms, with many ideas for improvements and new approaches. Monthly columns review trade books and nonprint media. The March issue contains "Out-standing Science Trade Books for Students, K–12" prepared by NSTA and the Children's Book Council. This is a well-annotated, authoritative bibliography arranged by subject (see entry in Chapter 3 under "Annu-als"). A companion periodical aimed at science teachers in middle and junior high schools is *Science Scope* (8/yr, $62 membership) also from the National Science Teachers Association.

230 *Science Teacher.* 1934, 9/yr., $62 (free to members). National Science Teachers Association, 1840 Wilson Blvd., Arlington, VA 22201; (703) 243-7100; www.nsta.org.

Like its companion periodical, *Science and Children* (see above), this is an official publication of the National Science Teachers Association and therefore contains association news. The emphasis in the articles is on teaching science at the secondary school level. Although its is not intend-ed as a major selection aid, each issue contains some reviews of trade books, professional literature, and software.

231 *Social Education.* 1937, 7/yr., $69 (free to members). National Council for the Social Studies, 8555 16th St., Silver Spring, MD 20910; www.ncss.org.

This, the official journal of the National Council for the Social Studies, concentrates on articles about teaching in the social sciences. Many of these articles contain useful bibliographies of materials both for students and professionals. The section in each issue called "Resources" includes articles about useful books and media lists on individual subjects. The May/June issue contains the annual list "Notable Social Studies Trade Books for Young People," which is an excellent selection aid (see entry in Chapter 3 under "Annuals").

232 *Storytelling Magazine.* 6/yr., $29.95 (free to members). National Storytelling Network, 132 Boone St., Suite 5, Jonesborough, TN 37659; (800) 523-4514; www.storynet.org.

This bimonthly publication is the official organ of the National Storytelling Network. It contains articles about storytelling projects from around the nation, gives advice on techniques, traces the development of themes and individual stories, and gives material on sources of information and other resources. The network also publishes the annual *NSN Source Book*, which is free to members and is a directory of the membership plus sections on regional activities, periodicals, and other resources.

233 *Teacher Librarian: The Journal for School Library Professionals.* 1974, 5/yr., $54. 15200 NBN Way, Blue Ridge Summit, PA 17214; (717) 794-3800 ext. 3597; www.teacherlibrarian.com.

Formerly known as *Emergency Librarian,* this periodical contains many useful hints for successful school library management and many practical suggestions for effective collection development. With readership in both Canada and the United States, it covers material from both countries in its articles and reviews. Each issue has a section on professional reading, plus reviews of books for children and young adults. The "Footnotes" section lists useful pamphlets and bibliographies, and "Portraits" contains author interviews. There are also best-sellers lists, one for Canada and one for the United States.

234 *Teaching and Learning Literature with Children and Young Adults (TALL).* 1985, 5/yr., $60. Essmont Publishing, P.O. Box 186, Brandon, VT 05733-0186; (802) 247-3488.

This periodical, which tries to bridge the gap between teachers and scholars, contains articles on literature-based reading programs, children's literature in the home, literary principles, genres, and authors. There are also reviews of current children's books and occasionally a lengthy article on a particularly important works of children's literature.

235 *Teaching K–8: The Professional Magazine for Teachers.* 8/yr., $32. 40 Richards Ave., Norwalk, CT 06854-2309; (800)-249-9363; www.teachingk-8.com.

Published monthly during the school year, this periodical is full of ideas and activities for teachers. Each issue also has articles about children's books and using the library, and frequently has interviews with children's authors and illustrators.

236   *Young Adult Library Services: The Journal of the Young Adult Library Services.* 2002, 2/yr., $40 (free to members). Young Adult Library Services Association/American Library Association, 50 E. Huron St., Chicago, IL 60611; (800) 545-2433, ext. 4390; www.ala.org/ala/yalsa/yalsa.htm.

This journal is directed at librarians serving young adults. It contains association news and articles on current trends and practices and it acts as a continuing education tool for its readers.

237   *Young Children.* 1944, 6/yr., $30. National Association for the Education of Young Children, 1509 16th St. N.W., Washington, DC 20036-1426; (800) 424-2460; www.naeyc.org.

This attractive magazine has as its goal to keep NAEYC members current on the latest developments and trends in early childhood education. It publishes research articles on classroom practice and on children's literature, plus reviews of children's and professional books. About 50 percent of the members of this organization are teachers; the rest are program directors, administrators, and college professors.

3. Australia and New Zealand

238   *Magpies: Talking About Books for Children.* 1986, 6/yr., $55. Australian Magpies, PO Box 98, Grange, Queensland 4051, Australia; www.magpies.net.au.

Although the emphasis in this periodical is on Australian children's literature, there is a section in each issue that contains articles and reviews pertaining to New Zealand. This lively, attractive, oversize publication features articles about authors, reviews of professional reading, lengthy reviews of children's books, and general news about events, prizes, and other related topics, The illustrations are in both color and black and white and consist mainly of reproductions of book jackets.

239   *Orana: Journal of School and Children's Librarianship.* 3/yr., A$63. Australian Library and Information Association, PO Box 6335, Kingston 2604, Australia; http://alia.org.au/publishing/orana.

Most issues of this official journal of the Children's and Youth Services division of the Australian Library and Information Association are devoted to articles about children's literature.

240 *Papers: Explorations into Children's Literature.* 1990, 3/yr., A$44.
Deakin University, 221 Burwood Highway, Burwood, Vic. 3125,
Australia.

Published annually in April, August, and December, this scholarly periodical covers all aspects of children's literature and is not confined to
material on Australian children's literature. For example, a recent issue
was devoted entirely to the life and works of C. S. Lewis. Its stated purpose is to provide "researchers into the historical background of children's literature, academic theoreticians and literary critics with an outlet
for their material."

241 *Reading Time.* 1969, 4/yr., $42. Children's Book Council of Australia,
PO Box 765, Rozelle, NSW 2039, Australia; www.cbc.org.au.

Each issue of this official journal of the Children's Book Council of Australia contains articles on Australian books, authors, and illustrators and
there are extensive reviews and news of children's books and professional
materials both from Australia and overseas. Annually, the CBCA Book of
the Year is announced in its pages and the acceptance speech is reprinted.

242 *Viewpoint: on Books for Young Adults.* 1993, 4/yr., University of
Melbourne, PO Box 4286, Parkville, Vic. 3052, Australia;
http://extranet.edfac.unimelb.edu.au/LLAE/viewpoint.

This Australian journal is devoted to different facets of literature for
young adults. With reviews, new items, topical articles, profiles of
authors, and discussion forums, this periodical reflects both Australian
and international viewpoints.

4. Canada

243 *Canadian Children's Book News.* 1978, 4/yr., C$19.95. The Canadian
Children's Book Centre, 40 Orchard View Blvd., Suite 101, Toronto,
ON M4R 1B9; (416) 975-0010; www.bookcentre.ca.

Dedicated to "informing readers about the world of Canadian children's
books," issues contain reviews of recent titles and often include profiles
of authors, illustrators, publishers, and booksellers. A section "Book
Bits," written by a different reviewer each issue, highlights three or four
new books. This is followed by a larger reviewing section, "We Recom-
mend," which features about 12 to 15 fiction and nonfiction books for
children and young adults. There are sections for both national and
regional news that include items on important conferences and activities,
awards, prizes, honors, and names of officers. The Book Centre is also

responsible for publishing an annual bibliography of the best books for young readers, arranged by subject, called *Our Choice: Choosing the Best for Canada's Young Readers.*

244   *CCL: Canadian Children's Literature/Littérature Canadienne pour la Jeunesse.* 1975, 4/yr., $39. Department of English, University of Winnipeg, 515 Portage Ave., Winnipeg, MB R3L 1V9.

This bilingual journal (some articles are in French, others in English, some in both) is the official publication of the Canadian Children's Literature Association and Canadian Children's Press. There are about seven or eight scholarly articles in each issue. Most focus on some aspect of Canadian literature, although more general topics are also covered (an issue in 2001 was devoted to Australian children's literature, for example). Many deal with the sociological aspects of children's literature and its cultural impact. Abstracts in French and English precede each article. The last section in each issue contains about 30 to 40 reviews of both English and French Canadian children's and young adult books.

245   *CM: Canadian Review of Materials.* 21/yr. 167 Houde Dr., Winnipeg, MB R3V 1C6; www.umanitoba.ca/cm.

This is an electronic journal that reviews Canadian books, video and audio recordings and electronic media produced for young people. It includes material produced for adults but useful in school libraries. A Canadian electronic journal that deals with children's literature is *The Looking Glass.*

246   *English Quarterly.* 4/yr. Canadian Council of Teachers of English and Language Arts, #10-730 River Rd., University of Manitoba, Winnipeg, MB R2M 5A4; www.cctela.ca/EQ.html.

The official publication of this organization, this quarterly features association news items and general articles about English teaching and literature for young people.

247   *French Canadian Children's and Young Adult Literature.* 3/yr., C$14. Association Lurelu, 4388 rue Saint Denis, Bureau 305, Montreal, Quebec H2J 2L1.

This periodical contains articles and reviews plus news, information about prizes, and interviews with authors and illustrators. It is a handsome publication with plenty of illustrations. It averages about 100 pages per issue.

248   *Resources Links: Connecting Classrooms, Libraries and Canadian Learning Resources.* 1995, 5/yr., C$29.95. PO Box 9, Pouch Cove, NF A0A 3L0.

The purpose of this reviewing journal is to promote "an awareness of the availability and use of Canadian learning resources" in various print and nonprint media. The reviews and news features are divided into sections such as picture books, nonfiction, fiction, audiovisual, Internet resources, awards and announcements, and professional resources.

249   *School Libraries in Canada.* Canadian Association for School Libraries, 328 Frank St., Ottawa, ON K2P 0X8; www.schoollibraries.ca.

The official journal of the Canadian Association for School Libraries, this free online publication features news items and articles on topics of concern to librarians in Canadian schools.

250   *YA Hotline.* 2/yr, C$20. School of Library and Information Science, Dalhousie University, Halifax, NS B7H 3J5; www.mgmt.dal.ca/slis/Publications/YA_Hotline.

This stimulating magazine for young adults and young adult services librarians appears twice a year. Each issue is devoted to a single theme—for example, witchcraft, sex stereotyping, drugs and alcohol, and feminism. There are essays, bibliographies, reviews, and many program ideas.

5. Ireland

251   *Inis.* 2002, 4/yr., 25 euros for membership; 45 euros overseas. Children's Books Ireland, 17 North Great Georges St., 1st Floor, Dublin 1; www.childrensbooksireland.com.

Inis (pronounced "inn-ish"), means "island" or "tell" in Gaelic. This colorful, attractive quarterly, previously known as *Children's Books in Ireland,* contains organization news, biographies of authors (each issue has a profile of a "living Irish author"), and interesting articles on topics relating to children's literature (for example, the Spring 2003 issue explored various aspects of the Der Struwwelpeter legend and publications). About half of each issue is devoted to reviews of children's books (not just Irish), divided by age groups from preschool through teenage. The reviews are lengthy and thorough. There is also a section of reviews of professional materials.

6. South Africa

252   *Bookchat.* 1976. Jay Heale, PO Box 541, Gradouw 7160.

At present, this is the only periodical in South Africa devoted to children's literature. It is ceaseless in spreading news about and promoting South African authors, their books, and the importance of reading in the lives of children. For his work, founder and editor Jay Heale was awarded the Carl Lahann Prize in 1992.

7. United Kingdom

253   *Books for Keeps: The Children's Book Magazine.* 1980, 6/yr., £20.50. 6 Brightfield Rd., Lee, London SE12 8QF, England; www.booksforkeeps. co.uk.

This colorful, often controversial British periodical is concerned with all aspects of British children's literature. There are articles on and by authors, reevaluation of classics, and accounts of current publishing practices. The latter appear in a section called "Books for Keeps Briefing," which also covers news about people, prizes, and events. In "Good Reads," young readers review their favorite books, and in "I Wish I'd Written," authors choose the books they wish they had written. About one third of the magazine is given over to reviews, divided by age groups and preceded by a short section on books about children's literature. There are about 100 reviews in each issue and books are rated by a star system—* means poor and ***** is unmissable. A groundbreaking, interesting publication with something for everyone involved with children's literature.

254   *Booktrusted News.* 2002, 4/yr., £25. Book Trust, Book House, 45 East Hill, Wandsworth, London SW18 2QZ, England; www.booktrust. org.uk.

Known for many years as *Children's Book News*, this newly redesigned, attractive publication is a theme-oriented periodical. For example, the Winter 2002 issue contained articles, booklists, and first-person accounts relating to refugees and children's literature around the world. In each issue there is also an in-depth author profile, an interview with an illustrator, "Desert Island Books" (in which an authority chooses favorite children's books), and a "News in Brief" section. The last third of each issue is devoted to reviews of children's books arranged by age level. There is also an "Our Choice" section in which young readers review books they particularly like. Book Trust also published an excellent annual bibliography, *Best Book Guide for Children and Young Adults* (formerly *100 Best Books*), which is a handy booklet that contains the best in children's and young adult paperback fiction published in the previous calendar year. This publication is £5 if ordered from the Book Trust.

255 *Carousel: The Guide to Children's Books.* 1995, 3/yr., £3.25 per issue. Saturn Centre, 54-76 Bissell St., Birmingham, B5 7HX, England; www.carouselguide.co.uk.

Known for 30 years as *Books for Young People*, the present periodical began publication with a Winter issue in 1995. The magazine contains detailed articles and interviews with authors, illustrators, and others working in the field of juvenile literature. There is also a section on news about children's literature that includes information on prizes and events. It is best known for its lively review section, which is divided by age groups, with headings including "Books for Babies," "Books for Sharing," and "Young Adult Fiction." This is a breezy, inviting publication that both entertains and informs readers about current developments in the field.

256 *The English and Media Magazine.* 1985, 3/yr., £15 (£30 overseas). The English and Media Centre, 18 Compton Terrace, London N1 2UN, England.

Intended for teachers of English and media studies, this publication contains articles about books, media, young people, and communication. There is news of the Centre and information on new publications, competitions, and changes in the school curriculum. Teacher-oriented, this magazine also includes reviews of teaching materials, professional books for teachers, and reports on media studies.

257 *English in Education.* 1966, 3/yr., £17.50. The National Association for the Teaching of English, 50 Broadfield Rd., Sheffield, S8 OXJ, England; www.nate.org.uk.

This is the official academic journal of the National Association for the Teaching of English, an organization covering preschool through college teaching of English. This publication is aimed at roughly the college level and contains articles on literacy, teaching practices, theoretical studies, and research reports. There are no reviews of children's literature. Two other professional publications from this organization are *The Secondary English Magazine* (1997, 5/yr., £17.50) and *The Primary Education Magazine* (1995, 5/yr., £17.50). Subscription information from Garth Publishing Service, PO Box 5034, Birmingham, B13 8JA.

258   *Literacy.* 1966, 3/yr., £30. United Kingdom Literacy Association, Upton House, Baldock St., Royston, Herts SG8 5AY, England; www.ukla.org.

This periodical, formerly known as *Reading*, reports on recent research in the field of literacy and gives accurate information on new and innovative programs in this area. UKLA also publishes *Journal of Research in Reading.*

259   *The School Librarian.* 1952, 4/yr., £45 (free to members). School Library Association, Lotmead Business Village, Lotmead Farm, Wanborough, Swindon SN4 0UY, England.

This attractive, colorful quarterly is the official journal of the British School Library Association. It consists of some general articles and a large review section written by teachers, librarians, and subject specialists. The reviews take up about half of each issue and are organized by age groups from "under 8" to "16–19." There are separate sections for poetry and plays, professional literature, and for Web sites, computer programs, and CD-ROMs.

260   *Signal: Approaches to Children's Books.* 1970–2003. Thimble Press, Lockwood, Station Rd., Woodchester, Stroud, Glos. GL5 5EQ, England.

From its founding in 1970 by children's literature authorities and authors Aidan and Nancy Chambers, until its last issue in August 2003, this periodical was considered the foremost children's literature journal in the United Kingdom. Published three times a year, it was an independent journal that contained no advertising. Each issue contained scholarly articles about children's books and their authors and lively discussions about literary criticism. The contributors read like a "who's who" in British children's literature. The focus was on British and Irish literature, but several of the articles were international in scope. The last oversize issue, *Signal 100*, contained the three 2003 issues in one volume, with articles by such luminaries as Anne Fine, Jan Mark, Elaine Moos, and Lissa Paul. Two book publications of note that came from this periodical are *The Signal Companion: A Classified Guide to 25 Years of Signal* (Thimble, 1996, o.p.) and a valuable selection from the magazine, *Signal Approach to Children's Books* (Kestrel, 1980, o.p.). The Signal Poetry Award was established in 1979 and is administered by the Centre for Literacy in Primary Education.

CHAPTER 2

Retrospective Bibliographies

       d. Historical Fiction
       e. Humor
       f. Mystery and Horror
       g. Poetry
       h. Pop-Up Books
       i. Romance
    4. Indexes and Related Reference Books

A. AUSTRALIA

261   Scutter, Heather Margaret. *Displaced Fictions: Contemporary Australian Books for Teenagers and Young Adults.* Melbourne University Press, 2000, o.p.

Scutter provides a scholarly study of the most important and relatively recent Australian books for teens, with critical analysis of such prominent writers as Gary Crew, Gillian Rubinstein, Paul Jennings, and John Marsden.

262   Simkin, John, and Margaret Dunkle. *Picture Books for Young Australians.* D. W. Thorpe, 1996, o.p.

This substantial work indexes by author, title, illustrator, and subject about 4,000 fiction and nonfiction picture books. About half of them are from Australia and New Zealand; the other half are from the United States and United Kingdom.

263   White, Kerry. *Australian Children's Fiction: The Subject Guide.* Jacaranda, 1993, o.p.

The body of this work analyzes 3,520 Australian fiction titles for children by a wide variety of subjects, including country life and crabs. The information on each entry is restricted to author, title, and genre. Extensive indexes follow—by author (where full bibliographic information is given for each book) and by genre, title, and illustrator. A separate update, covering the years 1992–1996 and analyzing 1,300 additional books, was published in 1996.

B. CANADA

264 Baker, Deirdre, and Ken Setterington. *A Guide to Canadian Books in English.* McClelland and Stewart, 2003, $24.95 (0-7710-1064-8).

This attractive bibliography lists and briefly annotates 500 recommended titles for preschool through junior high. Some old favorites, such as L. M. Montgomery and Farley Mowat, are here, but most of the titles were published within the past 20 years. Titles are arranged by age groups, with additional divisions by genres. Indexes are by author, title, subject, and Canadian setting. There is also a listing of where each author lives.

265 *Canadian Book Review Annual (year): Children's Literature.* Canadian Book Review Annual (annual), C$23.95 (2003 ed.).

Each year, this evaluative guide presents reviews of English-language books for young people by Canadian authors and illustrators. There are approximately 500 original reviews of both fiction and nonfiction in each issue, arranged in 13 categories, including picture books, science, and mathematics. Reviews average about 200 words. Each book is given an overall rating from "highly recommended" to "not recommended." There are indexes by author, title, and subject.

266 Egoff, Sheila A., and Alvine Belisle. *Notable Canadian Children's Books/Un Choix de Livres Canadiens pour la Jeunesse.* National Library of Canada, 1976, o.p.

The first edition of this volume, based on a National Library of Canada exhibition, was representative of the best Canadian books for children in English and French from early printed books to 1972. Supplements bring this record to 1980. This work is of great historical importance in chronicling the best in Canadian publishing for children.

267 Gagnon, Andre, and Ann Gagnon. *Canadian Books for Young People/Livres Canadiens pour la Jeunesse.* University of Toronto Press, 1995, o.p.

Though now in need of revision, this bibliography includes more than 2,500 titles in two sections, English and French. Each section is arranged by broad subjects, such as science and fiction, and covers material from preschool through junior high. Each book is annotated and there are extensive indexes.

268   *Our Choice: Your Annual Guide to Canada's Best Children's Books, Audio. Video, and CD-ROMs.* Canadian Children's Book Centre (annual), C$6.95.

This paperback lists materials chosen by committees of children's literature experts in Canada for excellence in writing, illustration, performance, and appeal. Exceptional titles are starred. Print materials are annotated and organized by subject—fiction, sports, and nature, for example. About 300 titles are included in each issue. There are also sections on professional materials and an author/title index. For more information, contact the Canadian Children's Book Centre, 40 Orchard View Blvd., Suite 101, Toronto, ON M4R 1B9; www.bookcentre.ca.

269   *Read All About It: Your Guide to Great Canadian Young Adult Fiction.* Canadian Children's Book Centre, C$5.95 per guide.

This series consists of a group of study guides each of which contains detailed information on a single book and ways to introduce it to young adults. Its purpose is to provide librarians with "exciting ways to connect teenagers to outstanding and challenging Canadian young adult novels." For more information on the Canadian Children's Book Centre, see the entry above.

C. IRELAND

270   Coghlan, Valerie, and Celia Keenan. *The Big Guide 2: Irish Children's Books.* Irish Children's Books Trust, 2000, $18 (1-8729-1706-2).

This is a sequel to Coghlan's *The Big Guide to Irish Children's Books* (Irish Children's Book Trust, 1996), which discussed the best in Irish children's literature in chapters divided by type, such as fantasy, poetry, and teenage fiction. The new volume consists of a series of short original articles on children's literature in general and on Ireland in particular. Sections cover books in the classroom, curricular materials, Ireland's past, cultural identity, and awards and research. Each section gives an overview of the new literature followed by a list of the books mentioned.

D. UNITED KINGDOM

271   Auchmuty, Rosemary, and Joy Wotton, eds. *The Encyclopedia of School Stories.* 2 vols., each $99.95, Ashgate, 2000.

The British invented the school story and this two-volume set (one for girls' novels [0-7546-0082-3] and one for boys' novels [0-7546-0083-1]) chronicles the development of the genre from *Tom Brown's Schooldays* (1857) to the adventures of Harry Potter. Each volume contains an alphabetical listing of all the known U.K. writers in the field, with biographical details, critical appraisals, and a full bibliography of their writings. There are also general articles on the genre under such topics as "Annuals" and "School Story Papers." Each volume has a critical history of its particular aspect of the school story (male or female) and each concludes with an extensive bibliography. This model of scholarly research took six years to produce.

272 *Children's Books: A Parent's Guide.* Puffin, 1995, o.p.

Though in need of an update, this book is a guide to some of the best-known writers of children's books in Britain. The six sections in the book are organized by age groups beginning with 5-year-olds and ending with 12 and over.

273 *Children's Books in Print: A Reference Catalogue.* Whitaker (annual).

Begun in 1984, this annual lists all the children's books currently in print in the United Kingdom. There are currently about 30,000 titles. Entries are by author and title, with a separate listing by subject and a directory of publishers.

274 *Families Just Like Us: The One Parent Families Good Book Guide.* Book Trust and National Council for One Parent Families, 2000 (1-85199-144-1).

With a foreword by J. K. Rowling, this book lists and annotates about 120 titles divided by age of appeal (from 0–5 to 11+). Some titles are nonfiction, but most are stories that deal with a wide range of family situations including divorce, separation, death, and stepfamilies. Some American titles are included, but most of the entries are British. The annotations are critical and often quote readers, both children and parents. There are author and title indexes.

275 Harrington, Sarah. *100 Best Books: The Pick of Paperback Fiction Published During (year).* Book Trust (annual).

Divided by age categories (from "First Books for Babies" to "Young Adult Readers of 14+," this annual bibliography gives bibliographic information for each book, a picture of the dust jacket, a six-line descriptive and critical annotation, and reading and interest levels. All titles are from British publishers, but some American titles are also included. As well as author, illustrator, and title indexes, there is an excellent subject listing. The address of Book Trust is Book House, 45 East Hill, London SW18 2QZ; www.booktrusted.com or www.booktrust.org.uk.

276   Harrington, Sarah, and Edward Zaghini. *Pop-Ups! A Guide to Novelty Books.* Book Trust, 2001, £5 (0-85353-491-8).

This book covers various facets of pop-up books, including a definition, discussion of appeal, different types (like movable books), and a history, beginning with the 13th century. There are profiles of two important pop-up artists (Jay Young and Kees Moerbeck) and an annotated list of about 30 important pop-up books, from preschool through the upper elementary grades. Other sections include a good list of background sources, a directory of organizations and book dealers that are involved with pop-ups (in both the United States and United Kingdom), and a glossary of terms.

277   Hoban, Margaret, and Jennifer Madden. *Children's Fiction Sourcebook,* 2nd ed. Scolar Press, 1995, $99.50 (1-85928-083-8).

This book covers fiction for children ages 6 to 13 through main entries on about 150 authors. The entry for each author includes biographical information, details of awards won, address, material on each of the author's important books (including age range and an annotation), and a list of other publications. There is a section at the back on classics, an appendix of awards, and a title index. Two other important bibliographies in this series are Keith Barker's *Information Books for Children,* 2nd ed. (Scolar Press, 1994, o.p.), which annotates 1,500 recommended nonfiction titles for ages 3 through 13, and Janet Fisher's *An Index to Historical Fiction for Children and Young People* (Scolar Press, 1994, $79.95 [1-85429-0781-1]), which covers 400 titles arranged by author and indexed by subject and title. The U.S. publisher of these bibliographies is Ashgate Publishing, Old Post Road, Brookfield, VT 05036.

278   Turner, Nicholas. *Rough Guide to Children's Books 0–5 Years.* Rough Guides, 2002, £5.99 (1-85828-787-1).

This attractive small-format book lists more than 100 titles and series for babies and toddlers. It is divided into four sections by age ranges, from 0 to 18 months to preschool 3½ to 5. Each section is subdivided by genre, such as stories, poetry, and interactive books. Each entry has a lengthy annotation that discusses format, content, illustrations, and developmental values, plus astute critical comments. The companion volume, also by Nicholas Turner, is *Rough Guide to Children's Books 5–11 Years* (Rough Guides, 2002, £5.99 [1-185828-788-X]). This work is also divided by age group and subdivided by such headings as classics, school stories, fantasy stories, and poetry. It features longer annotations of about one and a half pages each with good plot summaries, pithy critical comments, and an excellent analysis of possible readers. Both books are nicely illustrated, usually with dust jackets. More recently published is ***Rough Guide to Books for Teenagers*** (Rough Guides, 2003, £5.99 [1-8435-3138-0]). These are three useful overviews of the best of British children's books.

E. UNITED STATES

1. General Bibliographies

A. GUIDES TO COLLECTION DEVELOPMENT

279 Alabaster, Carol. ***Developing an Outstanding Core Collection: A Guide for Libraries.*** American Library Association, 2002, pap., $38 (0-8389-0819-5).

Although it is aimed at public libraries serving adult populations, this helpful book presents a sample collection development guide that can be used at other levels. After discussing the need for a core collection, the author explains how to determine candidates for such a collection (for example, by using bibliographies and reviews). The sample core lists would be helpful in libraries serving older teens.

280 DeLong, Janice A., and Rachel Schwedt. ***Core Collection for Small Libraries: An Annotated Bibliography of Books for Children and Young Adults.*** Scarecrow, 1997, $29.50 (0-8108-3252-6).

The purpose of this book is to help parents and librarians select "essential books for their collections appropriate for children and young adults." Chapters are divided by genres—picture books, modern fantasy, multicultural books, and so forth. For each chapter there is a general introduction outlining criteria and then an annotated list of recommended titles. A total of 494 titles are included. This is a highly selective list that ends with 1994 coverage.

281 Gillespie, John T., and Ralph J. Folcarelli. ***Guides to Collection Development for Children and Young Adults.*** Libraries Unlimited, 1998, $39 (1-56308-532-1).

This work contains more than 800 bibliographies of children's and young adult materials that would be useful for collection development in libraries. Both current and retrospective works are annotated and organized into five main sections according to age suitability. There is also a section on professional materials. Both print and nonprint materials are included, and there are thorough author, title, and subject indexes.

282   Jones, Dolores Blythe. *Building a Special Collection of Children's Literature in Your Library.* American Library Association, 1998, pap., $40 (0-838-90726-1).

This is a small but substantial handbook for librarians who wish to create a special collection of children's books—for example a collection of rare books, a subject specialization, or an archival collection. The ten essays in this volume, each written by an expert, cover such topics as acquisition, preservation, funding, and promotional techniques. There is also material on how to acquire out-of-print books and how to appraise rare books. Appendixes include directories of dealers and organizations.

283   Luckenbill, W. Bernard. *Collection Development for a New Century in the School Library Media Center.* Greenwood, 2002, $39.95 (0-313-31295-8).

This work contains an overview of the issues, problems, and possible solutions relating to developing collections in school libraries. There are also comprehensive lists of selection tools, a discussion of technology's role in the library, and discussion of censorship issues. This book supplies a scholarly base for making practical decisions; many useful tips are scattered throughout.

284   McGregor, Joy, et al. *Collection Management for School Libraries.* Scarecrow, 2003, $49.50 (0-8108-4488-5).

Thirteen essays by specialists are included in this volume that explores the theoretical aspects of collection management in school libraries. Among the topics covered are policies (sample policies are included), selection procedures, evaluation of collections, funding, management, weeding, presenting monetary requests, and grant writing.

285   Van Orden, Phyllis J. *Selecting Books for the Elementary School Library Media Center.* Neal-Schuman, 2000, $49.50 (1-55570-368-2).

This is a well-organized, handsomely illustrated guide for both novice and experienced librarians. It begins with four chapters that give a general picture of the selection process in elementary school libraries. An outline of useful guidelines is included. The next nine chapters deal with specific genres such as picture books, fiction, folk literature, and poetry. Each chapter presents criteria for evaluation, with many examples of recommended titles. Each chapter ends with lists of works cited, recommended professional sources, and representative authors and illustrators. A comprehensive, engaging work.

286   Van Orden, Phyllis J., and Kay Bishop. *The Collection Program in Schools: Concepts, Practices, and Information Sources*, 3rd ed. Libraries

Unlimited, 2001, $64.50 (1-56308-980-7); pap., $49.50 (1-56308-804-5).

Long considered the standard text in the field, this latest edition is divided into three main parts. The first part discusses the general environment of selection and looks at policies and procedures; the second part discusses the selection process, criteria by format, and educational perspectives; and the last part addresses such administrative concerns as acquiring materials, fiscal issues, and maintaining and evaluating the collection. There are excellent bibliographies, lists of organizations, and material on developing technologies, such as Web sites and e-books. An indispensable source.

B. GUIDES TO BOOKS IN SERIES

287 Anderson, Vicki. *Fiction Sequels for Readers 10 to 16: An Annotated Bibliography of Books in Succession*, 2nd ed. McFarland, 1998, pap., $29.95 (0-7864-0185-0).

In 154 pages, this work lists alphabetically by author about 3,000 titles of books in series. Each numbered entry includes titles in chronological order, with publisher and date plus an annotation of about four to six lines in length. About 400 authors are represented. There is a title index, which gives the entry number, and cross-references connect pen names to authors. There is no series name index. Both in-print and out-of-print titles are included. This is a straightforward, nonjudgmental work that could be updated.

288 Anderson, Vicki. *Sequels in Children's Literature: An Annotated Bibliography of Books in Succession or with Shared Themes and Characters, K–6.* McFarland, 1998, pap., $35 (0-7864-0285-7).

There are 7,500 titles arranged alphabetically by author in this index that is a companion to the Anderson book listed above. After the author name(s), each entry contains title, publisher, publication date, age range, and a few sentences about the book. In-print and out-of-print titles are included. There is a title index but no series index.

289 Makowski, Silk. *Serious About Series: Evaluations and Annotations of Teen Fiction in Paperback Series.* Scarecrow, 1998, pap., $26.50 (0-8108-3304-2).

After an introductory essay that gives background information on the genre, each chapter deals with a different series. Fifty paperback series of all types and varying quality (Tom Swift and Nancy Drew are included) are described, with an evaluation and an annotated title list that includes bibliographic information and publication dates. The writing style is lively and entertaining.

290   Thomas, Rebecca L., and Catherine Barr. *Popular Series Fiction for K–6 Readers: A Reading and Selection Guide.* Libraries Unlimited, 2004, $60 (1-59158-203-2).

This and the companion volume described later in this entry are extensions and revisions of Catherine Barr's *Reading in Series* (Libraries Unlimited, 1999, o.p.). This volume lists and annotates about 1,100 fiction series currently available for elementary school readers. Each entry gives brief bibliographic information and a grade-level notation and describes the appeal of the series and its characteristics, chief characters, location, and genre. Titles in the series are listed in chronological order with their dates of publication; where appropriate, a preferred reading order is also given. *Popular Series Fiction for Middle School and Teen Readers* (Libraries Unlimited, 2004, $50 [1-59158-202-4]), by the same authors, provides similar information for 700 additional series that are suitable for older readers.

291   Young, Philip H. *Children's Fiction Series: A Bibliography, 1850–1950.* McFarland, 1997, $55 (0-7864-0321-7).

Aimed at the serious collector and researcher, this comprehensive bibliography of fictional children's series lists 1,243 series arranged by series title. Some series contain more than 200 individual book titles! There are no annotations but author's and publisher's names are given, plus the date of publication when available. An interesting introduction provides historical background information on the origins and development of series publication. Author, title, and illustrator indexes are included.

c. Bibliographies of Books for All Ages

292   *Awards and Honors: A Guide to Selected Children's Books.* Children's Book Council, 2003, $3.95.

This attractive, 48-page pamphlet was produced to accompany an exhibition of award-winning books published from 1997 to 2002. A total of 227 books are listed by age group, beginning with fiction for toddlers and ending with books for young adults. Nonfiction titles are also included. Each entry has a brief annotation that gives a contents note and a list of awards and prizes won. There are no indexes except for a directory of publishers that participated in the project.

293 *Children's Books in Print: An Author, Title, and Illustrator Index to Books for Children and Young Adults.* Bowker, 2 vols. (annual).

This important tool for anyone involved with children's literature is now in two print volumes. Volume 1 is the title index. For each book listed, suitable bibliographic information is included (author/illustrator, publisher, date, and price). There is an interesting introduction that lists prize-winning books. Volume 2 is the author/illustrator index and gives the same bibliographic information, plus the title. There are numerous cross-references. About 250,000 books are included in each issue. The companion volume is *Subject Guide to Children's Books in Print* (Bowker, annual), which supplies an accessible way of identifying both fiction and nonfiction books via a thorough list of subjects. These titles are also available on CD-ROM. Bibliographic information for the 2004 publication is as follows: *Children's Books in Print*, 36th ed., 2005 (Bowker, 2004, $350; 0-8352-4706-6) and *Subject Guide to Children's Books in Print*, 2005 (Bowker, 2004, $250: 0-8352-4709-0).

294 *El-Hi Textbooks in Print* (year). Bowker (annual).

Textbooks and related materials currently in print in the United States are listed in this annual, non-evaluative publication. Approximately 193,000 materials from about 1,000 publishers are arranged under 21 basic subjects (art, literature, and business, for example) and 308 subdivisions. Citations include basic bibliographic information plus grade levels and an indication of additional teaching materials. There are author, title, and series indexes. The 2004 edition is in two volumes: *El-Hi Textbooks and Serials in Print, 2004*, Bowker, 2004, $265 (0-8352-4615-9).

295 Odean, Kathleen. *Great Books About Things Kids Love: More than 750 Recommended Books for Children 3 to 14.* Ballantine, 2001, pap., $14 (0-345-44131-1).

This work contains more than 750 titles arranged under such broad subjects as animals and sports, with subdivisions such as cats and soccer. Within each subject area, the books are organized by difficulty level, from preschool through junior high. Annotations give partial plot summaries. Additional material includes sections on children's magazines, book clubs, movie and TV tie-ins, reading-aloud tips, and other resources. There are author, title, and subject indexes.

296 *What Do Children and Young Adults Read Next?*, Vol. 6. Gale, 2004, $120 (0-7876-6580-0).

In 2001 Gale combined *What Do Children Read Next?* and *What Do Young Adults Read Next?* into a single entity. There were three volumes of each of these earlier titles; the first volumes of the combined text were Vol. 4 (Gale, 2001, $220 [0-7876-4799-3]; published as a set containing two books) and Vol. 5 (Gale, 2002, $120 [0-7876-4799-3]). For information on the earlier volumes, see the entries later in this chapter. The purpose of these combined volumes is to supply reading guidance for young people from the elementary grades through high school and to help match readers with suitable books. In a single alphabet, more than 1,500 books are listed by the author's last name. For each title, bibliographic information is given, plus an age range, plot summary, review citations, a list of other books by the author, and a briefly annotated bibliography of three other books of a similar nature. About one third of this oversize book is made up of indexes, which cover series, awards, time periods, locales, character names, character descriptions, age suitability, author, and title. This work—and its predecessors—are extremely valuable for both collection development and reading guidance.

D. BIBLIOGRAPHIES OF PICTURE BOOKS

297   Ammon, Bette D., and Gale W. Sherman. *Worth a Thousand Words: Annotated Guide to Picture Books for Older Readers.* Libraries Unlimited, 1996, pap., $28 (1-56308-390-6).

This innovative guide, though somewhat out of date, features 645 picture books published through 1994 that are suitable for use in grade 4 through senior high. Most were published in the 1980s and early 1990s and are still in print; most are also nonfiction works that are heavily illustrated. The books are arranged alphabetically by author's last name. Each entry includes a citation, brief summary, and subject list, along with specific suggestions for curriculum use. Subject, author/illustrator, and title indexes complete the volume.

298   Axel-Lute, Melanie. *Numbers! Colors! Alphabets! A Concept Guide to Children's Picture Books.* Linworth, 2003, $39.95 (1-58683-058-9).

This guide to concept books for young children is organized by concepts, both concrete and abstract, such as shapes, colors, same/different, real/pretend, the body, and change. Several titles are suggested for each concept. Bibliographic information and age-level suggestions are included for each title. There are helpful author and title indexes.

299   Benedict, Susan. *Beyond Words: Picture Books for Older Readers and Writers.* Heinemann, 1992, pap., $21.50 (0-435-08710-X).

A number of essays by different contributors celebrate the value of picture books beyond the elementary years. Teachers from the primary grades through high school show how picture books can be used in reading and writing programs to enrich the lives of older children. Professional writers and illustrators provide a glimpse into their creative processes, and poet Georgia Heard examines the relationship between poetry and picture books. There are many bibliographies of recommended titles from such writers as Maurice Sendak, Dr. Seuss, and Chris Van Allsburg.

300 Blakemore, Catherine. *Faraway Places: Your Source of Picture Books that Fly Children to 82 Countries.* Adams-Pomeroy, 2002, pap., $28.95 (0-9661009-2-1).

Arranged first by continent and then by country, this bibliography lists picture books that depict various peoples and places. Brief descriptions of each book are followed by basic bibliographic information. This work would be stronger if more information were given about each book (for example, quality of illustrations, curriculum applications, and suggested age or grade levels). Nevertheless, it supplies a basic geographical approach to picture books.

301 Cianciolo, Patricia J. *Informational Picture Books for Children.* American Library Association, 2000, pap., $36 (0-8389-0774-1).

After an interesting introduction that discusses informational picture books in general and the author's criteria for inclusion in this volume, approximately 250 recommended titles are organized in subject-oriented chapters—"Numbers and Arithmetic," "Peoples and Cultures," and so forth. A few fiction titles are included, but most are nonfiction. Lengthy annotations are provided for each book, with recommended age levels. This is a fine guide to high-quality picture books.

302 Cianciolo, Patricia J. *Picture Books for Children*, 4th ed. American Library Association, 1997, $40 (0-8389-0701-6).

Though now showing its age, this standard work lists 273 high-quality picture books. Titles chosen range from preschool to junior high school level. They are arranged by broad topics—"Other People" and "The World I Live In," for example—and then by author. Entries include full bibliographic data, illustrator, intended age level, and a perceptive, evaluative annotation.

303 Cooper, Cathie Hilterbran. *ABC Books and Activities: From Preschool to High School.* Scarecrow, 1996, $27.50 (0-8108-3013-2).

The general introduction lists criteria for use with different age groups and discusses the value of alphabet books. The 500 titles included are arranged in a series of topically oriented chapters (animals, science, and multiculturalism, to name a few). Annotations are given, plus suggested activities, games, projects, and worksheets that can be used at different grade levels. Many of the titles are still in print, and the variety of proposed activities makes this a valuable, if somewhat dated, resource.

304   Cooper, Cathie Hilterbran. *Color and Shape Books for All Ages.* Scarecrow, 2000, pap., $32.50 (0-8108-3542-8).

Although the title states "for all ages," the picture books discussed are for preschool through the primary grades. Chapters look at books about color and shapes in different formats (including board books) and on different subjects (for example, animals and social studies). Each chapter outlines a series of activities relating to the books listed.

305   Harms, Jeanne McLain, and Lucille Lettow. *Picture Books to Enhance the Curriculum.* H. W. Wilson, 1996, $60 (0-8242-0867-6).

The purpose of this bibliography is to identify and describe favorite, high-quality picture books that will be helpful in meeting curricular needs. About 1,500 picture books are included in this theme-oriented volume. Picture books are recommended within such areas as language arts, science, and social studies. Other features include a section in which each picture book is described and an alphabetical list of book titles. This innovative selective list is still of value.

306   Lima, Carolyn W., and John A. Lima. *A to Zoo: Subject Access to Children's Picture Books*, 6th ed. Libraries Unlimited, 2001, $75 (0-313-32069-1).

Long recognized as the most comprehensive subject guide to all types of picture books, both fiction and nonfiction, this sixth edition of *A to Zoo* contains nearly 23,000 in-print and out-of-print picture books; about 5,000 of them are new to this revision. The first section lists the 1,200 subject headings used, with many cross-references to help the user. In the next section, these subject headings are repeated, with appropriate books listed under each, by author and then by title. In the third section, "Bibliographic Guide," each of the books cited is listed alphabetically by author's last name. Full bibliographic information is given, plus material on the thematic material found in the book. Lastly, there are title and illustrator indexes. As one reviewer said, "Every library that serves children and teachers should own this source."

307   Matulka, Denise I. *Picture This: Picture Books for Young Adults: A Curriculum-Related Annotated Bibliography.* Greenwood, 1997, $49.95 (0-313-30182-4).

For this volume, the author defines picture books as books of 3,000 words of text or less and containing many illustrations. Young adults are classified as students in grades 8 through 12. Arranged by six curriculum areas (such as the arts, literature, and social science), this volume contains annotated bibliographic information for 424 books published in the late 1980s through 1996. Each book entry usually contains a listing of several other recommended titles on the subject. Although a few of the titles included are intended for a younger audience, most were published as young adult titles.

308 Odean, Kathleen. *Great Books for Babies and Toddlers: More than 500 Recommended Books for Your Child's First Years.* Ballantine, 2003, pap., $14.95 (0-345-45254-2).

This well-annotated, carefully selected listing of more than 500 books suitable for very young children contains a wide variety of formats and genres, including fingerplay and baby game books, board books, and conventional picture storybooks. All titles were published since 1990 and were in print as of 2003. Also included are excellent background material, tips concerning the use of books with this audience, and a list of books that have been translated into Spanish. A very useful resource.

309 Stephens, Claire Gatrell. *Picture This! Using Picture Story Books for Character Education in the Classroom.* Libraries Unlimited, 2003, $35 (1-59158-001-3).

In an unusual approach to picture storybooks, the author has searched the literature and compiled a bibliography that categorizes recommended picture books by the human qualities they portray. Arranged by "virtues," this annotated listing will be of importance in discussing values and character attributes with children. The appendix lists a wealth of supplemental resources to help convey each virtue to children.

E. BIBLIOGRAPHIES OF BOOKS FOR THE ELEMENTARY SCHOOL GRADES

310 Barstow, Barbara, and Judith Riggle. *Beyond Picture Books: A Guide to First Readers*, 2nd ed. Bowker, 1995, $52.50 (0-8352-3519-X).

Although this work is more than ten years old in its coverage, it is included here because of the comprehensive nature of its contents. The authors profile more than 2,500 first readers that are of interest to children ages 4 to 8 and that are both challenging and entertaining. Reading levels (from A for easiest to C for works with compound sentences) are given for each title. The bibliography is arranged alphabetically by author; for each entry, there is bibliographic material, subjects, reading category, and a brief annotation. About half of the book consists of indexes: by subject, title, illustrator, readability, and series.

311   Berman, Matt. *What Else Should I Read? Guiding Kids to Good Books, Vol. 2.* Libraries Unlimited, 1996, $24 (1-56308-419-8).

After an introduction that includes 15 to 20 types of activities for a literature program, the author highlights 30 popular children's books for grades 3 and up. He then links the books by webs to 9 to 12 topical bookmarks, with 4 to 8 books on each topic. A total of about 500 books are listed in this way. The webs and bookmarks are reproducible. Unfortunately, no grade or age levels are given. This is a continuation of Berman's earlier *What Else Should I Read? Guiding Kids to Good Books, Vol. 1* (Libraries Unlimited, 1995, $24.50 [1-56308-241-1]).

312   *Children's Catalog,* 18th ed. H. W. Wilson, 2001, $175 (includes 4 annual supplements) (0-8242-1009-3).

This work has been a mainstay for almost 100 years (the first edition was in 1909), supplying authoritative material for collection development in elementary schools and children's room in libraries. The body of the book consists of a listing of about 7,000 titles. The nonfiction titles are arranged by the Dewey Decimal system and the fiction titles are listed alphabetically by author (with separate sections for picture books, magazines, and story collections). Each entry contains full bibliographic information and excerpts from two reviews (one descriptive and the other critical). The remainder of the volume is given over to a combined author, illustrator, title, subject, and analytic index. Purchase of this volume entitles the owner to four annual paperback supplements that list about 600 new titles each. The 19th edition will appear in 2006. This highly recommended work is useful for book selection and evaluation.

313   Deeds, Sharon, and Catherine Chastain. *The New Books Kids Like.* American Library Association, 2001, pap., $32 (0-8389-3512-5).

Librarians from around the country were canvassed for suggestions of titles to include in this bibliography first published in 1991. The 500 books included are arranged under 44 topics of high interest, such as science fiction, humor, and survival stories. Each title is given a six-line annotation and was published since the last edition (i.e., since 1991). Under each subject, the books are classified as picture books, beginning readers, or chapter books. Although a few junior high books appear in this list, most of the books are for a K–6 audience. This attractive, practical volume also contains a combined author and title index.

314   Estes, Sally. *Popular Reading for Children IV: A Collection of Booklist Columns.* American Library Association, 1999, pap., $8.95 (0-8389-8010-4).

From time to time, the reviewing journal *Booklist* publishes retrospective bibliographies in its section on books for young people, under the heading "Popular Reading for Children." Most deal with specific topics and give good annotated lists that can be useful for librarians. This is the fourth collections of these well-received columns. See also *Popular Reading for Young Adults,* also by Estes, later in this chapter.

315   Freeman, Judy. *More Books Kids Will Sit Still For: A Read-Aloud Guide.* Libraries Unlimited, 1995, pap., $52.50 (0-8352-3520-3).

A supplement to the author's *Books Kids Will Sit Still For* (Libraries Unlimited, 1990, $52.50 [0-8352-3010-4]), this new volume, though more than ten years old, is still available. It recommends about 2,000 works that are fine read-alouds for K–6, organized under major genre headings. Each entry contains a brief annotation, suggested activities, similar titles, and subject headings. The lengthy introductory chapter discusses the effective use of different types of books with young people. *Books Kids Will Sit Still For 3* is scheduled for publication in late 2005.

316   Gillespie, John T. *Best Books for Children: Preschool Through Grade 6,* 7th ed. Libraries Unlimited, 2001, $65 (0-313-32068-3).

Hailed by one reviewer as "an essential book-collection development tool for all libraries serving children," this selection aid/collection evaluation tool is now in its seventh edition (new editions appear every four years). There are now more than 23,000 numbered entries (about 9,000 new to this edition) organized by broad subjects with subdivisions. Each entry contains full bibliographic information, including series notes, grade suitability, review citations, and a brief critical annotation. Each book listed has been reviewed favorably in such periodicals as *Booklist* and *School Library Journal.* All books listed were in print at the time of publication. There are extensive indexes, by author, illustrator, title, and subject. References are to book number rather than page number. The subject index is particularly helpful because it lists the books by reading level. A two-year supplement was published in 2003 (see entry below) and a new edition is planned for 2005.

317   Gillespie, John T., and Catherine Barr. *Best Books for Children: Preschool Through Grade 6: Supplement to the Seventh Edition.* Libraries Unlimited, 2003, $35 (1-59158-082-X).

Using the same main subject headings and subdivisions as in the parent volume, *Best Books for Children* (see entry above), this supplement lists about 6,000 new recommended titles published in the two years since the seventh edition (that is, from 2001 to 2003). As in the parent volume, each entry contains extensive bibliographic information, grade-level recommendations, and a brief annotation. The indexes are by author, illustrator, title, and subject/grade level.

318   Johnson, Miriam J. *Building a Child's Library: Inside 25 Classic Children's Stories.* Paulist Press, 2004, pap., $9.95 (0-8091-4229-5).

The author, who is a mother and former teacher and librarian, highlights 25 distinguished children's books. In addition to summaries, there are commentaries and suggestions for use from parents, teachers, clergy, and children. Without being preachy, this work discusses values found in each of these stories. The books are arranged under such headings as "God's Care and Forgiveness" and "World Religions."

319   *Kids Review Kids' Books.* Scholastic, 1999, $14.95 (0-5906-0346-9).

This attractive, engaging bibliography contains more than 400 lively book reviews by young readers. The organization is informal, but usually by subject or author. Each book is flagged with a genre designator, and scattered throughout the text are mini-biographies of authors, fun facts, and photographs. An inviting book that will be used mainly by young readers, parents, and teachers.

320   Lewis, Valerie V., and Walter M. Mayers. *Valerie and Walter's Best Books for Children: A Lively, Opinionated Guide*, 2nd ed. HarperResource, 2004, $17.95 (0-06-052467-7).

The authors, who have extensive experience in the field of children's literature, have compiled a list of more than 2,000 titles that they "couldn't live without." Arranged by age categories from birth to adolescence, the books are then entered alphabetically by title. The annotations are chatty and often witty and the selections include both classics and recent books. Sidebars feature particular authors or pertinent comments. There is an interesting cross-referenced theme appendix that helps relate titles with similar themes. This is a fine reading guidance tool for both professionals and parents.

321   Lipson, Eden Ross. *The New York Times Parent's Guide to the Best Books for Children*, 3rd ed. Three Rivers Press, 2000, $18 (0-8129-3018-5).

The author, who is the children's book editor at the *New York Times*, has compiled a listing of the top 1,700 children's books of the last century.

There are six divisions, roughly by age suitability, beginning with wordless books and ending with some books for young teens. Written in a user-friendly, informal way, the annotations are informative and helpful. In addition to the standard bibliographic data, entries contain award information and often related titles. The work is attractive, with interesting artwork in the margins. A very useful book for parents.

322   McClure, Amy A., and Janice V. Kristo. ***Adventuring with Books: A Booklist for Pre-K–Grade 6***, 13th ed. National Council of Teachers of English, 2002, $39.95 (0-8141-0073-2).

As in the previous 12 editions of this useful bibliography, coverage is for a specific publishing period (usually two to four years). This latest edition includes 850 titles published between 1999 and 2001. Books are arranged into 24 topical chapters ("Struggle and Survival," "Fantasy Literature," and "Science Nonfiction," for example), with subdivisions for picture books and chapter books. Each book is well annotated and each chapter has an introduction discussing criteria for inclusion. There are author, illustrator, title, and subject indexes. This is a highly respected bibliography. Libraries should retain old editions because coverage is not duplicated.

323   McElmeel, Sharron L. ***Great Nonfiction Reads***. Libraries Unlimited, 1995, $21 (1-56308-228-4).

Although in need of an update, this book gives an introduction to about 600 high-quality nonfiction titles suitable for grades 1 through 6. Using such topics as inventions, sports, and animals, the author highlights 120 books, providing extensive information, activities and projects, and three or four related titles. Many of the highlighted titles are suitable for reading aloud.

324   Silvey, Anita. ***100 Best Books for Children***. Houghton Mifflin, 2004, $14 (0-618-27889-3).

Particularly useful for parents, this volume is divided into six chapters by age grouping, beginning with Board Books (birth to age 2) and ending with Books for Older Readers (ages 11 and 12). Each book is given a page of text that not only supplies an introduction to the story and its characters, but also gives interesting background material on the author and the genesis of the book. As well as a name and title index, there is an appendix, "Beyond the 100 Best," in which about 250 other titles are listed under the same age groupings as in the main section. One reviewer claims that this title is "absolutely essential for every family."

325   Sullivan, Joanna. *The Children's Literature Lover's Book of Lists.* Jossey-Bass, 2004, pap., $29.95 (0-7879-6595-2).

The lists of recommended books in this work are divided into various sections according to grade level (for example, the first section covers preschool to grade 1). Each section lists books under such headings as "Books in Content Areas" (Science and Mathematics, for example) and "Favorite Books." There is also useful information about Web sites, teachers' resources, award-winning books, and publications about children's literature.

326   Sutherland, Zena, et al. *The Best in Children's Books: The University of Chicago Guide to Children's Literature, 1985–1990.* University of Chicago Press, 1991, o.p.

The late Zena Sutherland was for many years the highly respected editor of the *Bulletin of the Center for Children's Books*, then headquartered at the University of Chicago (for more information about the *Bulletin* see Chapter 3, "Current Reviewing Sources"). This compilation contains almost 1,200 titles, all chosen on the basis of literary merit, that were reviewed in the *Bulletin* from 1985 to 1990. Three previous volumes covered the years 1966 to 1972, 1973 to 1978, and 1979 to 1984. Though now only available through out-of-print dealers or in libraries, these volumes list and describe the best in children's literature published in the United States during these years.

327   Thompson, Sally Anne. *60 Years of Notable Children's Books.* American Library Association, 2004, pap., $25.95 (0-8389-8265-4).

Annually, a committee made up of members of ALA's Association for Library Service to Children compiles a "Notable Children's Books" list of the best children's books of the year. Organized by decade, Thompson's bibliography brings together more than 1,500 of those notable titles from 1940 through 1999. As well as author and title indexes, theme lists organize the books under popular subjects.

328   Trachtenberg, Ellen. *The Best Children's Literature: A Parent's Guide.* Parent's Guide Press, 2003, pap., $17.95 (1-931199-18-3).

In six main sections roughly based on age ranges, the author lists about 1,000 titles recommended for children ages 1 to 14. In addition to bibliographic information, entries include a short synopsis, other books by the author, and awards won. Sidebars provide information about select authors and quotations from parents and youngsters about reading. Also included are guidelines for parents on choosing books for children and activities to encourage reading. A good volume for parents who are help-ing their children to read and choose books.

329 *What Do Children Read Next?*, Vol. 3. Gale, 1999, $120 (0-7876-2466-7).

This is the last volume in this set to be published before the children's and young adult volumes were combined in 2001 into *What Do Chil-dren and Young Adults Read Next?* (see entry 296 earlier in this chapter). The first two volumes of the original children's set are: Vol. 1, Gale, 1994, $120 (0-8103-8886-3) and Vol. 2, Gale, 1997, $120 (0-8103-6448-4). In these volumes, each entry is numbered and arranged alpha-betically by the author's last name. Each entry also provides bibliographic information, age suitability, plot summary, review cita-tions, a selected bibliography of other books by the author, and an anno-tated list of three titles that are related to the main title by theme or subject. Extensive indexes cover awards, time periods, geographic locales, subjects, character descriptions, and age suitability, plus the usual author and title indexes. This is a remarkable book that is useful for reading guidance, the creation of bibliographies, and book selection.

330 Wilson, Elizabeth. *Books Children Love: A Guide to the Best Children's Literature.* Crossway Books, 2002, pap., $14.95 (1-58134-198-9).

Written and compiled by a home-schooling advocate and participant, this is a listing of tried and true fiction and nonfiction children's books, arranged first by such subjects as animals, biographies, and crafts and then by grade levels. Most have been given the ultimate test of being approved by children. Each selection has a six- or seven-line critical annotation plus a grade-level indicator. A particularly practical book for parents.

F. BIBLIOGRAPHIES OF BOOKS FOR MIDDLE SCHOOL, JUNIOR HIGH, AND SENIOR HIGH GRADES

331 Ayers, Rich, and Amy Crawford. *Great Books for High School Kids: A Teacher's Guide to Books that Can Change Teens Lives.* Beacon Press, 2004, pap., $15 (0-8070-3255-7).

The authors have compiled a guidebook on teaching a variety of signifi-cant works suitable for mature teen readers (for example, *Bastard Out of Carolina* and *Huckleberry Finn*). Lists of thematically related books are included for each of the highlighted works, plus an annotated list of "Recommended Great Books" and a number of useful indexes. This work is valuable in both the classroom and the library.

332   Beers, Kylene, and Teri Lesesne. *Books for You: An Annotated Booklist for Senior High*, 14th ed. National Council of Teachers of English, 2001, $33.95 (0-8141-0372-3).

Published every three years by the National Council of Teachers of English, this work has become a standard tool on library shelves. This volume annotates more than 1,000 fiction and nonfiction books and covers the publishing years of 1997, 1998, and 1999. The books are divided into 33 subject areas, such as Family Relationships, Friendships, and Choices; the largest number of titles (86) is found under Historical Fiction. The introduction is a history of young adult literature and there are appendixes on Web sites, multicultural titles, and award-winning books. Indexes are by author, title, and subject. Back volumes should be retained by libraries because of their retrospective coverage.

333   Bodart, Joni Richards. *Radical Reads: 101 YA Novels on the Edge.* Scarecrow, 2002, pap., $34.95 (0-8108-4287-4).

Bodart examines 101 books of contemporary young adult literature that explore "edgy, raw, and relevant" topics such as incest, teenage pregnancy, violence, and drugs. Arranged by title, the entries feature suitability levels, keywords that describe the book, descriptions of main characters, major themes, controversial elements, and booktalk material (a detailed booktalk and excerpts from reviews). There is also material on censorship and dealing with challenges. A well-organized and extremely useful source.

334   Bodart, Joni Richards. *The World's Best Thin Books: What to Read When Your Book Report Is Due Tomorrow.* Scarecrow, 2000, pap., $16.95 (1-57886-007-5).

Similar in content to the author's excellent *100 World Class Thin Books or What to Read When Your Book Report is Due Tomorrow* (Libraries Unlimited, 1993, o.p.), this work selects high-quality books of no more than 200 pages that are popular with middle and high school students. Titles are arranged into three categories: thin, thinner, and thinnest. For each title, there is a fine synopsis that can be used as a booktalk, plus information on plot, characters, and action. The booktalk materials are sure to grab reluctant readers. As well as useful indexes and advice on book reports, the newer volume includes an appendix, "Recent Titles Popular with Teens," that lists other recent thin books. A valuable, unique resource.

335 Brown, Jean E., and Elaine C. Stephens. *Your Reading: An Annotated Booklist for Middle School and Junior High*, 11th ed. National Council of Teachers of English, 2003, pap., $33.95 (0-8141-5944-3).

Divided first by broad subjects and then by chapters that cover such topics as adventure and survival, science fiction, and poetry, this bibliography contains more than 1,200 entries for books suitable for youngsters in grades 6 through 9. The books are well chosen by a committee from the National Council of Teachers of English and thoroughly annotated by the editors. There are author, title, and subject indexes. The books listed were all published between 1995 and 2002. Because there is no duplication from one edition to the next, older editions can be kept for reference purposes. This is a standard, highly respected work that is good for both reading guidance and book selection.

336 Carter, Betty, et al. *Best Books for Young Adults*, 2nd ed. Young Adult Library Services Association/American Library Association. 2000, pap., $35 (0-8389-3501-X).

This edition continues and updates coverage of the first edition, published in 1994, by including books that were selected annually from 1966 through 1999 by ALA's Best Book for Young Adults (BBYA) Committee. Other bibliographies of recommended YA titles compiled by the association were also consulted. A total of more than 1,800 books are listed. Part 1 tells how the books were selected and gives topical lists of the titles, under such subjects as adventure, animals, family, and fantasy. Part 2 lists all the titles alphabetically by author, and gives bibliographic information and a brief description for each. Unfortunately no grade levels are provided, nor is there indication of whether a book is an adult or a young adult title. Additional features include a list of the titles by year of selection, an appendix outlining procedures of the BBYA committee, and extensive indexes. A very helpful guide for both selection and reader guidance.

337 Estes, Sally. *Popular Reading for Young Adults: A Collection of Booklist Columns*. American Library Association, 1996, pap., $7.95 (0-8389-7835-5).

This collection of retrospective bibliographies on a number of subjects and genres popular with young adults serves as a companion to the author's *Popular Reading for Children* (see earlier in this chapter). Many of the bibliographies are reprinted from *Booklist*, but others are original to this paperback. Topics covered include self-image, poetry, historical fiction, and virtual reality. The author's previously published *Growing Up Is Hard to Do* (American Library Association, 1994, $7.95 [0-8389-7726-X]) is also a collection of columns containing literature aimed at adolescents and their problems.

338   Fenner, Pamela J., et al. ***Books for the Journey: A Guide to the World of Reading.*** Michaelmas Press, 2003, pap., $19.95 (0-9647832-4-X).

Aimed at the teenage reader, this bibliography contains about 1,500 annotated titles that bridge the gap between childhood and adulthood. Arranged by conventional genre categories (for example, fiction, nonfiction, drama, and poetry), this work contains both adult and adolescent literature. In a special final section, "Seniors Look Back,'" 12th-grade students list their best-loved books. This is a fine basic list.

339   Gillespie, John T., and Catherine Barr. ***Best Books for High School Readers, Grades 9–12.*** Libraries Unlimited, 2004, $75 (1-59158-084-6).

A companion volume to *Best Books for Children* (see entry earlier in this chapter) and *Best Books for Middle School and Junior High Readers* (see below), this bibliography contains 13,457 annotated entries with an additional 741 recommended titles mentioned within the entries. Using current reviewing sources (*VOYA* and *Booklist*, for example), the authors have compiled this list of recommended titles arranged by broad subjects with many subdivisions. Fiction titles are organized under such headings as "Science Fiction" and "Personal Problems." Both adult and young adult titles are included. As well as full bibliographic information, each entry contains series notes, grade-level suitability, and a three- or four-line annotation. Each entry is given an identifying number that is used in the author, title, and subject/grade-level indexes. This highly recommended volume is the largest, most comprehensive bibliography of books suitable for these grades. It is the successor to Gillespie's *Best Books for Senior High Readers* (Bowker, 1991, o.p.).

340   Gillespie, John T., and Catherine Barr. ***Best Books for Middle School and Junior High Readers: Grades 6–9.*** Libraries Unlimited, 2004, $75 (1-59158-083-8).

There are 13,523 entries in this bibliography of books suitable for grades 6 through 9, plus an additional 623 titles mentioned within the entries. Titles are arranged by broad subject areas—curriculum-oriented for nonfiction and interest categories for fiction—with numerous subdivisions. Each entry includes full bibliographic information including series notes, review citations, and a brief annotation. All titles are recommended in professional reviewing journals (usually two or more positive reviews per title). There are author, title, and subject/grade level indexes. This is considered a basic collection development and reading guidance tool for libraries. There are plans for a two-year supplement and a new edition in 2008. This work supercedes Gillespie's *Best Books for Junior High Readers* (Bowker, 1991, o.p.), Stephen J. Calvert's *Best Books for Young Adult Readers, Grades 7–12* (Bowker, 1996, $59.95 [0-8352- 3832-6]), and Gillespie's *Best Books for Young Teen Readers, Grades 7–10* (Bowker, 2000, $65 [0-8352-4264-1]) (the latter two volumes are available from Libraries Unlimited).

341 Jones, Patrick, et al. *A Core Collection for Young Adults.* Neal-Schuman, 2003, $65, pap. (1-55570-458-1).

Using both literary quality and popularity with readers as criteria, the authors have compiled an excellent list of more than 1,200 titles that would form a basic collection for young adults in grades 6 through 12. The breakdown is roughly 60 percent fiction, 30 percent nonfiction, and 10 percent in graphic format. Both adult and young adult titles are included. Nonfiction titles are arranged by broad Dewey classification numbers and the fiction and graphic novels are arranged by author. Each entry contains bibliographic information, an annotation, grade levels, and, sometimes, review sources. There are author and title indexes and many useful appendixes, such as tips for maintaining collections and a guide to "Best Books" lists. An accompanying CD-ROM presents lists in various formats. A useful work for any librarian working with teens.

342 Lewis, Marjorie. *Outstanding Books for the College Bound: Choices for a Generation.* American Library Association, 1996, $28 (0-8389-3456-0).

This respected bibliography lists more than 1,000 books in five categories: fiction, nonfiction, biography, drama, and poetry. Each entry contains a short annotation and indicates the year the title first appeared on a list prepared by the Young Adult Library Services Association. There is a separate chronological list (1959–1994), plus author and title indexes. The Preface explains how the books were selected and how frequently they have appeared on the lists. Though an update would be helpful, this is still a useful list of better books for better students.

343 *Middle and Junior High School Library Catalog,* 8th ed. H. W. Wilson, 2000, $250 (0-8242-0996-6).

This invaluable tool for acquisition work and reading guidance was first published in 1965 and is now on a five-year publishing schedule, with annual supplements for the four intervening years (the initial price includes the supplements). The main volume contains about 4,520 titles, each listed with full bibliographic information and extensive excerpts from reviews. The total number of new titles in the four supplements is about 2,500. Part 1 of the main volume contains nonfiction titles arranged by Dewey Decimal number and fiction titles arranged by author's last name. Part 2 is an extensive index that contains author, title, subject, and analytic entries. Part 3 is a directory of publishers and distributors. This is a companion volume to *Children's Catalog* (see earlier in this chapter) and *Senior High School Library Catalog* (see below); all three are available in electronic editions.

344   *Senior High School Library Catalog*, 16th ed. H. W. Wilson, 2002, $210 (0-8242-1008-5).

A new edition of this standard, reliable bibliography of books suitable for grades 9 through 12 appears every five years. Four annual supplements are published between editions; these supplements are included in the basic purchase price. There are about 5,400 entries in the main volume and a total of more than 2,400 in the supplements. The nonfiction titles are arranged by Dewey numbers, and the fiction titles are arranged by the author's last name. About half of the book consists of a massive index that contains title, author, subject, and analytic listings. As with the other titles in Wilson's Standard Catalog series, titles are voted in by a group of experienced librarians. This work first appeared in 1926, and since then it has maintained its status as an essential tool for core collection development in libraries serving older teens.

345   Snodgrass, Mary Ellen. *Literary Treks: Characters on the Move.* Libraries Unlimited, 2003, pap., $32 (1-56308-953-X).

This companion to the author's *Literary Maps for Young Adult Literature* (Libraries Unlimited, 1995, o.p.) contains maps and itineraries for 28 young adult books that feature real and imaginary terrains. Titles span such genres as historical fiction, fantasy, and science fiction and are standard literary works, both classic and contemporary. Full bibliographic information is given for each book, along with a detailed geographic summary and maps that feature routes and travels described in the book. A unique source for young adult collections.

346   *What Do Young Adults Read Next? Vol. 3.* Gale, 1999, $120 (0-7876-2467-5).

This is the last of the three volumes issued before this title was merged with the children's volumes in 2001 to become *What Do Children and Young Adults Read Next?* (see entries earlier in this chapter). The first two volumes in the young adult set are: Vol. 1, Gale, 1994, $120 (0-8103-88887-1) and Vol. 2, Gale, 1997, $120 (0-8103-6449-2). Each volume contains about 1,500 entries arranged alphabetically by author's last name. For each title, the information supplied includes bibliographic material, subjects, age ranges, a plot summary, a list of other books by the author, and an annotated bibliography of three related books useful in giving reading guidance. There is an amazing array of indexes, including author, title, location, subject, character name, character descriptor, age suitability, and time period. This set is valuable for matching readers with books and for bibliography preparation and book selection.

347 Zitlow, Connie S. *Lost Masterworks of Young Adult Literature.* Scarecrow, 2002, $31.50 (0-8108-4360-9).

Twenty-six essays, by such authorities in young adult literature as Michael Cart and Joni Richards Bodart, discuss books that were critically acclaimed but are now out of print. Each essay focuses on a single work or series and explores why it is a "masterwork" for young adults. For each book or series, biographical information is given about the author and there is a detailed examination of the plot, characters, and literary quality. Authors featured include John Rowe Townsend, Robert Lipsyte, Aidan Chambers, and the Mazers. Part of the Scarecrow Studies in Young Adult Literature series, this work offers a unique look at the past glories of young adult literature.

348 Zwirin, Stephanie. *The Best Years of Their Lives: A Resource Guide for Teenagers in Crisis*, 2nd ed. American Library Association, 1996, $26 (0-8389-0686-9).

The many problems, chiefly social, that trouble today's teenagers are the focus of this listing of resources. It is a wonderful guide for teachers, librarians, and parents seeking suitable books and videos dealing with topics important to young adults who are coping with the pangs of adolescence. Sample chapter headings include "Family Matters," "Wellness," and "Sex Stuff." The second edition has expanded coverage on fiction and videos, and includes an interview with Michael Pritchard, head of the PBS series *Power of Choice*.

2. Specific Audiences

A. GAY AND LESBIAN

349 Cart, Michael. *Gay and Lesbian Fiction for Young Adults.* Scarecrow, 2005, $40 (0-8108-5071-0).

Young people's difficulties finding nonjudgmental literature on homosexuality and positive gay and lesbian role models in their reading are among the issues addressed in this book. It features a critical evaluation of the books published for young adults that feature homosexual themes or characters. There are also lists of resources (magazines, Web sites, and hotlines), an annotated bibliography of other printed sources, and an index by author, title, and subject. Part of the Scarecrow Studies in Young Adult Literature series.

350   Day, Frances Ann. *Lesbian and Gay Voices: An Annotated Bibliography and Guide to Literature for Children and Young Adults.* Greenwood, 2000, $38.95 (0-313-31162-5).

The body of this comprehensive work consists of two parts. The first part contains six bibliographies organized by genre—picture books, fiction, and biography, for example. The entries total 275, with the largest number (70 entries) appearing in the fiction section for ages 8 through 18. The choice of books is outstanding. Each entry contains bibliographic information, age suitability, detailed content notes, and a list of subject headings. The second part contains brief profiles of authors who have written on gay or lesbian themes, including M. E. Kerr and Michael Cart. Supplementary material includes lists of hotlines and organizations and guidelines for evaluating books with gay or lesbian content. This is an excellent bibliographic source.

351   Lobban, Marjorie, and Laurel A. Clyde. *Out of the Closet and into the Classroom: Homosexuality in Books for Young People.* Bowker, 1993, o.p.

Although now out of date, this bibliography supplies a good backward glance at how themes and characters relating to homosexuality were treated in earlier books for young people. A total of 120 books are discussed in alphabetical order by author. Most of the books are for junior and senior high school students. The annotations describe and critically analyze each book. This is a pioneering effort, still of some value.

B. GENDER-RELATED BIBLIOGRAPHIES

i. Boys

352   Bilz, Rachelle Lasky. *Life Is Tough: Guys, Growing Up, and Young Adult Literature.* Scarecrow, 2004, $40 (0-8108-5055-9).

This book (part of the Scarecrow Studies in Young Adult Literature series) explores the types of male protagonists found in important young adult novels and shows how these characters can act as role models for today's male teenagers as they experience the problems of adolescence. The novels are dealt with thematically, based on such issues as coming-of-age, sexuality, and making decisions. Annotated book lists, useful for acquisition purposes, conclude each chapter. A fine work for both reading guidance and selection.

353 Odean, Kathleen. *Great Books for Boys: More than 600 Books for Boys 2 to 14.* Ballantine, 1998, pap., $12.95 (0-345-42083-7).

The purpose of this bibliography is to suggest good books for boys so that they continue to read through adolescence. Titles are organized by reader age and then by genre. The well-annotated entries include novels with strong protagonists of both sexes, as well as some nonfiction titles. The books selected express a wide range of emotions and experiences. Graphic novels are not included, but there is a list of magazines for young readers. This unique resource is a companion to *Great Books for Girls* (see entry below).

ii. Girls

354 Bauermeister, Erica, and Holly Smith. *Let's Hear It for the Girls: 375 Great Books for Readers 2–14.* Penguin, 1997, $15 (0-14-025732-2).

Each of the 375 annotated titles in this bibliography furnishes an entertaining reading experience and features a heroine who can serve as a suitable role model. The titles are arranged by broad age groupings, beginning with picture books (such as *Madeline*), continuing through story books and chapter books, and ending with more complex works (for ages 10 and up, such as *A Wrinkle in Time*). Entries include good summaries but give no specific age-level suitability, name of publisher, or price. Both old favorites and more recent titles are included, all featuring a strong, interesting female character. The second part of this work contains five indexes that cross-reference titles by dates, genres, setting, and subjects.

355 Cooper-Mullin, Alison, and Jennifer Marmaduke Coye. *Once Upon a Heroine: 400 Books for Girls to Love.* McGraw-Hill, 1998, $16.95 (0-8092-3020-8).

Using recommendations from librarians, teachers, and their own experiences as mothers, the authors have compiled a bibliography of current and classic titles that will "nurture a young girl's spirit of independence, competence, and self-esteem." Books range in interest and reading levels from preschool through young adult and all contain positive female role models. The annotations are concise and informative. There is a special section in which 70 prominent women (including Sandra Day O'Connor, Beverly Sills, and Julia Child) reveal their own childhood reading favorites. This is a worthwhile addition to collections of gender studies in literature for youth.

356   Dodson, Shireen. *100 Books for Girls to Grow On.* HarperCollins, 1998, pap., $14 (0-06-095718-2).

In this companion volume to the author's recommended *The Mother-Daughter Book Club* (HarperCollins, 1997, $14 [0-06-095242-3]), the author has chosen 100 books, both classic and current titles, that will interest girls from age 9 through 13. The books are arranged by author's last name; the annotations contain material on authors and plot, discussion questions, recommended additional titles, and ideas for crafts, projects, and field trips. Although there are some inconsistencies in matching the book with appropriate activities, and there is an absence of bibliographic material in the citations, this is nevertheless an excellent book, particularly for those starting a book discussion group.

357   Fisher, Jerilyn, and Ellen S. Silber. *Women in Literature: Reading Through the Lens of Gender.* Greenwood, 2003, $65 (0-313-31346-6).

This book contains 96 short but provocative essays on literary works frequently studied in high schools and colleges, beginning with *Huckleberry Finn* and ending with *A Yellow Raft in Blue Water.* The books are examined from the standpoint of portrayal of women and of masculinity and femininity. Each essay includes teaching suggestions that aim to heighten students' understanding of how gender influences writing. Bibliographies for further reading follow each essay. An appendix lists the books discussed according to themes and subjects, to promote the use of these titles in a variety of situations. This work presents a new and stimulating way of looking at some standard titles taught in English classrooms.

358   Odean, Kathleen. *Great Books for Girls: More Than 600 Books to Inspire Today's Girls and Tomorrow's Women.* Ballantine, 2002, pap., $14.95 (0-3454-5021-3).

Aimed at raising a girl's self-image, this resource guide lists 600 books with strong female protagonists for girls from age 2 to 14. Beginning with picture books and ending with popular adult titles, there are subdivisions in each age group by fictional genre and nonfiction. Annotations include plot summaries and sometimes a comparison to other books, as well as full bibliographic material. An appendix lists additional titles that are out of print but remain important; and a parental resource section gives many good ideas for promoting reading. The book concludes with author, title, and subject indexes. A fine reference work for both parents and professionals.

359   O'Dell, Katie. *Library Materials and Services for Teen Girls.* Libraries Unlimited, 2002, pap., $45 (0-313-31554-X).

After a short history of the struggle for gender equality, the author discusses the development of library collections that contain nonsexist literature. As well as a wealth of program ideas, this book contains many bibliographies, including "Essential Nonfiction" (biographies, careers, history) and "Essential Fiction" (divided by genres including historical fiction and romance). There are also lists of important Web sites and a bibliography of films and videos relevant to teen girls. A useful tool for attracting girls to libraries.

360 O'Keefe, Deborah. *Good Girl Messages: How Young Women Were Misled by Their Favorite Books.* Continuum, 2000, $26.95 (0-8264-1236-X).

This is a study of the "good girl" stereotype seen in books that once were popular and recommended for reading by young people. Examples include Pollyanna and Tarzan's Jane. The final chapter tells how this image is changing in today's children's literature through the works of such writers as Katherine Paterson and Brock Cole. Bibliographies are included. This is a stimulating look at sexism in respected titles from the past.

C. GIFTED READERS

361 Halsted, Judith Wynn. *Some of My Best Friends Are Books: Guiding Gifted Readers from Pre-School to High School,* 2nd ed. Great Potential Press, 2002, pap., $26 (0-910707-51-0).

Beginning with general information about the development of gifted students and their reading, this book discusses these students' interests and psychology, as well as bibliotherapy, reading guidance, and selecting books for the gifted. Annotated lists of about 300 fiction and nonfiction titles follow, arranged by grade levels and covering preschool through the 12th grade. These lists tend to include the tried-and-true rather than recent, more stimulating works. However, this is a valuable work, particularly for its background material.

362 Polette, Nancy J. *Gifted Books, Gifted Readers: Literature Activities to Excite Young Minds.* Libraries Unlimited, 2000, pap., $34 (1-56308-822-3).

The author shows how professionals can promote critical thinking, decision making, and problem solving through the use of challenging books with gifted students in kindergarten through 8th grade. Activities are suggested to link the content of the books to the experiences of the students. The heart of the book, however, is the resources that are listed, including bibliographies of stimulating books suitable for all of the elementary grades. A unique resource that is valuable both for program planning and collection building.

D. PHYSICALLY DISABLED

363   Ward, Marilyn. *Voice from the Margins: An Annotated Bibliography of Fiction on Disabilities and Differences for Young People.* Greenwood, 2002, $44.95 (0-313-31798-4).

This work covers a broad spectrum of disabilities, from physical handicaps to other conditions that make youngsters feel different (including emotional problems such as bullying). The 200 books included in this bibliography are intended to be used to comfort, advise, and ease the psychological pain felt by the students who have these problems. The titles range in reading level from picture books through young adult literature and are presented under 90 subject headings. The annotations are both descriptive and critical, with good grade-level indications. Most of the titles were published between 1998 and 2001. There are subject, author/title, and age-level indexes. A useful resource.

E. RELUCTANT AND READING–DISABLED READERS

364   Ammon, Bette D., and Gale W. Sherman. *More Rip-Roaring Reads for Reluctant Teen Readers.* Libraries Unlimited, 1998, pap., $26.50 (1-56308-571-2).

Following the same successful format as the authors' *Rip-Roaring Reads for Reluctant Teen Readers* (Libraries Unlimited, 1993, pap., $24 [1-56308-094-X]), this work features 40 titles (20 for middle school and 20 for high school), chosen for their high interest, appealing formats, reading levels, outstanding writing, and popularity. Various genres and themes are represented. Each entry includes author information, bibliographic material, themes, interest and reading levels, review citations, plot summaries, and sample booktalks. Both titles are extremely valuable for work with reluctant readers.

365   Backes, Laura. *Best Books for Kids Who (Think They) Hate to Read: Books that Will Turn Any Child into a Lifelong Reader.* Prime Lifestyles, 2001, pap., $15.95 (0-76152-755-9).

The 125 books included in this bibliography are listed under specific age groups: 5–8, 7–10, 8–12, and books for ages 12 and up. Each book is intended to ignite a child's interest in reading and have appeal for the reluctant reader. Each entry provides a synopsis, ways to introduce the book, a picture related to it, reading and interest levels, and an excerpt from the book. Practical tips on making reading an enjoyable and rewarding experience are scattered throughout the text. An appendix lists additional titles. One reviewer called this book "a fantastic resource."

366   Brommer, Shawn, and Carolyn Vang Schuler. *Choices: A Core Collection for Young Reluctant Readers, Vol. 5.* John Gorden Burke, 2001, $45 (0-934272-67-0).

This is the fifth installment of an ongoing series that highlights books of fiction and nonfiction suitable for reluctant readers in grades 1 through 6. This volume contains 217 titles, published from 1997 through January 2000, that have been evaluated for literary merit, motivational value, and interest levels. The books are arranged by author's last name. Each entry contains a full overview of the plot, some critical comments, interest and reading levels, and a list of related subjects. Indexes are by title and subject. The two most recent previous volumes are Vol. 3, 1994, $45 (0-934272-30-1) and Volume 4, 1997, $45 (0-934272-36-0). Each has the same scope, treatment of material, title, and publisher as the fifth volume.

367   Fredericks, Anthony D. *The Integrated Curriculum: Books for Reluctant Readers, Grades 2–5,* 2nd ed. Teacher Ideas Press/Libraries Unlimited, 1998, pap., $24 (1-56308-604-2).

This teacher handbook is in three parts. The first part outlines strategies to motivate students to read. The second part lists 35 children's books that can be used in an integrated curriculum. In addition to a summary, each entry gives critical-thinking questions and suggests activities relating to the book. Other reading sources are also listed. The last section gives various additional resources, including a list of children's books to use with reluctant readers, useful Web sites, and teachers' reviews of books. This book is useful in both the library and the classroom.

368   LiBretto, Ellen V., and Catherine Barr. *High/Low Handbook: Best Books and Web Sites for Reluctant Teen Readers,* 4th ed. Libraries Unlimited, 2002, $48 (0-313-32276-7).

This work lists and annotates more than 500 of the best new (published since 1990) titles for reluctant teen readers. The first part presents a core collection of high/low books with reading levels up to and including the sixth grade. These books are from publishers' high interest/low-reading-level series. Both fiction and nonfiction titles are included and arranged under subjects such as sports, health and fitness, and history. The second part lists regular young adult material suitable for the reluctant reader. All titles are annotated and reading and interest levels are given. All titles are new to this edition. Suggested Web sites and lists of magazines are included along with thorough author, title, and subject indexes. This continues to be one of the standard works in this field.

369   Nakamura, Joyce. *High Interest Books for Teens: A Guide to Book Reviews and Biographical Sources*, 3rd ed. Gale, 1996, o.p.

Listed alphabetically by author, more than 3,500 young adult and adult books that Nakamura believes have appeal to adolescents are presented. Each entry includes biographical sources for the author(s) and review citations. Fiction and nonfiction titles are included, but a number of factors limit the use of this book: its age, the lack of consistent criteria for inclusion, the absence of interest and reading levels, and the fact that many titles listed are out of print.

370   Reynolds, Marilyn. *I Won't Read and You Can't Make Me: Reaching Reluctant Teen Readers*. Heinemann, 2004, pap., $17 (0-325-00605-9).

The main body of this work describes the author's experiences and techniques in dealing with teenage nonreaders. Each chapter contains letters she has received about reading problems, along with her answers. Topics covered include censorship, bibliotherapy, and various reading programs. The section "Tricks of the Trade" offers good, practical advice on dealing with reluctant readers. There are also lists of recommended books that deal with the topics that most interest young readers. A fine manual on reaching reluctant readers.

371   Sullivan, Edward T. *Reaching Reluctant Young Adult Readers: A Handbook for Librarians and Teachers*. Scarecrow, 2002, $24.50 (0-8108-4343-9).

Sullivan focuses on young adults who can read but don't, a group known as the aliterates. In separate chapters, he describes how to approach reluctant readers, explores real-life situations, and presents case studies of high school students. The heart of the book consists of a discussion of books of high interest to teens. Different genres are highlighted with lists of specific titles and books whose characters and themes are appropriate for this group are profiled. Literature for Asian, black, and Latino students is also a focus. This book offers some solutions to the age-old problems of getting teens to read.

3. Specific Genres and Formats

A. GENERAL

372   Buss, Kathleen, and Lee Karnowski. *Reading and Writing Literary Genres*. International Reading Association, 2000, $22.95 (0-87207-257-6).

Aimed at teachers of grades 3 through 6, this volume advocates exposing children to a variety of literary genres, such as realistic fiction, mysteries, folk tales, pourquoi stories and fables, fantasy, and biography. Back-

ground information is given on each genre's characteristics and evaluation points, along with strategies for teaching, suggested student activities, and lists of recommended titles. A companion volume by these two
authors, **Reading and Writing Nonfiction Genres** (International Reading
Association, 2002, $20.95 [0-87207-346-7]), covers nonfiction for ele-
mentary students and gives information on the purposes, structure, and
instructional devices associated with nonfiction genres.

373   Herald, Diana Tixier. **Teen Genreflecting: A Guide to Reading Interests**,
       2nd ed. Libraries Unlimited, 2003, $40 (1-56308-996-3).

This expanded and improved second edition contains more than 2,000
popular titles (most published in the late 1990s and early 2000s),
arranged by genre, then by subgenres and themes. Examples of the main
headings are "Adventure," "Mystery," "Contemporary Life," and "Multicultural Fiction." Publication dates, reading levels, and awards are noted,
along with informative annotations and good cross-referencing. There is
also introductory material on the different genres and their relative popularity. This work is very useful in choosing books for young adults and
for teenagers who are seeking reading guidance.

374   McElmeel, Sharron L. **Educator's Companion to Children's Literature,
       Vol. 2: Folklore, Contemporary Realistic Fiction, Fantasy, Biographies,
       and Tales for Here and There.** Libraries Unlimited, 1996, pap., $24 (1-
       56308-330-2).

After introductory material on how to establish student-led book discussion groups and on other ways to promote reading at the elementary
school level, this work focuses on the literary genres outlined in the title.
Each chapter is accompanied by an annotated bibliography of read-aloud
and independent reading choices for elementary students. The companion volume *Educator's Companion to Children's Literature, Vol. 1: Mysteries, Animal Tales, Books of Humor, Adventure Stories, and Historical
Fiction* (Libraries Unlimited, 1995) is now out of print.

375   Volz, Bridget Dealy, et al. **Junior Genreflecting: A Guide to Good Reads
       and Series Fiction for Children.** Libraries Unlimited, 2000, $29.50 (1-
       56308-556-9).

Using a variety of sources, including reviews and best books lists, the
authors compiled a list of recommended books for grades 3 through 8
published from 1990 through 1998. Titles are arranged by genres
including adventure, animals, contemporary life, fantasy, science fiction,
and mysteries. The first chapter provides an overview of genre fiction for
children, and author, title, and subject indexes provide access to the
main body of the work. As well as bibliographic information, each entry

contains an annotation, award citations, a list of sequels, and reading levels. Most of the titles are for grades 3 to 6, but some are for grades 6 through 8. This clearly organized and well-researched volume provides valuable reading guidance.

B. FANTASY AND SCIENCE FICTION

376   Barron, Neil. *Fantasy and Horror: A Critical and Historical Guide to Literature, Illustration, Film, TV, Radio, Internet.* Scarecrow, 1999, $85 (0-8108-3596-7).

This guide to about 3,000 works of fiction by more than 950 authors and more than 800 works of related nonfiction is aimed primarily at adult readers; however, books suitable for young adults are identified through the indexes and through material within the entries. There are also chapters on fantasy in other genres, such as comics and poetry, and in nonprint media, including films, television, and radio. Also use Barron's 5th edition of *Anatomy of Wonder* (Libraries Unlimited, 2004, $80 [1-59158-171-0), in which there are discussions of more than 1,400 of the best science fiction titles. Titles that are appropriate for teens are flagged, and there is a chapter on teaching science fiction.

377   Buker, Derek M. *The Science Fiction and Fantasy Readers' Advisory: The Librarian's Guide to Cyborgs, Aliens, and Sorcerers.* American Library Association, 2002, $38 (0-8389-0831-4).

Although this bibliography is meant for adults and does not contain some of the standard young adult fantasy and science fiction titles, the completeness of its coverage makes it a valuable reading guidance tool in senior high schools, particularly for use by librarians who are not familiar with the literature. The book is divided into two parts—science fiction and fantasy—with many subdivisions containing short annotated lists of recommended titles and longer lists without annotations. A wide range of titles is included and there are author and title indexes.

378   Gates, Pamela S., et al. *Fantasy Literature for Children and Young Adults.* Scarecrow, 2003, $45 (0-8108-4637-3).

After a general discussion of the meaning of fantasy and of criteria for evaluating it, the authors cover a sizable number of fantasy titles in this annotated bibliography. It is divided into three large chapters: "Fairy Tales," which includes folk tales; "Mixed Fantasy," in which books that combine realism and fantasy are covered; and "Heroic-Ethical Traditions," which covers "pure" or "high" fantasy. Each of these chapters is divided into subgenres. A final chapter covers the rationale behind using fantasy with children. This is a basic introduction to fantasy and, although some reviewers have commented on its omissions and its confusing organization, this is still a good place to begin an exploration of this important genre.

379 Herald, Diana Tixier, and Bonnie Kunzel. *Strictly Science Fiction: A Guide to Reading Interests.* Libraries Unlimited, 2002, $55 (1-56308-893-2).

This bibliography of 900 mainly adult titles is organized by such subgenres as action/adventure and high tech. The titles range from classics, such as *Frankenstein*, to works published in 2002. Most of the titles are recent and suitable for young adults, but there are also brief sections containing books written specifically for young adults and children. There are author, title, and main character indexes.

380 Hintz, Carrie, and Elaine Ostry. *Utopian and Dystopian Writing for Children and Young Adults.* Routledge, 2003, $99 (0-41594-017-6).

A collection of essays that examine utopian and dystopian writing for children and young adults from the 18th century to the present. It defines and explores this genre as part of literary fantasy. Essays describe thematic conventions and discuss landmark authors and books in the field, such as E. Nesbit, H. G. Wells, Zilpha Keatley Snyder, and the Redwall series. There is also an interview with Lois Lowry, as well as the first fully annotated bibliography of utopian fiction for children and young adults.

381 Hunt, Peter, and Millicent Lenz. *Alternative Worlds in Fantasy Fiction.* Continuum, 2001, pap., $24.95 (0-8264-4937-9).

This scholarly work analyzes the work of three important fantasy writers for young people. Hunt writes about important British writer Terry Pratchett, and Lenz covers Ursula Le Guin and Philip Pullman. The section on Pullman concentrates on the His Dark Materials trilogy. As well as a discussion of important books of fantasy, this work supplies a strong defense of a genre that is frequently criticized as being childish and formulaic.

382 Kunzel, Bonnie, and Suzanne Manczuk. *First Contact: A Reader's Selection of Science Fiction and Fantasy.* Scarecrow, 2001, pap., $21.50 (0-8108-4028-6).

Grouping books under such headings as "Brain Power" and "Time Warp," this is an annotated bibliography of the authors' favorite fantasy and science fiction stories for young people in grades 6 through 12. Brief synopses are accompanied by reading-level designations, a listing of sequels, and often other titles by the same author. This is a well-organized, useful work for both collection development and readers' advisory.

383   Lynn, Ruth Nadelman. *Fantasy Literature for Children and Young Adults: A Comprehensive Guide*, 5th ed. Libraries Unlimited, 2005, $65 (1-59158-050-1).

Hailed as "a monumental achievement" when it first appeared, this work is now in a new edition. The book lists and briefly annotates more than 7,500 recommended works of fantasy for children and young adults published over a 100-year period ending in 2004. About 2,800 titles are new to this edition. The titles are organized into chapters based on fantasy subgenres and themes, such as alternate worlds and time travel. There are author and illustrator, title, and subject indexes.

384   O'Keefe, Deborah. *Readers in Wonderland: The Liberating Worlds of Fantasy Fiction: From Dorothy to Harry Potter*. Continuum, 2003, $29.95 (0-8264-1469-9).

More than 200 modern fantasies are discussed in this survey, in an arrangement that begins with simple, obvious fantasies and progresses to the deeper, more complex books where the battles between good and evil reach epic proportions. Using material from psychologists and social historians rather than from established literary critics, the author nevertheless presents a comprehensive—and interesting—overview of the genre.

385   Perry, Phyllis J. *Teaching Fantasy Novels: From The Hobbit to Harry Potter and the Goblet of Fire*. Teacher Ideas Press/Libraries Unlimited, 2003, pap., $29 (1-56308-987-4).

Perry highlights 20 fantasy classics such as *A Wrinkle in Time, The Amber Spyglass, Ella Enchanted,* and *The Giver,* providing for each title vocabulary exercises, comprehension and discussion questions, research activities, and reading projects. This guide is full of interesting, inspiring ideas and will be ideal for teachers using fantasy literature, particularly with students in grades 4 through 8.

386   Reid, Suzanne Elizabeth. *Presenting Young Adult Science Fiction*. Twayne, 1998, $30 (0-8057-1653-X).

This volume traces the history of science fiction from its beginning in the works of Mary Shelley and Jules Verne to some of the most popular current writers. Separate chapters are devoted to several major authors, such as Orson Scott Card, Douglas Hill, H. M. Hoover, Pamela Service, Piers Anthony, and Douglas Adams. There is also a chronology of major events and works, plus a section on current trends. This is a useful work for both teachers and students who need an overview of the subject. A valuable companion volume by Cathi Dunn MacRae, *Presenting Young Adult Fantasy Fiction* (Twayne, 1998, $30 [0-8057-8220-6]), gives similar coverage for young adult fantasy.

387   Sullivan, C. W., III. *Young Adult Science Fiction.* Greenwood, 1999, $87.95 (0-313-28940-9).

Twelve scholarly essays are presented in three parts. The first part surveys the past and present of science fiction writing for young adults in Australia, Canada, Britain, Germany, and the United States. The second part presents thematic survey articles that deal with such topics as coming-of-age in science fiction, war, treatment of women, and science fiction in other media. The third part is a 55-page bibliography of secondary sources, including "sources of information on every author who has published children's or young adult science fiction of consequence." This very successful book is particularly valuable for researchers and serious students of science fiction. A companion volume is Sullivan's *Science Fiction for Young Readers* (Greenwood, 1993, o.p.).

388   Wadham, Tim, and Rachel L. Wadham. *Bringing Fantasy Alive for Children and Young Adults.* Linworth, 1999, $39.95 (0-938865-80-3).

The authors suggest ways in which books of fantasy can be incorporated into the curriculum, providing material on using fantasy in social studies, mathematics, language arts, science, and the humanities. Lesson outlines are supplied, along with booktalk material, program ideas, and storytime suggestions. Other features include a useful bibliography of fantasy books and an appendix of online resources.

389   Westfahl, Gary. *Science Fiction, Children's Literature, and Popular Culture: Coming of Age in Fantasyland.* Greenwood, 2000, $87.95 (0-313-30847-0).

The essays in this intriguing volume cover three main areas—science fiction, children's literature, and pop culture—and the relationship of each to growing up in the contemporary world. The essays involving children's literature range from a discussion of little-known book series to such popular topics as Superman, Horatio Alger, and the Hardy Boys. The ideas are provocative and the relationship between the content of the books presented and the actual problems faced by children growing up makes for stimulating reading.

C. GRAPHIC NOVELS

390   Gorman, Michel. *Getting Graphic! Using Graphic Novels to Promote Literacy with Preteens and Teens.* Linworth, 2003, $36.50 (1-58683-089-9).

This fine book about the world of modern fiction and nonfiction comic books contains material on collection policies for this genre, how to process these books, and how to use these materials constructively. There is also material on how to integrate them into classroom curricula. Additional features include an annotated bibliography of "50 Graphic Novels" recommended for readers in grades 6 and up, and another list of 10 basic novels suitable for beginning collectors.

391   Lyga, Allyson A. W., and Barry Lyga. *Graphic Novels in Your Media Center: A Definitive Guide.* Libraries Unlimited, 2004, pap., $35 (1-59158-142-7).

As well as recommended lists of graphic novels suitable for young people in grades K–12, this volume gives a wealth of background material on this genre, including lesson plans, reviewing media, Web sites, interviews with librarians who use graphic novels, and hints on how these novels can be used with reluctant readers. This work is attractively illustrated with pages from popular graphic novels.

392   Miller, Steve. *Developing and Promoting Graphic Novel Collections.* Neal-Schuman, 2004, $49.95 (1-55570-461-1).

In addition to presenting a carefully chosen, annotated list of graphic novels that could be considered a core collection suitable for teen readers, this work gives plenty of background material. Included are an overview of the genre, its evolution, categories, and types; material on collection development; and tips on display preparation, acquisition, cataloging, and maintenance of these collections.

393   Weiner, Stephen, and Keith R. A. DeCandido. *The 101 Best Graphic Novels.* Nantier Beall Minoustchine Publishing, 2001, pap., $8.95 (1-5616-3284-8).

This very selective list is arranged alphabetically by author, with brief annotations. Entries are marked "C" for all ages, "Y" for ages 12 and up, and "A" for adult. It is an eclectic list, covering titles that range from Maurice Sendak's *In the Night Kitchen* to Art Spiegelman's *Maus.* There is also an introduction that describes the nature and evolution of graphic novels and gives hints on how to use them with reluctant readers.

D. HISTORICAL FICTION

Note: See also the section on "Social Studies, History, and Geography" in Chapter 4.

394 Adamson, Lynda G. *American Historical Fiction: An Annotated Guide to Novels for Adults and Young Adults.* Oryx, 1999, $49.95 (1-57356-067-7).

A comprehensive guide to historical fiction for young people published through 1998 and dealing with the United States. Divided into 13 chronological periods, starting with "North America Before 1600" and ending with "The Late 20th Century," books in each section are arranged alphabetically by author. As well as bibliographic information, there are brief annotations and genre designations. Appendixes list award winners and books for young adults; indexes are by author, title, genre, location, and subject. An equally successful companion volume by the same author is *World Historical Fiction: An Annotated Guide to Novels for Adults and Young Adults* (Oryx, 1999, $49.95 [1-57356-066-9]). Together, these two volumes contain listings for about 10,000 titles.

395 Anderson, Vicki. *Cultures Outside the United States in Fiction: A Guide to 2,875 Books for Librarians and Teachers, K–9.* McFarland, 1994, $35 (0-89950-905-3).

This extremely ambitious work lists 2,875 works representing 150 countries. The books listed emphasize daily life and customs and were published, with a few exceptions, between 1960 and 1993. Titles are arranged by country name and each entry gives bibliographic information, a short annotation, and grade level. There are author, title, and subject indexes. (For more up-to-date bibliographies by this author that include fiction, nonfiction, and multimedia entries and cover roughly the same subjects, see Chapter 4's section on Social Studies, History, and Geography.)

396 Barnhouse, Rebecca. *Recasting the Past: The Middle Ages in Young Adult Literature.* Boynton/Cook, 2000, pap., $15 (0-86709-470-2).

In addition to introducing and evaluating in detail 19 novels set in the Middle Ages (A.D. 500 to 1500), this critical work gives a fine overview of the period. Chapters examine such topics as literacy, religion, dress, historical figures, and fantasy as presented in books for teens, and shows how inaccuracies and misconceptions can be incorporated in fiction. Suggestions are given for classroom projects, and an extensive background bibliography is provided. See also the author's *The Middle Ages in Literature for Youth* in Chapter 4.

397   Coffey, Rosemary K., and Elizabeth F. Howard. *America as Story: Historical Fiction for Middle and Secondary Schools.* American Library Association, 1997, $25 (0-8389-0702-4).

This highly selective bibliography contains entries for 201 high-quality historical novels "arranged in eight broad chronological and topical categories." For each entry, there is bibliographic information, a sizable plot summary, suggestions for activities, and a reading-level designation. At the end of each section is a briefly annotated list called "More Challenging Books for Advanced Readers." Although not up to date, this remains a valuable bibliography.

398   Gordon, Lee, and Cheryl Tanaka. *World Historical Fiction Guide for Young Adults.* Highsmith, 1995, o.p.

There are entries in this paperback covering 800 historical novels written for young adults. Old favorites are included as well as books of the early 1990s. Each entry supplies bibliographic information, along with a plot summary, material on the book's setting, and suggested reading levels.

399   Hartman, Donald K., and Gregg Sapp. *Historical Figures in Fiction.* Oryx, 1994, $45 (0-89774-718-6).

Historical figures from Abigail Adams to Emiliano Zapata are arranged alphabetically in this comprehensive guide to characters in historical fiction. About 1,500 individuals are listed and 4,200 novels cited. The dates of publication range from 1940 to 1993, but most of the books were published before 1970. Symbols are used to indicate novels for children and young adults. Bibliographic information and review citations are given for each title.

400   Holsinger, M. Paul. *The Ways of War: The Era of World War II in Children's and Young Adult Fiction: An Annotated Bibliography.* Scarecrow, 1995, $57.50 (0-8108-2925-8).

This work lists and annotates more than 750 works of fiction published in the United States. The focus is on the military and domestic aspects of the war years, beginning with China in 1937 and extending beyond the cessation of hostilities. Each entry contains bibliographic information, an excellent, often lengthy, contents note, and an indication of the book's historical and literary merit.

401   Lucas, Ann Lawson. *The Presence of the Past in Children's Literature.* Praeger, 2003, $63.95 (0-313-32483-2).

Lucas explores how children's writers of fiction around the world present themes and facts concerning times past. Beginning with applying literary theory to historical novels, this account also examines changing fashions in criticism and publishing. It then considers such specific topics as adaptations of myths and colonial and postcolonial children's fiction. This is a scholarly treatise, with some helpful evaluation of selected historical novels for children.

402   Taylor, Desmond. *The Juvenile Novels of World War II: An Annotated Bibliography.* Greenwood, 1994, $65.95 (0-313-29194-2).

In this bibliography, books are listed chronologically by year, from 1940 through 1992, and then alphabetically by author. As well as bibliographic information, there are extensive annotations. A total of 438 English-language books are included, and a fine introduction discusses World War II literature and mentions some of the landmark books. The work ends with author, title, and subject indexes.

403   Van Meter, Vandelia L. *America in Historical Fiction: A Bibliographic Guide.* Libraries Unlimited, 1997, $40.50 (1-56308-496-1).

Most of the 1,168 titles listed in this bibliography are best suited for young adult and adult readers. After a lengthy introduction on national education standards in U.S. history, the entries are arranged under broad chronological headings. Classic as well as contemporary novels are included, with brief annotations, but not all of the selections have appeal for today's readers. Nevertheless, this is a very extensive, if not too selective, list.

404   Zarian, Beth Bartleson. *Around the World with Historical Fiction and Folktales: Highly Recommended and Award-Winning Books, Grades K–8.* Scarecrow, 2004, pap., $48 (0-8108-4816-3).

This is a bibliography of about 800 historical novels and volumes of folktales, many of which have won awards. The book is divided into three main parts—American history, world history, and myths and folklore. Each is subdivided, first chronologically from prehistoric time to today, and then by grade level. Each title is well annotated.

E. HUMOR

405   Hogan, Walter. *Humor in Young Adult Literature.* Scarecrow, 2004, $40 (0-8108-5072-9).

The author examines humorous young adult literature as it exists in family stories, adventure stories, problem novels, satire, romance, and coming-of-age stories. The books are examined in light of adolescent developmental stages and goals, as well as from the standpoint of various theories relating to comedy and humor. The books, their protagonists, and the humorous situations are analyzed. This guide is both informative and entertaining.

406   Roberts, Patricia L. *Taking Humor Seriously in Children's Literature: Literature-Based Mini-Units and Humorous Books for Children Ages 5–12.* Scarecrow, 1997, pap., $45 (0-8108-3209-7).

This book is divided into two sections, for children ages 5 to 8 and 9 to 12. Each section contains a series of short study units and an annotated bibliography. Humorous books are then categorized into such areas as animals, humans, humorous humans, jokes, nonsense, and family. Each unit describes a book appropriate to the age group and explains why it is funny. There are appropriate indexes and a glossary of terms.

F. Mystery and Horror

407   Fonseca, Anthony J., and June Michele Pulliam. *Hooked on Horror: A Guide to Reading Interests in Horror Fiction*, 2nd ed. Libraries Unlimited, 2003, $55 (1-56308-904-1).

Intended for reading guidance with adult readers, this work does contain a listing of young adult titles. Annotated listings of recommended books of horror fiction are arranged under such chapter headings as "Ghosts and Haunted Houses" and "Small-Town Horror." Each chapter contains an introductory essay that surveys each of the subgenres. A helpful appendix lists a variety of resources for librarians and teachers, including awards, Web sites, and further reading.

408   Larson, Jeanette. *Bringing Mysteries Alive for Children and Young Adults.* Linworth, 2004, pap., $39.95 (1-58683-012-0).

The body of this informative work contains chapters on the history of mystery stories, their place in the reading of young people, the different subgenres, the most popular mystery series, and suggestions for use in the classroom, with examples that include crafts, speakers, Web sites, and writing assignments. Most helpful is the annotated bibliography of all the titles mentioned in the text. There is also a listing of resources for librarians and teachers that contains award information, Web sites, and suggestions for further reading.

409   Reynolds, Kimberley, et al. *Frightening Fiction: Contemporary Classics in Children's Literature.* Continuum, 2001, pap., $29.95 (0-8264-5309-0).

This volume takes a serious and scholarly look at the most important contemporary horror fiction for young people. Various aspects of the genre are explored, including its increasing commercialization, the fascination horror has for children and young adults, and the important themes that are often explored—fear, loss of control, and death, for example. There are close studies of a number of titles, and separate reviews of the work of such authors as David Almond. Bibliographies are included for each of the authors discussed, plus a thorough index and a list of Web sites of interest.

410 Schembri, Pamela. *Scary Stories You Won't Be Afraid to Use: Resources and Activities for a K–6 Audience.* Linworth, 2001, pap., $39.95 (1-58683-002-3).

More than 500 books are listed and annotated in this guide that is arranged by format and grade levels and covers such areas as ghost stories, haunted houses, Halloween stories, and monster stories. The activities are based on major curriculum areas and include detailed lesson plans. Each entry contains bibliographic information, grade level, review citations, and an annotation. There are subject, author, and title indexes.

G. POETRY

411 Hopkins, Lee Bennett. *Pass the Poetry Please!*, 3rd ed. HarperCollins, 1998, $25 (0-06-027746-7).

An attractive update and revision of the title last published in 1987, this is a good manual on how to effectively introduce young people to poetry. Hopkins provides brief biographies of poets read by young people, suggests poems and poetry collections to use, and includes a number of poetry-related activities and projects. There are examples of many poetry forms and characteristics. A fine starting place for teachers.

412 Schwedt, Rachel, and Janice DeLong. *Young Adult Poetry: A Survey and Theme Guide.* Greenwood, 2002, $52.95 (0-313-31336-9).

This work contains an annotated bibliography of 198 anthologies and poem collections recommended for use with young people in grades 6 through 12. It also contains a thematic guide to more than 6,000 individual poems found in these volumes, arranged by such subjects as "love" with subdivisions like "love, first love." The choice of the volumes of poetry (both collections and by individual poets) is excellent. This work can serve as both a selection guide and a poetry index.

413 Wade, Barrie. *A Guide to Children's Poetry for Teachers and Librarians.* Scolar, 1996, $23 (1-85928-141-9).

Approximately 400 sources—volumes by individual poets as well as anthologies—are featured here. The entries cover poetry from Blake through the 20th century. Some audiotapes are also included. Each entry gives bibliographic information, age ranges, and themes covered. Other features are a list of organizations, contacts, competitions, and hints on how to get poetry published.

H. POP-UP BOOKS

414   Carter, Daria A. *The Elements of Pop-Up.* Simon, 1999, $35 (0-689-82224-3).

Subtitled *A Pop-Up Book for Aspiring Paper Engineers,* this is an excellent primer on how to create pop-ups. After a history of this format, there are step-by-step directions on the "hows" and "whys" of producing pop-ups. As one critic said, "This is the definitive reference book on the subject."

415   Montanaro, Ann R. *Pop-Up and Movable Books: A Bibliography.* Scarecrow, 1993, $59.50 (0-8108-2650-X).

This is an unusual, extensive bibliography of books that have movable parts. The author, a professor at Rutgers University, founded the Movable Book Society, which exceeds 400 members. More than 1,600 books published from the 1850s through 1991 are described. An introduction traces the history of these fascinating books. The main entries are arranged by author's name and contain both bibliographic information and an informative annotation. There are indexes by series, author/illustrator, paper engineer and designer, and title, but, unfortunately not by subject. The work is continued in the supplement described below.

416   Montanaro, Ann R. *Pop-Up and Movable Books: A Bibliography, Supplement I, 1991–1997.* Scarecrow, 2000, $95 (0-8108-3728-5).

A continuation of the main volume discussed above, this supplement covers six years of pop-up books and adds ones that were missed in the first edition. The material given on each entry is quite detailed and includes bibliographic information and annotations that describe important aspects of the book and the types of movables it contains. The various indexes cover both the main volume and the supplement. A date index tries to organize this vast output in a chronological order. This work is crammed with facts and figures and is an invaluable source on this genre.

I. ROMANCE

417   Carpan, Carolyn. *Rocked by Romance: A Guide to Young Adult Romance Genre Fiction.* Libraries Unlimited, 2004, $39 (1-59158-022-6).

Books suitable for students in grades 5 through 12 are discussed in this bibliography of about 500 recommended titles on love and romance. Organized by such teen preferences as humorous love stories, historical romance, the paranormal, and romantic suspense, the entries contain a brief plot summary and highlight elements of appeal such as setting or action-packed stories. Appendixes include award information, profiles of important authors, a core collection, and listings of research materials.

4. Indexes and Related Reference Books

418   Anderson, Vicki. *Fiction Index for Readers 10 to 16: Subject Access to Over 8,200 Books, 1960–1990.* McFarland, 1992, $40 (0-89950-703-4).

Although in need of a supplement, this amazing reference has great historical value. It is divided into two main parts. The first part is a subject index to the 8,200 novels analyzed, from Acting, Adoption, and Adventure to World War II and Writing. Only the author and title are given in the first part. In the second, much larger, section, these books are arranged by author; for each book, there is bibliographic information and a two-line annotation. A title index closes the volume.

419   *Children's Book Review Index.* Gale (annual).

This annual spinoff from Gale's *Book Review Index* began in 1975. Culling reviews from about 600 reviewing publications, this publication is invaluable for locating reviews of children's and young adult books. About 250 of the chief reviewing sources are listed in the front of the book. The main alphabet is arranged by author (with a title index at the back of the book). For each entry, reviews are listed with locations and length and an indication of the book's suitability for young adults. Recent annual volumes have been priced at $175 each, and there are frequent cumulations (for example, the 1985 cumulation covers the years 1965 through 1985).

420   Graff Hysell, Shannon. *Recommended Reference Books for Small and Medium-Sized Libraries and Media Centers.* Libraries Unlimited, 2005, $70 (1-59158-288-1).

The 500 titles included in this volume have been selected from past volumes of *American Reference Books Annual* as the best books for smaller libraries. The emphasis is on adult titles, but there are entries for reference books suitable for children's collections.

421   *Index to Fairy Tales.* Scarecrow Press, many volumes.

This long-established reference series was originally compiled by Mary Huse Eastman in 1915, later edited by Norma O. Ireland, and most recently edited by Joseph W. Sprug. Each volume indexes collections of fairy tales by author, title, and subject. In print are *Index to Fairy Tales 1949–1972* (1973, $78 [0-8108-2011-0]); *Index to Fairy Tales, 1973–1977* (1979, $45 [0-8108-1855-8]); *Index to Fairy Tales, 1978–1986* (1989, $88 [0-8108-2194-X]), and *Index to Fairy Tales, 1987–1992* (1994, $85 [0-8108-2750-6]). This latest supplement (number 7) indexes 310 collections.

422   *Index to Poetry for Children and Young Adults.* H. W. Wilson, many volumes.

This series of poetry indexes began in 1942 and was edited by John E. and Sara W. Breton. Now, many supplements and many editors later, this continues to be the authoritative index to collections of poetry for children and young adults. There are now nine volumes in the set, indexing a total of more than 1,000 collections. The current volume is *Index to Poetry for Children and Young People, 1993–1997* (1998, $95 [0-8242-0939-7]). For information on previous volumes, see www.hwwilson.com.

423   *Magazines for Libraries*, 13th ed. Bowker, 2004, $240 (0-8352-4661-2).

The standard selective guide to recommended magazines for libraries, this work now contains about 7,000 reviews by 200 media specialists. There is a special section on important magazines for children and young adults.

424   *Plays for Children and Young Adults: An Evaluative Index and Guide. Supplement 1, 1989–1994.* Garland, 1996, $65 (0-8153-1493-0).

This supplement to the 1991 main volume, *Plays for Children and Young Adults*, lists 2,158 plays (in anthologies and published separately), including those found in *Play* magazine. Entries are listed alphabetically by title, with material on age suitability, cast analysis, playing time, settings, plot, and so forth. There are seven indexes, including author, cast, grade level, and subject.

425   Safford, Barbara Ripp. *Guide to Reference Materials for School Library Media Centers*, 5th ed. Libraries Unlimited, 1998, $49.50 (1-56308-545-3).

When this book appeared in 1998, it was well received as a guide to reference books suitable for elementary and secondary libraries. All the sources were published between 1992 and 1997. They are organized into major subject areas, such as social sciences and humanities, with many subdivisions. A new edition would be welcome.

CHAPTER 3

CURRENT AMERICAN REVIEWING TOOLS, ANNUAL BIBLIOGRAPHIES, AND CHILDREN'S MAGAZINES

Note: See also Chapter 1's coverage of general periodicals and Chapter 9's listings of professional organizations and agencies, many of which have publications.

A. PERIODICALS

426   *Appraisal: Science Books for Young People.* 1967, 4/yr., $44. Children's Science Book Review Committee, School of Education, 605 Commonwealth Ave., Boston, MA 02215; 617-353-4150.

This journal reviews trade books in science and mathematics for children from preschool to high school. Approximately 90 books are reviewed in each issue, arranged alphabetically by author. For each book there are two reviews of about 15 lines each—one by a librarian and the other by a subject specialist. Each review contains a rating from E for Excellent to U for Unsatisfactory and an indication of age suitability. Each issue also contains a section that indicates and annotates new titles that have been added to existing series. There are about 40 of these reviews in each issue. The index is cumulated annually by author, title, and subject.

427   *Bayviews.* 1990, 13/yr., $30. Association of Children's Librarians of Northern California, Box 12471, Berkeley, CA 94701.

A journal with a Western U.S. perspective, *Bayviews* appears 13 times a year. Reviews are signed by the participating librarians, and the total number of reviews printed each year now averages about 1,200. An annual selection of the best books of the year is printed in a separate publication, ***The ACL Distinguished Book List.*** A single copy is available for $3 from the address above.

The Book Report see ***Library Media Connection.***

428   *Booklist.* 1905, 22/yr., $95. American Library Association, 50 E. Huron St., Chicago., IL 60611; 313-944-6780; www.ala.org/booklist.

Booklist is one of the oldest and most trusted reviewing journals in America. It is published twice a month, except for July and August, and the January issue is usually also a single issue. After the section "Upfront: Advance Reviews," which gives early notification of important adult fiction and nonfiction titles expected to be in demand in libraries, each issue contains a series of reviews of adult books arranged by subjects—gardening, recreation and sports, history, mystery, romance, and SF/fantasy, for example. After the review, there is sometimes a short additional annotation for books that are suitable for young adult collections. These are indicated by a YA symbol. The "Books for Youth" section that follows is subdivided into three sections: Book for Older Readers (junior and senior high books), Books for Middle Readers (roughly grades 3 through 6), and Books for the Young (preschool through the primary grades). Highly recommended titles are starred and found in a separate section. Series books are listed separately once each month. Issues often highlight a particular theme or subject, such as religion, first novels, science fiction, graphic novels, or black history. The editors' choices of best books of the year appear in the January issues; the March 15 issue features the year's best books lists from the American Library Association. Finally, there are sections that review both adult and children's nonprint media and an important "Reference Books Bulletin," which reviews reference books and professional material. Semiannual and annual indexes are included in the February 15 and the August issues, respectively. This is considered a basic selection aid for all libraries.

429   *Bulletin of the Center for Children's Books.* 1947, 11/yr., $75 (individuals $50). University of Illinois at Urbana-Champaign, Graduate Library School, 501 E. Daniel St., Champaign, IL 61820-6211; 217-244-0324; www.lis.uiuc.edu/puboff/bccb.

One of the most respected sources of reviews of books for children and young adults (preschool through junior high), this periodical contains approximately 60 in-depth reviews in each issue. The reviews are usually written by members of the editorial staff, although some are contributed by specialists who are members of the editorial committee. Books are arranged in one alphabet by author's last name. Each review is about 10 to 15 lines in length and contains a rating: *=special distinction; R= recommended; Ad= additional purchase; M= marginal; and NR= not recommended. Books of borderline quality, including some series books, are not reviewed. Reviews in this journal are astute and perceptive. Subjects at the end of each review indicate curricular use and developmental values. The last page is an unannotated bibliography of new books, articles, and pamphlets of interest to professionals. A combined author and title index appears each year in the July/August issue. This journal is highly recommended for elementary schools and children's rooms in public libraries.

430   *Chicago Tribune Books.* 1847, 52/yr.

Reviews of children's books are included in this respected newspaper's weekly book review section approximately once a month. Sometimes there are special articles on particular books and their authors.

431   *Children's Magazine Guide: A Subject Index to Children's Magazines.* 1948, 9/yr., $69.95. Libraries Unlimited, 88 Post Rd. W., Westport, CT 076881-5007; (800) 225-5800; www.lu.com.

This title would more accurately be called "Children's Magazine Index" because it supplies an index to the nonfiction contents of about 54 popular children's magazines geared to ages 6 through 14. Each issue also includes citations to carefully selected Web sites. Among the magazines indexed are *American Girl, Sports Illustrated for Kids,* and *National Geographic World.* Entries are arranged by subject and there is an annual cumulation in the August issue. Useful for elementary and middle-school students, this can also be used as a buying guide for librarians who want to subscribe to the best and most popular children's magazine.

432   *Essential Resources for Schools and Libraries.* 1979, 5/yr., $30. Connaught Education Services, Box 34069, Dept. 349, Seattle, WA 98124; (604) 689-1568.

Formerly called *Free Materials for School Libraries,* this newsletter recommends free and inexpensive materials and services including Web sites and research materials. This publication also contains informative articles and reviews.

433   *The Horn Book Guide to Children's and Young Adult Books.* 1990, 2/yr., $45. The Horn Book, 56 Roland St., Suite 200, Boston, MA 02129; (617) 227-1555; www.hbook.com.

A companion volume to *The Horn Book Magazine* (see following entry), this is solely a reviewing journal. It tries to review virtually every children's and young adult book published in the United States. About 4,000 books are reviewed every year. Each review consists of a brief summary of the contents plus critical statements. Fiction books are arranged by genre and grade level; nonfiction are arranged by Dewey Decimal number. Books are rated from 1 (Outstanding) to 6 (unacceptable). A pointer indicates those receiving a 1 or a 2.

434   *The Horn Book Magazine: About Books for Children and Young Adults.* 1924, 6/yr., $48 (individuals). The Horn Book, 56 Roland St., Suite 200, Boston, MA 02129; (617) 227-1555; www.hbook.com.

This is one of the oldest and most prestigious reviewing sources in the field of children's literature. Each issue contains articles about individual authors or illustrators and scholarly essays on topics relating to young people, their reading, and their education. The review section is divided by age group and genre. Most of the reviews are favorable—books are screened in advance so that only important new works are highlighted. About 60 books are reviewed in each issue. There are also sections on professional news and publications, new editions and reprints, and outstanding paperbacks. The January–February issue contains the Fanfare List, an annotated bibliography of the books considered to be the best of the preceding year. This periodical co-sponsors and administers the annual Boston Globe-Horn Book Awards (see Chapter 6), and the January–February issue also contains the acceptance speeches of the winners as well as background information on each recipient.

435   *Kirkus Reviews: A Pre-Publication Review Service.* 1933. 24/yr., $255. Kirkus Service, 200 Park Ave. S., New York, NY 10013; (212) 777-4554.

Noted for its realistic, straightforward reviews, this publication evaluates books from prepublication galleys. A loose-leaf format is used for easy filing in binders. Each issue is divided into two main parts: one on adult books and one on books for children and young adults. These are subdivided into fiction and nonfiction. Books of unusual merit are given a diamond and are highlighted at the beginning of each section.

436 *KLIATT.* 1967, 6/yr., $39. Kliatt, 33 Bay State Rd., Wellesley, MA 02481; (617) 237-7577; http://hometown.aol.com/Kliatt.

Each bimonthly issue of *KLIATT* offers hundreds of reviews of recommended paperbacks, hardcover fiction, and audiobooks for young adults. It reviews more than 1,200 paperbacks and more than 300 audiobooks each year, plus dozens of educational software programs. All types of paperbacks are reviewed: trade and mass market young adult titles and adult titles suitable for young adults. Symbols indicate suitability and merit. Each issue also includes a lead article of interest to librarians and teachers. The title of this periodical is derived from the names of the two founders.

Library Talk: The Magazine for Elementary School Librarians see *Library Media Connection.*

437 *LMC: Library Media Connection.* 2002, 7/yr., $69. Linworth Publishing Inc., 480 E. Wilson Bridge Rd., Suite L, Worthington, OH 43085; (614) 436-7107; www.linworth.com.

In 2002, Linworth combined two publications, *The Book Report* (for young adult literature and librarianship) and *Library Talk* (for children's literature and librarianship), into this single expanded publication that covers grades Pre-K–12. After introductory news and special articles, a lengthy review section is divided into departments—picture books, fiction K–5, fiction 6–8, fiction 9–12, folk literature, graphic books, poetry, and nonfiction subdivided by subject. There are also reviews of professional and nonprint materials. Each review ends with a recommendation judgement, from "not recommended" to "highly recommended." Reviews are by librarians or subject specialists. This is a very attractive, extremely useful reviewing journal.

438 *Los Angeles Times Book Review.* 52/yr.

The weekly book review section of this daily newspaper frequently contains reviews of children's and young adult books.

439 *Multicultural Review.* 1992, 4/yr., $65. Goldman Group, 14497 N. Dale Mabry Hwy., Suite 205N, Tampa, FL 33618; www.mcreview.com.

This periodical's subtitle is *Dedicated to a Better Understanding of Ethnic, Racial and Religious Diversity.* In addition to penetrating reviews of material associated with American ethnic, racial, and religious experiences, each issue contains several articles giving overviews of various facets of these subjects. The reviews, which are organized by subject area, cover new books, magazines, audiovisual materials, and software for children, young adults, and adults. An effort is made to include material from both mainstream and alternative publishers. Where this coverage is needed, this is an excellent selection tool for school, public, and academic libraries.

440   *New York Times Book Review.* 52/yr.

This standard book reviewing source can be purchased as part of the Sunday edition of the *New York Times* or separately by subscription. There is sometimes a separate section called "For Younger Readers," in which five or six books are reviewed (with more mentioned in the "In Brief" section). There are also two or more special supplements a year: usually one in November for gift-giving time and one in the spring. In these 50-page supplements, there are many more reviews (usually about 50 lengthy ones). The November issue contains a colorful section on the ten best illustrated books of the year.

441   *Publishers Weekly.* 52/yr., $189. Cahners Business Information, 360 Park Ave. S., New York, NY 10010; (646) 746-6758; www.publishers weekly.com.

This is the most important periodical for the book trade. As well as newsy articles on publishers and book selling, it contains advance reviews of new books soon to be on the market. There is a section on children's books in each issue. The reviews are divided into three sections: picture books, fiction, and nonfiction. Age levels are given and highly recommended books receive a star (*). Special editions and reprints are mentioned in a "Children's Notes" section.

442   *San Francisco Chronicle Review.* 52/yr.

As part of its Sunday book review section, the *Chronicle* often prints reviews of children's books.

443   *SB&F: Science Books and Films.* 1965, 6/yr., $45. American Association for the Advancement of Science, 1200 New York Ave. N.W., Washington, DC 20005; (202) 326-6454; http://sbfonline.com.

Subtitled *Your Guide to Science Resources for All Ages,* this periodical is an excellent source of reviews of science materials for students from the elementary grades through college and adulthood. The reviews are arranged by Dewey Decimal classification in sections such as "Adult Books,"

"Junior High and Young Adult Books," "Children's Books," "Audio-Visual Materials," and "Electronic Media." Levels of difficulty are noted and an overall rating from "not recommended" to "highly recommended" is given.

444 *School Library Journal: The Magazine of Children's, Young Adult, and School Librarians.* 1934, 12/yr., $124. School Library Journal, 360 Park Ave. S., New York, NY 10010; (646) 746-6758; www.slj.com.

School Library Journal is an excellent all-purpose magazine for school librarians and public librarians who work with children and young adults. The first sections are devoted to features and articles that deal with various aspects of publishing, authors, and concerns of those who work with young people in libraries. Recent news, a calendar of events, and similar updates are also included. The review sections compose more than two thirds of each issue. The book reviews follow reviews of non-print materials and are divided into four age groups, from preschool and primary grades to adult books for young adult readers. There are about 3,200 book reviews each year. Not all reviews are favorable. The December issue contains a list of the best books of the year and a cumulated index by author and title. This is a must-purchase for all libraries involved with young readers.

445 *VOYA: Voice of Youth Advocates.* 1975, 6/yr., $39.95. Scarecrow Press, 4501 Forbes Blvd., Suite 200, Lanham, MD 20706; www.voya.com.

No other publication for teachers and librarians so accurately conveys the needs, concerns, and attitudes of young adults as *VOYA*. Each issue has several interesting and sometimes controversial articles on young adult reading and recreational interests, important authors, and library service. There are also professional news items and bibliographies on specific topics. The review section (about two thirds of each issue) is divided into different departments, such as media, fiction, science fiction (a special strength), nonfiction, professional, reference, and reprints. Each book is coded according to quality and popular appeal. Grade levels are also indicated. This lively, provocative publication deserves a place in all libraries serving a young adult audience.

446 *Washington Post Book World.* 52/yr.

Every Sunday's edition of the *Washington Post* features a book-reviewing supplement called *Book World*. A section is usually devoted to reviews of children's books.

B. ANNUALS

447   *Best Children's Books of the Year.* $8. Children's Book Committee at
Bank Street College, 610 W. 112th St., New York, NY 10025-1895.

The Children's Book Committee at Bank Street College was founded
more than 90 years ago. At present it reviews about 4,000 books each
year. From this massive number, the committee chooses the 600 best for
inclusion in this annual bibliography. Titles are attractively presented,
with bibliographic information and a short annotation. They are divided
by age and subject category. This has become one of the most respected
of the annual booklists. Information about this and other publications
from the college is available from the address above or by telephoning
(212) 875-4400.

448   *Bibliography of Books for Children.* $5. Association of Childhood
Education International, 17904 Georgia Ave., Suite 215, Olney, MD
20832; www.acei.org.

Published since 1937, this standard bibliography contains entries
arranged by type—picture books, fiction, nonfiction, references, sources,
periodicals, and so forth. Each entry provides full bibliographic information as well as a reading level and a brief annotation. This is a reliable
source for annual assessments of the best books for children.

449   *Books for the Teen Age (year).* $10. New York Public Library, Office of
Branch Libraries, 455 Fifth Ave., New York, NY 10016; (212) 340-
0897; http://teenlink.nypl.org.

This annual list has been especially prepared by the Office of Young
Adult Services of NYPL for teenagers in New York City since 1929. The
current list is in a slick, magazine-like format that is attractive to young
people. About 1,000 titles that would be of interest to teenagers
throughout the country, especially urban youngsters, are included each
year. The titles are grouped into roughly 70 broad subjects and the selections emphasize current interests and tastes (although some time-tested
titles are included). Brief bibliographic information is given for each
book plus a catchy one-line descriptive phrase.

450   *CCBC Choices (year).* $7. Cooperative Children's Book Center, School
of Education, University of Wisconsin–Madison, 600 N. Park St.,
Madison, WI 53706-1403.

An excellent annual guide to the best books for children published within a particular year. (The 2004 edition, for example, covers books published during 2003.) Each issue contains a lengthy introductory section,
"Observations About Publishing in (year)," that surveys publishing

trends and characteristics during the period. The body of the work is an extensive, well-annotated bibliography of recommended books arranged by such subjects as the arts, issues in today's world, biography, picture books, and fiction for various age groups. Suitable age levels are indicated at the end of the review. Issues contain about 200 to 225 titles. Appendixes include detailed information about the purposes and activities of the center. There is also a detailed author, title, and subject index.

451 *Children's Books (year)*. $3. New York Public Library, Office of Branch Libraries, 455 Fifth Ave., New York, NY 10016; (212) 340-0897; http://kids.nypl.org.

This attractive annual publication lists 100 of the best children's books published in the preceding year as judged by a committee of NYPL children's librarians. The list is divided into several sections according to age group, with special sections for folk and fairy tales, poetry, and nonfiction. Each entry is given a brief one- to three-line annotation.

452 *Children's Choices*. International Reading Association, 800 Barksdale Rd., PO Box 8139, Newark, DE 19714-8139; http://reading.org/resources/tools/choices_childrens.html.

Begun in 1974, this is a joint project of the International Reading Association and the Children's Book Council. About 100 fiction and nonfiction books are chosen annually by about 10,000 participating children ages 5 through 13 from different regions of the United States. The books must be published within a given year. The annotated list is published in the October issue of the IRA journal *The Reading Teacher*. The list can be downloaded from the Web site, where lists from the past several years can also be found. Multiple copies are available for a nominal price. A 256-page book, ***Celebrating Children's Choices: 25 Years of Children's Favorite Books***, by Arden DeVries is also available from IRA (2000, $23.95). As well as giving historical background on the project, this resource tells how one can use these children's favorites in the classroom, with activity-based chapters that group sample titles by grade levels.

453 *Not Just for Children Anymore!* Children's Book Council, 12 W. 37th St., New York, NY 10018; (212) 966-1990; www.cbcbooks.org.

This annual bibliography, which was discontinued in 2002, was published to help booksellers increase the market for children's books. Each list represents a sampling of children's books that are appropriate for adults. About 150 books were highlighted each year, arranged under broad subject headings such as "Art and Architecture," "Biographies and History," and "Novels." A concluding section listed classics and perennial favorites. No reading levels were indicated. Each book was annotated and there were indexes by title and author/illustrator plus a list of participating publishers.

454   *Notable Children's Books in the Language Arts.* National Council of Teachers of English; www.ncte.org/elem/notable.

Prepared by the Children's Literature Assembly of the National Council of Teachers of English, this annual list of about 30 of the best books in the language arts appears in the fall issues of *Language Arts* and *The Journal of Children's Literature.*

455   *Notable (year) Social Studies Trade Books for Young People.* $2. Children's Book Council, 132 W. 37th St., New York, NY 10018; www.socialstudies.org/resources/notable/, www.cbcbooks.org.

This eight-page list, which has been issued annually since 1972, is a project of the Children's Book Council's joint committee with the National Council for the Social Studies. About 150 notable books written for children in grades K–12 are included each year. They are chosen by social studies and language arts teachers and are divided by broad subjects. The list is published first in the journal *Social Education* and is then reprinted for distribution by CBC. Single copies are available from CBC for $2 and a 6" by 9" self-addressed envelope with 83 cents postage. Previous years' lists are available online.

456   *Outstanding Science Trade Books for Students K–12.* $2. Children's Book Council, 12 W. 37th St., New York, NY 10018; www.nsta.org/ostbc.

Issued annually since 1973, this list is a joint project of CBC and the National Science Teachers Association. Each year's list is eight pages long and contains about 100 outstanding science books chosen by science educators and librarians. The list appears first in the periodical *Science and Children* and then is reprinted by CBC. Lists are available at the Web sites.

457   *Teacher's Choices.* International Reading Association, 800 Barksdale Rd., PO Box 8139, Newark, DE 19714-8139; http://reading.org/resources/tools/choices_teachers.html.

This annotated annual list is the result of a project involving teachers, librarians, and reading specialists that began in 1989. The list highlights about 30 new trade books for children and young adults that professionals find to be exceptional in curriculum use. It consists primarily of non-fiction titles and is first printed in the November issue of *The Reading Teacher.* The list can be downloaded from the Web site, where lists from the past several years can also be found. Multiple copies are available for a nominal price.

458 *Young Adult Choices.* International Reading Association, 800 Barksdale Rd., PO Box 8139, Newark, DE 19714-8139; http://reading.org/ resources/tools/choices_young_adults.html.

The books on this list are chosen annually by teams of middle school and high school students from across the United States who vote for the title they consider the most enjoyable and informative. The list, which usually contains about 30 titles, first appears in the November issue of the association's *Journal of Adolescent and Adult Literacy.* The bibliography is later available, along with retrospective lists, free of charge on the Web or in printed form for a small fee from the organization.

C. CHILDREN'S MAGAZINES

This section lists a selection of recommended magazines that contain literature (stories, poetry) for children. It does not include subject magazines, such as those that deal with science or geography. With the exception of *Babybug,* the magazines are indexed in *Children's Magazine Guide.*

459 *American Girl.* 6/yr., $22.95. 8400 Fairway Place, Middleton, WI 53562; (800) 234-1278; www.americangirl.com (Grades 3–7).

460 *Babybug.* 12/yr., $35.97. Carus Publishing Co., PO Box 300, Peru, IL 61354; (800) 821-0115; www.babybugmag.com (Ages 6 months to 2 years).

461 *Boys' Quest.* 6/yr., $22.95. Bluffton News Publishing Co., PO Box 227, Bluffton, OH 45817-0227; (800) 358-4732; www.boysquest.com (Grades 2–7).

462 *Child Life.* 6/yr., $22.95. Children's Better Health Institute, PO Box 420235, 11 Commerce Blvd., Palm Coast, FL 32142; (386) 447-6302; www.childlifemag.org (Grades 2–4).

463 *Children's Digest.* 6/yr., $22.95. Children's Better Health Institute, PO Box 420235, 11 Commerce Blvd., Palm Coast, FL 32142; (386) 447-6302; www.childrensdigestmag.org (Grades 2–5).

464 *Children's Playmate.* 6/yr., $32.95. Children's Better Health Institute, PO Box 420235, 11 Commerce Blvd., Palm Coast, FL 32142; (386) 447-6302; www.childrensplaymate.org (Grades K–2).

465   *Cricket.* 12/yr., $35.97. Carus Publishing Co., PO Box 300, Peru, IL 61354; (800) 821-0115; www.cricketmag.com (Grades 2–7).

466   *Highlights for Children.* 12/yr., $29.64. PO Box 2182, Marion, OH 43306-8282; (888) 876-3809; www.highlights.com (Grades Preschool–6).

467   *Jack and Jill.* 6/yr., $22.95. Children's Better Health Institute, PO Box 420235, 11 Commerce Blvd., Palm Coast, FL 32142; (386) 447-6302; www.jackandjillmag.org (Grades 1–3).

468   *Ladybug.* 12/yr., $35.97. Carus Publishing Co., PO Box 300, Peru, IL 61354; (800) 821-0115; www.ladybugmag.com (Ages 2–6).

469   *Muse.* 9/yr., $32.97. Carus Publishing Co., PO Box 300, Peru, IL 61354; (800) 821-0115; www.cricketmag.com (Ages 4–8).

470   *New Moon.* 6/yr., $44. New Moon Publishing, 34 E. Superior St., #200, Duluth, MN 55802; (800) 381-4743; www.newmoon.org (Grades 3–8).

471   *Read.* 18/yr., $34.50. Weekly Reader Corp., 3001 Cindel Dr., Delran, NJ 08075; (800) 446-3355; www.weeklyreader.com/read (Grades 6–9).

472   *Sesame Street* (supplement to *Parenting*). 11/yr. Sesame Street Workshop, One Lincoln Plaza, New York, NY 10023; (813) 910-3601 (Grades Preschool–1).

473   *Spider.* 12/yr., $35.97. Carus Publishing Co., PO Box 300, Peru, IL 61354; (800) 821-0115; www.spidermag.com (Grades 1–3).

474   *Stone Soup.* 6/yr., $34. Children's Art Foundation, PO Box 83, Santa Cruz, CA 95063; (800) 447-4569; www.stonesoup.com (Grades 3–7).

CHAPTER 4

BIBLIOGRAPHIES OF CURRICULUM-RELATED SUBJECTS

A. GENERAL AND MISCELLANEOUS

475   Cornog, Martha, and Timothy Perper. *For Sex Education, See Librarian: A Guide to Issues and Resources.* Greenwood, 1996, $55.95 (0-313-29022-9).

This important, unique work is divided into two parts. The first part supplies all sorts of good background information, from the history of libraries regarding sex education to evaluation of materials, censorship, and the necessity of building a wide range of materials. The second part, in five chapters, is a selective list of recommended titles on such broad topics as sexuality and behavior, homosexuality and gender issues, and sexual problems. The annotations are lengthy and excellent. About 600 titles are listed in age ranges from childhood through adult. The titles are considered by the authors to be the best available through a publication date of 1995.

476   Forgan, James W. *Teaching Problem Solving Through Children's Literature*. Teacher Ideas Press/Libraries Unlimited, 2002, pap., $25 (1-56308-981-5).

Using lesson plans for 40 popular children's literature books, the author examines how characters in the books solved problems similar to those faced by children today. Each lesson plan includes bibliographic information, a concise book summary, points to consider before reading, discussion questions, and outlines of many classroom activities.

477   Matthew, Kathryn I., and Joy L. Lowe. *Neal-Schuman Guide to Recommended Children's Books and Media for Use with Every Elementary Subject*. Neal-Schuman, 2002, pap., $55 (1-55570-431-X).

More than 1,200 books, videos, software, CDs, cassettes, and Internet sites are listed in this bibliography, arranged under broad subject areas such as science, mathematics, and social studies. Background information on national curriculum standards is found at the beginning of each chapter. A valuable introduction describes how educators can use learning materials, particularly literature, to help individual students and groups. Each entry gets a brief annotation and there are activity suggestions throughout each chapter. Appendixes include lists of professional organizations, teacher resources, and Internet sites. This book offers fine suggestions for integrating literature into every subject in the elementary school curriculum.

478   Wright, Cora M. *Hot Links: Literature Links for the Middle School Curriculum*. Libraries Unlimited, 1998, pap., $31.50 (1-56308-587-9).

This work contains about 280 recommended children's literature titles that would be of use in specific curricular areas such as poetry, fine arts, mathematics, and science. Genres covered include fiction, folktales, and biographies. Entries are annotated and contain basic citation information. A chart at the end lists the books alphabetically and indicates the content and genre areas covered by each title. This book is of value in finding uses for superior titles in children's literature for the middle grades.

B. THE ARTS AND RECREATION

479   Crowe, Chris. *More Than a Game: Sports Literature for Young Adults*. Scarecrow, 2004, $40 (0-8108-4900-3).

Chapters trace, with many examples from the literature, the evolution of the sports book (fiction, nonfiction, poetry) from formula writing to a complex, diverse genre where the great themes of literature are often explored. Sports books for both girls and boys are discussed, and there is material on various situations and conflicts commonly found in these books. More than 3,000 titles are introduced and annotated, and there are lists of additional adult sources on this topic. Extensive appendixes give excellent bibliographies of books past and present.

480 Englebaugh, Debi. *Integrating Art and Language Arts Through Children's Literature.* Teacher Ideas Press/Libraries Unlimited, 2002, pap., $25 (1-56308-958-0).

The first part of this valuable resource focuses on art techniques and suggests a variety of interesting projects for each. The second part, organized by title, suggests activities for more than 140 well-known books. Each book is briefly annotated and relevant Web sites are given. Most of the titles are of recent publication.

481 Jurenka, Nancy Allen. *Hobbies Through Children's Books and Activities.* Teacher Ideas Press/Libraries Unlimited, 2001, pap., $28 (1-56308-773-1).

Each of the 30 chapters in this book focuses on a different hobby, such as bird watching and tap dancing. Each chapter features a picture book in which the hobby plays an important part. For each entry, there is a starter activity, a language arts activity, a poem citation, a glossary of important words, references to related societies and associations, and an annotated list of five nonfiction informational books.

482 Levene, Donna B. *Music Through Children's Literature.* Teacher Ideas Press/Libraries Unlimited, 2001, $24.50 (1-56308-021-4).

This collection of musical activities has sections that explore rhythm, melody, form, instruments, music history, and dance forms. Coverage includes folk songs, rhythmic poems, stories with musical themes, and references to books (chiefly picture books) with strong musical links. These activities can be adapted to accommodate time limitations and different levels of the teacher's musical proficiency.

C. FOLKLORE

483 Helbig, Alethea K., and Agnes Regan Perkins. *Myths and Hero Tales: A Cross-Cultural Guide to Literature for Children and Young Adults.* Greenwood, 1997, $49.95 (0-313-29935-8).

After an introduction that gives background material on folklore, this book is divided into eight sections. The first, and largest, gives material on 189 books published between 1985 and 1996 that contain 1,455 myths and hero tales. Scholarly accuracy and literary quality were the two criteria for inclusion. A majority of entries are from Native American and African sources, but tales from other cultures are included. The annotations are clear, direct, and interesting. The other sections are detailed indexes that list the stories by writer, tale type, culture, character and place names, grade level, title, and illustrator. This is the most comprehensive guide to myths and hero tales currently available.

484   Kraus, Anne Marie. *Folktale Themes and Activities for Children: Pourquoi Tales.* Libraries Unlimited, 1998, pap., $22.50 (1-56308-521-6).

This solid, well-organized, and well-researched volume shows how traditional "how and why" folktales can be integrated into all areas of the curriculum. Throughout, the author emphasizes the importance of choosing authentic, well-written stories and, to facilitate this selection, she provides extensive bibliographies. Stories are organized by theme and motif, as well as by cultural and geographic groups. Many interesting activities are also suggested. Both the theoretical and practical are combined effectively in this volume. There is an excellent sequel by the same author: *Folktale Themes and Activities for Children: Trickster and Transformation Tales* (Libraries Unlimited, 1999, pap., $24.95 [1-56308-608-5]).

D. MATHEMATICS

485   Braddon, Kathryn L., et al. *Math Through Children's Literature: Making the NCTM Standards Come Alive.* Teacher Ideas Press/Libraries Unlimited, 1993, $25 (0-87287-932-1).

This resource shows how to integrate nonfiction books on mathematics into the curriculum by incorporating them into real-life situations in the classroom. In a well-organized manner, each book is introduced with a summary and each is related to the standards developed by the National Council of Teachers of Mathematics (now superceded by a new set of standards). Each book is also explained in relation to the concept it demonstrates. In addition, many math-related activities are outlined for the elementary grades. Although geared to the old standards, this work is still of value.

486   Copper, Cathie Hilterbran. *Counting Your Way Through 1-2-3: Books and Activities.* Scarecrow, 1996, $33.50 (0-8108-3125-2).

The 663 counting books for young children described in this annotated guide are divided into ten subject areas. Each section includes a description of the subject area, an annotated bibliography of books relating to this area, and a number of book-related activities. There is also a brief look at the history of counting books.

487 Evans, Caroline W., et al. *Math Links: Teaching the NCTM 2000 Standards Through Literature.* Teacher Ideas Press/Libraries Unlimited, 2001, $32.50 (1-56308-787-1).

In 2000, the National Council of Teachers of Mathematics adopted new standards. The 36 lesson plans in this volume reflect these new standards. Each detailed lesson plan integrates library materials into primary-grade math teaching and utilizes both reading and writing skills. Each has a suggested time frame, an annotated list of materials, activities, ideas for assessment, and suggestions for adapting the lesson for special situations. There are also reproducible charts and literary resource lists.

488 Kacmarski, Kathryn. *Exploring Math with Books Kids Love.* Fulcrum, 1998, pap., $19.95 (1-55591-960-X).

Aimed at teachers of grades 4 through 8, this book is divided into six chapters, each of which covers a different math concept, such as number relationships, systems, and theory. Each chapter lists several books and gives examples of exercises and activities based on those books. For each book, there is a lesson plan, a list of applicable standards from the National Council of Teachers of Mathematics, and an indication of which parts of the book are related to these standards. This manual gives students an opportunity to study math in the context of many real-life situations and offers links to literature, art, history, and other subjects.

489 Perry, Phyllis J. *Guide to Math Materials: Resources to Support the NCTM Standards.* Libraries Unlimited, 1997, pap., $20 (1-56308-491-0).

All types of math materials for the elementary grades can be located with this guide. A variety of materials—from scales, cubes, and calculators to books, puzzles, activity cards, and games—are organized under such topics as problem solving, number sense, and geometry. Annotations include a description, grade levels, applications, and an indication of quality. Addresses of publishers and suppliers are also given.

490 Thiessen, Diane, et al. *The Wonderful World of Mathematics: A Critically Annotated List of Children's Books in Mathematics,* 2nd ed. National Council of Teachers of Mathematics, 1998, pap., $17.95 (0-87353-439-5).

This excellent resource for selecting high-quality books for children provides reviews of more than 550 trade books relating to mathematics. Each section of the book is arranged by topics that range from counting books for the youngest to geometry books for older children. Each topic is introduced with examples of how these books have been used successfully. This is followed by a list of the recommended books, with good bibliographic data, a grade-level indication, a usefulness rating, and a full annotation. All books were in print as of 1997.

491   Whitin, David J., and Sandra Wilde. *It's the Story that Counts: More Children's Books for Mathematical Learning, K–6.* Heinemann, 1995, pap., $25.50 (0-435-08369-4).

In this sequel to the authors' *Read Any Good Math Lately?* (Heinemann, 1992, $23.50 [0-435-08334-1]), the purpose is again to show how library materials can be integrated into the teaching of mathematics. Written in an accessible style with many anecdotes, conversations, and interviews with well-known authors (such as Tana Hoban), this work makes teaching math fun. There are bibliographies of recommended books, including fiction, nonfiction, poetry, and books of games and puzzles. The materials are organized around a wide range of mathematical topics, such as estimation, geometry, and fractions.

E. RELIGION AND CHARACTER DEVELOPMENT

492   Cecil, Nancy Lee, and Patricia L. Roberts. *Families in Children's Literature: A Resource Guide, Grades 4–8.* Teacher Ideas Press/Libraries Unlimited, 1998, $18.50 (1-56308-313-2).

Using a wide variety of family situations, this bibliographic guide lists and annotates recommended books for grades 4 through 8. The titles chosen present a positive view of family structure while promoting an appreciation of the diversity in families. This book offers professionals a unique but valid way of introducing the complexities of modern families to today's students.

493   Dole, Patricia Pearl. *Children's Books About Religion.* Libraries Unlimited, 1999, $32 (1-56308-515-1).

Approximately 700 critically annotated books are included in this bibliography that covers all aspects of world religion. The book is divided into three sections. The first section has chapters on general concepts in religion, such as God, prayer, and the Bible. The middle section deals with books on the Judeo-Christian tradition, and the last section covers books on other world religions, such as Buddhism, Hinduism, and Native American religious beliefs. A variety of genres is represented, including prayer books, creation stories, song books, holiday tales, and biographies. Unfortunately, grade levels are not indicated. All books were published after 1990 (but each chapter ends with an "Older and Noteworthy" section). Dole also edited a briefer bibliography titled *Helping Children Through Books* (Church and Synagogue Library Association, 2001, $10 [0-915324-45-8]). Another fine bibliography is Carol Campbell's *Classic Religious Books for Children* (Church and Synagogue Library Association, 2001, $11 [0-915324-44-X]).

494   Jweid, Rosann, and Margaret Rizzo. *Building Character Through Literature.* Scarecrow, 2001, $32.50 (0-8108-3951-2).

The primary purpose of this book is to present 50 novels that show strength of character. The titles range from Mark Twain's *Puddn'head Wilson* to Christopher Paul Clark's prize-winning *Bud, Not Buddy*. The treatment for each book ranges from three to five pages and covers such material as plot, author information, characters, setting, discussion topics, vocabulary study, and a number of interesting project and activity ideas.

495   Livo, Norma J. *Bringing Out Their Best.* Libraries Unlimited, 2003, $28 (1-56308-934-3).

Subtitled *Values Education and Character Development Through Traditional Tales*, this work highlights 60 stories that exemplify, support, and promote strong values and character traits for today's youth. This book will be of particular value with the elementary grades.

496   McElmeel, Sharron L. *Character Education: A Book Guide for Teachers, Librarians, and Parents.* Libraries Unlimited, 2002, $32.50 (1-56308-884-3).

After an introduction that discusses character education in general, how it relates to the home and classroom, and the strengths of various formats and genres, this tool is organized into 17 chapters each dealing with a different quality, such as humility, initiative, and patience. For each quality, there is a definition and an annotated list of books that demonstrate the trait. The books are suitable for children in kindergarten through grade 5. There are thorough author, title, and concept indexes.

497   Mort, John. *Christian Fiction: A Guide to the Genre.* Libraries Unlimited, 2002, $55 (1-56308-871-1).

Although this book is intended for building collections for adults, the author uses icons to indicate young adult books and adult books suitable for young adults. All books are recommended; starred items are especially recommended. There are almost 2,000 titles in this bibliography, most of which are from religious publishers. However, mainstream authors such as John Irving and Stephen King are also represented.

498   Roberts, Patricia L. *Family Values Through Children's Literature and Activities, Grades 4–6.* Scarecrow, 2004, pap., $42 (0-8108-5057-5).

This bibliography, aimed at the middle grades, highlights children's books that feature characters who display positive family-oriented values in their relations with others. Related activities and lessons expand on the themes explored in each book.

499   Stephens, Claire Gatrell. *Picture This! Using Picture Story Books for Character Education in the Classroom.* Libraries Unlimited, 2003, $35 (1-59158-001-3).

As well as listing recommended picture books under the virtue they demonstrate, this book contains lesson plans and reproducible worksheets to use in teaching these virtues. Ideas for curriculum integration are also presented. There is good background material on each title, plus a list of related Web sites. This book will be useful for both teachers and librarians involved in character education projects.

500   Walker, Barbara J. *Developing Christian Fiction Collections for Children and Adults.* Neal-Schuman, 1998, pap., $35 (155570-292-9).

Part I of this guide to collection development supplies all sorts of background information, from a definition of Christian fiction and discussion of its audience to guidelines for building and promoting collections of Christian fiction. Part II provides recommendations for core collections for children, young adults, and adults. The books are listed by genre, such as mysteries and romances. Each entry contains bibliographic information, a brief summary, and, usually, a quote from reviews. Most titles are recent, but classics like C. S. Lewis's Narnia books are included. There are also a section on videos of interest, a list of fiction award winners, and several helpful indexes.

F. SCIENCE

501   Butzow, Carol M., and John W. Butzow. *Exploring the Environment Through Children's Literature: An Integrated Approach.* Teacher Ideas Press/Libraries Unlimited, 1999, $24 (1-56308-650-6).

The authors have organized their exploration of children's literature about the environment into 15 chapters geared to grades K through 4. Each highlights a different book from classic and contemporary children's literature that demonstrates environmental themes. In addition to detailed lesson plans, there are puzzles, word searches, and a variety of other activities to interest young readers.

502 Butzow, Carol M., and John W. Butzow. *Intermediate Science Through Children's Literature: Over Land and Sea.* Libraries Unlimited, 1995, $26, o.p.

Focusing on the middle grades and environmental science, the authors build each chapter's complete interdisciplinary lesson plan around a single book. Chapters cover such topics as oceans, rivers, mountain formations, weather, the tundra, fossils, and environmental quality. There are many classroom-tested activities for each unit.

503 Butzow, Carol M., and John W. Butzow. *Science Through Children's Literature: An Integrated Approach*, 2nd ed. Libraries Unlimited, 2000, pap., $27.50 (1-56308-651-4).

In more than 30 thematic units that feature trade science books for the primary grades, the authors demonstrate how interesting, appealing books can be integrated into the instructional program. The book is packed with activity ideas and each chapter ends with lists of related resources. The first edition of this book produced a sequel that is still in print, *More Science Through Children's Literature* (Libraries Unlimited, 1998, pap., $28 [1-56308-266-7]).

504 Cecil, Nancy Lee. *Developing Environmental Awareness Through Children's Literature: A Guide for Teachers and Librarians, K–8.* McFarland, 1996, pap., $28.50 (0-7864-0221-0).

There are more than 200 books in this bibliography; each portrays characters who respect their environments and act on their beliefs. The books are organized in five genres: contemporary fiction, folklore, historical fiction, biography, and fantasy. After bibliographic information, a descriptive annotation is given, plus an indication of the appropriate grade levels.

505 Cerullo, Mary M. *Reading the Environment: Children's Literature in the Science Classroom.* Heinemann, 1997, pap., $21 (0-435-08383-X).

This book covers science books on the environment for preschool through grade 6. After discussing basic criteria for selecting science books and making a plea for integrating trade books into the curriculum, the author devotes separate chapters to reviewing recommended fiction and nonfiction science titles under the following headings: earth science, the oceans, weather and the seasons, and the movement of water from mountains to the sea. Science activities and discussion topics are included, plus a list at the end of each chapter of all the recommended titles.

506   Dwyer, Jim. *Earth Works: Recommended Fiction and Nonfiction About Nature and the Environment for Adults and Young Adults.* Neal-Schuman, 1996, $39.95 (1-55570-194-9).

This extensive bibliography lists and briefly annotates 2,601 new and classic titles divided into chapters by broad subject areas. Grade levels are given for each title; some go as low as 4th grade.

507   Fredericks, Anthony D. *From Butterflies to Thunderbolts: Discovering Science with Books Kids Love.* Fulcrum, 1997, $17.95 (1-55591-946-4).

The author believes that children learn science best through the discovery method and that trade books play an important part in this process. This book consists of nine parts on such subjects as plants, animals, and dinosaurs. Three or four chapters are devoted to each subject and each chapter focuses on a single title. Chapters include brief summaries, discussion questions, suggested activities, and a bibliography of related literature. Unfortunately, there is no overall bibliography of works cited, and many of the books are now more than ten years old.

508   Fredericks, Anthony D. *Investigating Natural Disasters Through Children's Literature: An Integrated Approach.* Teacher Ideas Press/Libraries Unlimited, 2001, pap., $26.50 (1-56308-861-4).

Children (and many adults) have a fascination for natural disasters—storms, volcanic eruptions, hurricanes, earthquakes, tornadoes, floods, avalanches, landslides, and tsunamis. These disasters are all covered in this bibliographic guide that uses trade books to open children's minds to wonders and power in the natural world. Books are highlighted for each phenomenon, along with short activities and longer projects.

509   Lowe, Joy L., and Kathryn I. Matthew. *Discoveries and Inventions in Literature for Youth.* Scarecrow, 2004, $49 (0-8108-4915-1).

This bibliography includes a varied collection of books and other resources useful in grades K–12 for the study of scientific discoveries and inventions from ancient Greece to the present. As well as bibliographic listings for inventors and discoverers, there is coverage of the fields of energy, the environment, industry, technology, medicine, science, space, transportation, and weapons. Genres included are picture books, general fiction and nonfiction, biographies, reference books, and professional and electronic resources. There is also a directory of museums and organizations and a collection of booktalks.

510 Pilger, Mary Anne. *Science Experiments Index for Young People*, 3rd ed. Libraries Unlimited, 2001, $65 (1-56308-899-1).

This is the standard reference tool for locating science experiments as they appear in science trade books for children and young adults. Apart from this important use, librarians have found that the listing of books indexed has some value in collection development and gaining familiarity with science publishing in various areas.

511 Roberts, Patricia L. *Language Arts and Environmental Awareness: 100+ Integrated Books and Activities for Children.* Linnet/Shoe String Press, 1998, $35 (0-208-02427-1).

Books on environmental education are combined here with language arts activities. The books are grouped under specific activities, such as listening, folk literature, reading, speaking, and writing. The books listed for each of these activities are subdivided into two age groups: 5 through 8 and 9 through 14. Each book is given an environmental context, a synopsis, a language arts activity, and an activity for the home. The activities are imaginative, interesting, and make children aware of the environment and its conservation.

512 Sosa, Mary, and Tracy Gath. *Exploring Science in the Library: Resources and Activities for Young People.* American Library Association, 2000, $32 (0-8389-0768-7).

Co-published with the American Association for the Advancement of Science (AAAS), this excellent resource is an update of *Great Explorations: Discovering Science in the Library* (AAAS, 1995, o.p.). Its purpose is to bring science educators together and to help librarians develop science, math, and technology resources for K–12 students. A multitude of topics are covered, including education reform, collection development, videos and software, ways to integrate trade books into the curriculum, Internet resources, and cooperative efforts between the library and the classroom. There are also lists of basic recommended books and other materials. This useful book also describes 47 successful science projects and gives hints on how to collect funds to support science activities in libraries.

G. SOCIAL STUDIES, HISTORY, AND GEOGRAPHY

Note: See also Chapter 2's coverage of historical fiction.

513   Adamson, Lynda G. *Literature Connections to American History, K–6: Resources to Enhance and Entice.* Libraries Unlimited, 1997, $37 (1-56308-502-X).

The first part of this bibliography contains a series of book lists arranged by time periods from "North America Before 1600" to "Since 1975." The materials are subdivided by grade levels and then by genres: historical fiction, biography, nonfiction histories, and multimedia. In the second and larger section, all these materials are divided by format. These entries are arranged alphabetically by author and each entry is annotated. There are author/illustrator, title, and subject indexes. This volume lives up to its subtitle: it does supply resources to enhance and entice, and in a well-organized fashion. A companion volume by the same author uses the same basic format and arrangement. It is *Literature Connections to American History, 7–12: Resources to Enhance and Entice* (Libraries Unlimited, 1997, $39.50 [0-56308-503-8]).

514   Adamson, Lynda G. *Literature Connections to World History, K–6: Resources to Enhance and Entice.* Libraries Unlimited, 1998, $34 (1-56308-505-4).

Like the American history set described above, this work and its companion highlight recommended resources, this time for world history. This volume is divided into three sections. In the first section, the materials are organized by continent and time period, followed by further divisions by grade level and then genre (fiction, biography, nonfiction, and multimedia). The second section is an annotated bibliography of all these entries, arranged by format and then by author. The third section consists of a number of thorough indexes. This is a valuable asset for collection building even though it is now showing its age. A companion volume by the same author uses the same arrangement and format: *Literature Connections to World History, 7–12: Resources to Enhance and Entice* (Libraries Unlimited, 1998, $36.50 [0-67308-505-4]).

515   Austin, Mary C., and Esther C. Jenkins. *Literature for Children and Young Adults About Oceania: Analysis and Annotated Bibliography, with Additional Readings for Adults.* Greenwood, 1996, $69.50 (0-313-26643-3).

The title gives a very good description of this book's contents. After an introduction to Oceania, its people, and environments, the work is divided into three main parts: Australia, New Zealand, and Melanesia/Micronesia/Polynesia. Each section includes annotated bibliographies of fiction and nonfiction for young people with supplemental listings of background books for adults.

516   Barnhouse, Rebecca. *The Middle Ages in Literature for Youth.*
Scarecrow, 2004, pap., $30 (0-8108-4916-X).

This work covers material on the Middle Ages (500–1500 A.D.) written
for both children and teenagers. It focuses on Western Europe and is
organized around geographic locations, time periods, and subjects. Each
section begins with a short, descriptive explanation concerning the period or subject, followed by annotated critical bibliographies. Materials
included are picture books, historical fiction, nonfiction including biographies, and reference books. There are additional lists of professional
resources including Web sites and classroom activities. For an earlier bibliography by this author that includes only fiction, see Chapter 2, "Historical Fiction."

517   Barr, Catherine. *From Biography to History: Best Books for Children's
Entertainment and Education.* Libraries Unlimited, 1998, $59.95 (0-
8352-4012-6).

Books for grades 3 through 9 are listed in this guide to recommended in-
print biographies of nearly 300 notable men and women, plus related
histories. Included are such diverse personalities as Pocahontas, Oprah
Winfrey, Charles Darwin, Davy Crockett, Jane Goodall, and Jesse
Owens. Although biographies of people currently in the news will be
somewhat out of date, this is nevertheless a good selection and readers'
advisory tool.

518   Bosmajian, Hamida. *Sparing the Child: Children's Literature About
Nazism and the Holocaust.* Garland, 2002, $95.50 (0-8153-3856-2).

This innovative, well-researched work examines texts for children that
have either a Holocaust survivor or a former member of the Hitler Youth
as a protagonist. The texts examined and analyzed in this prize-winning
monograph include juvenile fiction, picture books, and general nonfiction. The choice of material represents two opposite juvenile points of
view (Nazi German and Jewish) toward the Holocaust.

519   Brazowski, Antoinette, and Mary J. Katt. *Children's Books on Ancient
Greek and Roman Mythology: An Annotated Bibliography.* Greenwood,
1994, $49.50 (0-313-28973-5).

This bibliography lists 381 books, published from the mid-19th century
through 1992, dealing with classical mythology and written for children
in grades 4 through 8. There are also scholarly articles on the importance
of the study of mythology, a history of children's books on mythology,
and a section on how to introduce mythology to youngsters. The bibliography is arranged by author and gives grade levels for each book.

Though most of these books are out of print, this bibliography is interesting historically.

520   *Exploring the United States Through Literature.* Oryx, 1994–1995, $24.95 per volume.

Each volume in this seven-volume set (volumes are available individually) covers a specific region of the United States (for example, Great Lakes States, Mountain States, Northeast States). Volumes are subdivided into chapters by states and further by format—nonfiction, biography, fiction, periodicals, and computer programs. The titles (usually about 700 per volume) are for use with children from grades K through 8. Unfortunately, this splendid set has been allowed to languish unrevised.

521   Fredericks, Anthony D. *More Social Studies Through Children's Literature: An Integrated Approach.* Teacher Ideas Press/Libraries Unlimited, 2000, pap., $29.50, o.p.

A continuation of the author's earlier *Social Studies Through Children's Literature* (Libraries Unlimited, 1991, o.p.), this volume begins with an explanation of literature-based instruction and a review of the current standards for teaching social studies. The main text is divided into seven major areas (for example, "Nation and Country") and five titles are highlighted for each of these areas. After a summary and a list of appropriate study areas, each entry contains thematic material, critical-thinking questions, related books, and many thoughtful activities. This is an easy-to-use manual on integrating literature into the social studies classroom for grades K to 5.

522   Khorama, Meena. *Africa in Literature for Children and Young Adults: An Annotated Bibliography of English-Language Books.* Greenwood, 1994, $59.95 (0-313-25488-5).

This is an annotated bibliography of 676 English-language books about Africa published between 1873 and 1994 and written by European, American, and African writers. The three-part introduction is a discussion of juvenile literature about Africa under the headings "Colonial Literature," "Post-Colonial Western Literature," and "Post-Colonial African Literature." The bibliography is arranged by geographical regions and then by genres: fiction, biography, and informational books. The annotations supply content notes, an indication of bias, and a critical comment. This work will be of value to scholars of children's literature.

523   Lowe, Joy L., and Kathryn I. Matthew. *Colonial America in Literature for Youth: A Guide and Resource Book.* Scarecrow, 2003, $42 (0-8108-4744-2).

Approximately 800 annotated titles on aspects of American colonial history (1607–1776) form the body of this work. They range in difficulty from picture books through adult titles suitable for young adults. The seven chapters are organized by genres, including fiction, nonfiction, picture books, poetry and song reference books, and books on specific subjects such as slavery and exploration. The appendixes contain much valuable material: a core collection, booktalks, lists of professional materials, and electronic resources.

524   MacDonald, Eleanor Kay. *A Window into History: Family Memory in Children's Literature.* Oryx, 1996, $24.95 (0-89774-879-4).

The 203 books and audiocassettes included in this bibliography on American history range from picture books to works geared to the elementary through middle school grades. They are arranged by seven main topics, including "The Immigrant Experience" and "The Frontier Experience." Each entry contains critical annotations, period notes, geographic locations, and recommended grade levels. Appendixes describe oral history projects and list books for further reading. There is a useful index by ethnic origin, historical period, and location.

525   Matthew, Kathryn I., and Joy L. Lowe. *Neal-Schuman Guide to Celebrations and Holidays Around the World.* Neal-Schuman, 2004, $59.95 (1-55570-479-4).

Organized in a calendar fashion, this book highlights holidays and other special events celebrated around the world. For each holiday, there is a comprehensive annotated list of books and other materials plus an outline of a number of activities. There are also chapters on such events as birthdays and weddings. This guide can be used as a sourcebook for media involving both familiar holidays and those associated with lesser-known multicultural traditions.

526   Miller, Wanda J. *Teaching History Through Children's Literature: Post-World War II.* Libraries Unlimited, 1998, pap., $27.50 (1-56308-581-X).

Individual chapters in this teacher's guide are devoted to the Korean War, the civil rights movement, the women's rights movement, space exploration, the Vietnam War, multicultural heritage, and the first Persian Gulf War. In each of these chapters, specific books are recommended for the entire class to read, with accompanying material about the author, group activities, and discussion questions. The books are aimed at roughly grades 4 through 8. The final chapter identifies professional and computer resources and gives suggestions on how to evaluate students. The companion volume by the same author, *U.S. History Through Children's Literature from the Colonial Period to World War II* (Libraries Unlimited, 1997, $25 [1-560308-440-6]), also uses a broad topical approach with headings such as "Exploration," "Native Americans," and "The Civil War." For each topic, the author suggests two books—one for the entire class and one for small reading groups—and extensive accompanying material.

527   Perez-Stable, Maria A., and Mary Hurlbut Cordier. *Understanding American History Through Children's Literature: Instructional Units and Activities for Grades K–8*. Oryx, 1994, $24.95 (0-89774-795-X).

This book is divided into two parts by grade levels—K–3 and 4–8. Each part is subdivided chronologically by major periods or events. In turn, each of these sections contains annotated lists of appropriate books, along with detailed activities. There are also many tables, charts, and diagrams and an extensive general bibliography and index at the end.

528   Perry, Phyllis J. *Exploring Our Country's History: Linking Fiction to Nonfiction*. Teacher Ideas Press/Libraries Unlimited, 1998, pap., $23.50 (1-56308-622-0).

The author supplies lists of recommended fiction and nonfiction on different eras in U.S. history and shows how to use the historical fiction as a bridge to related nonfiction. As well, there is material on discussion topics, multidisciplinary activities, and topics for further investigation. This book is useful for working with children in grades K to 5.

529   Raum, Elizabeth. *Every Day a Holiday: Celebrating Children's Literature Throughout the Year*. Scarecrow, 2001, pap., $32.50 (0-8108-4043-X).

At least one holiday is highlighted for every day of the year. Each entry includes a description of the holiday, one or more featured picture books, additional books, and suggested activities. Classics, long-time favorites, and current books are included. The subject index helps users find topics for programs, but there is no index by holiday.

530   Snodgrass, Mary Ellen. *Celebrating Women's History: A Women's History Month Resource Book*. Gale, 1996, $44.95, o.p.

Arranged in 29 subject chapters (art, geography, science, and so forth), this book contains more than 300 ideas for activities and projects relating to Women's History Month in March. Each of these entries provides grade level suitability and an annotated list of sources (mainly books and videos).

531 Stephens, Elaine C., and Jean E. Brown. *Learning About . . . the Civil War: Literature and Other Resources for Young People.* Shoe String, 1998, $32 (0-208-02449-2).

After a general discussion about integrating literature into the curriculum, and specifically the study of the Civil War, this book focuses separate chapters on various aspects of the war. Important "Focus Books" are then listed, with complete summaries and grade-level indicators. Teaching considerations are also included, plus about four suggested student follow-up activities. The highlighted books are of good quality, by such authors as Ann Rinaldi and Russell Freedman. A final chapter lists additional resources including recordings, laser discs, Web sites, and historical sites. Another valuable book in this series by Elaine C. Stephens is *Learning About . . . the Holocaust: Literature and Other Resources for Young People* (Shoe String, 1995, $29.50 [0-208-02398-4]). After a brief historical overview, this bibliography of nearly 300 titles is arranged by types of materials—nonfiction, photoessays, personal narratives, poetry, biography, drama, and fiction. Additional resources, such as organizations and nonprint materials, are listed in a final section.

532 Sullivan, Edward T. *Appalachian Literature for Youth.* Scarecrow, 2004, pap., $30 (0-8108-5070-2).

This is an annotated bibliography of books and nonprint materials relating to the Southern Appalachian region (Kentucky, North Carolina, Tennessee, Virginia, and West Virginia). The listings cover children's, young adult, and appropriate adult literature, organized by such genres as autobiography and memoir, fiction, nonfiction, picture books, poetry, and reference tools. There are also sections on teacher resources, discs, and videos, plus some booktalks and lesson plans.

533 Sullivan, Edward T. *The Holocaust in Literature for Youth: A Guide and Resource Book.* Scarecrow, 1999, $29.50 (0-8108-3607-6).

This comprehensive bibliography is suitable for use with youngsters from the primary grades through high school. Approximately 600 titles are listed by genres—autobiography and biography, drama, fiction, nonfiction, picture books, and reference works. A separate section lists books on related subjects, such as anti-Semitism and genocide. Helpful annotations contain a book synopsis, evaluation (good, mediocre, or poor), grade levels, and notes on special features. Additional sections list electronic resources, directories of museums and organizations, and professional materials. A suggested core collection is given, as well as sample booktalks and thorough indexes. This is an outstanding resource on the subject.

534   *Teaching About the Holocaust: A Resource Book for Educators.* U.S. Holocaust Memorial Museum, 2000, free (no ISBN).

After detailed information about visiting the museum and strategies for effective teaching about the Holocaust, there is an extensive annotated bibliography and list of videos. These are grouped by reading level (middle school, high school, adult) and by genre (for example, fiction, history, memoir, and art). A new edition is planned. This one is available free from the museum: Resource Center for Educators, U.S. Holocaust Memorial Museum, 100 Raoul Wallenberg Place S.W., Washington, DC 20024-2150; (202) 488-2661. The contents of this booklet can also be downloaded at www.ushmm.org.

CHAPTER 5
MULTICULTURAL SOURCES

A. GENERAL SOURCES

535 Anderson, Vicki. *Immigrants in the United States in Fiction: A Guide to 705 Books for Librarians and Teachers, K–9.* McFarland, 1994, $23.50 (0-89950-906-1).

This work has been criticized for the number of suitable titles that are not included. Keeping this criticism and the age of the volume in mind, this should be considered a secondary source. However, it does supply annotated listings, arranged by ethnic groups, of novels for the elementary and junior high grades.

536 Beck, Peggy. *GlobaLinks: Resources for World Studies, Grades K–8.* Linworth, 2002, pap., $39.95 (1-58683-040-6).

Part I of this helpful bibliography lists print and nonprint resources involving world cultures. Within broad subjects, the books are listed alphabetically by the author's last name. The subjects include ancient civilizations, biography, festivals, foods, holidays, customs, games, myths and fairy tales, flags, geography, human rights, racism, and social issues. Part II provides Web sites for the study of other countries and cultures and Part III gives a webography of key pal/pen pal resources.

537   Braus, Nancy, and Molly Geidel. *Everyone's Kids Books: A Guide to Multicultural, Socially Conscious Books for Children.* Everyone's Books, 2000, pap., $19.95 (0-97038-160-3).

Aimed at parents, teachers, and librarians, this book lists and annotates books for children relating to peace, social justice, and understanding diversity. Among the topics covered are African American history, African American picture books and literature, the Caribbean region, Latin American heritage, Asian heritage, adoption, gays and lesbians, war and peace, violence, strong women in picture books and literature, and Irish, Russian, and Jewish cultures. This book is excellent for collection development and reading guidance in the elementary grades.

538   Brown, Jean E., and Elaine C. Stephens. *United in Diversity: Using Multicultural Young Adult Literature in the Classroom.* National Council of Teachers of English, 1998, pap., $22.95 (0-8141-5571-5).

This excellent resource is divided into four parts. The first part includes seven essays, by such writers as Eve Bunting and Christopher Paul Curtis, on how the authors handle diversity and multiculturalism in their writing. The essays in the second part are written by practicing teachers who tell how they make connections between their students and multicultural literature. The third part, "Expanding the Curriculum," gives examples of using multicultural literature in various subject areas. The fourth part contains a list of professional resources as well as an annotated bibliography of young adult titles mentioned throughout the book.

539   Cai, Mingshui. *Multicultural Literature for Children and Young Adults: Reflections of Critical Issues.* Greenwood, 2002, $64.95 (0-313-31244-3).

In nine chapters, the author examines various issues in the writing and use of multicultural literature. After making a convincing argument about the difference multicultural literature makes to young lives, he examines the struggle between literary values and pedagogical purposes. He also examines questions of criticism and evaluation, and tackles the question of what makes a good multicultural book. A section on how to use multicultural books in education describes the results of good programs in this area. Bibliographies of recommended books are appended along with other resources such as Web sites, books for further reading, and indexes.

540   *Children's Booklist: Over 350 Classic and Current Books Reflecting Many Cultures and Traditions, Chosen for Their Contributions to the Child's Inner Development.* Theosophical University Press, 1998, $9.95 (1-55700-012-3).

Chosen by the Children's Committee of the Theosophical Society, this excellent volume covers a wide range of books on different cultures and peoples. Arranged by broad subject, the well-annotated list is valuable for choosing books in the elementary grades and for offering reading guidance for ages 5 through 12.

541   Cotton, Penni. *Picture Books Sans Frontières.* Trentham Books, 2001, pap., £14.95 (1-85856-183-3).

This project was devised and carried out in Europe. Its purpose was to allow children in primary grades in European Community schools a glimpse at the cultures of other EC countries. One picture book was chosen from each country, with two from Belgium, Wales, Scotland, and Northern Ireland, for a total of 19 books. Minimal text, a specific cultural setting, and a universal theme were among the criteria used in choosing the books. The complete kit sent to schools includes general material on the development of the picture book plus material on how to use this package in a six-week curricular unit. Accompanying each book is a cassette of the book's text in the original language, plus a summary in English, and several ideas on how the book could be used in the classroom. This is an excellent way to introduce children to other cultures and to explore similarities and differences.

542   Darby, Mary Ann, and Miki Pryne. *Hearing All the Voices: Multicultural Books for Adolescents.* Scarecrow, 2002, $29.90 (0-8108-4058-8).

The largest part of this extremely useful volume consists of an annotated bibliography of more than 500 books suitable for grades 6 through 9, with an emphasis on recent publications. In addition to the usual cultural subjects, the authors explore related areas—drug use, nontraditional families, neglect, and homosexuality, for example. The first part gives hints for using these materials at home and at school and the third part covers literary circles and cross-curricular study. One appendix lists the books by genre, theme, culture, and country; the other offers suggestions for subject-area reading. This work opens doors for young adults studying diversity in our society.

543   Day, Frances Ann. *Multicultural Voices in Contemporary Literature: A Resource for Teachers.* Heinemann, 1999, pap., $28 (0-325-00130-8).

Following the same format as the 1994 edition, the author presents 40 contemporary multicultural authors and illustrators. For each entry there is a photograph, a biographical sketch, and a comprehensive bibliography of the subject's work. Then several of the most important books by the author are highlighted with a plot summary, critical analysis, and suggested activities. Approximately 120 new books are featured in this edition. Additional sections cover evaluating books for bias, offer further lists of resources, and provide a multicultural assessment plan to evaluate how a school program is succeeding in its multicultural studies. This work is a solid asset for both teachers and librarians.

544   Freeman, Evelyn B., and Barbara A. Lehman. *Global Perspectives in Children's Literature.* Allyn and Bacon, 2000, $29.50 (0-205-30862-7).

This book provides a basic overview of multiculturalism in children's literature and how it can be used in the classroom. Criteria for evaluating multicultural books are given and many examples cite titles published in the late 1990s.

545   Gates, Pamela S., and Dianne L. H. Mark. *Cultural Journeys: Multicultural Literature for Children and Young Adults.* Scarecrow, 2004, pap., $39.50, o.p.

As well as providing the criteria for evaluating multicultural literature, this volume supplies methods for using these materials in the classroom. All forms of multiracial literature for grades K–8 are introduced, with examples including picture books, folklore, fairy tales, myths, legends, fantasy, historical fiction, realistic fiction, and nonfiction. The book includes unit plans and an extensive annotated bibliography.

546   Hansen-Krening, Nancy, et al. *Kaleidoscope: A Multicultural Booklist for Grades K–8*, 4th ed. National Council of Teachers of English, 2003, $30.95 (0-8141-2539-5).

This work highlights recommended works of fiction and nonfiction published between 1999 and 2001 and dealing with people of color. The hundreds of titles are organized by type of literature, such as informational and educational books, or by contemporary issues such as families, friends, and community. Each annotation gives a summary, critical comment, and an indication of reader suitability. The three previous editions had different editors but are basically the same in organization and format. Volume 1 (now out of print) covers more than 400 titles published from 1990 to 1992. Volume 2 (NCTE, 1997, pap., $12.95 [0-8141-

2541-7]) lists about 600 titles published between 1993 and 1995, and Volume 3 (NCTE, 1999, $29.95 [0-8141-2540-0]) has about 600 entries covering 1996 through 1998. All editions are available at www.ncte.org.

547   Harris, Violet J. *Using Multicultural Literature in the K–8 Classroom.* Christopher-Gordon, 1997, pap., $37.95 (0-926842-60-9).

This is a fine collection of essays that explore issues relating to the creation, publication, and dissemination of multiethnic literature for children. The author discusses techniques of sharing this literature with young people and fostering an appreciation of other peoples and their cultures.

548   Helbig, Alethea K., and Agnes Regan Perkins. *Many Peoples, One Land: A Guide to New Multicultural Literature for Children and Young Adults.* Greenwood, 2001, $59.95 (0-313-30967-1).

In this continuation of *This Land Is Our Land* (see below), the authors offer information on more than 500 books of fiction, poetry, and the oral tradition published from 1994 through 1999 that are suited for preschool through high school. The books deal with four principal ethnic groups in the United States: Native Americans, African Americans, Hispanic Americans, and Asian Americans. In general, works set in other countries are not cited; adult titles of interest to young adults may be included. Along with bibliographic information and a brief summary, each entry contains comments on literary merit and possible objectionable material and offers age suggestions. There are five indexes, including a very helpful and detailed subject and thematic index.

549   Helbig, Alethea K., and Agnes Regan Perkins. *This Land Is Our Land: A Guide to Multicultural Literature for Children and Young Adults.* Greenwood, 1994, $49.95 (0-313-28742-2).

Of the 559 titles analyzed in this book, 60 percent were published between 1990 and 1993. (Coverage for 1994 through 1999 is contained in *Many Peoples, One Land*, discussed above). These titles, recommended for children in grades K through 12, cover the ethnic experiences of four American minorities: African Americans, Asian Americans, Hispanic Americans, and Native Americans. Bibliographic information for each title is followed by age and grade levels, a plot summary, and critical comment. The indexing is particularly strong and includes a broad subject index of themes, attitudes, and situations as well as the obvious subjects. Both this book and its successor continue to be of great value in school and public libraries.

550   Horning, Kathleen T., et al. *Multicultural Literature for Children and Young Adults: A Selected Listing of Books By and About People of Color, Vol. 2, 1991–1996.* Cooperative Children's Book Center, 1997, pap., $17 (0-931641-07-1).

This is a list of 350 recommended books published in the United States and Canada between 1991 and 1996. (Volume 1 covers books published between 1980 and 1990.) The titles in this book feature Africans, people of Afro-Caribbean origins, African Americans, Native Americans, Latinos, Asians, people of Asian Pacific origins, and Asian Americans. Covering works for preschoolers through teenagers, the entries contain bibliographic information, an annotation of several sentences, a brief evaluation, and age levels. The books are suitable for youngsters in preschool through age 14. Titles are arranged into 16 categories by genre or theme. There is also a supplementary listing of reference resources and material on literary awards.

551   Kuharets, Olga R. *Venture into Cultures: A Resource Book of Multicultural Materials and Programs,* 2nd ed. American Library Association, 2001, $34.50 (0-8389-3513-3).

Each section of this work represents a different ethnic group, such as African, Caribbean, Indian, Jewish American, Korean, Latin American, Middle Eastern, Native American, and Russian. List of resources for each area include books and stories. There are also dozens of ideas for programs for children in the elementary grades.

552   Lind, Beth Beutler. *Multicultural Children's Literature: An Annotated Bibliography, Grades K–8.* McFarland, 1996, $34.50 (0-7864-0038-2).

More that 1,100 fiction and nonfiction titles written for young people in grades K through 8, and published from 1980 through 1995, are listed in this annotated bibliography. The selections are arranged first by ethnic groups (African Americans, Asian Americans, Hispanic Americans, and Native Americans) and then by grade levels (K–3 or 4–8). They are further subdivided under each of these grade levels into such areas as informational nonfiction, biographies, historic/realistic fiction, and folklore. Each entry contains a brief annotation and complete bibliographic information. There are also lists of children's literature publishers, curricular resources for teachers, and an integrated author/title index.

553   Manna, Anthony L., and Carolyn S. Brodie. *Art and Story: The Role of Illustration in Multicultural Literature for Youth.* Highsmith, 1997, $30 (0-917846-77-X).

Presentations exploring the role that illustration plays in multicultural books for children have been collected from various Virginia Hamilton

Conferences from 1985 through 1996. The 14 contributors, mainly illustrators but also authors and editors, include Vera B. Williams, Pat Cummings, and Jerry Pinkney. The selections provide a critical and analytical look at multicultural books and examine such qualities as authenticity, stereotyping, and accuracy. Appendixes feature bibliographies of multicultural trade books, nonprint resources, and information about the conference.

554 Marantz, Sylvia, and Kenneth Marantz. *Multicultural Picture Books: Art for Understanding Others.* Linworth, 1994, pap., 28.95 (0-938865-22-6).

This work is unusual in that it focuses almost entirely on identifying and analyzing illustrations in picture books that portray many cultures in America. Included are representations of Asian, Middle Eastern, African (including African American and Caribbean), Native American, and some European ethnic cultures, such as Russian Jews. The book begins with a rationale for exposing children to the depiction of various cultures and an evaluation of various picture books. Then, for each culture, the authors list folktales and stories of the past, depictions of contemporary life, books of personal experiences, and other works on the immigrant experience. Each entry contains a brief summary, a detailed description of the artwork, and a comparison with other works. Grade levels are also given. The book ends with a list for further reading and a complete index.

555 Muse, Daphne. *The New Press Guide to Multicultural Resources for Young Readers.* The New Press, 1997, $60 (1-56584-339-8).

Arranged by thematic chapters subdivided by age levels from kindergarten to 8th grade, this is a thoughtful collection of reviews and essays from a number of distinguished contributors. The approximately 1,000 reviews average 250 to 500 words. Each gives a detailed summary plus extensive critical material (some reviews are not favorable). The essays are on key issues in multicultural education, such as recent immigrant experiences and human rights. One strength of this book is the breadth of its coverage; material back to the 1950s is included and the definition of multiculturalism includes religious, sexual, and disabled groups. This book was well received on publication but now needs updating.

556 Pilger, Mary Anne. *Multicultural Projects Index: Things to Make and Do to Celebrate Festivals, Cultures, and Holidays Around the World,* 3rd ed. Libraries Unlimited, 2001, $55 (1-56308-898-3).

Arranged by subjects that cover important events celebrated by different cultures around the world, this work indexes thousands of books useful for work with children from preschool through 8th grade. Although this is really a reference book rather than a bibliography, the extensive listing in the back of all the books indexed can serve as both a checklist and acquisition tool. There is also an author index.

557   Pratt, Linda, and Janice J. Beaty. *Transcultural Children's Literature.* Prentice Hall, 1999, $52 (0-134-32816-7).

The authors of this book maintain that transcultural children's literature is a definite complement to the field of children's literature. This work is organized first by nine geographical regions and then by individual countries. For each of these divisions, there are lists of books. Each entry gives bibliographic information, a detailed plot summary, critiques of illustrations, and suggested uses in the classroom. The authors stress the need to take into consideration young readers' cultures and concerns when reviewing books on other countries.

558   Roberts, Patricia L. *Multicultural Friendship Stories and Activities for Children Ages 5–14.* Scarecrow, 1998, pap., $36 (0-8108-3359-X).

The titles in this bibliography are divided into two age levels (5–8 and 9–14) and then by the topics "Family Friendships," "Community, Neighborhood, and School Friendships," and "Friendships Around the World." For each entry, there is an annotation, a cultural note, and several related activities (each with goals, materials needed, and instructions) geared to promoting understanding and friendships. A listing of additional stories is appended, along with suggested readings and resources for adults.

559   Rochman, Hazel. *Against Borders: Promoting Books for a Multicultural World.* American Library Association, 1993, $25 (0-8389-0601-X).

Although this book is more than ten years old, it is still "must" reading for anyone interested in promoting multiculturalism through the use of children's literature. In a series of essays on cultural issues, the author discusses numerous books representing a variety of ethnic groups and explains how these books can be used to help young people understand and appreciate cultures other than their own. There are bibliographies of the books listed in the text.

560   Stan, Susan. *The World Through Children's Books.* Scarecrow, 2002, pap., $27.95 (0-8108-4198-3).

A continuation of Carl M. Tomlinson's *Children's Books from Other Countries* (see below), this volume covers children's books published in the United States from 1996 to 2000 that originated in foreign countries, plus some American titles published in the same time period that are set in foreign countries. Entries are arranged by broad areas, such as Latin America, and then subdivided by country. Each gets a lengthy annotation, a grade-level designation, and good bibliographic information. Two opening chapters give an overview of international children's literature and tell how to use these books with children. The last part of the book contains material on book awards, organizations, publishers, and sources of foreign-language and bilingual books. This is a valuable guide to literature from other cultures.

561 Steiner, Stanley F. *Promoting a Global Community Through Multicultural Children's Literature.* Libraries Unlimited, 2001, $35 (1-56308-705-7).

More than 800 titles for kindergarten through 8th grade are featured in this book, whose purpose is to help build an understanding of world cultures. Five main sections—on such topics as different cultures, refugees and homeless people, and multicultural books in series—each contain annotated lists of books in many genres. Chapters end with a list of ideas and applications to build on the issues raised in the book lists. These range from reading passages aloud to discussion topics. There is also an appended listing of professional materials and resources. This book has been called "an invaluable resource."

562 Stones, Rosemary. *A Multicultural Guide to Children's Books.* Books for Keeps, 2002, £7.50 (no ISBN).

From the offices of *Books for Keeps,* one of Britain's leading periodicals on children's literature, comes this interesting book on multicultural children's books. There are several fine articles by such writers as Beverley Naidoo and some profiles of other authors, but the main body consists of lists of recommended titles arranged by age group, from picture books to age 16+. The titles are annotated and represent a wide range of genres, including nonfiction, novels, poetry, and biographies. There is also information on publishers and important organizations. This is a useful, attractive work, particularly for British and Canadian libraries.

563 Thomas, Rebecca L. *Connecting Cultures: A Guide to Multicultural Literature for Children.* Bowker, 1996, $40 (0-8352-3760-5).

This is a comprehensive subject index to more than 1,600 titles published between the 1970s and the mid-1990s that are suitable for use with preschoolers through 6th-grade students. Included are fiction titles, folktales, poetry, and songbooks that reflect a diversity of cultures, current interests, and timely topics. Each entry has complete bibliographic information, a cultural designation, use levels, subjects, and a summary.

Standard sources including *Children's Catalog* were consulted in compiling this bibliography.

564   Tomlinson, Carl M. ***Children's Books from Other Countries.*** Scarecrow, 1998, pap., $24.50 (0-8108-3447-2).

Sponsored by USBBY (the United States Board on Books for Young People), this work lists and annotates 724 children's books published between 1950 and 1996 in 29 foreign countries. Many are now out of print, but this bibliography presents an accurate picture of publishing in this area over a period of almost 50 years. The books are organized by genre, with information that includes the original title and country, year, age ranges, and an evaluative annotation. Introductory material discusses the field of international publishing and appendixes list awards, organizations, and publishers. A sequel by Susan Stan, *The World Through Children's Books* (see above), continues the coverage from 1996 through 2000.

565   Totten, Herman L., and Risa W. Brown. ***Culturally Diverse Library Collections for Children.*** Neal-Schuman, 1994, $38.50 (1-55570-140-X).

A total of 1,300 books are recommended for the development of multiethnic collections in elementary and middle schools. The bibliography is divided into four large sections: African Americans, Hispanic Americans, Asian Americans, and Native Americans. Under these headings are further divisions by genre: general nonfiction, biographies, folklore, fiction, reference works, and scholarly works for adults. Each entry provides good bibliographic information, a brief annotation, and suggested ages or grades. Indexes are by author, illustrator, and title. This well-organized, reliable guide would benefit from a revision.

566   Totten, Herman L., et al. ***Culturally Diverse Library Collections for Youth.*** Neal-Schuman, 1996, $38.50 (1-55570-141-8).

A companion to the title above, this bibliography provides annotated entries for books and videos that deal with Asian Americans, African Americans, Hispanic Americans, and Native Americans. An additional section is devoted to multiethnic materials. Each of these sections is divided by genre—biographies, general nonfiction, folklore, fiction, and so forth. Each title is annotated and has full bibliographic data and suggested ages and grades. A revision of this useful title would be welcome. Another companion volume is Irene Wood's ***Culturally Diverse Videos, Audios, and CD-ROMs for Children and Young Adults*** (Neal-Schuman, 1999, $35 [1-55570-377-1]).

567 Webber, Desiree, et al. *Travel the Globe: Multicultural Story Times.* Libraries Unlimited, 1998, $30.30 (1-56308-501-1).

Primarily an activity workbook, this volume contains an annotated list of "Books to Read Aloud" on multicultural themes that makes it valuable for collection development. In the main body of the work, 14 geographic regions are featured, with at least one country per continent. Two sample programs are presented for each region, one for preschool and the other for K–3. Each program includes a story, plus directions for a number of different activities and projects. This is a practical manual with a useful bibliography.

568 *What Do I Read Next? Multicultural Literature.* Gale, 1997, $155 (0-7876-0814-9).

This volume guides children and young adults to recommended titles about Asian Americans, African Americans, Latinos, and Native Americans. Each title entry contains a great deal of information, including author, title, awards, major characters, time period, locale, plot summary, other books by the author, and other recommended books with similar themes and subjects. As with other books in this series, there are many indexes (including an excellent subject approach), which allow readers to locate books from various access points. Though a few years old, this is still a valuable resource.

B. SPECIFIC CULTURES

1. African Americans

569 *The Black Experience in Children's Literature.* New York Public Library, 1999, $8.

This trusted bibliography has gone through many editions; the previous one appeared in 1995. This inexpensive edition contains more than 400 briefly annotated titles dealing with the African American experience. The books are arranged by age groups starting with picture books, continuing with ages 6 to 8, and ending with ages 8 to 12. Books are then subdivided by genres—fiction, folklore, poetry, history, biography, celebrations, and reference. A list of Coretta Scott King Award winners is appended. Copies can be obtained from The Black Experience, Office of Branch Libraries, New York Public Library, 455 5th Ave., New York, NY 10016.

570   Kutenplon, Deborah, and Ellen Olmstead. *Young Adult Fiction by African American Writers, 1968–1993: A Critical and Annotated Guide.* Garland, 1996, $99.95 (0-8153-0873-6).

After an introduction that gives a useful overview of African American literature and an outline of criteria for inclusion, this extensive bibliography lists about 200 novels for young adults written by about 50 African Americans between 1968 and 1993. Each entry gets about two pages of text, including a detailed plot summary and a paragraph of candid evaluations that explore themes, character development, literary quality, and the handling of racial issues. Some may disagree with the author's critical assessments, but they are always stimulating.

571   Rand, Donna, and Toni Trent Parker. *Black Books Galore! Guide to Great African American Children's Books About Boys.* Wiley, 2001, pap., $15.95 (0-471-37527-6).

This work and its companion volume by the same authors, *Black Books Galore! Guide to Great African American Children's Books About Girls* (Wiley, 2001, pap., $15.95 [0-471-37526-8]), each present about 300 gender-specific titles that contain positive depictions of African American characters. The books are arranged first by age/interest level (preschool through early teens) and then by author's last name. In addition to bibliographic information, there are useful annotations, and frequent sidebars contain quotations from famous authors, illustrators, and public figures as well as testimonials from parents and children. There are also indexes by title, author, illustrator, and subject. Though intended for parents, these bibliographies will also be helpful to teachers and librarians.

572   Rand, Donna, and Toni Trent Parker. *Black Books Galore! Guide to More Great African American Children's Books.* Wiley, 2001, pap., $15.95 (0-471-37525-X).

This is a sequel to the authors' *Black Books Galore! Guide to Great African American Children's Books* (Wiley, 1998, pap., $15.95 [0-471-19353-4]), which highlighted 500 titles chosen by black parents for children from birth through young teens. This volume recommends an additional 450 titles, again selected by black parents. Arrangement is by grade level and then alphabetically by title. After extensive bibliographical information, each title is given a brief annotation and an indication of awards, sequels, and series information. Frequent sidebars give profiles of authors and illustrators. Appendixes include a listing of Coretta Scott King Award winners and a bibliography of books for parents and families.

573   Toussaint, Pamela. *Great Books for African-American Children.* Plume, 1999, pap., $12.95 (0-452-28044-3).

In addition to bibliographic information and a brief descriptive annotation, many of the entries in this bibliography of about 250 recommended titles contain usage tips and information about series titles. There are also frequent sidebars that give material on black authors and illustrators and quotations from readers young and old. Lists of out-of-print titles, magazines, videos, Web sites, and other resources are also included.

2. Asian Americans

574 Beck, Peggy. *GlobaLinks: Resources for Asian Studies, Grades K–8.* Linworth, 2002, pap., $39.95 (1-58683-009-0).

GlobaLinks explores both print and nonprint materials in the area of Asian studies and is divided into three parts. The first, and largest, part lists more than 400 items, including fiction, nonfiction, folktales, videos, and CD-ROMs arranged by country and then by author. Each item is annotated and indicates grade-level suitability. Related groups such as Chinese Americans are included under the name of the parent country. Part 2 gives about 500 recommended Web sites, again arranged by country, and Part 3 discusses online key pal/pen pal resources. The appendixes include Web sites that cover multiple countries, and a title index of all the sites mentioned. The many indexes include a thorough one by subject.

575 Blake, Barbara. *A Guide to Children's Books About Asian Americans.* Scolar Press, 1995. $49.95, o.p.

Although the coverage in this bibliography is now more than ten years old, it contains interesting background material that is still of value. The first part covers immigrants and refugees from East Asia, Southeast Asia, and South Asia, with historical and demographic background material. Part 2, the largest section, lists fiction and nonfiction published between 1970 and 1993, each divided by grade level (preschool through 3rd grade and 4th grade through 6th grade). No nonprint material is included. Each entry is well annotated, and the several indexes include one by culture.

3. Hispanic Americans

576 Augenbraum, Harold, and Margarite Fernandez Olmos. *U.S. Latino Literature: A Critical Guide for Students and Teachers.* Greenwood, 2000, $49.95 (0-313-31137-4).

The subjects of the 18 essays in this volume were suggested by 15 high school teachers as those most relevant to their students. The essays, written by Latino scholars, discuss the works of important U.S. Latino authors, among them Piri Thomas, Tomas Rivera, Oscar Higuelos, and Sandra Cisneros. Most essays include a brief biography, analysis of a major work, teaching suggestions, criticism, and suggestions for further reading. The essays cover various ethnic groups, including Cuban Americans and Mexican Americans. A sample outline for a course in Latino literature is appended along with important Web sites, a list of gay Latino writers, and areas for independent study.

577   Dale, Doris Cruger. *Bilingual Children's Books in English and Spanish: An Annotated Bibliography, 1942–2001*. McFarland, 2003, pap., $39.95 (0-7864-1316-6).

This is an updated and revised edition of the author's *Bilingual Books in Spanish and English for Children* (Libraries Unlimited, 1985, o.p.). This edition contains material on 433 books in English and Spanish, chiefly picture, alphabet, and counting books, arranged by author's last name. Each entry is annotated and review sources are cited. There is an interesting introduction on the history of bilingual books in the United States from 1942 through 2001. Appendixes list publishers and review journals and there are author, title, and subject indexes.

578   Day, Frances Ann. *Latina and Latino Voices in Literature: Lives and Works*. Greenwood, 2003, $55 (0-313-32394-1).

This is a revision and expansion of the author's *Latina and Latino Voices in Literature for Children and Teenagers* (Heinemann, 1997, o.p.). After an introductory section on how to detect bias in literature, the main body of this work consists of a series of critical essays on 35 writers, arranged alphabetically by author. For each author, there is a photograph, a biographical sketch, a list of works with summaries, and selections from some of these works, with indications of age suitability and subject content. The works range in reading level from elementary school through adult. Appendixes include material on awards, activities, and additional resources.

579   Immroth, Barbara, and Kathleen de la Peña McCook. *Library Services to Youth of Hispanic Heritage*. McFarland, 2000, pap., $42.50 (0-7864-0790-5).

This valuable collection of essays surveys the strengths and shortcomings of current practices in libraries that serve Hispanic American youngsters. Survey results are cited in chapters that discuss such topics as demographics, successful programs, bilingual education, workshops for parents, and services to migrant workers. A section called "Collections" contains lists of outstanding literature, including Hispanic works. Lists of vendors and book fair sources are appended. This is a practical, no-nonsense guide to collection development and programming in this area.

580   Schon, Isabel. *The Best of Latino Heritage: A Guide to the Best Juvenile Books About Latino People and Cultures.* Scarecrow, 1997, $37.50 (0-8108-3221-6).

This is a revision and continuation of a series of five books first published under the title *A Hispanic Heritage* and then *A Latino Heritage.* The author is the founder and director of the Center for the Study of Books in Spanish for Children and Adolescents at California State University at San Marcos. The present volume contains 21 chapters, each of which lists books in English about a different Spanish-speaking country (a final chapter is on Hispanics in the United States). It covers a variety of books, including fiction, nonfiction, biographies, folklore, and cultural studies, suitable for kindergarten through high school grades. The number of books for each country reflects publishing practices; therefore there are 92 entries for Spain and 160 for Mexico but only one for Bolivia. The annotations are direct and objective and include grade-level suitability. This work is continued in *The Best of Latino Heritage, 1996–2002: A Guide to the Best Juvenile Books About Latino People* (Scarecrow, 2003, $37.50 [0-8108-4669-1]). In both volumes, material on individual countries is followed by surveys of various series, such as Latinos in Baseball. Of great help in each of these volumes is the extensive grade-level index.

581   Schon, Isabel. *Recommended Books in Spanish for Children and Young Adults: 2000 Through 2004.* Scarecrow, 2004, $45 (0-8108-5196-2).

Originally published as a series of six volumes that appeared about every four years under the title *Books in Spanish for Children and Young Adults* (all Scarecrow, various dates and prices), this set had a name change in 1997 with the publication of *Recommended Books in Spanish for Children and Young Adults, 1991–1995* (Scarecrow, 1997, $42.50 [0-8108-3235-6]). That volume was followed by *Recommended Books in Spanish for Children and Young Adults, 1996 Through 1999* (Scarecrow, 2001, $45 [0-8108-3840-0]). The present volume contains more than 1,300 entries divided into four sections: reference, nonfiction (divided by Dewey subject divisions), publishers' series, and fiction, which includes easy books as well as general fiction. Book titles are translated into English for non-Spanish-speaking readers. Entries include extensive annotations and, in addition to author, title, and subject indexes, there is an appendix that lists dealers of books in Spanish by country. This is a unique and very useful selection aid.

582   Schon, Isabel, and Sarah Corona Berkin. ***Introducción a la Literatura Infantil y Juvenil.*** International Reading Association, 1996, pap., $15.95 (0-87207-144-8).

Available only in a Spanish-language edition, this work explains why children's literature is significant, and recommends many Spanish-language books for the young. Each of the 12 chapters deals with a different type of book and includes titles for beginning readers up to young adults. Both original titles and those translated into Spanish are included. Though in need of updating, this work is still of value to the Spanish-speaking population.

583   Wadham, Tim. ***Programming with Latino Children's Materials: A How-to-Do-It Manual for Librarians.*** Neal-Schuman, 1999, $45 (1-55570-352-6).

This work combines a collection development manual with ideas for programs and other usage tips. The first part gives an overview of Latino culture and literature followed by the text in English and Spanish for 100 fingerplays and rhymes, two bilingual puppet shows, and more than 20 programs for use in libraries. The second part discusses criteria for evaluation and selection of material, followed by an 86-page annotated bibliography of professional resources and children's books. Other features include a list of online resources, the Dewey Decimal Classification in Spanish, material on Latino holiday programs, and bilingual publicity materials. A useful, practical guide.

584   Webster, Joan Parker. ***Teaching Through Culture: Strategies for Reading and Responding to Young Adult Literature.*** Arte Publico Press, 2003, pap., $16.95 (1-55885-376-6).

Webster offers an organized approach to the teaching of six young adult novels with Latino themes and characters. Each chapter deals with a different book and gives a story summary, background information, reading activities, and interdisciplinary links to curricular areas—science, social studies, and art, for example. Imaginative writing projects are suggested plus a wide variety of research activities. This is a practical resource for cultural awareness undertakings.

585   York, Sherry. ***Children's and Young Adult Literature by Latino Writers: A Guide for Librarians, Teachers, Parents, and Students.*** Linworth, 2002, pap., $36.95 (1-58683-062-7).

Following an introductory chapter on Latino literature, the remaining chapters are divided by genres such as novels, chapter books, short stories, drama, poetry, nonfiction (arranged by Dewey numbers), and other resources including videos and Web sites. Full bibliographic information is given for each entry plus brief summaries and review citations. Brief biographical information about the authors can be found in the remaining chapters. Two appendixes feature publishers of Latino materials and a directory of "Nearly Latinos" (bilingual storytellers and authors). There are also helpful indexes in this practical book that is a boon to collection development.

586 York, Sherry. *Picture Books by Latino Writers: A Guide for Librarians, Teachers, Parents, and Students.* Linworth, 2002, pap., $36.95 (1-58683-052-X).

This short, useful work highlights 65 picture books that meet the author's criteria—that the work be written in English, in print (as of 2002), set in the United States, and written by an American Latino writer. The main section contains material on each of these books, including bibliographic data, review citations, an annotation, and notes on awards and Web sites. Another section gives brief biographical information on each of the writers and illustrators. Additional features include a subject-title index, a listing of awards, a directory of publishers, and a list of additional titles that did not meet all the criteria for inclusion. This is an excellent guide to a specialized area of publishing.

4. Native Americans

587 Anderson, Vicki. *Native Americans in Fiction: A Guide to 765 Books for Librarians and Teachers, K–9.* McFarland, 1994, $14.95 (0-89950-907-X).

This work is now more than ten years old, but many of the books listed are still in print—most were originally published between 1960 and 1993. The book deals with 116 tribes, and entries are listed alphabetically by tribe and geographical area. As well as bibliographic material, entries include grade level, subjects, and a brief summary. In an appendix, books are arranged by grade level. There are also many indexes.

588 Harvey, Karen, et al. *How to Teach About American Indians: A Guide for the School Library Media Specialist.* Greenwood, 1995, $41.50 (0-313-29227-2).

The purpose of this book is to help anyone (but particularly school librarians) who wants to learn and teach about Native American people and their history, culture, and contemporary issues. Harvey supplies guidelines for selecting resources and gives lists of recommended materials. Individual chapters deal with such topics as Indian lands, spiritual practices, environments, tribal governments, policies, and lifestyles. Various activities are suggested and sample lesson plans are included. This is an excellent sourcebook but it is in need of updating.

589   Jones, Guy W., and Sally Moomaw. *Lessons from Turtle Island: Native Curriculum in Early Childhood Classrooms.* Redleaf, 2002, pap., $29.95 (1-929610-25-4).

After examining how Native Americans have been depicted in children's books in the past, the authors suggest appropriate literature and materials and give strategies for incorporating the study of contemporary Native American cultures into the curriculum. This nicely illustrated volume also deals with "problem books" (and why they are problems) and presents criteria for evaluating the depictions of Native Americans in material for young people.

590   Kuipers, Barbara J. *American Indian Reference and Resource Books for Children and Young Adults.* Libraries Unlimited, 1995, $27.50 (1-56308-258-6).

In an effort to supply accurate, unstereotyped information to her Native American school population, the author developed a checklist for evaluating books that deal with this subject. The application of these criteria to available books on Native Americans led to the development of this list of recommended titles. It is arranged by the Dewey Decimal Classification and then alphabetically by author. For each of the roughly 200 titles, a reading level is given along with bibliographic information, a lengthy annotation, reasons for the book's recommendation, and subject headings. This highly recommended work would benefit from a revision.

591   Molin, Paulette F. *Native American Characters and Themes in Young Adult Literature.* Scarecrow, 2004, $40 (0-8108-5081-8).

This work analyzes Native American characters and themes in young adult literature. After outlining the plot, the author evaluates each book's content in light of the tribal culture depicted. Both old and new titles have been selected for review, some by Native Americans and others not. By using this cross-section of literature that features Native American characters and stories, the author has developed evaluation criteria that can be applied to other books and materials.

592   Slapin, Beverly, and Doris Seale. *Through Indian Eyes: The Native Experience in Books for Children,* 4th ed. University of California, 1998, pap., $25 (0-9356-2646-8).

An expansion of the authors' earlier, now out-of-print editions. this volume consists in large part of book reviews of titles from standard sources and from less familiar presses. A resource section gives information on acquiring print and nonprint materials, curriculum materials, and periodicals, all ranging from preschool through the high school level. There is also a well-selected bibliography of materials by and about Native

Americans. This dependable, honest resource lacks coverage of recently published materials.

593   Stott, Jon C. *Native Americans in Children's Literature.* Oryx, 1995, pap., $24.50 (0-89774-782-8).

In a carefully sequenced series of essays, the author examines and rejects stereotypes relating to Native Americans in children's literature and explores the selection problems that librarians face in this area. The first chapter gives a history of the misrepresentation of Native Americans in children's literature by examining five popular books published between 1901 and 1991. In subsequent chapters, the works of contemporary authors including Paul Goble, Gerald McDermott, Scott O'Dell, and Jean Craighead George are examined and evaluated. There is also a chapter on adaptations of Native American folklore. Each chapter ends with an annotated bibliography of recommended sources, with related reading and classroom suggestions. Although the titles examined and listed are not the most recent, this is still a stimulating work that invites the thoughtful reader.

594   York, Sherry. *Children's and Young Adult Literature by Native Americans: A Guide for Librarians, Teachers, Parents, and Students.* Linworth, 2003, pap., $36.95 (1-58683-119-4).

Organized by such literary types as fiction, folklore, storytelling/drama, poetry, and nonfiction, this work lists and annotates about 390 books written by Native Americans for young readers. (Inclusion does not necessarily imply recommendation.) Each entry includes a summary, subject headings, reading levels, review citations, awards, and relevant Web sites. Other sections cover such resources as important books by non-Native American authors, a list of publishers, and author/illustrator biographies. There are the usual indexes plus an index of the nations represented. This is a fine resource for those seeking books for young people by Native Americans.

C. ENGLISH AS A SECOND LANGUAGE

595   McCaffery, Laura Hibbets. *Building an ESL Collection for Young Adults: A Bibliography of Recommended Fiction and Nonfiction for Schools and Public Libraries.* Greenwood, 1998, $39.95 (0-313-29937-4).

After an introduction on the need for ESL material in the United States, the author lists and annotates more than 500 titles appropriate for English-as-a-second-language students. Entries are organized by genre or topic and then arranged alphabetically by author. Clearly written annotations are accompanied by bibliographic information, Fry reading levels, and interest designators. Most works fall in the 4th- to 6th-grade reading level and have publication dates between 1992 and 1998. An appendix lists distributors of nonprint materials and important Web sites. One of the indexes is by ethnic group. This is a useful publication in this area.

596   Reid, Suzanne. *Book Bridges for ESL Students: Using Young Adult and Children's Literature to Teach ESL.* Scarecrow, 2002, $32.50 (0-8108-4213-0).

Beginning with the basics, such as the first steps an ESL teacher should take with a new class, this clear, straightforward book describes how to use literature from picture books on up as teaching tools. One chapter is aimed at special populations, such as children of migrant workers. There is a bibliography of recommended titles for children and young adults, an annotated bibliography of resources for teachers, and an index that includes titles discussed throughout the text.

597   Rosow, La Vergne. *Light 'n' Lively Reads for ESL, Adult and Teen Readers.* Libraries Unlimited, 1996, $42 (1-56308-365-5).

The author builds this bibliography of high-interest, low-reading-level fiction and nonfiction around 17 thematic units, such as sports, the arts, parenting, racism, science, and biography. Each of these units is subdivided by level of difficulty. The lengthy annotations include material on the usefulness of the titles and often suggest language activities. There are two chapters on preparing for the GED and U.S. citizenship test. This valuable resource for all involved with ESL students is now somewhat dated.

CHAPTER 6

LITERARY AWARDS AND PRIZES

Note: For Web sites devoted to information on awards and prizes, see Chapter 11.

A. GUIDES TO AWARDS AND PRIZES

1. General Guides

598   Allen, Ruth. *Children's Book Prizes: An Evaluation and History of Major Awards for Children's Books in the English-Speaking World.* Ashgate Publishing, 1998, $84.95 (1-85928-237-7).

In separate chapters for each award, the author examines 40 of the most prominent English-language awards, such as the Newbery, Carnegie, Caldecott, and Kate Greenaway medals, the Boston Tribune-Horn Book Awards, and the Coretta Scott King Awards. As well as major awards given in the United States and Great Britain, this work covers Canada, New Zealand, Australia, South Africa, and Ireland. For each award, the author describes its creation and the criteria applied; discusses how it is viewed by authors, publishers, librarians, and booksellers; and provides an assessment of its success in meeting its goals. There are also annotated lists of winners and runners-up, ending with 1997. In addition to being a valuable directory, this is a refreshingly critical look at these awards and the status they hold in various elements of the literary world.

599   *Awards and Prizes Online.* Children's Book Council, 2003. Annual subscription $150; 24-hour usage fee $9.95; http://awardsandprizes. cbcbooks.org.

This online revision and expansion of the 1996 edition now contains information on more than 300 major domestic and international English-language children's book awards. Each entry provides a description of the award, its history and when it is awarded, the name of the sponsor, its address, contact information (e-mail, Web site, fax, and so forth), and a complete but unannotated list of winners and honor books since the award's inception. Publisher and publication date are given for each title; publisher contact information is also supplied. This online version (although a print edition was announced, it was canceled just before publication) gives additional access points such as keywords, award types, and grade and age levels. It also supplies information on discontinued awards and winners. This is the most complete and most current directory of prizes and prize winners presently available.

600   Berman, Matt, and Marigny J. Dupuy. *Children's Book Awards Annual 1998.* Libraries Unlimited, 1998, $18.50, pap. (1-56308-649-2).

Though intended as an annual, this publication lasted for only one volume. Arranged by age groups (picture books, chapter books, and young adult books), this bibliography gives detailed, evaluative information on the 150 books that were in the winner's circle of nine of the most prestigious American children's book awards for the year 1998.

601   Jones, Dolores Blythe. *Children's Literature Awards and Winners: A Directory of Prizes, Authors, and Illustrators*, 3rd ed. Neal-Schuman and Gale, 1994, $120 (0-8103-6900-1).

Although now out of date, this thoroughly researched volume continues to give valuable background information on about 300 awards, both American and international. The first part is a directory that describes each award and lists the winners and runners-up through the early 1990s. Part 2 lists authors and illustrators and the awards they have won; Part 3 is a bibliography of materials (books, articles, and so forth) about these awards. The last part consists of indexes by author, title, illustrator, subject, and award.

602   *Literary Laurels, Kid's Edition: A Guide to Award-Winning Children's Books.* Hillyard, 1996, $11.95 (0-96473-611-X).

Thirty-three American and British children's book awards are highlighted in this volume now in need of an update. Every winning book from each award's inception to 1995 or 1996 is listed with indexes by author, illustrator, and title. Awards are also indexed by age level and specialty. More than 1,200 books are included. This is a companion to the work that features adult titles, *Literary Laurels: A Reader's Guide to Award-Winning Fiction* (Hillyard, 1996).

603   Smith, Laura. *Children's Book Awards International, 1990 Through 2000.* McFarland, 2003, $49.95 (0-7864-1288-7).

This is a companion to the author's now out-of-print *Children's Book Awards International: A Directory of Awards and Winners, From Inception to 1990* (McFarland, 1992), which listed alphabetically by country more than 400 awards that were given in the field of children's literature. After a brief description of the award, there followed a list of winners through 1989 with full bibliographic information. The present volume, a continuation of this valuable resource, uses the same scope and arrangement. A total of 370 awards from 34 countries are included. The United States has the greatest coverage with 142 awards, followed by Canada with 33 and Great Britain with 29. Only awards given to authors and illustrators are cited. Each entry briefly describes the award, establishment date, qualifying conditions, its sponsor, and a contact person and address. There follows a list of the winners and runners-up from 1990 through 2000. Indexes are by author, illustrator, title, and award/sponsoring agency.

2. Guides to Specific Awards

Note: Sources of background information on each of these awards are given in the Directory of Major Awards and Prizes later in this chapter.

A. CARNEGIE AND GREENAWAY MEDALS

604   Barker, Keith. *Outstanding Books for Children and Young People: The Library Association Guide to Carnegie/Greenaway Winners, 1937–1997.* Library Association (distributed by Bernan Associates of Lanham, Md.). 1998, pap., $35 (1-85604-287-1).

The first half of this book deals with Carnegie Medal winners, the second with Kate Greenaway Medal recipients. After general material on each medal and the criteria applied in the deliberations, the author gives full bibliographic material for each winner, an annotation describing the story, and illustrations when appropriate, plus a critical comment on the book's relevance today. Two other guides to these medal winners, now both out of print, are Keith Barker's *In the Realms of Gold* (Library Association, 1986) and Derek Lomas's *50 Years of the Carnegie Medal* (Library Association, 1986).

B. CORETTA SCOTT KING AWARDS

605   Polette, Nancy. *Celebrating the Coretta Scott King Awards: 101 Ideas and Activities.* Alleyside, 2000, pap., $16.95 (1-57950-055-2).

With a chapter for each highlighted book, this activity resource features 19 of the most important award-winning books. Material includes a plot synopsis, reading levels, biographical material on authors and illustrators, before and after reading activities, and Internet links of interest. The project material is printed on reproducible, workbook-like pages. A concluding section lists all the King Awards winners and honor books from 1970 through 2000.

606   Smith, Henrietta M. *The Coretta Scott King Awards Book: 1970–2004,* 3rd ed. American Library Association, 2004, pap., $35 (0-8389-3540-0).

This is both an extension of and companion volume to the 1994 and 1999 publications by the same author with the same title (some material in the old editions is not included in the new work, therefore hold on to both old and new). The updated 2004 work begins with a general discussion of the prize and how it is awarded. The main body is in three parts. The first part lists chronologically the Author Award winners and generously annotates the award winners and honor books. The second part does the same for the Illustrator Award. Material on the New Talent Award Winners is integrated into these two sections depending on whether the recipient is an author or illustrator. The third section contains about 90 brief biographies of prize winners. There are 16 gorgeous, full-color pages of illustrations from recent winners, plus profiles of two writers and alphabetical listings of both author and illustrator winners. This excellent resource is a treasure trove of material on this important award that honors African American talent and culture.

607 Stephens, Claire Gatrell. *Coretta Scott King Award Books: Using Great Literature with Children and Young Adults.* Libraries Unlimited, 2000, pap., $26 (1-56308-685-9).

This activity book helps teachers and librarians use these award winners and integrate them into the curriculum through a series of projects, games, and discussion topics. After a general introduction to the award, its history, and significance, each winner and honor book is listed with a plot description and some selected biographies of authors and illustrators. The most useful section of this work is the variety of activities that can be used to better understand the book, appreciate its importance, and highlight its themes. This book will be useful in both the library and the classroom.

C. NEWBERY AND CALDECOTT MEDALS

608 Bankston, John. *Randolph J. Caldecott and the Story of the Caldecott Medal.* Mitchell Lane, 2003, $19.95 (1-58415-200-1).

Part of the Great Achievement Awards series, this is a simple biography for middle graders that gives a brief profile of Caldecott with examples of his work plus a history of the prizes awarded in his name. There is also a list of winners. Companion volumes in the same series are Bankston's *Michael L. Printz and the Story of the Michael L. Printz Award* (Mitchell Lane, 2004, $19.95 [1-58415-182-X]) and Russell Roberts's *John Newbery and the Story of the Newbery Medal* (Mitchell Lane, 2003. $19.95 [1-58415-201-X]).

609 Bostrom, Kathleen Long. *Winning Authors: Profiles of the Newbery Medalists.* Libraries Unlimited, 2003, $52 (1-56308-877-0).

Covering medal winners from 1922 through 2001, this biographical dictionary supplies 75 interesting profiles of the Newbery Award recipients with details on their personal and writing lives and a complete list of each author's published works. Also included are numerous black-and-white photographs of the authors and a brief history of the award. Simple enough to be used by youngsters, this is a helpful tool for both librarians and students.

610   Comfort, Claudette Hegel. *The Newbery and Caldecott Books in the Classroom.* Incentive Publications, 1999, pap., $14.95 (0-86530-178-6).

This work gives practical advice on how to integrate specific prize-winning books into the curriculum using imaginative activities and goals. Though intended for the classroom, this book will also be of value in planning library programs.

611   Englebaugh, Debi. *Art Through Children's Literature: Creative Art Lessons for Caldecott Books.* Libraries Unlimited, 1994, pap., $25 (1-56308-154-7).

Focusing on such principles and elements as line, color, texture, shape, value, and space, the author has created a series of lessons that involve 57 Caldecott books from 1938 to 1994. Each lesson contains projects with step-by-step instructions, materials lists, and illustrations to help teachers and librarians without art training. Various art media—pencil, marker, chalk, and watercolor, for example—are explored. This is a fine activity book that will inspire an appreciation for Caldecott medal winners.

612   Gillespie, John T., and Corinne J. Naden. *The Newbery Companion: Booktalk and Related Materials for Newbery Medal and Honor Books,* 2nd ed. Libraries Unlimited, 2001, $56 (1-56308-813-4).

This update of the 1996 edition covers Newbery Medal winners and honor books from 1922 through 2001. Arranged chronologically, material on each medal winner includes an introduction giving background information about the author and the book, a detailed plot summary, a discussion of themes and subjects found in the book, an indication (with page numbers) of particular episodes suitable for booktalking, an annotated list of several books related by subject and/or theme, and an extensive bibliography of references about the book and author. There is also a lengthy plot summary for each honor book. Introductory material includes a chapter titled "John Newbery—The Man and the Medal." Also included are an extensive general bibliography and author, title, and subject indexes. Reviewers have called this an "invaluable resource" that should be "a part of any children's library collection."

613   Glandon, Shan. *Caldecott Connections to Social Studies.* Libraries Unlimited, 2000, pap., $25 (1-56308-845-2).

Using 11 Caldecott medal winners as a beginning point, the author describes how these books can be integrated into the language arts curriculum of students in preschool through 3rd grade. After suggestions for studying each title and background information on the illustrations, there is material on curriculum connections, lesson plans, and support materials, many of which will foster cooperation between the library media specialist and classroom teachers. Individual and group projects outlined for each book involve writing, crafts, art, and dramatic presentations. The resources of both the library and the classroom are used. Two companion volumes in this series by the same author are similar in scope and treatment but highlight different medal winners: *Caldecott Connections to Science* (Libraries Unlimited, 2000, $29 [1-56308-687-5]) and *Caldecott Connections to Language Arts* (Libraries Unlimited, 2000, $28.50 [1-56308-846-0]).

614 Goetting, Denice, et al. *Newbery and Caldecott Awards: A Subject Index.* Linworth, 2003, pap., $35 (1-58683-083-X).

This index covers the 622 winners and honor books designated from the beginning of the awards (1922 for the Newbery and 1938 for the Caldecott) through 2003 in an alphabetical subject analysis. Although such a subject index is valuable, this needs some improvements. The subject headings are awkward, and the coverage is inconsistent and often incomplete. Nevertheless, something is better than nothing and this might be of value, however flawed it is.

615 Hegel, Claudette. *Newbery and Caldecott Trivia and More for Every Day of the Year.* Libraries Unlimited, 2000, pap., $26 (1-56308-830-4).

Arranged in calendar format, this book includes more than 1,000 facts and tidbits of information pertaining to the award-winning and classic books and their authors. Useful for bulletin boards, newsletters, and introducing lessons on these books, this compendium of out-of-the-way information can also be used in constructing book contests, observing literary celebrations, and creating interest in these prize winners.

616 Horn Book, Inc., and Association for Library Service to Children. *The Newbery and Caldecott Medal Books 1986–2000: A Comprehensive Guide to the Winners.* American Library Association, 2001, pap., $38 (0-8389-3505-2).

This is the most comprehensive guide available to the winners of the Newbery and Caldecott medals during the 15 years covered in this volume. The body of the book is arranged chronologically. For each of the two annual prize winners, the material supplied includes a plot summary, an interesting personal biographical essay (often by a friend of the author or a family member), a reprint of the author's acceptance speech, an excerpt from the book (in the case of Caldecott winners, this includes a reproduction of the cover illustration), and *Horn Book* and *Booklist* reviews that appeared at the time of the book's publication. Introductory material includes a general preface and three background essays by Kathleen Horning, Maria Salvadore, and *Horn Book* editor Roger Sutton. These essays discuss the history, trends, and significant developments involving these awards during the period covered. In summary, this volume gives an excellent in-depth look at the Newbery and Caldecott, supplies a wealth of background material, and captures the excitement and importance of these awards. Previous volumes in this series that contain similar coverage but for different time periods are available from *Horn Book*. They are (in chronological order by coverage dates):

> Miller, Bertha M., and Elinor Field, eds. *Newbery Medal Books: 1922–1955 with Their Author's Acceptance Papers and Related Material.* Horn Book, 1955, $22.95 (0-87675-396-8).

> Miller, Bertha M., and Elinor Field, eds. *Caldecott Medal Books: 1938–1957.* Horn Book, 1957, o.p.

> Kingman, Lee, ed. *Newbery and Caldecott Medal Books: 1956–1965 with Acceptance Papers, Biographies and Related Material.* Horn Book, 1965, o.p.

> Kingman, Lee, ed. *Newbery and Caldecott Medal Books: 1966–1975 with Acceptance Papers, Biographies and Related Material.* Horn Book, 1975, $22.95 (0-87675-003-4).

> Kingman, Lee, ed. *Newbery and Caldecott Medal Books: 1975–1985 with Acceptance Papers, Biographies and Related Material.* Horn Book, 1985, $24.95 (0-87675-004-8).

617 Lacy, Lyn. *Art and Design in Children's Picture Books: An Analysis of Caldecott Award-Winning Illustrations.* American Library Association, 1986, o.p.

Though now out of print and out of date, this is a pioneering study of the illustrations in Caldecott winners and honor books with an analysis of techniques, materials, composition, and quality. It is still useful for its material on early winners and the opportunity it gives to look at these illustrations in a new way.

618 Lamb, Annette, and Nancy R. Smith. *Newberys and the Net: Thematic Technology Connections.* Vision to Action, 2000, $28.95 (1-891917-02-1).

This wonderful, innovative resource supplies amazing Internet connections for each Newbery Medal winner and runner-up from 1923 through 1999 in reverse chronological order. For each book, there are two or three pages of resource material—overview facts (author, title, etc.), a brief summary of the plot, Internet sites relating to the author and to the book, and classroom connections, some of which are pure entertainment and others that explore themes and subjects found in the book. For example, for Louis Sachar's *Holes*, the 1999 winner, there are sites listed relating to juvenile delinquency, homelessness, desert life, buried treasure, and Texas. Each of the sites is annotated and there are author, title, and subject indexes.

619   Lewis, Marguerite. *Hooked on the Caldecott Award Winners: 60 Crossword Puzzles Based on the Caldecott Gold Medal Books.* Center for Applied Research in Education, 1997, pap., $6.95 (0-87628-424-1).

To increase the knowledge and appreciation of Caldecott winners and to encourage young readers to explore more of them, this slender volume contains 60 unique, pleasantly illustrated crossword puzzles that will add fun to classroom or library exploration of these books. The puzzles cover winners from 1938 through 1997. There is a companion volume for older readers by the same author, *Hooked on the Newbery Award Winners: 75 Wordsearch Puzzles Based on the Newbery Gold Medal Books* (Center for Applied Research in Education, 1996, $6.95 [0-87628-398-9]). Also by Marguerite Lewis is an earlier volume of games and puzzles: *Hooked on Reading: 128 Wordsearch and Crossword Puzzles Based on the Newbery and Caldecott Award Winners* (Center for Applied Research in Education, 1986, $27.95 [0-87628-406-3]).

620   Licciardo-Musso, Lori. *Teaching with Favorite Newbery Books.* Scholastic, 1999, pap., $9.95 (0-590-01975-9).

This book highlights 25 Newbery Award winning books and for each supplies (as the subtitle states) "engaging discussion questions, vocabulary builders, writing prompts, and great literature response activities." Many examples of student work are included. This book is suitable for work with grades 4 through 8.

621   Marcus, Leonard S. *A Caldecott Celebration! Six Authors Share Their Paths to the Caldecott Medal.* Walker, 1998, $19.95 (0-8027-8658-8).

In individual chapters, the author highlights one Caldecott winner for each decade of the medal's existence, beginning with Robert McCloskey's *Make Way for Ducklings* (1942) and ending with David Wiesner's *Tuesday* (1992). Between these books are winners by Marcia Brown, Maurice Sendak, William Steig, and Chris Van Allsburg. For each title, the author/illustrator explains the work's genesis and evolution in text and in sketches and scribbles that show the book's progress to becoming a final prize-winning product. The author/illustrator also describes what winning the award has meant to him or her. This book is filled with wonderful pictures and witty anecdotes (McCloskey bringing 16 ducks to his

Greenwich Village apartment to study their ways and anatomy, for example). A glossary explains artistic and related terms. As the title suggests, the book is a celebration.

622   *The Newbery and Caldecott Awards: A Guide to the Medal and Honor Books.* American Library Association, annual (2004 ed.), $19, pap. (0-8389-3542-7).

This annual comprehensive guide supplies a quick, inexpensive paperback listing of all winning titles and honor books since the inception of the awards (Newbery, 1922; Caldecott, 1938) to the present. Listed in reverse chronological order by year, each title is given a brief (three- or four-line) descriptive annotation. There are author, title, and illustrator indexes. Introductory material includes histories of each award and the criteria for selection. Each edition contains distinctive additional material. For example, the 2003 volume contains an essay on children's reactions to the Newbery Award and material on the media used in Caldecott picture books. Suitable for both the reference and circulating collections, this indispensable work will have many uses, including reading guidance and collection development. Leaflets listing winners and providing other material about these awards are available from the American Library Association and the Association for Library Service to Children. Phone (800) 545-2433 or contact the ALA Order Department at 50 E. Huron St., Chicago, IL 60611.

623   *The Newbery Award* (videocassette). International Reading Association, 2000, $19.95.

The Newbery Medal, its origins and sponsors, and the criteria and mechanics involved in choosing and awarding the medal are the subjects of this 17-minute video for students in the 5th through 8th grades. Highlights of the favorite medal winners and honor books are also presented. A reproducible bookmark and a guide to using the books in the classroom are included.

624   Novelli, Joan. *Using Caldecotts Across the Curriculum.* Scholastic, 1999, pap., $12.95 (0-590-11033-0).

Geared to teachers in K–2 classrooms, this valuable book gives innovative literature-based activities for a number of key Caldecott winners. Each title is allotted four or five pages that include an introduction to the book, lesson plans with instructional materials outlined, general activities, word activities, extensions into various subject areas such as social studies and science, and other books of interest. This is a valuable, well-organized resource.

625   Sharkey, Paulette Bochnig, and Jim Roginski, eds. *Newbery and Caldecott Medal and Honor Books in Other Media.* Neal-Schuman, 1992, $35, o.p.

Though now in need of revision, this volume supplies valuable information about print and nonprint media relating to past Newbery and Caldecott Medal and Honor Books. It lists large-print books, Braille books, talking books, videos, and filmstrips available both commercially and in the public domain. Media about the authors and illustrators, including interviews, are also listed after the book's title. This is a companion to Jim Roginski's *Newbery and Caldecott Medalists and Honor Book Winners* (2nd ed., Neal-Schuman, 1992, o.p.).

626   Sherman, Gale W., and Bette D. Ammon. *Handbook for the Newbery Medal and Honor Books, 1990–1999.* Alleyside, 2000, pap., $19.95 (1-57950-046-3).

In the two or three pages given to each medal winner and honor book, there is a wealth of information—plot summary, ideas for sharing the book, author information, a sample booktalk, curriculum connections, and related titles. Both print and nonprint resources are cited. Sidebars supply additional information such as themes, genre, ordering information, readability and interest levels, and review citations. Appendixes list all the medal and honor books and supply a general list of resources. There are indexes by author/title and by subject/genre. This useful, attractive volume is a continuation of the authors' earlier *Handbook for the Newbery Medal and Honor Books, 1980–1989* (Alleyside, 1991, pap., $19.95 [0-913853-15-1]).

627   Story-Huffman, Ru. *Caldecott on the Net*, 2nd ed. Upstart Books, 2002, pap., $17.95 (1-57950-076-5).

Subtitled *Reading and Internet Activities*, this book outlines more than 20 lesson plans each of which is devoted to a single Caldecott winner and contains activities that involve searching subjects on the Internet and reading titles on the subject. Specific assignments and activities are given along with Web site addresses and lists of books to be consulted. Each lesson also has a section on Web sites suitable for teacher research. The book begins with information on evaluating Web sites and ends with a rundown on important general children's literature sites. This is a valuable resource for both teachers and librarians.

628   Story-Huffman, Ru. *Newbery on the Net*, 2nd ed. Upstart Books, 2002, pap., $17.95 (1-57950-077-3).

A companion to the book listed above, this volume outlines lesson plans for 24 Newbery winners. Each lesson plan involves an assignment, Internet resources, activities, educator notes (with important related Web sites), and lists of follow-up books. The activities are imaginative and easily accomplished. The appendix on additional general Web sites is very useful. This is a practical, unintimidating handbook on using the Internet in worthwhile activities.

Additional out-of-print titles about the Newbery and Caldecott medals are:

629   Brown, Muriel W., and Rita S. Foudray. *Newbery and Caldecott Medalists and Honor Book Winners: Bibliographies and Resource Material Through 1991*, 2nd ed. Neal-Schuman, 1992, o.p.

630   Comfort, Claudette H., and Rita S. Foudray. *Distinguished Children's Literature: The Newbery and Caldecott Winners: The Books and Their Creators*. Denison, 1990, o.p.

631   Peterson, Linda K., and Marilyn L. Solt, eds. *Newbery and Caldecott Medal and Honor Books, 1922–1981*. Hall, 1982, o.p.

632   Woolman, Bertha, and Patricia Litsey. *The Newbery Award Winners: The Books and Their Authors*. Denison, 1992, o.p.

D. KERLAN AWARD

633   Berman, Ruth. *The Kerlan Awards in Children's Literature (1975–2001)*. Pogo Press, 2003, pap., $17.95 (1-880654-25-3).

The Kerlan Award is presented annually "in recognition of singular attainments in the creation of children's literature and in appreciation for generous donation of unique resources to the Kerlan Collection." This volume is a collection of the acceptance speeches, biographical information, pertinent artwork, and related materials for the first 26 years of the award. Madeleine L'Engle, Barbara Cooney, Mary Stolz, Phyllis Reynolds Naylor, and Lois Lenski are among the writers and illustrators included.

E. ORBIS PICTUS AWARD

634   Zarnowski, Myra, et al. *The Best in Children's Nonfiction: Reading, Writing, and Teaching Orbis Pictus Award Books*. National Council of Teachers of English, 2001, pap., $21.95 (0-8141-0489-4).

Past and present members of the selection committee of this award discuss the process and issues involved in selecting each year's winner, honor books, and recommended titles. The world of children's nonfiction literature is introduced, with tips on how to present and teach the award-winning texts. Many of the winning authors are highlighted, reflecting on their work during the 1990s.

F. PHOENIX AWARD

635   Helbig, Alethea, and Agnes Perkins, eds. *The Phoenix Award of the Children's Literature Association, 1995–1999.* Scarecrow, 2001, pap., $37.50 (0-8108-4014-6).

This annual award, established in 1985, honors books whose merits were not fully recognized when first published. The present volume covers the five-year period from 1995 through 1999. For each year's winners, the acceptance speeches of the authors are reprinted as well as relevant papers that were presented at that Children's Literature Association conference. These papers are usually three to five pages long for winning titles and a single page for honor titles. Biographical information about each of the winners is also given. In this volume the main award winners are Laurence Yep, Robert Cormier, Alan Garner, Jill Paton Walsh, and E. L. Konigsburg. Honor book writers include Natalie Babbitt and William Steig. This valuable resource is the third in a series by Helbig and Perkins. The previously published titles are:

> *The Phoenix Award of the Children's Literature Association 1985–1989* (Scarecrow, 1996, o.p.) and *The Phoenix Award of the Children's Literature Association 1990–1994* (Scarecrow, 1996, $45 [0-8108-3191-0]). Also available from the publisher is a packaged set of all three volumes, priced at $98.50 (0-8108-4053-7).

B. DIRECTORY OF MAJOR AWARDS AND PRIZES

1. International

636   *Astrid Lindgren Memorial Award for Literature;* www.alma.se.

This award was founded by the Swedish government to honor the memory of Astrid Lindgren, the beloved Swedish author and creator of Pippi Longstocking. Its aim is to increase global interest in literature for children and young adults. This annual award consists of prize money valued at 5 million kronor or roughly $500,000. It was awarded for the first time in June 2003, to two writers: the author-artist Maurice Sendak of the United States and the Austrian Christine Noestlinger, whose stories have enchanted millions of children worldwide. Brazilian author Lygia Bojunga was given the 2004 award.

637   *Hans Christian Andersen Award*; www.ibby.org/index.php?id=273.

This prestigious award (often called "the little Nobel Prize") is administered by the IBBY Secretariat (Nonnenweg 12, Postfach, CH-4003, Basel, Switzerland) and consists of a gold medal and a diploma awarded biennially to an author and an artist based on the entire body of their work and the fact that they are considered to have made a lasting contribution to children's and young adult literature. The author prize was established in 1956 and the medal for illustrators in 1966. Winners are elected by a jury composed of its president, the president of IBBY, and eight elected children's literature experts. Some recent American prize winners include Virginia Hamilton, Katherine Paterson, and Tomi Ungerer. In 2004, Ireland's Martin Waddell won the author award and Max Velthuijs from the Netherlands received the illustrator award.

638   *IBBY Honour List*; www.ibby.org/index.php?id=270.

Every two years since 1956, the year the Hans Christian Andersen Award was established, IBBY has issued its list of honor books. Each national section can submit three entries for recently published books—one for excellence in writing, one for illustration, and one for translation.

639   *UNICEF-Ezra Jack Keats International Award for Excellence in Children's Book Illustration.*

This award, established in 1986 by the Ezra Jack Keats Foundation in New York, was given to one to five picture books published in the previous five years that showed at least one of the goals of the United Nations and UNICEF, including family, peace, nature, cultural unity, and diversity. The award was given biennially and consisted of $5,000 and a medal. Since 1994, this award has been put "on hold"; but it is hoped to reinstate it in the future.

2. Australia

640   *Bilby (Books I Love Best Yearly) Awards*; www.pa.ash.org.au/cbc/bilbyawards.

Established in 1990, these awards named for the bilby, a rare species of bandicoot, are given to books selected by children in three categories: Early Readers (8 years and younger), Younger Readers (9 to 11 years), and Older Readers (12 and older). The award is administered by the Queensland branch of the Children's Book Council of Australia.

641   *Children's Book Council of Australia Children's Books of the Year Awards*; www.cbc.org.au/awards.htm.

These, the most prestigious children's book awards in Australia, were established in 1946 and are given annually in four categories: Early Childhood, Younger Readers, Older Readers, and Picture Book of the Year. The award consists of A$30,000 divided among these categories. The council also administers the Eve Pownall Award for Non-Fiction (see below). The books are selected by the Children's Book Council of Australia. A short list is published in March, followed by the announcement of winners during Children's Book Week in July or August.

642   *Children's Peace Literature Award*, www.psychology.org.au/aps/awards/ 1.4_10.asp.

Founded in 1987 by Psychologists for the Prevention of War, this award is given biennially to the author of a book published in the preceding two years by an Australian writer or resident that promotes peace, international relations, and racial tolerance.

643   *Dromkeen Medal*, www.scholastic.com.au/common/dromkeen.

Named after the estate where Joyce and Courtney Oldmeadow established the Dromkeen collection of Australian children's literature, this prize is awarded annually to an Australian citizen who has made a significant contribution to the appreciation and development of children's literature. Winners include Mem Fox and Colin Thiele.

644   *Environment Award for Children's Literature*; www.cbc.org.au/ awards.htm.

This award, established in 1994, is given annually to the authors of fiction and nonfiction books that encourage positive attitudes toward the caring and understanding of the natural world and promote an awareness of environmental issues.

645   *Eve Pownall Award for Information Books*; www.cbc.org.au/ awards1.htm.

Administered by the Children's Book Council of Australia, this award is the counterpart of the American Robert F. Silbert Award, which honors the best informational book published for youngsters within a given year. Established in 1993, the award consists of cash prize of A$10,000.

646   *Western Australia Young Readers Book Award*, www.wayrba.iinet.net.au.

This is one of several prizes awarded by state and other regional associations and agencies. Founded in 1980, the award (a wooden trophy designed as a book) is given for a book published within the past five years and nominated and voted on by young readers. Frequent winners include Brian Jacques, John Marsden, and Roald Dahl. Another award selected by children is the Young Australia Best Book Award (YABBA) begun in 1987 and sponsored by the Young Australian Best Book Award Council in Victoria. For a longer list of regional Australian children's book awards—for example, the Patricia Wrightson Award (New South Wales) and COOL (Canberra's Own Outstanding List)—consult one of the directories of international children's book awards mentioned above or the Web sites listed in Chapter 11 that have material on awards and prizes.

3. Canada

647   *Amelia Frances Howard-Gibbon Illustrators Award*; www.cla.ca/awards/ afhgwinners.htm.

Established by the Canadian Library Association in 1971, this annual award of a silver gilt medal is given to the illustrator of the outstanding children's book published during the previous year. The book must by suitable for children up to age 14, and the illustrator must be a Canadian or resident of Canada.

648   *Canadian Library Association Book of the Year for Children*; www.cla.ca/awards/boyc.htm.

The Canadian Association of Children's Librarians of the Canadian Library Association (headquarters in Ottawa) founded this award in 1946. This is an annual award given by vote of a committee from the association "for an outstanding children's book by a Canadian author or an author resident in Canada." The book must be suitable for children up to age 14. The award, considered the most prestigious in Canada, consists of a bronze medal.

649   *Canadian Library Association Young Adult Canadian Book Award*; www.cla.ca/awards/yawinners.htm.

A companion to the award described above, this annual award is given to the author of an outstanding English-language book for young adults (ages 13 to 18) published in Canada within a given year and written by a citizen or resident of the country. Established in 1980, the award consists of a leather-bound copy of the book with the award seal embossed on the cover.

650   *Elizabeth Mrazik-Cleaver Canadian Picture Book Award*; www.ibby-canada.org/cleaver.html.

Administered by IBBY Canada, whose headquarters are in Toronto, this award of a scroll and C$1,000 is given annually to a Canadian illustrator of a picture book published in Canada in English or French during a given year. All genres (fiction, nonfiction, folktales, and so forth) are considered.

651 *Geoffrey Bilson Award for Historical Fiction for Young People*; www.bookcentre.ca/awards/bilson/index.shtml.

Administered by the Toronto-based Canadian Children's Book Centre, this annual award, established in 1988, is given to the author of an outstanding work of historical fiction for young people published within a given year. The prize is C$1,000 and the winner must be a Canadian.

652 *Governor General's Literary Awards*; www.canadacouncil.ca/prizes/ggla.

These awards are given annually to the best English-language and French-language books published in the previous year in seven categories including adult fiction and nonfiction. Two of the categories are Children's Literature (Text) and Children's Literature (Illustration). The awards, sponsored by the Canada Council in Ottawa, were established in 1987 and are for C$10,000 each.

653 *Information Book Award*; www.library.ubc.ca/edlib/table/awards/information.html.

The Children's Literature Roundtables of Canada sponsor this annual award of C$500 for the outstanding informational book published in Canada for children ages 5 to 15. The book must be in English and written by a Canadian or resident of Canada.

654 *Mr. Christie Book Award.*

These annual awards, which were established in 1990 and continued through 2004, were sponsored by Christie Brown and Co. in Toronto. Six awards (three for English-language books and three for French-language books) were given in three different categories (ages 7 and under, ages 8 to 11, and ages 12 and up) for books written or illustrated by a Canadian and published in the previous year.

655 *Norma Fleck Award for Canadian Children's Nonfiction*; www.bookcentre.ca/awards/norma_fleck.

Sponsored by the Fleck family and administered by the Canadian Children's Book Centre in Toronto, this award, established in 1999, consists of a C$10,000 prize (one of the largest in Canadian children's book publishing) and is presented annually to an author and illustrator of a Canadian nonfiction book for children.

656   *Ruth Schwartz Children's Book Award*, www.arts.on.ca/English/
The-Ruth-Schwartz-Childrens-Book-Awards.html.

Administered by the Ontario Arts Council in Toronto, this award was
founded in 1976 by the Ruth Schwartz Foundation to "reward the best
creative effort in children's literature for a particular year." Nominations
come from members of the Canadian Booksellers Association and the
final selection is made by a jury of high school children. All books must
be published in Canada and be by a Canadian author or illustrator.

There are additional regional and provincial agencies and organizations in
Canada that award prizes for excellence in children's literature—for example
the Sheila A. Egoff Children's Book Prize (British Columbia) and the Ontario
Red Maple Award. There are also many awards for books published in French.
For more details, check the directories mentioned above and the Web sites list-
ed in Chapter 11.

4. Ireland

657   *CBI/Bisto Book of the Year Award*, http://childrensbooksireland.com/
bisto_book_awards.

Administered by Children's Books Ireland, this award, established in
1990, is given for the best book of the year written or illustrated by a
native or resident of Ireland. Three merit awards are also given annually.
Books must be written in English or Irish. In addition to a cash prize,
the overall winner receives a bronze trophy by Joseph Sloane.

658   *Eilis Dillon Memorial Award*, http://childrensbooksireland.com/
bisto_book_awards.

Named after the famous Irish writer who published almost 40 books for
children before he died in 1994, this award—established in 1994 and
administered by Children's Books Ireland—is given annually to the Irish
author of an outstanding first children's book.

659   *Reading Association of Ireland Children's Book Award*, www.reading.ie/
book_awards.html.

Given every two years for outstanding books for children and adolescents published in Ireland in the preceding year, these awards are judged
by teachers and librarians. Also awarded biennially is the Special Merit
Award, given to the book the judges believe has made a significant contribution to publishing for children in Ireland.

5. New Zealand

660   *Esther Glen Award*; http://lib.cce.ac.nz/nzcba/estherg.

This annual award was established in 1945 and is administered by the Library and Information Association of New Zealand Aotearoa. It is given to the book by a New Zealand author that represents the most distinguished contribution to literature for children. Margaret Mahy has won the award five times; in some years no award has been granted.

661   *Gaelyn Gordon Award*; http://lib.cce.ac.nz/nzcba/gaelyn.

Administered by the Children's Literature Foundation of New Zealand, this annual award, established in 1998, honors a book from New Zealand that has been a favorite of children for a long time. The author must be still living and the book must have been in print for at least five years.

662   *LIANZA Young People's Non-fiction Award*; http://lib.cce.ac.nz/nzcba/nonfic.

Established by the Library and Information Association of New Zealand Aotearoa in 1987, this award is made annually to the New Zealand author of the most distinguished contribution to nonfiction for young people.

663   *Margaret Mahy Medal Award*; http://lib.cce.ac.nz/nzcba/mahy.

Named for the important New Zealand writer of books for both children and young adults, this award, established in 1991, is administered by the Children's Literature Foundation of New Zealand, and is given to an individual in recognition of excellence in children's literature, publishing, and literacy in New Zealand.

664   *New Zealand Post Children's Book Award*; www.nzbooks.com/nzbooks/static/nzpost.asp.

Sponsored by Booksellers New Zealand and formerly known as the AIM Children's Book, this award is given in different categories—picture books, fiction at various levels, first books, nonfiction, and a "children's choice" award. From these is chosen the Book of the Year.

665   *Russell Clark Award*; http://lib.cce.ac.nz/nzeba/clark.

Named after the prominent New Zealand illustrator, this annual award, first presented in 1978, is given to a New Zealand illustrator for the most distinguished illustrations for a book for children or young adults.

666   *Te Kura Pounamu Award*; http://lib.cce.ac.nz/nzcba/tekura.

Established in 1995 by the Library and Information Association of New Zealand Aotearoa, this award is given annually to the author of a book for young people written in the Maori language. The author must be a citizen or resident of New Zealand.

667   *Tom Fitzgibbon Award*; http://lib.cce.ac.nz/nzcba/fitz/.

Named for the man who contributed richly to New Zealand's children's literature, this award is administered by the Children's Literature Foundation of New Zealand. Established in 1996, it is given annually to the best first manuscript of a previously unpublished writer who is a citizen or resident of New Zealand.

6. South Africa

668   *Percy Fitzpatrick Award*; www.childlit.org.za/percyfitzpatrick.html.

Sponsored by the English Academy of Southern Africa, this biennial award is given to the author of a children's book in English. The author must be living in South Africa or the book must be from a South African perspective.

Many literary prizes are awarded in South Africa for books written in languages other than English.

7. United Kingdom

669   *Angus Book Award*; www.angus.gov.uk/bookaward/information.htm.

To encourage teenagers to read more, participating students read five short-listed titles chosen by teachers and librarians written by British writers and published in paperback within the preceding 12 months. The winner is announced in March at a ceremony at which many of the students participate.

670   *Aventis Prizes for Science Books*; www.aventisprizes.com.

In conjunction with the Science Museum in London, these two annual awards are given to authors of nonfiction books on popular science and technology. The first is a General Prize for the best book written for the general reader; the second, the Junior Prize, is awarded to the best book written for children under 14. The prize winners and short-listed authors share a prize of £30,000. The award was established in 2000 and was formerly known as the Rhone-Poulenc Prize for Science Books.

671   *Blue Peter Book Award;* www.bbc.co.uk/cbbc/bluepeter.

Begun in 2000, these awards are sponsored by the BBC children's program Blue Peter and operated with the cooperation of public libraries
throughout the UK. The awards are determined by votes of youngsters
nationwide. The three categories are "The book I couldn't put down,"
"The best book to read aloud," and "The best book with facts in it."
From these three winners is chosen the Blue Peter Book of the Year.

672   *Books for Children Award* (formerly Mother Goose Award).

The Mother Goose Award, which was discontinued in 2000, has been
revived using different criteria. An award of £1,000 is administered by
the magazine *Books for Children* and is presented annually to the most
exciting newcomer to British children's literature whether writer or illustrator.

673   *Booktrust Teenage Prize;* www.booktrusted.co.uk/booktrust/teenage.

Begun in 2003 by Book Trust in London, this award recognizes and celebrates contemporary teenage fiction. A shortlist of about ten titles is
selected in the spring and the winner is announced in November.

674   *Carnegie Medal;* www.carnegiegreenaway.org.uk.

First awarded in 1937, the Carnegie Medal is the most prestigious award
presented to an author of children's books in the UK. It is given to an
outstanding work of fiction or nonfiction for children or young people,
written in English and published first or concurrently in the UK during
the year preceding the year in which the award is presented. Until 1969,
the award was restricted to British writers. Previously under the aegis of
the Library Association, the medal is now awarded by CILIP (the Chartered Institute of Library and Information Professionals). Recent winners
include Philip Pullman, David Almond, and Aidan Chambers. The
2004 winner was an American writer, Jennifer Donnelly, for *A Gathering
Light*.

675   *Children's Laureate;* www.childrenslaureate.org.

Administered by the British section of the International Board on Books
for Young People, this biennial award recognizes and highlights the
importance of exceptional children's authors. It celebrates both a lifetime's achievement and the author's role in creating readers of the future.
The judges receive nominations from a variety of sources, including children, librarians, critics, writers, and booksellers. The first laureate was
Quentin Blake; the second, Anne Fine; and the third, the 2003–2005
winner, is Michael Morpurgo.

676   *Eleanor Farjeon Award*; no Web site located.

Founded in 1965 and named after the outstanding British children's book author, this award, which consists of a certificate and £500, is sponsored by the Children's Book Circle in London. Awarded annually, the prize is given to an individual in recognition of his or her distinguished contribution to the world of children's books. The 2004 winner was Jacqueline Wilson.

677   *Guardian Children's Fiction Award*; www.booktrusted.co.uk/prizes.

This award, established in 1966, was administered for many years by the distinguished young adult author John Rowe Townsend, who was also a literary editor of the *Guardian* newspaper. It is given annually for a work of fiction published in British by a British or Commonwealth author in the preceding year. Picture books and books by previous winners are included. This award, now of £1,500, is similar in its criteria to the Carnegie Medal, discussed above.

678   *Kate Greenaway Medal*; www.carnegiegreenaway.org.uk.

The most important award for picture books in the UK, this was established in 1955 and is now awarded by the Chartered Institute of Library and Information Professionals. It is named for the distinguished Victorian book illustrator and is given annually to the artist who, in the opinion of a committee of librarians, has created the best illustrations for a picture book. The book must have been published in the UK during the year preceding the year in which the award is presented.

679   *Kurt Maschler Award*; www.literature-awards.com/kurt_maschler_award_for_children.htm.

Established in 1982 by Kurt Maschler to honor the memory of Erich Kästner and Walter Trier, the author and illustrator of *Emil and the Detectives*, this annual award is given to the author and illustrator of a children's book that combines excellence in both text and illustration. The prize is £1,000 and an "Emil," a bronze figure of Kästner's famous character.

680   *Marsh Award*; no Web site located.

Administered by the University of Surrey Roehampton and first awarded in 1996, this biennial award honors the best translation into English of a children's book, by a British translator and published in the UK by a British publisher. The 2004 winner was the translator of *Eye of the Wolf* by Daniel Pennac, a French author.

681   *Red House Children's Book Award*; www.redhousechildrensbookaward.
co.uk/about.htm.

Known as the Children's Book Award when it was established in 1980,
this prize is now sponsored by Red House Books, a bookseller and children's book club organizer, but continues to be administered by Federation of Children's Book Groups. The award is selected entirely by
children. Books are furnished by publishers and sent out for review to
ten of the federation's children's books groups. Votes are tabulated, and
the prizes are given annually in three categories: Books for Younger Children, Books for Younger Readers, and Books for Older Readers.

682   *Sainsbury's Baby Book Award*; www.booktrust.org.uk/prizes/btprizes/baby.

Sponsored by the British supermarket chain and administered by Book
Trust, this is an annual award for the best book for babies. The prize is
intended to emphasize the importance of the first book a baby receives
and to highlight the importance of sharing books with babies. Both the
author/illustrator and the publisher receive trophy obelisks and, in addition, the author is given a check for £2,000.

683   *Signal Poetry Award.*

Founded by Aidan and Nancy Chambers in 1979 and named after their
now also defunct periodical, the purpose of this award was to highlight
excellence in poetry published for children and in the work done to promote poetry with children. The award was given from 1979 through
2001, and was presented annually in the spring. One hopes that the gap
left by this award will be filled by the one proposed to begin in 2005
that will be sponsored by *The Lion and the Unicorn* periodical (Johns
Hopkins Press).

684   *Smarties Prize*; www.booktrusted.com/nestle/prize.html.

Begun in 1985, sponsored by the Nestle chocolate company (maker of
Smarties) and administered by Book Trust, these three annual prizes—
one for children 5 years and under, another for children 6 to 8 years, and
the last for children 9 to 11—are awarded for books of excellence published in English and written by a UK citizen or resident within the preceding year. Recent winners have included J. K. Rowling, Philip
Pullman, and David Almond.

685   *Times Educational Supplement Information Book Awards*;
www.booktrusted.co.uk/prizes.

Established in 1972 and sponsored by the *Times Educational Supplement*,
this award is given to the author and illustrator of the best information

books published in the UK or Commonwealth during a given year. There are two awards: the junior award for children up to age 11, and the senior award for the 11 to 16 age group.

686   *Tir Na n-Og Awards*; www.cllc.org.uk/child_tirnanog.html.

Sponsored by the Welsh Book Council and established in 1976, there are awards in three categories: best fiction book of the year in the Welsh language, best nonfiction book in the Welsh language, and best English book of the year that depicts an authentic Welsh background.

687   *W. H. Smith Book Awards*; www.whsmith.co.uk.

Sponsored by the famous book chain and begun in 2001, these are the only nationwide British book awards that are voted for entirely by the public. The top accolades are given to the authors who are truly the people's favorites. There is a main prize and several runners up annually. The 2002 book of the year was *Artemis Fowl* by Eoin Colfer.

688   *Whitbread Children's Book of the Year Award*; www.whitbread-book awards.co.uk.

This important and lucrative literary award, sponsored by the Whitbread Breweries and administered by the Booksellers Association of Great Britain and Ireland, was established in 1972. To be eligible, the book must have been published in the UK or Ireland and written by a resident of either country. Past winners include Rumer Godden, Leon Garfield, Roald Dahl, Peter Dickinson, and David Almond.

A number of important children's book awards originate with regional agencies or organizations. Some of the most prominent are the Stockton Children's Book of the Year (Stockton Borough Schools), Lancashire County Library Children's Book of the Year, South Lanarkshire Book Awards, Sheffield Children's Book Award, North East Book Award, and the Scottish Arts Council Children's Book Award.

8. United States

A. National Awards

689   *Aesop Prize*; www.afsnet.org/sections/children/.

Established by the American Folklore Society (Mershon Center, Ohio State University, 1501 Neil Ave., Columbus, OH 43201-2602; (614/292-3375 4350 N. Fairfax Dr., Arlington, VA 22203), this annual award is given to an outstanding book published in English for children or young adults that incorporates folklore into its text. Past winners have included Paul Goble in 1993 for *Love Flute* and Julius Lester in 1994 for *John Henry*.

690   *ALAN Award;* www.alan-ya.org.

This award, founded in 1974 by the Assembly on Literature for Adolescents (ALAN) of the National Council of Teachers of English, is given annually to honor "outstanding contributions to the field of adolescent literature by a publisher, author, librarian, scholar, editor, or anyone whose gift to the ALAN community calls out for recognition." The 2002 award was given to Paul Zindel shortly before his death; the 2003 co-winners were Norma Fox Mazer and her husband Harry Mazer; and in 2004 Jacqueline Woodson was the recipient.

691   *Alex Awards*; www.ala.org/yalsa/booklists/alex/.

Founded in 1993, the Alex Awards are funded by the Margaret Alexander Edwards Trust and cosponsored by *Booklist*. They honor the top ten adult books most suitable for teenagers published during the previous calendar year. The award is named for a respected young adult librarian who worked at the Enoch Pratt Free Library in Baltimore and who was known to her friends as Alex. The books are selected by a nine-member committee of the Young Adult Library Services Association and are judged on literary quality, readability, and appeal to readers age 12 to 18.

692   *Americas Award for Children and Young Adult Literature*; www.uwm.edu/Dept/CLACS/outreach/americas.html.

Sponsored by the Consortium of Latin American Studies Programs (CLASP) at the University of Wisconsin-Milwaukee (2513 E. Hartland Ave., Pearse Hall 168, Milwaukee, WI 5321), this annual award, now in existence for more than ten years, recognizes children's and young adult fiction, poetry, folklore, or nonfiction that "authentically and engagingly portrays the cultures of Latin America, the Caribbean, or Latinos in the United States" in English or in Spanish. The range is wide—from picture books to works for young adults—and only two winning works are chosen each year: a picture book and a work of fiction.

693   *Anne Spencer Lindbergh Prize in Children's Literature*; www.lindberghfoundation.org/events/lind-prize.html.

Sponsored by the Charles A. and Anne Morrow Lindbergh Foundation in Anoka, Minnesota, this prize is awarded biannually to the author of a children's fantasy judged to be the best published in English over a two-year period. In 1998, the winner was J. K. Rowling's *Harry Potter and the Sorcerer's Stone*.

694   *Bank Street College of Education Annual Book Awards*;
www.bankstreet.edu/bookcom/awards.html.

Each year, the Children's Book Committee of the Bank Street College of
Education (610 W. 112th St, New York, NY 10025) awards three prizes
for distinguished children's books published the previous year. They are:
the Josette Frank Award for fiction, the Flora Stieglitz Straus Award for
nonfiction, and the Claudia Lewis Award for poetry. The awards began
in 1943 and sometimes include a Lifetime Achievement Award.

695   *Book Sense Book of the Year Award*; www.bookweb.org/news/awards/
3433.html.

Formerly known as the American Booksellers Book of the Year (ABBY)
Award, this prize was founded by the American Booksellers Association
(828 South Broadway, Tarrytown, NY 10591) and honors the book that
ABA member bookstores most enjoyed recommending to their customers during the previous year. The children's book award was established in 1993. The 1999 winner was J. K. Rowling's *Harry Potter and
the Sorcerer's Stone*.

696   *Boston Globe-Horn Book Awards*; www.hbook.com/awards/bghb/
default.asp.

Established in 1967 and co-sponsored by the *Boston Globe* and the *Horn
Book Magazine*, these annual awards are now given in three categories:
Fiction and Poetry, Nonfiction, and Picture Book. The nonfiction award
was added in 1976. These are now considered among the most prestigious prizes awarded in the United States. It is customary to designate
several honor books in each of these divisions. Acceptance speeches and
related material are reprinted in the January-February issue of the *Horn
Book Magazine*.

697   *Caldecott Medal*; www.ala.org/alsc/caldecott.html.

Correctly called the Randolph Caldecott Medal, this award was named
after the great 19th-century English book illustrator and was founded in
1937 through the generosity of Frederic G. Melcher, then editor of *Publishers Weekly*. Chosen by a committee of the Association for Library Service to Children (ALSC) of the American Library Association, the award
is given to "the artist of the most distinguished picture book for children
published in the United States during the preceding year." The award is
restricted to artists who are citizens or residents of the United States.
Considered the most important award for picture book art in this country, the committee also designates honor books each year.

698 *Carter G. Woodson Book Award;* www.socialstudies.org/awards/woodson/.

Administered by the National Council for the Social Studies (8555 16th St., Silver Spring, MD 20910), this annual award is given for a nonfiction book with an American setting. The book should also contain material on one or more racial or ethnic minority groups and accurately portray the group's values and culture.

699 *Charlotte Zolotow Award;* www.soemadison.wisc.edu/ccbc/books/zolotow.asp.

Named after the distinguished author/editor of children's books, this annual award recognizes the author of the best text in a picture book published in the United States in the preceding year. In addition to the main winner, there are designated honor books each year. The sponsor is the Cooperative Children's Book Center of the School of Education of the University of Wisconsin-Madison (4290 Helen C. White Hall, 600 N. Park St., Madison, WI 53706). This agency also sponsors the annual Charlotte Zolotow Lecture.

700 *Chicago Tribune Young Adult Fiction Prize;* http://about.chicago tribune.com/community/literaryawards.htm.

This annual prize honors the author of a book that the newspaper feels is worthy by its high literary quality and inclusion of subjects and themes pertinent to a young adult audience. The selection is made from books suitable for ages 12 through 18.

701 *Child Study Children's Book Award;* www.bankstreet.edu/bookcom/awards.html.

Established in 1943 by the Children's Book Committee at Bank Street College of Education (610 W. 112th St., New York, NY 10025), this annual award is given to the best book written for children ages 8 through 13 that best portrays realistically and in a positive way, a universal problem such as war, poverty, or personal problems. The book is chosen from the College's annual "Children's Books of the Year" bibliography.

702 *Christopher Awards;* www.christophers.org/awardsmm.html.

Sponsored by the Christophers (12 E. 48th St., New York, NY 10017), these awards honor writers, illustrators, and others in the arts and entertainment fields whose work affirms "the highest values of the human spirit." The children's book awards have categories for picture books, middle grades, and young adult. Picture books, fiction, and nonfiction are eligible, but books must have been published during the preceding calendar year.

703   *Coretta Scott King Award*; www.ala.org/ala/emiert/
corettascottkingbookawards/corettascott.htm.

Established in 1969, these awards are administered by the Coretta Scott
King Task Force of the American Library Association's Social Responsi-
bilities Round Table. Each year, they honor African American authors
and illustrators of outstanding books for children and young adults. The
author award was first given in 1970; the illustrator award was established in 1974. A third award, now known as the Coretta Scott King/
John Steptoe New Talent Award, was begun in 1995. In addition to the
main author and illustrator awards, honor books are usually designated
each year.

704   *Dolly Gray Award*; www.dddcec.org/dolly_gray_award.htm.

This biannual award recognizes fictional books for children that give
positive portrayals of individuals with developmental disabilities. It is
sponsored by the Division on Developmental Disabilities of the Council
for Exceptional Children.

705   *Edgar Allan Poe Awards*; www.mysterywriters.org/pages/awards/
index.htm.

Also known as the "Edgars," these awards were established by the Mystery Writers of America (17 E. 47th St, 6th Floor, New York, NY 10017)
in 1945. There are currently two annual awards in the juvenile category:
one for the best mystery for children published in the United States and
one for the best book for a young adult audience. The award is a citation
and a ceramic bust of Poe.

706   *Ezra Jack Keats New Writer and Illustrator Award*; www.ezra-jack-keats.
org/programs/nyplawards.htm.

This award was established in 1983 and honors the memory of the
much-loved illustrator. It is jointly sponsored and administered by the
Ezra Jack Keats Foundation and the New York Public Library. Its purpose is to encourage new talent in the field of children's literature and
illustration. Two awards are given annually, one for the text of a picture
book and one for illustrations in a picture book.

707   *Golden Kite Award*; www.scbwi.org/awards/gk_main.htm.

Founded in 1971, these awards are given annually by the Society of
Children's Book Writers and Illustrators (8271 Beverly Blvd., Los Angeles, CA 90048) in four categories: fiction, nonfiction, picture book text,
and picture book illustrations. Eligible books are written and/or illustrated by members of the society, and members of the society select the win-

ners. These are the only awards given to writers and illustrators by their peers.

708   *Grolier Foundation Award*; http://www.ala.org/
Template.cfm?Section=awards.

Presented annually by the Grolier Foundation, this award is given to a librarian whose contributions to the "stimulation and guidance" of children's and young adult reading exemplify outstanding achievement in the profession. The 2000 winner was Michael Cart.

709   *Gryphon Award for Children's Literature*; www.lis.uiuc.edu/~ccb/
gryphonaward.html.

This newly established (2003) award—a $1,000 prize—is given annually to the author of an outstanding English-language work of fiction or non-fiction whose audience is roughly kindergarten through grade 4. The title chosen should best exemplify qualities of writing that successfully bridge the gap between picture books and chapter books. This award is sponsored by the Center for Children's Books at the Graduate School of Library and Information Science at the University of Illinois in Urbana-Champaign. The first winner (in 2004) was Douglas Florian for his collection of poetry *bow wow, meow meow: it's rhyming cats and dogs.*

710   *Henry Bergh Children's Book Awards and Honors*; www.aspca.org/site/
PageServer?pagename=al_bookaward.

These awards are given annually by the ASPCA to a number of books that "promote a humane ethic of consideration for all living things." Eleven fiction and nonfiction titles were honored in 2002.

711   *Hope S. Dean Memorial Award*

Established in 1990, sponsored by the Foundation for Children's Books (Box 284, Boston, MA 02132) and administered by the Boston Public Library, this annual award was given to individuals and groups who made a lasting contribution to and/or promoted the appreciation and knowledge of children's literature. Authors, teachers, and book editors were among those who received this award. For example, Ethel and Paul Heins of *Horn Book* are winners, as is author Virginia Hamilton. The award was discontinued in 2004.

712   *International Reading Association Children's Book Award*;
www.reading.org/association/awards/childrens_ira.html.

These cash awards, given by the International Reading Association (Box 8139, Newark, DE 19714), were established in 1975. They are intended to encourage newly published authors who show unusual promise in the children's book field. Four annual awards are given: two in fiction (ages 4 to 10 and 10 to 17) and two for nonfiction (for the same age groups). The books must be the author's first or second published book.

713   *James Madison Book Award*; www.jamesmadisonbookaward.org.

Established in 2003, this award honors books on American history for children. The award was established by Lynne Cheney, author and wife of the U.S. vice president, and consists of a $10,000 prize. The first winner was a biography of the Wright brothers, *First to Fly* by Peter Busby and David Craig. The award goes to a work "that best represents excellence in bringing knowledge and understanding of American history to children ages 5 to 14."

714   *Jane Addams Book Award*; www.janeaddamspeace.org/index.asp.

Sponsored jointly by the Women's International League for Peace and the Jane Addams Peace Association (777 United Nations Plaza, New York, NY 10017), this award now consists of two prizes, the first for a picture book and the second for a book suitable for older readers. Established in 1953, these annual awards are given to books that "effectively promote the cause of peace, social justice, a world community, and equality of the sexes and the races." As well as prize winners, there are also honor books. The books must be published in the previous year and may be translated or published in English in other countries as well as the United States.

715   *Jefferson Cup Award*; www.vla.org.

Since 1983, this award has been given annually by the Virginia Library Association to honor distinguished nonfiction, biography, or historical fiction about American's past. As well as a grand prize winner, several honor books are designated annually.

John Newbery Medal see ***Newbery Medal.***

716   *Judy Lopez Memorial Medal for Children's Literature*; no Web site located.

Given annually by the Women's National Book Association (1225 Selby Ave., Los Angeles, CA 90024) and the Judy Lopez Memorial Foundation, this award was established in 1985 "for excellence in a children's book written for ages 9 to 12."

717   *Kerlan Award*; http://special.lib.umn.edu/clrc/awards.php#3.

Established in 1975 by the Kerlan Collection Twenty-fifth Anniversary Committee (see also "Chapter 10: Special Collections and Resources"), this annual award is given "in recognition of singular attainments in the creation of children's literature, and in appreciation for generous donations of unique resources to the Kerlan Collection." The award is administered by the Children's Literature Research Collections at the University of Minnesota (113 Andersen Library, 222 21st. Ave., Minneapolis, MN 55455). Past winners include Madeleine L'Engle, Lois Lenski, and, in 2004, Lois Lowry.

718 *Laura Ingalls Wilder Award*; www.ala.org/ala/alsc/awardsscholarships/ literaryawds/wildermedal/wildermedal.htm.

This award was established in 1954 to honor the beloved author of the Little House series. Originally presented every five years, the award is now made every three years "to the author or illustrator whose books, published in the United States, have over a period of time made a substantial and lasting contribution to literature for children." The winner is selected by a committee of the Association of Library Service to Children of the American Library Association. The first winner was the award's namesake.

719 *Lee Bennett Hopkins Award for Children's Poetry*; www.pabook.libraries. psu.edu/hopkins.

This award is given annually for the best book of poetry written for children by a single author. It is usual also to name three or four honor books. The award is administered jointly by Penn State's College of Education, the University Libraries, and the Pennsylvania Center for the Book.

720 *Margaret A. Edwards Award*; www.ala.org/ala/yalsa/booklistsawards/ margaretaedwards/margaretedwards.htm.

Sponsored by *School Library Journal* and administered by the Young Adult Library Services Association of the American Library Association, this annual award honors, by a citation and $2,000, an author's lifetime achievement in writing books for young adults. Named after the young adult library pioneer, this award was established in 1988, the year of Edwards's death. Winners include Robert Cormier, Judy Blume, and Paul Zindel. Winners' acceptance speeches are reprinted in the Fall issue of *Young Adult Library Services*.

721 *May Hill Arbuthnot Honor Lecture Award*; www.ala.org/ Template.cfm?Section=awards.

Administered by the Association of Library Service to Children of the American Library Association, this award is presented annually to an individual of distinction in the field of children's literature. It is named after the distinguished author and teacher whose introductory text on children's literature was highly regarded. In 2003, the lecture was delivered by Maurice Sendak; in 2004, by Ursula K. Le Guin; and, in 2005, by Richard Jackson.

722 *Michael L. Printz Award;* www.ala.org/yalsa/printz.

The first Printz awards for high-quality young adult literature were given in 2000. They honor the memory of Michael L. Printz, a champion of young adult literature, a high school librarian in Kansas, and a beloved college teacher. They are sponsored by *Booklist* but administered by the Young Adult Library Services Association of the American Library Association. Criteria for selection include, when applicable, excellence in "story, voice, style, setting, accuracy, characters, theme, illustration, and design." The award-winning book can be fiction, nonfiction, poetry, or an anthology. A prizewinner and up to four honor books are selected each year. The first prizewinner was *Monster* by Walter Dean Myers.

723 **Mildred L. Batchelder Award**; www.ala.org/ala/alsc/awardsscholarships/ literaryawds/batchelderaward/batchelderaward.htm.

Founded in 1966 to honor the former director of the American Library Association's Association for Library Service to Children, this award honors "the most outstanding children's book originally published in a foreign language and subsequently translated into English for publication in the United States." The first award, given in 1968, was for Erich Kästner's novel *The Little Man.*

724 *Mythopoeic Fantasy Award for Children's Literature;* www.mythsoc.org/ awardwinners.html.

Founded in 1992, this award is given to multi-volume or single-volume epics that follow in the tradition of *The Hobbit* and show quality in the field of fantasy writing.

725 *National Book Award for Young People's Literature;* www.nationalbook. org/nba.html.

Once known as the American Book Award, this award, which was established in 1996 and consists of a sculpture and a $10,000 check, is part of the National Book Awards program. Although there are many finalists, there is only one annual award. The deliberating committee considers books of all genres written for children and young adults by U.S. writers, with an emphasis on literary merit. The prize is sponsored by the National Book Foundation (95 Madison Ave., Suite 709, New York, NY 10016).

726 *National Council of Teachers of English Award for Excellence in Poetry for Children*; www.ncte.org/about/awards/sect/elem/106857.htm.

This award, sponsored by the NCTE, was begun in 1977. It is presented every three years to a living American poet, for a body of work suitable for children or young adults. Two previous winners are Eloise Greenfield (1997) and X. J. Kennedy (2000).

727 *Neustadt Prize for Children's Literature*; www.ou.edu/worldlit/NSK/NSK.htm.

Begun in 2004, this award is given by the University of Oklahoma and its quarterly *World Literature Today*, to honor on a biannual basis an accomplished contemporary writer of children's books. The first winner was Mildred D. Taylor.

728 *Newbery Medal*; www.ala.org/alsc/newbery.html.

Along with the Caldecott Medal for illustration, this award is the most prestigious given in the United States for children's literature. Established in 1922 by Frederic G. Melcher, American bookseller and publisher, it is given to the author of the most distinguished book published for children in the United States by an American citizen or resident within a given year. The award honors the first important English publisher of books for children, John Newbery (1713–1767). The winning book sports a medallion of gold color and the honor books (sometimes numbering as many as five) have silver ones. The award is administered by the Association of Library Service to Children of the American Library Association. Although the awards are announced at the Midwinter Conference of ALA, they are actually presented at the Annual Conference held usually in the following June or July.

729 *Orbis Pictus Award for Outstanding Nonfiction for Children*; www.ncte.org/about/awards/sect/elem/106877.htm.

Named after the *Orbis Sensualium Pictus*, published by Johannes Comenius in 1657 and considered to be the first informational book for young people, this award was founded in 1990 by the National Council of Teachers of English to recognize and promote quality in nonfiction books for young people. It is now administered by the NCTE's Committee on Using Nonfiction in the Elementary Language Arts Classroom. A prize winner and as many as four or five honor books are announced each year. The 2005 winner was *York's Adventures with Lewis and Clark* by Rhoda Blumberg.

730   *Osborne Award for Humor in Children's Literature*;
www.worthingtonlibraries.org/kids/jo.htm.

Given to an author and/or illustrator "whose humor is delivered with
heart, wit, and insight," this national award is named in memory of Jo
Osborne, Children's Librarian at Worthington (Ohio) Public Library
and administered by the Ohio Library Foundation (35 E. Gay St., Suite
305, Columbus, OH 43215-3138).

731   *Parents' Choice Award*; www.parentschoice.org/awards_portal.cfm.

First presented in 1980, this award has as its purpose to "recognize children's books with illustrations of more than remarkable charm." Nominations are made by parents who have enjoyed particular books with
their children. The final selections are made by the Parents' Choice
board and announced in *Parents' Choice* magazine. The award is now
given in several categories—fiction, doing and learning books, nonfiction, reference books, picture books, paperbacks, story books, poetry,
homework helpers, and historical fiction.

732   *Phoenix Award*; http://ebbs.english.vt.edu/chla/Phoenix.html.

This award, founded in 1985 and administered by the Children's Literature Association (PO Box 138, Battle Creek, MI 49016), is built on the
unusual concept of recognizing books of merit that were underestimated
when first published. The award-winning books (plus runners-ups) are
those of high literary merit that did not receive major awards when they
were first published 20 years before. The 2000 winner was the novel *The
Keeper of the Isis Light* by Monica Hughes, first published in 1979.

733   *Pura Belpre Awards*; www.ala.org/ala/alsc/awardsscholarships/
literaryawds/belpremedal/belprmedal.htm.

These biennial awards honor Latino authors and illustrators whose work
best portrays and celebrates the Latino cultural experience in children's
literature. Administering the awards are the Association for Library Services to Children (a division of the American Library Association) and
REFORMA, the National Association to Promote Library and Information Services to Latinos and the Spanish Speaking. In addition to the
two awards for narrative and illustration, honor books are designated.

Randolph Caldecott Medal see *Caldecott Medal.*

734   *Regina Medal*; www.cathla.org/regina.html.

This annual award, established in 1959, is given by the Catholic Library
Association (100 North St., Suite 224, Pittsfield, MA 01201) to honor

an individual's lifetime of achievement in children's literature. The award, which is presented at the association's annual conference, goes to an author, illustrator, editor, or publisher. Recent winners include Jean Craighead George and E. L. Konigsburg.

735 *Robert F. Sibert Informational Book Award*; www.ala.org/ala/alsc/ awardsscholarships/literaryawds/sibertmedal/Sibert_Medal.htm.

The Robert F. Sibert Award is given annually to the most distinguished informational book for children published within a given year. The award is administered by the Association of Library Service to Children, a division of the American Library Association, and sponsored by Bound to Stay Bound Books. Several honor books are also chosen each year.

736 *Scott O'Dell Award for Historical Fiction*; www.scottodell.com/ sosoaward.html.

Donated by the distinguished writer of historical novels for young people in 1982, this prize was first awarded in 1984. It is now given annually to the author of a distinguished work of historical fiction set in the New World. The book must be published in English for children or young adults by a United States publisher and written by an American. The selection committee, chaired by Zena Sutherland until her death in 2002, is now chaired by Hazel Rochman of *Booklist*. A recent (2005) winner is A. LaFaye's *Worth*.

737 *Spur Awards*; www.westernwriters.org/spur_awards.htm.

These awards, established by the Western Writers of America (60 Sandpiper, Conway, AZ 72032) in 1953, are given annually to a juvenile fiction and nonfiction book that portray life in the Old West. The award consists of a plaque with a mounted golden spur. Winners include Gary Paulsen, Ben Mikaelson, and Will Hobbs.

738 *Sydney Taylor Awards*; www.jewishlibraries.org/ajlweb/awards/ st_books.htm.

Sponsored by the Association of Jewish Libraries (330 Seventh Ave., 21st floor, New York, NY 10001), this award, which was established in 1968, is given annually to the book published in the previous year and considered to have made the most outstanding contribution to the field of Jewish literature for young people. The award is made in honor of the author who wrote the All-of-a-Kind Family books that depict Jewish life in New York City at the turn of the 20th century. The Sydney Taylor Body-of-Work Award is also awarded from time to time.

739   *Tomás Rivera Mexican American Children's Book Award*;
www.education.txstate.edu/subpages/tomasrivera.

Founded in 1995, this annual award is given to "the most distinguished books for children and young adults that authentically reflect the lives and experiences of Mexican Americans in the United States." Sponsored by Texas State University at San Marcos and administered by the National Committee of Mexican American Literature, this prestigious award consists of $3,000 and a certificate.

740   *University of Southern Mississippi's de Grummond Award*; no Web site located.

This medallion is given annually by the university (Southern Station, Box 5148, Hattiesburg, MS 39406) in recognition of a children's author or illustrator's distinguished body of work in the field of children's literature. The 2005 recipient was Kenneth Henkes (a recent Caldecott Award winner).

741   *Washington Post Children's Book Guild Nonfiction Award*;
www.childrensbookguild.org/awardnonfiction.htm.

This annual award, which was started in 1977, is given to "an author or illustrator whose total body of work has contributed significantly to the quality of nonfiction for children."

742   *WILLA Literacy Award*; http://www.womenwritingthewest.org/willamain.html.

Outstanding books that are set in the West and feature women's stories are honored by this award. There is one annual award in the category of children's and young adult literature; others are given for adult books in categories including historical fiction, contemporary fiction, nonfiction, and memoirs.

B. REGIONAL AWARDS

In the United States there are also a number of regional awards, most of them sponsored by state library associations to honor books that feature a particular state or region or, in some cases, honor an important writer or illustrator who is a native or resident of that state. Other awards signify favorite books as voted on by children in a particular area or state. Some, but not all, of these awards are listed below in alphabetical order with brief explanations in parenthesis.

743   *Anne V. Zarrow Award for Young Readers' Literature*;
www.tulsalibrary.org/eventguide/press/zarrow.htm.

Sponsored by the Tulsa Library Trust, this annual award is given to an author for lifetime achievement in literature for children and young adults. Winners have included Walter Dean Myers, Lois Lowry, and Madeleine L'Engle.

744   *Arizona Young Readers' Awards*; www.azla.affiniscape.com.

School-aged readers in Arizona vote for books in three categories: picture book, intermediate book, and teen book.

745   *Beehive Awards*; www.clau.org/index.html.

The Children's Literature Association of Utah sponsors this award in which Utah children in four age groups vote on their favorite books.

746   *Black-Eyed Susan Book Award*; www.tcps.k12.md.us/memo/whatbes.html.

Administered by the Maryland Educational Media Organization, this annual award is given to an outstanding children's book published in the past three years.

747   *California Book Awards*; www.commonwealthclub.org/features/caBookAwards/2004/index.html.

Established in 1931, these awards, sponsored by the Commonwealth Club of California, are given annually to honor a California author of fiction or nonfiction for young people. There are two categories for children: one for ages up to 10, and one for ages 11 to 16.

748   *California Young Reader Medal*; www.cla-net.org/awards/cyrm.php.

Young readers in California vote on favorite books in four age categories for these medals sponsored by the California Library Association.

749   *Carolyn W. Field Award*; www.jvbrown.edu/youth/cwf.htm.

The Pennsylvania Library Association sponsors this annual award, which is given to a Pennsylvania author or illustrator of the best fiction or non-fiction book published in the preceding year.

750   *Charlie May Simon Children's Book Award*; www.asl.lib.ar.us/childaward/charlie_may_main.htm.

Sponsored by the Arkansas Elementary School Council and voted on by children in grades 4 through 6 who choose their favorite books, this award aims to promote better reading for children.

751   *Colorado Children's Book Award*; http://ccira.org/w/w?cmd=goccba.

Sponsored by the Colorado Council of the International Reading Association, this award is given for books selected by Colorado children as their favorites.

752   *Dorothy Canfield Fisher Award*; http://homepage.mac.com/ crowleyvt/dcfaward/dcf/index.html.

Vermont schoolchildren in grades 4–8 participate in choosing the winner of this award sponsored by the Vermont Department of Education.

753   *Elizabeth Burr/Worzalla Award*; www.wla.lib.wi.us/yss/cba/ burr-winners.html.

Given by the Wisconsin Library Association to the best children's book published in the previous year by a Wisconsin author or illustrator.

754   *Empire State Award*; www.nyla.org/index.php?page_id=411.

Awarded by the Youth Services Section of the New York Library Association to a living author or illustrator currently residing in New York State, this prize honors a significant body of work.

755   *Evelyn Sibley Lampman Award*; www.olaweb.org/csd/lampman.html.

Given by the Children's Section of the Oregon Library Association to an Oregon author, librarian, or educator.

756   *Flicker Tale Children's Book Award*; http://ndsl.lib.state.nd.us/ndla/ ftaward.htm.

This award is administered by the North Dakota Library Association and the prize-winning book is chosen by North Dakota children.

757   *Garden State Children's Book Award*; www.njla.org/honorsawards/book.

Four awards—for easy-to-read series book, easy-to-read book, young fiction, and young nonfiction—are awarded annually by the New Jersey Library Association. There is also a New Jersey Teen Book Award.

758   *Georgia Children's Book Award and the Georgia Children's Picture Storybook Award*; www.coe.uga.edu/gachildlit.

These two awards are sponsored by the College of Education of the University of Georgia and are selected by an estimated 1000,000 schoolchildren who vote for their favorite books.

759   *Golden Dolphin Award*; www.socalkidsbooks.com/golden_dolphin.htm.

This award is given annually by the Southern California Children's Booksellers' Association to a Southern California author and/or illustrator for excellence in the field of children's literature.

760   *Golden Sower Award*; www.nebraskalibraries.org/golden/sower.htm.

Sometimes called the Nebraska Gold Sower Award, this prize involves school-aged children in Nebraska, who vote for their favorites in three areas: picture books, grade 3–6 books, and young adult books.

761   *Great Stone Face Award*; www.chilisnh.org/gsf/gsfaward.html.

New Hampshire children in grades 4 through 6 vote on their favorite book in this annual award sponsored by the New Hampshire Library Association.

762   *Heartland Award for Excellence in Young Adult Literature*; www.writingconference.com/heartlan.htm.

Sponsored by the Writing Conference, Inc., an organization of English teachers, this award is presented on the basis of votes from students in grades 6 through 10 in Kansas, Nebraska, Oklahoma, Missouri, Colorado, and Iowa, who vote for their favorite book from a master list of 10 titles.

763   *Indian Paintbrush Book Award*; www.wyla.org/paintbrush.

An award administered by the Wyoming Library Association, in which Wyoming children in grades 4 through 6 vote for their favorite books.

764   *Iowa Children's Choice Award and Iowa Teen Award*; www.iema-ia.org/icca.html

Iowa children vote for their favorite books in this program sponsored by the Iowa Educational Media Association.

765   *Kentucky Bluegrass Award*; http://kba.nku.edu/.

Sponsored by Northern Kentucky University, this book award is voted on by Kentucky children in two age groups: kindergarten through grade 3 and grades 4 through 8.

766   *Knickerbocker Award*; www.nyla.org/index.php?page_id=632.

An award given annually to a New York State author for a distinguished body of work.

767   *Land of Enchantment Book Award*; www.loebookaward.com/.

This annual award, sponsored by the New Mexico Library Association, honors a book of high quality that has appeal for readers in grades 3 through 9.

768   *Lupine Award*; www.mainelibraries.org/yss/lupine.htm.

Sponsored by the Youth Services Section of the Maine Library Association, this award honors a living author or illustrator who has created a work whose focus is Maine.

769   *Maine Student Book Award*; www.mainelibraries.org/yss/msba.htm.

This award, sponsored by the Maine Library Association, Maine Reading Association, and Maine Association of School Librarians, is given to the book selected as best by students in grades 4 through 8 from a pre-selected list of 42 titles.

770   *Mark Twain Award*; www.maslonline.org/awards/books/MarkTwain.

This award is given annually by the Missouri Association of School Librarians to the author who receives the most votes from the children of the state.

771   *Maud Hart Lovelace Book Award*; www.isd77.k12.mn.us/lovelace/lovelace.html.

Honoring the famous author of the Betsy-Tacy books, this award, sponsored by the Minnesota Valley Regional Library, is given to an author selected by Minnesota children in grades 3 to 8.

772   *Nene Award*; www.librarieshawaii.org/information/nene.htm.

The winning book must be suitable for grades 4 through 6 and published in the last six years in this annual award sponsored by the Hawaii Library Association.

773   *New England Book Award*; www.newenglandbooks.org.

Administered by the New England Booksellers Association, this award is given to a New England author who has produced a body of work that stands as a significant contribution to the region's literature. Writers who have received this award include Steven Kellogg and Karen Hesse.

774   *Ohioana Book Awards*; www.oplin.org/page.php?Id=66-59&msg=.

This annual award for the best book by an Ohio author or the best book about Ohio in juvenile literature is sponsored by the Ohioana Library Association.

775 *Pacific Northwest Booksellers Association*; www.pnba.org/awards.htm.

This association of independent booksellers in Washington, Oregon, Idaho, Montana, and Alaska honors Northwest authors annually.

776 *Pacific Northwest Young Reader's Choice Awards*; www.pnla.org/yrca/index.htm.

Annually students from Alaska, Alberta, British Columbia, Idaho, Montana, Oregon, and Washington vote on the best book for children in this award sponsored by the Pacific Northwestern Library Association.

777 *Pennsylvania Young Reader's Choice Award*; www.psla.org/grantsandawards/pyrcapurpose.php3.

Pennsylvania children vote on favorite books in three age groups—K–3, 3–6, and 6–8—for these annual awards administered by the Pennsylvania School Librarians Association.

778 *Red Clover Award*; www.mothergooseprograms.org/html/redclover.html.

Vermont children vote for their favorite picture book in this annual award sponsored by the Vermont Center for the Book.

779 *Sequoyah Children's Book Award*; www.yukon.lib.ok.us/sequoyah.html.

Oklahoma children in grades 2 through 6 vote for their favorite books in this annual award administered by the Oklahoma Library Association. There is also a Sequoyah Young Adult Book Award.

780 *Society of Midland Authors Book Awards*; www.midlandauthors.com/contest_about.html?1.

Established in 1961 to honor the outstanding books of the year by natives or residents of the 12 Midwestern Heartland states, these awards are administered by the Chicago-based Society of Midland Authors.

781 *South Carolina Children's Book Award, South Carolina Junior Book Award, and South Carolina Young Adult Book Award*; www.scasl.net/bookawards.htm

These three awards are administered by the South Carolina Association of School Librarians and are presented on the basis of votes by schoolchildren for their favorite authors and books.

782 *Southern California Council on Literature for Children and Young People*; www.childrensliteraturecouncil.org/book_awards.htm.

These awards are given in a variety of areas each year to authors and illustrators living in Southern California. Other awards administered by the organization are the Dorothy C. McKenzie Award and the Myra Cohn Livingston Award.

783   *Sunshine State Young Readers Award*; www.firn.edu/doe/instmat/ ssyrap.htm

The Florida Department of Education sponsors these annual awards in which schoolchildren in grades 3 to 5 and 6 to 8 vote for their favorite books.

784   *Texas Bluebonnet Award*; www.txla.org/groups/tba.

Texas students in grades 3 through 6 vote for their favorite book in this award administered by the Texas Library Association.

785   *Time of Wonder Awards*; www.mainearts.com.

Presented by the Maine Discovery Museum, these annual awards are given to books that capture "the sense of wonder and imagination of the most enduring children's literature."

786   *Virginia State Reading Association Young Readers Award*; www.vsra.org/ ags.htm.

Virginia schoolchildren vote on these awards in four age groups.

787   *Volunteer State Book Award*; www.korrnet.org/tasl/vsba.htm.

The Tennessee Library Association and Tennessee School Library Association sponsor these annual awards for intermediate and young adult readers; Tennessee students vote on the choices in a master list.

788   *William Allen White Children's Book Award*; www.emporia.edu/libsv/ wawbookaward.

Sponsored by Emporia State University and Trusler Foundation, this award is given to the author who receives the most votes from the children of Kansas.

789   *Young Hoosier Book Awards*; www.ilfonline.org/Programs/YHBA/ yhba.htm.

Organized by the Association for Indiana Media Educators, more than 75,000 schoolchildren in Indiana participate annually in this program in which they vote in three different grade groupings for their favorite books.

CHAPTER 7

GUIDES TO WRITING, USING, AND PROMOTING LITERATURE AND SERVICES FOR CHILDREN AND YOUNG ADULTS

A. GUIDES FOR SPECIFIC AGES AND GRADE LEVELS

1. General (Preschool Through Grade 12)

790 Bauer, Caroline Feller. *Leading Kids to Books Through Crafts*. American Library Association, 2000, pap., $30 (0-8389-0769-5).

This is one of a series of books by the author that shows how enthusiasm for reading can be promoted through projects that involve children's interests. Geared for the elementary grades, these books are enhanced by delightful line drawings and easy step-by-step directions—in this case, for several interesting craft projects that lead to reading. Two other volumes by this author are *Leading Kids to Books Through Magic* (ALA, 1996, $30 [0-8389-0684-2]) and *Leading Kids to Books Through Puppets* (ALA, 1996, $30 [0-8389-0684-2]).

791   Beers, Kylene. *When Kids Can't Read: What Teachers Can Do: A Guide for Teachers, 6–12.* Heinemann, 2003, pap., $27.50 (0-86709-519-9).

Written by a veteran of more than 20 years in the classroom, this book suggests strategies for teachers who have students who are unable to read. Beers presents practical strategies rather than theoretical generalizations. One reviewer said this book should be "required reading for all current English teachers and those preparing for the profession."

792   Blecher-Sass, Hope, et al. *A Travel Guide Through Children's Literature.* Alleyside, 2001, pap., $16.95 (1-57950-074-9).

This guide is rich in ideas for creating interesting travel activities based on children's books. Trips can be real or imaginary and involve standard titles such as *Stuart Little* and *Old Yeller.* In addition to marking charts and maps, activities for the highlighted titles include songs, shoebox dioramas, travel brochures, paper crowns, games, and field trips. There is a chapter on children's activities using the Internet, plus good background on each of the books.

793   Bouchard, David, and Wendy Sutton. *The Gift of Reading: A Guide for Educators and Parents.* Orca, 2001, pap., $16.95 (1-55143-214-5).

This Canadian book suggests practical ways to promote reading at various levels. In the first part, parents are shown how important reading is; in the second part, teachers and librarians are introduced to concepts involving student literacy (word comprehension, for example); and the third part provides suggestions for administrators on promoting reading in the community. There is additional material on various reading theories, quotations about books and reading, and lists of favorite read-alouds.

794   Codell, Esmé Raji. *How to Get Your Child to Love Reading: For Ravenous and Reluctant Readers Alike.* Algonquin, 2002, pap., $18.95 (1-5651-2308-5).

An experienced teacher of language arts offers thousands of suggestions for making reading fun. Using a common-sense approach, the author shows how to stimulate children's interests through such devices as storytimes, book-based birthday parties, experiments, cooking adventures, crafts, storytelling, and other techniques. There are 3,000 recommended titles and extensive indexes in this attractive volume.

795 Doll, Beth, and Carol Doll. *Bibliotherapy with Young People: Librarians and Mental Health Professionals Working Together.* Libraries Unlimited, 1997, $24 (1-56308-407-4).

This well-researched volume first introduces the often-conflicting definitions of the controversial subject of bibliotherapy. There follows a discussion of the mental health of children and how bibliotherapy can help achieve the desired goals in this area. The authors stress the risks involved, and there is a blueprint of a five-step method of developing programs in this area through cooperation between librarians and mental health experts.

796 Fiore, Carole D. *Running Summer Library Reading Programs: A How-to-Do-It Manual.* Neal-Schuman, 1998, $45 (1-55570-312-7).

Tried-and-true program ideas are presented in this practical guide to administering successful summer reading programs. Among the subjects covered are ways to motivate children's and teen reading, staffing and budgeting considerations, and working with community organizations and the private sector. There are also sample program outlines and detailed material on such activities as puppets, discussion groups, and theater workshops.

797 Greeson, Janet. *Name that Book! Questions and Answers on Outstanding Children's Books*, 2nd ed. Scarecrow, 1998, pap., $32.50 (0-8108-3151-1).

Using books popular with elementary and middle school readers as a basis, this book tells how to stage a "Battle of the Books" trivia quiz. Approximately 800 books published between 1986 and 1998 are included, with questions involving their plots and characters. The questions are arranged by grade level. There are author and title indexes and an appendix that includes additional activities such as crossword puzzles that use the same books.

798 Hall, Susan. *Using Picture Storybooks to Teach Literary Devices: Recommended Books for Children and Young Adults, Vol. 3.* Oryx, 2001, $32.50 (1-57356-350-1).

This work helps to promote the use of picture books beyond the primary grades, examining 41 literary devices found in 120 books published almost entirely between 1995 and 2000 (the two previous volumes cover earlier years). The devices are arranged alphabetically and range from "alliteration " to "understatement." Each is accompanied by a definition, descriptions of the appropriate picture books, discussion of the art style featured, and curriculum tie-ins.

799   Herb, Steven, and Sara Herb. ***Connecting Fathers, Children and Reading: A How-to-Do-It Manual for Librarians.*** Neal-Schuman, 2002, pap., $45 (1-55570-390-9).

Many aspects of the importance of a father's involvement in children's reading are covered in this well-organized volume. After looking at the role of fathers in modern times, the authors discuss the changing aspects of fatherhood and its importance in the reading and literacy of children. There are program ideas for librarians and tips to ensure father participation, plus a bibliography of 450 children's books that feature fathers and fathering.

800   Johnson, Wayne L., and Yvette C. Johnson. ***Summer Reading Program Fun: 10 Thrilling, Inspiring, Wacky Board Games for Kids.*** American Library Association, 1999, pap., $28 (0-8389-0755-5).

This work features ten board games that provide innovative approaches to planning summer programs, particularly in public libraries. The ideas presented are simple, easily adapted to various types of libraries and programs, and should help stimulate a love of reading in children.

801   Knowles, Elizabeth, and Martha Smith. ***The Reading Connection: Bringing Parents, Teachers, and Librarians Together.*** Libraries Unlimited, 1997, pap., $20 (1-56308-436-8).

The authors explore every aspect of forming a book club in a school or community. The focus is on parent groups who are studying literature for children in preschool through 8th grade, but these ideas could be used in intergenerational groups. The role of the moderator and various forms of publicity are discussed, and separate chapters look at genres including horror, poetry, and historical fiction. Each of these chapters contains a bibliography of recommended books and suggestions for further reading.

802   Knowles, Elizabeth, and Martha Smith. ***Talk About Books! A Guide for Book Clubs, Literature Circles, and Discussion Groups.*** Libraries Unlimited, 2003, pap., $30 (1-59158-023-4).

Each of the 15 chapters focuses on a different book, detailing how to use the book in discussion groups. For each title, there is introductory material on the author, a summary of the plot, discussion questions, activities for all areas of the curriculum, lists of related titles, Web sites, other books by the author, and publisher information. The highlighted books represent various genres and include some nonfiction titles. Although sometimes vague on recommended grade and interest levels for the designated books, this is nevertheless a good practical guide to running effective book discussion groups with elementary and middle school students.

803 Kropp, Paul. *How to Make Your Child a Reader for Life.* Broadway, 1995, pap., $12.95 (0-3854-7913-1).

Full of fresh ideas to cultivate young readers, "must read" lists, and sections on "reading solutions," this book stresses the importance of building literate households where all kinds of reading materials abound. There are chapters on the developmental stages of reading, from floating vinyl books in a baby's bath through the teenage years, as well as information on special readers such as the gifted and reluctant. This useful book is crammed with material on catching the attention of prospective readers.

804 Leonhardt, Mary. *99 Ways to Get Kids to Love Reading: And 100 Books They Will Love.* Three Rivers, 1997, pap., $10 (0-60980-113-9).

Tip number one in this book is "Resolve that a love of reading will be your most important educational goal for your children." With this in mind, the book supplies good, practical tips on inspiring and supporting a child's lifelong reading habit. A separate section identifies books suitable for various types of readers.

805 Lesesne, Teri S. *Making the Match: The Right Book for the Right Reader at the Right Time, Grades 4–12.* Stenhouse, 2003, pap., $21 (1-57110-381-3).

In spite of its title, this book concentrates on young adult readers in middle school, junior high, and senior high. It is divided into three parts. "Knowing the Kids" discusses adolescent development and interests, "Knowing the Books" explores various genres and information books, and "Making the Match" outlines such techniques as reading aloud, booktalking, and other motivational methods. Extensive appendixes contain annotated lists of recommended books, material on alternatives to book reports, and online resources. This work covers key issues relating to young adult reading and offers practical tips for promoting reading.

806 Miller, Pat. *Reaching Every Reader: Promotional Strategies for the Elementary School Library Media Specialist.* Linworth, 2001, pap., $39.50 (1-58683-001-5).

The first seven chapters in this oversized volume look at ways to enrich and promote the reading program in elementary schools—working with teachers in specific curriculum areas, storytelling and booktalking, and using puppets, games, songs and chants, dramatics, and field trips. The final (and most lengthy) chapter presents more than 100 detailed activity plans, grouped under such topics as Groundhog Day and African folktales. Each plan gives step-by-step instructions and final evaluations. Useful appendixes include bibliographies of recommended books, Internet sites, software, and publisher Web sites.

807   Nash, Jennie. *Raising a Reader: A Mother's Tale of Desperation and Delight.* St. Martin's, 2003, pap., $19.95 (0-312-31534-1).

This is a charming, enjoyable guide in which the author reports her gradual progress in developing her children's literacy. She shares anecdotes, insights, and practical tips—recommending, for example, that parents and children all keep reading journals. An appended list cites books that were enjoyed and recommended.

808   Neamen, Mimi, and Mary Strong. *More Literature Circles: Cooperative Learning for Grades 3–8.* Greenwood, 2001, $27 (1-56308-895-9).

Designed to help in schools that have literature-based curricula, this work highlights 38 novels and 5 picture books and organizes them around key concepts. Questions essential to understanding each book are given, along with many examples of activities that could be incorporated into the reading of each book.

809   Post, Arden DeVries, et al. *Celebrating Children's Choices: 25 Years of Children's Favorite Books.* International Reading Association, 2000, pap., $23.95 (0-87207-276-2).

Every year, a poll conducted jointly by the Children's Book Council and the International Reading Association determines the reading choices of children across the nation. This is a history of this project and how it has mirrored changes in reading instruction and research. A series of activity-based chapters include practical tips on using these children's favorites in the classroom.

810   Ray, Virginia Lawrence. *School Wide Book Events: How to Make Them Happen.* Libraries Unlimited, 2003, pap., $25 (1-59158-038-2).

The author outlines various "Book Events" that cut across grade levels and involve teachers, administrators, students, and librarians. Organized around 17 different themes and subjects, including sports and poetry, this practical guide covers such topics as preparation, delivering the program, sample reading lists, and resources needed. This book is particularly useful for librarians new to the field.

811   Reid, Rob. *Something Funny Happened at the Library: How to Create Humorous Programs for Children and Young Adults.* American Library Association, 2002, pap., $32 (0-8389-0836-5).

The ideas presented in this book are divided by age groups, from preschool to high school. Reid discusses preparing the audience, selecting appropriate material, using facial and vocal expressions, and suitable props. Each program is outlined clearly, and there are chapters on readers' theater, hosting library tours, and rap songs that discuss the virtue of libraries. An annotated bibliography lists more than 300 of the funniest books available, arranged by category and age.

812   Short, Kathy G., and Kathryn Mitchell Pierce. *Talking About Books: Literature Discussion Groups in K–8 Classrooms.* Heinemann, 1998, pap., $24 (0-325-00073-5).

This is a reissue of a collection of articles on the purposes and results of book discussion groups at the elementary school level. There are many practical suggestions on preparing for these groups, on conducting the sessions, and on potential pitfalls. Lists of recommended titles are appended.

813   Skaggs, Gayle. *Reading Is First: Great Ideas for Teachers and Librarians.* McFarland, 2003, pap., $28.50 (0-7864-1576-2).

Skaggs offers simple, practical advice on stimulating elementary students to read. Twenty chapters focus on different topics and themes—from castles to outer space to careers. Each gives many suggestions for activities, usually with resources that will be on hand or involve very little expenditure. Most of the ideas are workable and would be useful in involving everyone in the reading program.

814   Steele, Anitra T. *Bare Bones Children's Services: Tips for Public Library Generalists.* American Library Association, 2001, pap., $32 (0-8389-0791-1).

This companion volume to *Bare Bones Young Adult Services* (see below) aims to supply basic information to library workers on how to provide essential services to children in public libraries. After chapters on child development and a discussion of basic services, there are separate chapters on storytimes and storytelling, various kinds of programs, summer reading programs, displays, library instruction, and outreach activities. There are also chapters on selection and collection development, as well as record keeping, professional development, censorship, and Internet access. Many sample programs are outlined and there are useful appendixes on highly recommended children's books, selection aids, and basic professional publications.

815   Stover, Lynne Farrell. *Magical Library Lessons.* Upstart, 2003, pap., $16.95 (1-57950-094-3).

Written for librarians working with students in grades 4 through 8, this book contains 15 lesson plans built around the works of such authors as Brian Jacques and J. K. Rowling. The lessons are designed to introduce the library, research techniques, and literary concepts. For the highlighted books, there is a plot outline, indication of time requirement, a materials list, and lists of activities.

816   Sullivan, Michael. *Connecting Boys with Books: What Libraries Can Do.* American Library Association, 2003, pap., $32 (0-8389-0849-7).

Based on his experiences in educational and library settings, the author supplies useful programming ideas for boys in middle school and beginning junior high grades. He shows how cultural and developmental challenges such as stereotyping and lack of role models can be overcome and how vital, involving reading programs can be developed. From chess playing to programs that create opportunities to respond to reading (discussion groups, for example), this book is full of practical ideas that take into consideration boys' developmental needs and their interests.

817   Walter, Virginia. *Children and Libraries: Getting It Right.* American Library Association, 2001, pap., $32 (0-8389-0795-4).

This well-researched, carefully cited book discusses the past, present, and possible future of public library service to children. Walter discusses the wide gap that often separates children from the library and how this can change. A provocative work that describes the essence of children's librarianship and stirs thinking about its future.

2. Preschool Through Primary Grades (PK–3)

818   Fountas, Irene C., and Gay Su Pinnell. *Matching Books to Readers: Using Leveled Books in Guided Reading K–3.* Heinemann, 1999, pap., $30 (0-325-00193-6).

Organized by title and reading level, this is a guide to 7,500 texts, series, and general children's literature books. Several hundred books are suggested at each reading level, with notes on their text characteristics, topics, and formats. There are also sections on matching books to readers, creating a classroom collection, starting a school bookroom, acquiring books, writing grant proposals, and the use of book clubs and gifts of books.

819 Greene, Ellin. ***Books, Babies, and Libraries: Serving Infants, Toddlers,***
Their Parents, and Caregivers. American Library Association, 1991,
pap., $25 (0-8389-0572-2).

Although this is now considered an old title, it still offers great practical
advice to librarians who are trying to give service to the very young.
There are many tips on programming for this age group and ways to
involve parents in this process.

820 Herb, Steven, and Sara Herb. ***Using Children's Books in Preschool***
Settings: A How-to-Do-It Manual for School and Public Librarians.
Neal-Schuman, 1994, $49.95 (1-55570-156-6).

This useful resource is a manual that not only shows how to use children's books effectively with children ages 2½ to 5 but also surveys literature for the very young and provides tips on how to find and introduce
the best of these books. Topics covered include creating a proper reading
environment, planning storytime programs, techniques for reading
aloud, storytelling, how to work with special children such as the disabled, and how to involve parents.

821 Kaye, Peggy. ***Games with Books.*** Farrar, Straus, 2002, $35 (0-374-
52815-2).

Subtitled *28 of the Best Children's Books and How to Use Them to Help*
Your Child Learn: From Pre-School to Third Grade, this book suggests
imaginative games, projects, and other activities involving such standard
titles as *The Carrot Seed* and *Charlotte's Web.*

822 Marino, Jane. ***Babies in the Library!*** Scarecrow, 2003, $23.50 (0-8108-
4576-8).

This book, by a valued expert in the field, offers a variety of pointers on
supplying library services to babies and their parents. Among the topics
covered are making babies comfortable in libraries, creating programs for
various growth stages, and suggestions for planning and executing these
programs. Many fingerplays are included, along with lists of books,
recordings, videos, and other sources useful to both librarians and parents.

823 Marsh, Valerie. ***Stories that Stick: Quick and Easy Storyboard Tales.***
Upstart, 2002, pap., $15.95 (1-57950-068-4).

Twenty-two rhymes, songs, and stories—"Old MacDonald" and "The
Little Red Hen," for example—are highlighted for use in storyboard presentations. Instructions are given for each title. Another recommended
book in this field is Judy Sierra's *The Flannel Board Storytelling Book*
(Wilson, 1997, $60 [0-824-20932-X]).

824   Nespeca, Sue McCleaf, and Joan B. Reeve. *Picture Books Plus: 100 Extension Activities in Art, Drama, Music, Math, and Science.* American Library Association, 2002, pap., $40 (0-8389-0840-3).

The purpose of this work is to promote the use of well-known picture books through a series of activities in five curriculum areas. After brief book annotations, 20 activities are outlined for each of the disciplines, with a materials list, tips for success, alternative activities, and additional resources. Many useful ideas are presented.

825   Raines, Shirley, et al. *Story S-t-r-e-t-c-h-e-r-s for Infants, Toddlers, and Two: Experiences, Activities, and Games for Popular Children's Books.* Gryphon House, 2002, pap., $19.95 (0-87659-274-4).

This work offers a variety of program suggestions for use with very young children. There are sections on choosing the right books for programs and techniques for introducing these books. There is a plot summary for each recommended title, along with reading hints and several activities or story stretchers—object play, movements, and songs, for example.

826   Webber, Desiree, and Sandy Shropshire. *The Kid's Book Club: Lively Reading and Activities for Grades 1–3.* Libraries Unlimited, 2001, pap., $32 (1-56308-818-5).

Each of the 16 chapters in this book suggests a theme and a particular book to be used for discussion in a book club for primary school students. For each title, there are discussion questions, games, crafts, material on the book and author, and list of related titles. Introductory material explores resources on establishing book clubs and gives general discussion guidelines and advice on obtaining multiple copies. Useful for both public and school libraries.

3. Middle Grades (4–6)

827   Beers, Kylene. *Into Focus: Understanding and Creating Middle School Readers.* Christopher-Gordon, 1998, pap., $42.95 (0-926842-64-1).

This excellent resource identifies the developmental goals and reading needs of middle school children and suggests ways to develop reading programs that build on these needs and goals. Throughout the text there are suggestions of specific titles, genres, and activities that can be useful in promoting reading with this age group. Twenty-four experts—educational specialists and authorities in library science and children's literature—have contributed to the handbook, which one reviewer called a "must-have for all middle schools."

828 *"Books Are Cool!" Keeping Your Middle School Student Reading.*
International Reading Association, 1999, free.

This 22-page brochure is aimed at parents who want to make reading and writing more attractive to their middle school children. There is advice on reading to children, providing reading time, and helping in the selection of suitable high-quality books. Also included are lists of recommended books, magazines, and parent resources. Single copies are available from International Reading Association, Dept. E. G., 800 Barksdale Rd., PO Box 8139, Newark, DE 19714-8139. Send a self-addressed stamped envelope.

829 Evans, Karen S. *Literature Discussion Groups in the Intermediate Grades: Dilemmas and Possibilities.* International Reading Association, 2001, pap., $19.95 (0-87207-293-2).

Drawing on her experience, the author presents the problems and benefits of literature discussion groups in classrooms of highly diverse students. Real-life situations in the middle grades are explored and many tips are given for conducting discussion groups that are effective and rewarding.

830 Fountas, Irene C., and Gay Su Pinnell. *Guiding Readers and Writers, Grades 3–6: Teaching Comprehension, Genre, and Content Literacy.* Heinemann, 2001, pap., $38 (0-325-00310-6).

Designed for teachers of writing and literature in the middle grades, this work explores the essential components of a high-quality upper elementary literacy program. Topics covered include promoting reading and writing, the goals of the intermediate literacy program, development of independent readers, giving effective reading guidance, the basics of literature study, comprehension and word analysis, and the reading–writing connection. A companion book by the same authors that lists more than 6,000 titles at various middle school reading levels is *Leveled Books for Readers, Grades 3–6* (Heinemann, 2001, pap., $30 [0-325-00307-6]).

831 Polette, Nancy J., and Joan Ebbesmeyer. *Literature Lures: Using Picture Books and Novels to Motivate Middle School Readers.* Libraries Unlimited, 2002, pap., $24 (1-56308-952-1).

This work uses well-written, well-illustrated picture books as a starting place from which to advance to more mature literature. For example, in the "Wages of War" section, the topic of courage is explored first in a picture book and then in two more-mature novels suitable for older readers. Other topics similarly explored include homelessness, civil disobedience, suicide, and the price of freedom. In a second section, literary devices such as alliteration, personification, puns, parodies, and biography are introduced through their use in picture books.

832   Stover, Lois Thomas. *Young Adult Literature: The Heart of the Middle School Curriculum.* Heinemann, 1996, pap., $20 (0-86709-376-5).

The author, on the faculty of St. Mary's College of Maryland, makes a case for putting young adult literature at the center of the process by which a concept-based curriculum is developed for middle school students. Throughout the text there are examples of specific novels and nonfiction trade books and discussion of their relationship to multidisciplinary units.

833   Tiedt, Iris McClellan. *Teaching with Picture Books in the Middle School.* International Reading Association, 2000, pap., $22.95 (0-87207-273-8).

Tiedt shows how some picture books can be appropriate for middle school students and outlines lesson plans and activities using picture books that will foster reading and writing skills within this group. Genres such as fables and pourquoi tales are explored in picture books suitable for older readers, and Tiedt looks at ways in which older students can share picture books with younger children and polish their reading and presentational skills while also creating programs to engage these younger readers.

834   Wilson, Patricia Potter, and Roger Leslie. *Center Stage: Library Programs that Inspire Middle School Patrons.* Libraries Unlimited, 2002, pap., $35 (1-56308-796-0).

This book focuses on school library programs for grades 5 through 8, with material on the planning, implementation, and evaluation of such programs, plus a wide range of suggestions for programs both for students and for professional development with teachers. There are many checklists and sample forms, material on useful Web sites, and a chapter that highlights 70 model programs from middle schools around the country. Much of the material in this volume is duplicated in the authors' earlier *Premiere Events: Library Programs that Inspire Elementary School Patrons* (Libraries Unlimited, 2001, pap., $37 [1-56308-795-2]).

4. Young Adults (7–12)

835   Booth, David. *Even Hockey Players Read: Boys, Literacy, and Learning.* Stenhouse, 2002, pap., $19 (1-55138-147-8).

In this comprehensive, sympathetic account, the author—a teacher and parent—draws on his experiences to describe the reading habits of boys and how to improve them. Topics covered include the need for adult role models, the status of reading among boys, the selection of suitable material, ways to improve instruction, and techniques for making reading popular. There is also an interview schedule to be used in assessing reading activities, a list of recommended books for boys, and a bibliography of professional reading on the topic.

836   Bowman, Cynthia Ann. *Using Literature to Help Troubled Teenagers Cope with Health Issues.* Greenwood, 2000, $39.95 (0-313-30531-5).

Each chapter in this collection is written by a different teacher/therapist team. Topics covered include blindness, birth defects, cancer, diabetes, hyperactivity, depression, eating disorders, and Alzheimer's disease. In each chapter, a single important book is highlighted, with material on plot, characters, strategies for teaching and counseling, and follow-up activities. An annotated list gives approximately 30 recommended fiction and nonfiction titles dealing with the same subject. An excellent source of material on these topics.

837   Brown, Jean E., and Elaine C. Stephens. *Teaching Young Adult Literature: Sharing the Connection.* Wadsworth, 1994, pap., $46.95 (0-534-19938-0).

This volume offers practical advice to teachers on incorporating young adult literature into the language arts curriculum and suggests strategies for using YA literature effectively. The connection between literature and literacy is explored, and there are interviews with award-winning YA authors and lists of hundreds of books suitable for classroom use.

838   Bushman, John, and Kay Parks Haas. *Using Young Adult Literature in the English Classroom*, 3rd ed. Prentice-Hall, 2001, $56 (0-1302-6455-5).

The authors list four goals for this publication: (1) to encourage the use of quality young adult literature to promote lifelong reading, (2) to use reader's responses to foster literary analysis, (3) to show that the literature that young adults read can be a bridge to the classics, and (4) to promote the use of multicultural young adult literature as a way to reach a diverse student population. The text shows teachers how to make appropriate reading choices and develop ideas for teaching them. This is a standard text on the subject.

839   Carroll, Pamela S. *Using Literature to Help Troubled Teenagers Cope with Societal Issues.* Greenwood, 1999, pap., $39.95 (0-313-30526-9).

This collection of chapters by specialists in the field deals with such topics as body image, sexuality, gang membership, sports, and leaving home. Each chapter gives material on current research and thinking on the topic and then highlights one or two books that deal with the topic, suggesting ways to use this material with teenagers. There are also lists of related fiction and nonfiction in each chapter, and a bibliography of further professional reading.

840   Chelton, Mary K., and the Young Adult Library Services Association. *Excellence in Library Services to Young Adults: The Nation's Top Programs*, 3rd ed. American Library Association, 2000, pap., $28 (0-8389-0786-5).

The third edition of this respected work presents 30 public library programs that offer excellent services to their young adult population. As well as outlining services, this book delves into adult and teen perceptions of libraries and reading, and explores the relationship between these constituents. Factors such as positive attitudes and willingness to expend a lot of energy emerge as important ingredients for success.

841   Dickerson, Constance. *Teen Book Discussion Groups @ the Library*. Neal-Schuman, 2004, pap., $49.95 (1-55570-485-9).

The first part of this book gives practical and philosophical information on how and why to run a teenage book discussion group. The remaining chapters present 50 suitable fiction and nonfiction titles with detailed background information on each, ways of presenting the title to a group, and a list of thoughtful and provocative discussion questions. There is also a short chapter on using online resources.

842   Edwards, Kirsten. *Teen Library Events: A Month-by-Month Guide*. Greenwood, 2001, $45 (0-313-31482-9).

This chronologically arranged book outlines in detail two or three programs for each month. Material is given on the three important elements in programming: advertising, preparation, and presentation. Sample flyers, letters, checklists, display ideas, craft projects, and ideas for games and skits are included along with lists of supplies and directions for use. Although intended for public libraries, many of these events can be adapted for school library use. Bibliographies of professional titles and young adult fiction and nonfiction are provided. There is a list of Internet sites. This is an excellent practical guide.

843   Elliott, Joan B., and Mary M. Dupuis. *Young Adult Literature in the Classroom: Reading It, Teaching It, Loving It*. International Reading Association, 2002, $28.95 (0-87207-173-1).

A collection of practical readings covering topics related to young adult literature—multiculturalism, reader response, book reviewing, poetry, picture books for teens, author studies and author visits, and genres including historical fiction—this book suggests new ways to view and teach young adult literature. An appendix highlights Web sites relating to YA literature.

844 Herz, Sarah K., and Donald R. Gallo. *From Hinton to Hamlet: Building Bridges Between Young Adult Literature and the Classics.* Greenwood, 1996, $29.95 (0-313-28636-1).

In the first third of this book, the authors make a case for teaching young adult literature in the classroom and using it as a bridge to the classics. For example, the themes and plot of Avi's *Nothing But the Truth* can be used to introduce *The Scarlet Letter.* In one section, 12 classics are paired with three or four young adult books. The remaining sections outline stages of literary appreciation, describe how to promote young adult literature in schools, and give helpful tips on running successful library programs. This is an important work for both teachers and librarians.

845 Honnald, Rose Mary. *101+ Teen Programs that Work.* Neal-Schuman, 2002, pap., $49.95 (1-55570-453-0).

A wide range of ages and interests are represented in this manual that describes more than 100 program ideas. Sample program titles are "Misheard Lyrics" and "The Body in the Book Drop." Instructions are given on planning and presentation, with material on the books in the collection that are to be used. Also covered are evaluation, teen feedback, and further reading resources. A companion Web site supplies easy access to other programming resources. This is a useful volume for those seeking year-round programming ideas.

846 Jones, Jami Biles. *Helping Teens Cope: Resources for School Library Media Specialists.* Linworth, 2003, pap., $39.95 (1-58683-121-6).

This work is divided into three main parts. The first explores the importance of books and bibliotherapy in helping teens cope; the second covers ten common problems, such as eating disorders and bullying; and the third shows how the library can explore these problems through programs, booktalks, and other devices. Many Web sites are listed and each chapter concludes with annotated lists of books for adolescents.

847 Jones, Patrick, and Joel Shoemaker. *Do It Right! Best Practices for Serving Young Adults in School and Public Libraries.* Neal-Schuman, 2001, pap., $45 (1-55570-394-1).

Principles that apply to customer service in general are here applied to the service given to young adults in school and public libraries. The first five chapters discuss the nature of school library service, how to develop it, the importance of staff and evaluation, and what would constitute an ideal school library center. In the next part, similar topics are explored in relation to public libraries and 20 steps are outlined that will develop and improve interactions with teenagers. This is a helpful volume for librarians reaching out to a young adult audience.

848   Jones, Patrick, with the Young Adult Library Services Association. *New Directions for Library Service to Young Adults.* American Library Association, 2002, pap., $32 (0-8389-0827-6).

This important work supplies an overview of current purposes and practices in the field of public and school library service to young adults, with material on goals and their implementation. The wider view of youth services in the entire community is also discussed and there are examples of exemplary programs currently in existence. Policies that should be in place to ensure that teens receive necessary library service are gathered together in this single volume. The appendix includes important supportive documents on the subject from a variety of governmental and professional sources.

849   Kan, Katharine L. *Sizzling Summer Reading Programs for Young Adults.* American Library Association, 1998, $25 (0-8389-3480-3).

A practical, witty resource, this looks at a number of successful, field-tested summer programs for teens. Each program is thoroughly described, with discussion of its goals, materials, promotions, and outcomes. The library activities are interesting, appropriate, and have as their overall purpose to make teens enjoy reading and, one hopes, turn them into lifelong lovers of books.

850   Kaplan, Jeffrey S. *Using Literature to Help Troubled Teenagers Cope with Identity Issues.* Greenwood, 1999, $39.95 (0-313-30532-3).

Therapists and literary experts combine forces to explore specific identity issues—sexual identity and body image, for example—and match them with one or two young adult novels that feature the issue. For example, M. E. Kerr's *Deliver Us from Evie* is used in the sexual identity chapter. Each chapter also features an annotated list of other fiction and nonfiction titles on the same subject.

851   Kaywell, Joan F. *Adolescent Literature as a Complement to the Classics, Vol. 4.* Christopher-Gordon, 2000, pap., $32.50 (1-929024-04-5).

In each chapter of this book, a noted teacher/scholar of young adult literature presents a unit plan that includes at least one literary classic (*Oliver Twist,* for example) and relates it to important young adult novels. The relationship might be by theme, subject matter, or genre. The volume contains a wealth of information for teachers who want to create and foster a love of literature in their students. Appendixes include separate bibliographies for classic and young adult works. The three previous volumes in this set (with the same editor, publisher, and title) are still in print: Volume 1 (1993, pap., $35.95 [0-926842-23-4]), Volume 2 (1995, pap., $35.95 [0-926842-43-9]), Volume 3 (1997, pap., $35.95 [0-9268429-61-7]).

852 Kaywell, Joan F. *Using Literature to Help Troubled Teenagers Cope with Family Issues.* Greenwood, 1999, $39.95 (0-313-30335-5).

Therapists and literacy experts combine their skills in this volume. Each team covers a specific issue—school and family conflicts, eating disorders, and gay and lesbian situations. Each issue is discussed at length and at least one young adult novel on the subject is thoroughly analyzed. In each case, the relationship between the real-life problem and the characters in the novels is stressed. Each chapter also contains an annotated list of related fiction and nonfiction titles.

853 Knowles, Elizabeth, and Martha Smith. *Reading Rules! Motivating Teens to Read.* Libraries Unlimited, 2001, $33.50 (1-56308-883-5).

For use with students in grades 6 through 8, this work is filled with ideas, practical tips, useful statistics, and other helpful data on teen reading. It gives details on numerous methods used to get young teens to read. Reading workshops, literature circles, book clubs, and booktalks are covered, and there is an overview of young adult literature. There are also annotated bibliographies of young adult books and professional titles.

854 Koelling, Holly. *Classic Connections: Turning Teens on to Great Literature.* Libraries Unlimited, 2004, $40 (1-59158-072-2).

The author offers a variety of techniques to attract teenagers to classic literature. A number of different lures are introduced, including the genre approach and using the aspects of each book that will be appealing to teens. Programs are outlined that will help teens appreciate the classics they read. The use of booktalks, booklists, displays, book clubs, discussions, reviews, and other ways to stimulate reading is explained with plenty of practical examples.

855 Kuta, Katherine Wiesolek. *What a Novel Idea! Projects and Ideas for Young Adult Literature.* Teacher Ideas Press/Libraries Unlimited, 1997, $21.50 (1-56308-479-1).

Sixty projects that are adaptable to any novel are introduced here. These activities are divided into three sections: Reading and Writing, Representing and Viewing, and Speaking and Listening. For each activity, there is information on its purpose, use, evaluation points, and possible variations. The activities can be used with individuals or with groups reading the same or different novels. A particular strength is the suggestions for book discussion groups.

856   Leslie, Roger, and Patricia Potter Wilson. *Igniting the Spark: Library Programs that Inspire High School Patrons.* Libraries Unlimited, 2001, pap., $35 (1-56308-797-9).

This is an excellent tool that introduces the concept of programming to school librarians. (Public librarians will also find it of value.) Beginning with the goals and purposes of school library programs, the authors cover each aspect of programming from determining students' interests and formulating a plan through executing the program and conducting evaluations. The book contains forms, sample formats, checklists, and other aids, as well as useful tips and helpful strategies. Two chapters are devoted to Internet resources and materials of interest to high school students.

857   Mondowney, Joann G. *Hold Them in Your Heart: Successful Strategies for Library Services to At-Risk Teens.* Neal-Schuman, 2001, pap., $45 (1-55570-393-3).

The purpose of this volume is to alert librarians to what they need to know about adolescent development and the creation of successful programs for at-risk teens. After introductory material, the author showcases several programs in the ambitious San Francisco Bay Area Youth-at-Risk Project. The issues faced involve such problems as pregnancy, drugs, school failure, and delinquency. Later chapters discuss strategies for gaining support and funding, conducting a needs assessment, planning programs, and measuring success. Outreach activities such as homework centers and tutoring are covered. The book ends with a more detailed discussion of successful programs and a useful appendix that provides contact information.

858   Monseau, Virginia R. *Responding to Young Adult Literature.* Heinemann, 1996, pap., $18.50 (0-86709-401-X).

The author presents a passionate case for the use of young adult literature in the classroom and gives practical advice to teachers who want to teach YA literature but are unsure how to do it. She also cites results of studies that show how student attention and literary appreciation increase when high-quality young adult novels are used either alone or in conjunction with established classics. Interesting class projects and other creative assignments are outlined.

859 Monseau, Virginia R., and Gary M. Salver. *Reading Their World: The Young Adult Novel in the Classroom*, 2nd ed. Heinemann, 2000, pap., $25 (0-86709-473-7).

This is a collection of essays by various authors on the use of young adult novels in the classroom. In addition to a critique of this literary form, there are many practical tips on how to teach language arts through these novels. Topics covered include literary response and interpretation, censorship, gender considerations, and multicultural concerns. Authors including Will Hobbs and M. E. Kerr contribute essays on writing for young adults. As a bonus, a companion CD features almost 2,000 critiques and synopses from *The ALAN Review*.

860 Nichols, Mary Anne. *Merchandising Library Materials to Young Adults*. Libraries Unlimited, 2002, pap., $40 (0-313-31382-2).

This volume shows how marketing principles can be applied in libraries to reach young adults, particularly reluctant readers. Chapters discuss the interests of young adults and how to capitalize on these interests in library collections. Nichols looks at techniques that can be used to market library collections and services—displays (she provides tips on collecting inexpensive display items), book lists, bulletin boards, readers' advisory, and so forth. This guide will be useful in both public and school libraries.

861 Reid, Louann. *Rationales for Teaching Young Adult Literature*. Heinemann, 1999, pap., $22.50 (1-893056-04-X).

Reid stresses the importance of teaching high-quality young adult literature in middle schools and high schools and discusses how to handle any controversies that may arise. In separate chapters, 22 important young adult novels are introduced by several experienced English teachers. Each entry contains an excerpt from the book, a plot summary, intended audience, a discussion of how the book relates to the curriculum, possible controversial subjects, and a list of alternative and related works.

862 Shipley, Roberta Gail. *Teaching Guides for 50 Young Adult Novels*. Neal-Schuman, 1995, $32.50 (1-55570-193-0).

Fifty excellent, thought-provoking, popular young adult novels are featured in this practical guide for classroom teachers. For each book there is a teaching guide that includes lesson plans, vocabulary words, discussion questions, writing exercises, research questions, and activities. There is also an appendix that contains information on each author.

863 Simpson, Martha Seif. ***Reading Programs for Young Adults: Complete Plans for 50 Theme-Related Units for Public, Middle School, and High School Libraries.*** McFarland, 1997, $45 (0-7864-0357-8).

This readable, well-organized book begins with an introduction that points up the need for programs in libraries for teenagers. There follow 50 units, each of which presents a program theme—fantasy literature or famous people, for example. For each unit there are suggestions for promotional materials and displays; ten activity ideas; lists of appropriate books, films, periodicals, and computer software; and curriculum tie-ins and activities. Finally, there is a bibliography of resources for youth-oriented programs. The material in this manual is clever and creative and will be of value in all types of libraries.

864 Vaillancourt, Renee J. ***Bare Bones Young Adult Services: Tips for Public Library Generalists.*** American Library Association, 2000, pap., $33 (0-8389-3497-8).

In a clear and straightforward style, the author answers basic question concerning services to young adults in public libraries. Aimed at personnel without experience with this age group, material is presented on the needs of the young adult in such areas as reference, reader's advisory, collections, and programs, along with guidelines for meeting these needs. There is a good discussion on how to build effective collections. Appendixes cover online safety, booktalking, pathfinders, program evaluation, and competencies for library personnel. This is an outstanding resource for public libraries.

865 Walter, Virginia, and Elaine Meyers. ***Teens and Libraries: Getting It Right.*** American Library Association, 2003, pap., $32 (0-8389-0857-8).

This is an inspiring yet practical look at young adult services in libraries, as well as a needed definition of the unique and indispensable role that the young adult librarian plays in this process. Beginning with a historical overview of the field, this book emphasizes the need for distinct young adult librarian positions. It also covers such areas as print and electronic resources, ways of working with young adult customers, methods of listening to teen voices, advice on forming teen advisory committees, and ways in which evaluation and accountability can help create effective programs. Many important documents are included in the appendixes. This is an important book in the field of young adult librarianship.

B. GUIDES ON SPECIFIC TOPICS

1. Author Visits

866   Buzzeo, Toni, and Jane Kurtz. *Terrific Connections with Authors, Illustrators, and Storytellers: Real Space and Virtual Links.* Libraries Unlimited, 1999, pap., $28 (1-56308-744-8).

A practical handbook, this supplies a lot of useful information on planning and executing library visits by authors, illustrators, and storytellers. There are many descriptions of actual visits and the factors that made them successful. A unique aspect of this book is the material on "virtual visits"—ways in which students and authors can communicate with each other online or by using television/satellite links.

867   East, Kathy. *Inviting Children's Authors and Illustrators: A How-to-Do-It Manual for School and Public Librarians.* Neal-Schuman, 1995, pap., $35 (1-55570-182-5).

This work chronicles the process of conducting an author or illustrator program in a library—from getting the right people involved in the selection process and choosing and contacting the authors and illustrators to budgeting, planning, correspondence, publicity, the timeline, logistics of the visit, evaluation, and thank-you letters. This is a commonsense manual that supplies information that should ensure a successful visit.

868   Spencer, Gwynne. *Have Talent, Will Travel: Directory of Authors, Illustrators, and Storytellers East of the Mississippi.* Linworth, 2002, pap., $36.95 (1-58683-050-3).

The author has compiled a list of more than 500 authors, illustrators, and storytellers who are willing to meet and interact with young readers. As well as providing contact information (often including e-mail addresses), this directory describes presentation content, target grade levels, typical fees, equipment necessary, and up to three published works by the person. There is an appendix of additional resource materials and a last name and geographical index. A companion volume by the same author is *Have Talent, Will Travel: Directory of Authors, Illustrators, and Storytellers West of the Mississippi* (Linworth, 2002, pap., $36.95 [1-58683-051-1]).

2. Booktalking

869   Baxter, Kathleen A., and Marcia Agness Kochel. *Gotcha! Nonfiction Booktalks to Get Kids Excited About Reading.* Libraries Unlimited, 1999, pap., $26.50 (1-56308-683-2).

This is a collection of 350 nonfiction booktalks arranged in seven thematically organized chapters including "Great Disasters," "Fun Stuff," "Unsolved Mysteries," "Science," and "Fascinating People." Along with the booktalk, there are excerpts for reading aloud and reading levels from grades 1 through 8. Packed with great ideas, this book has an equally useful sequel by the same authors, *Gotcha Again! More Nonfiction Booktalks to Get Kids Excited About Reading* (Libraries Unlimited, 2002, pap., $30 [1-56308-940-8]), which contains an additional 350 titles.

870   Blass, Rosanne J. *Booktalks, Bookwalks, and Read-Alouds: Promoting the Best New Children's Literature Across the Elementary Curriculum.* Libraries Unlimited, 2002, pap., $30 (1-56308-810-X).

The author has chosen more than 150 quality fiction and nonfiction titles published in the four-year period from 1998 to 2001 that the author thinks are suitable for booktalking (or bookwalking). The books are arranged in four subject areas: "Language Arts and Literature," "Mathematics and Science," "Social Studies," and "Arts and Recreation." Each entry gives bibliographic information, age level, a book summary, a booktalk or read-aloud, curriculum connections, and a list of several related books. The books chosen represent a wide range of reading levels and interests, from picture books and first readers to junior novels and biographies. This is a useful guide, particularly with a younger age group.

871   Bodart, Joni Richards. *Booktalking Series.* H. W. Wilson.

Bodart, perhaps the most renowned authority on booktalks using children's and young adult literature, has written and edited a number of time-tested works over the years that have aided librarians, teachers, reading specialists, and others working with children and young adults. Each volume contains a number of booktalks written by a staff of experienced booktalkers. Each is about three to five paragraphs in length (about two to three minutes in duration). The titles represent a variety of genres and styles and range from those written for middle school children through adult books suitable for young adults. There are now ten titles in this valuable series:

> *Booktalk! 2: Booktalks for All Ages and Audiences*, 2nd ed. 1985, $55 (0-8242-0716-5).

> *Booktalk! 3: More Booktalks for All Ages and Audiences.* 1988, $55 (0-8242-0764-5).

Booktalk! 4: Selections from The Booktalker for All Ages and Audiences. 1992, $55 (0-8482-0835-8).

Booktalk! 5: More Articles and Booktalks from The Booktalker, 1990–1992. 1993, $55 (0-8242-0836-6).

Booktalking the Award Winners, 1992–1993. 1994, $55 (0-8284-0866-8).

Booktalking the Award Winners, 1993–1994. 1995, $55 (0-8242-0876-5).

Booktalking the Award Winners, Children's Retrospective Volume. 1997, $50 (0-8242-0901-X).

Booktalking the Award Winners: Young Adult Retrospective Volume. 1997, $55 (0-8242-0877-3).

Booktalking the Award Winners 3. 1997, $55 (0-8242-0898-6).

Booktalking the Award Winners 4. 1998, $55 (0-8242-0923-0).

There is a cumulative index, also edited by Joni Bodart: *Index to the Wilson Booktalking Series: A Guide to Talks from Nine Volumes* (H. W. Wilson, 1997, $55 [0-8242-0905-2]).

872 Bromann, Jennifer. *Booktalking that Works.* Neal-Schuman, 2001, $35 (1-55570-403-4).

Using a hip approach to reach teens, the author gives step-by-step guidance in preparing and delivering booktalks. After a chapter on what teens want, there are sections on how to choose the right books, booktalking basics, writing booktalks, presentation factors, and school visits. A 33-page section contains 50 sample booktalks covering ten genres. One reviewer called this "a fresh grab-and-go compendium" of resources.

873 Cox, Ruth E. *Tantalizing Tidbits for Teens: Quick Booktalks for the Busy High School Library Media Specialist.* Linworth, 2002, pap., $36.95 (1-58686-017-1).

After an introduction on booktalking basics, the author presents 150 award-winning books suitable for grades 9 through 12. For each title, there is bibliographic information, an annotation, and a brief description of the plot, followed by the booktalk. Each booktalk lasts one or two minutes. The titles have been carefully chosen from authoritative lists prepared by professional organizations. This is a handy, useful volume that will help active high school librarians.

874 Gillespie, John T., and Corinne J. Naden. *Teenplots: A Booktalk Guide to Use with Readers Ages 12–18.* Libraries Unlimited, 2003, pap., $48 (1-56308-921-1).

This guide provides abundant information on 100 recommended fiction and nonfiction titles, with references to several hundred more. After a general introduction on booktalking, the highlighted books are arranged by central themes, such as "Sports in Fact and Fiction." There is background information on each book and author, a list of characters, a detailed plot summary, comments on suitability, lists of themes and subjects, passages for booktalking, and an annotated list of related titles. This is one of a series of books on booktalking by these authors. The titles still in print (initially published by R. R. Bowker) are:

Juniorplots 3: A Book Talk Guide for Use with Readers Ages 12–16. 1987, $35.50 (0-8352-2367-1).

Juniorplots 4: A Book Talk Guide for Use with Readers Ages 12–16. 1993, $44 (0-8352-3167-4).

Middleplots 4: A Book Talk Guide for Use with Readers Ages 8–12. 1994, $47 (0-8352-3346-0).

Seniorplots: A Book Talk Guide for Use with Readers Ages 15–18. 1989, $45 (0-8352-2513-5).

875   Keane, Nancy J. *Booktalking Across the Curriculum: The Middle Years.* Libraries Unlimited, 2002, pap., $30 (1-56308-937-8).

About 90 percent of the books highlighted in this useful work are fiction. There are short booktalks on 170 recommended in-print titles of interest to middle school children with an additional 330 related titles introduced by short annotations. The entries are arranged in subject areas such as United States historical fiction and mathematics, and contain reading and interest levels, background information, the booktalk (usually about 100 words), related titles, and ideas that promote comprehension, writing, and research. This is an excellent tool for librarians and teachers.

876   Langemack, Chapple. *The Booktalker's Bible: How to Talk About the Books You Love to Any Audience.* Libraries Unlimited, 2003, pap., $30 (1-56308-944-0).

A superb one-volume compendium of basic and advanced information on the art of booktalking. The 14 chapters cover such topics as choosing the books, delivery tips, booktalking to various age groups (including adults), booktalking in schools, and evaluation. Many personal anecdotes are included, and each chapter ends with sample booktalks and lists of resources. This compact, good-natured volume lives up to its title as a booktalker's bible.

877 Littlejohn, Carol. *Talk That Book! Booktalks to Promote Reading.* Linworth, 1999, pap., $36.95 (0-938865-75-7).

Three hundred field-tested booktalks range from the classics to popular titles of the time. For each entry, there is a half-page booktalk, plus material on the genre, themes, awards, and series information. The entries are divided into three groups: grades 4 to 6, grades 6 to 8, and grades 9 to adult. An introduction includes material on how to write and deliver booktalks, and there are sidebars on curriculum tie-ins and related material. This is a useful tool for both teachers and librarians. A sequel is *Keep Talking That Book: Booktalks to Promote Reading, Vol. 2* (Linworth, 2000, pap., $36.95 [1-938865-7]). Cathlyn Thomas joined Littlejohn in two further sequels: *Keep Talking That Book! Booktalks to Promote Reading, Grades 2–12, Vol. 3* (Linworth, 2001, $36.95 [1-58683-020-1]), which contains—in addition to many new booktalks—an introductory section called "The ABCs of Booktalking"; and *Still Talking That Book! Booktalks to Promote Reading, Grades 3–12, Vol. 4* (Linworth, 2003, $36.95 [1-58683-123-2]). Littlejohn has also culled 100 booktalks from this series that are suitable for middle school use and presented them in a single volume: *Promote Reading with Booktalks: Highlights of 100 Exciting Books for Middle School Students* (Linworth, 2002, $10.95 [1-58683-086-4]).

878 Rochman, Hazel. *Tales of Love and Terror: Booktalking the Classics, Old and New.* American Library Association, 1987, pap., $22 (o.p.).

In this, a classic in the field, the author demonstrates how to promote the pleasure of reading through booktalking. Using a thematic approach, she suggests many appropriate titles throughout the text and gives plenty of tips on preparing and delivering booktalks. Lists in the appendix are arranged by theme and genre. This is a more thoughtful, philosophical approach to booktalking than those found in many of the popular manuals.

879 Schall, Lucy. *Booktalks Plus: Motivating Teens to Read.* Libraries Unlimited, 2001, pap., $35 (1-56308-817-7).

The author has highlighted 100 books recommended for teen reading and published between 1996 and 1999. The booktalks are arranged into four thematic units that deal with teens' problems and conflicts, the world around them, self-image, and reaching out to others. For each entry, there is a summary, a brief booktalk, a list of related activities, and annotated bibliographies of related works. Both fiction and nonfiction are included. The author has also written a sequel, *Booktalks and More:*

Motivating Teens to Read (Libraries Unlimited, 2003, pap., $35 [1-56308-982-3]), that includes 100 more booktalks for titles published between 1997 and 2001. Both are valuable manuals that provide clear and effective material on relevant sources.

3. Censorship

880   ***Banned Books Resources Guide.*** American Library Association, Office for Intellectual Freedom, 2004, $35 (0-8389-8279-4).

This thick annual guide gives a cornucopia of information on book banning in the United States. Included are exhaustive booklists, material on banned books and why they were banned, landmark court cases, an action guide to be used when books are questioned, and a wealth of ideas for raising awareness in your library or classroom concerning issues about censorship. There is also a great deal of related material available at the Web site www.ala.org/ala/oif/bannedbooksweek/bannedbooksweek.htm.

881   Becker, Beverley C., and Susan Stan. ***Hit List for Children 2: Frequently Challenged Books.*** American Library Association, 2002, pap., $25 (0-8389-0830-6).

After a general introduction on censorship and its causes and effects, this book highlights the children's books that are most frequently challenged in libraries. The entries are arranged by author. Each entry has a lengthy annotation with material on plots and characters, a discussion of recent challenges (and reasons for the challenges), review sources, and sources recommending the book. A concluding chapter explains how ALA can help librarians faced with a censorship challenge. This work is an update of the earlier *Hit List: Frequently Challenged Books for Children* by Donna Reidy Pistolis (ALA, 1996, o.p.).

882   Foerstel, Herbert N. ***Banned in the U.S.A.: A Reference Guide to Book Censorship in Schools and Public Libraries***, 2nd ed. Greenwood, 2002, $54.95 (0-313-31166-8).

This, a complete revision and update of the earlier 1994 edition, continues to offer a complete analysis of the current state of book banning. The introduction supplies a history of the topic, and the text continues with a survey of major book banning incidents and a legal analysis of recent cases. Detailed information is given on each incident. A section called "Voices of Banned Authors" includes remarks from writers such as Judy Blume. A final chapter covers the most frequently banned or challenged books of the years 1996 through 2000 (the Harry Potter series leads). Though the subject matter is heavy, the writing style is light and this book is highly recommended for both public and school libraries.

883 Karolides, Nicholas J. *Censored Books II: Critical Viewpoints.* Scarecrow, 2002, $45 (0-8108-4147-9).

A continuation of the editor's earlier *Censored Books: Critical Viewpoints* (Scarecrow, 1993, o.p.), which covers the years 1950 to 1985, this volume looks at the years from 1985 through 2000. After a general background introduction by the editor, there are 64 essays on books for children, teens, and adults that have been frequently challenged. Each brief essay gives material on why the book was challenged, the outcome, and specific reasons why the book should be retained on library shelves. This material will help provide a foundation on which to build a defense for each book.

884 Kravitz, Nancy. *Censorship and the School Media Center.* Libraries Unlimited, 2002, pap., $40 (0-313-31437-3).

This excellent volume supplies all sorts of good material for school libraries on the subject of intellectual freedom and censorship. It discusses the types of challenges that come from parents and other groups, a brief history of school censorship, case law on obscenity, and the nature of challenges relating to religion, politics, sex, language, and other taboos. The need for selection policies and procedures for acquiring different formats is stressed. The many appendixes include one dealing with important documents and another that lists frequently challenged books.

885 Lesesne, Teri S., and Rosemary Chance. *Hit List for Young Adults 2: Frequently Challenged Books.* American Library Association, 2002, pap., $25 (0-8389-0835-7).

In addition to providing strategies for dealing with censorship challenges of young adult materials, this book looks at approximately 20 frequently challenged titles by such authors as Judy Blume, Robert Cormier, and S. E. Hinton, devoting two to four pages to each. For each book, there is a concise plot summary, awards and prizes, a history of the challenges, relevant Internet sites, and important reviews. There is an outstanding introduction by YA writer Chris Crutcher, and numerous appendixes list germane resources, tips for dealing with censorship, and give advice to librarians on "How to Write a Book Rationale." This is an update of an earlier title, *Hit List*, that was published in 1996 and is now out of print.

886   Nilsen, Alleen Pace, and Hamida Bosmajian. *"Censorship in Children's Literature," Para·Doxa Studies in World Literature,* Vol. 2, Number 3–4 (double issue), 1996, $25.

A special issue of the periodical that devotes separate issues to articles on a specific literary genre, this covered a wide range of topics and perspectives relating to censorship and children's literature. Several of the essays address the concerns of authors, publishers, teachers, librarians, and academics. Particularly valuable were the separate articles written by experts on censorship and children's literature in countries including Australia, New Zealand, Japan, Canada, the United States, Great Britain, and various European countries such as Germany. The articles are authoritative and well written. Two focus on writers M. E. Kerr and Lois Lowry. In her article, Nilsen classifies censorship in four ways: political, educational, economic, and personal. For more information about this issue, write: Para·Doxa, P.O. Box 2237, Vashon Island, WA 98070.

887   Reichman, Henry. *Censorship and Selection: Issues and Answers for Schools,* 3rd ed. American Library Association, 2001, $37 (0-8389-0798-9).

Now in its third edition, this work focuses on the problems librarians face in balancing materials selection on the one hand and censorship on the other. This manual provides practical advice on handling problems involving challenged material and informs school personnel how to prepare for these situations. The author supplies a concise summary of laws and legal decisions relating to these matters and gives a three-page checklist for school administrators, outlining steps to be taken in handling possible confrontations. This work is particularly recommended for all levels of public school administration.

888   Scales, Pat R. *Teaching Banned Books: 12 Guides for Young Readers.* American Library Association, 2001, pap., $28 (0-86709-504-0).

This text outlines strategies for teaching books that have been banned. The issues are covered in five sections that look at such topics as First Amendment rights, the outcast and the bully, race and bigotry, and multiculturalism. Eleven banned books are highlighted with plot summaries, discussion questions, pre-reading strategies, suggested activities, and an annotated list of related fiction and nonfiction titles. Though specifically aimed at middle school and junior high readers, this book could also be used by discussion groups involving teachers, administrators, and parents.

889   Simmons, John S., and Eliza T. Dresang. *School Censorship in the 21st Century: A Guide for Teachers and School Library Media Specialists.* International Reading Association, 2001, $24.95 (0-87207-288-6).

The authors offer guidance in confronting censorship in a variety of educational contexts. There is a focus on the nature of current censorship issues; the historical, legal, and social contexts in which these occur; and resources available to counter and prevent these occurrences.

890   Sova, Dawn B. *Banned Books: Literature Suppressed on Social Grounds.* Facts on File, 1998, $35 (0-8160-3303-X).

This book covers fiction and nonfiction titles that have been challenged because of their social content. Although it deals primarily with adult material, there is some coverage of material associated with children and young adults, such as *Huckleberry Finn, Little House on the Prairie, Annie on My Mind,* and *Bridge to Terabithia.* This volume is part of a Banned Books series from Facts on File, which also includes, by the same author, *Banned Books: Literature Suppressed on Sexual Grounds* (Facts on File, 1998, $35 [0-8160-3305-X]).

891   West, Mark I. *Trust Your Children: Voices Against Censorship in Children's Literature,* 2nd ed. Neal-Schuman, 1997, pap., $19.95 (1-55570-251-1).

West looks at the devastating effects of censorship of children's materials from a variety of viewpoints. Interviews with authors, publishers, and leaders of the anticensorship movement are reprinted. The publishers often speak of the negative effects of censorship on their handling of controversial authors and their writing. Among the censored children's authors interviewed are Katherine Paterson, Phyllis Reynolds Naylor, Gail Haley, Maurice Sendak, and Roald Dahl. Mark West has also furnished an excellent, lucid introduction to the topic and a fine bibliography.

4. Storytelling

892   Bauer, Caroline Feller. *Caroline Feller Bauer's New Handbook for Storytellers.* American Library Association, 1995, $48 (0-8389-0664-8).

This is a revision of the highly successful 1977 title with new material on videos, poetry, and promotion, and an update of the entire text including bibliographies. This is a comprehensive overview (550 pages) of the entire field of storytelling without a concentration on any one area. It contains imaginative suggestions for presentations, and tips, tricks, and techniques for choosing and preparing stories. Bauer offers many innovative ideas for using film, music, crafts, puppetry, magic, and other media in storytelling programs. This is a standard work in the field.

893   Cabral, Len, and Mia Manduca. *Len Cabral's Storytelling Book*. Neal-Schuman, 1997, $32.95 (1-55570-253-8).

An easy-to-follow guide by an acclaimed professional storyteller, this work helps the novice develop the skills to tell stories effectively and with confidence. Chapters cover participation, stories for the young, humorous tales, multicultural folktales, and "why" stories. Within these chapters is advice on telling tales and dealing with various situations. There is also material on how to expand a story presentation into a discussion session. An additional section gives an overview of techniques and props, and answers questions most commonly asked by teachers and librarians.

894   Champlin, Connie. *Storytelling with Puppets*, 2nd ed. American Library Association, 1997, pap., $38 (0-8389-0709-1).

A revision of a well-received 1985 book, this work contains fresh illustrations and pays close attention to literature-based instruction and multicultural themes. Among topics discussed are puppet types and styles, developing a puppet collection, participatory storytelling, and presentation formats. Champlin provides a wealth of information on good stories and how to present them.

895   Collin, Rives, and Pamela J. Cooper. *The Power of Story: Teaching Through Storytelling*. Allyn and Bacon, 1996, pap., $32.50 (0-13776-709-9).

The authors effectively share the heritage of the oral tradition in storytelling and the craft and skills necessary to become an expert storyteller. Each chapter ends with an interview with a storyteller, ranging from children to librarians and teachers. Each storyteller conveys the satisfaction one feels when telling stories and gives tips for success. There is a wealth of teaching material and examples of how to incorporate stories into the curriculum. Another excellent source on using storytelling in the classroom comes from the National Storytelling Association and Sheila Dailey: *Tales as Tools: The Power of Storytelling in the Classroom* (National Storytelling Association, 1994, o.p.).

896   Cox, Allison, and David H. Albert. *The Healing Heart—Communities: Storytelling to Build Strong and Healthy Communities*. New Society, 2003, $39.95 (0-86571-469-X).

With its companion volume by the same authors, *The Healing Heart—Families: Storytelling to Encourage Caring and Healthy Families* (New

Society, 2003, $39.95 [0-86571-467-3]), this volume can be used to help promote understanding, resolve conflicts, and encourage peace in homes, communities, and the world. To advance this form of bibliotherapy through storytelling, these two volumes contain a number of excellent stories, with material on how to tell them effectively, and extensive bibliographies arranged by subject. This is a valuable tool for all kinds of storytellers, in schools, community centers, libraries, churches, and hospitals.

897   De Vos, Gail. *Storytelling for Young Adults: A Guide to Tales for Teens,* 2nd ed. Libraries Unlimited, 2003, $35 (1-56308-903-3).

For use with students in grades 7 through 12, this is an update of the original edition that appeared in 1996. It is essentially an annotated bibliography of stories for young adults from around the world and throughout the ages. After explaining the value of storytelling to young adults and reviewing storytelling basics, the author lists hundreds of suitable stories in such thematically arranged chapters as "Tales of the Fantastic," "Tales of the Folk," "Tales of the Spirit," and "Tales of Laughter." Each entry contains a brief synopsis of the story (sometimes it is reprinted in full), gives presentation hints, and explains where the text can be found. Each chapter ends with an extensive bibliography. There are multiple indexes, including a subject index that suggests curriculum connections and a list of the story collections in which the stories appear. Because there is no duplication between the editions, librarians will want to consult both volumes.

898   Greene, Ellin. *Storytelling: Art and Technique,* 3rd ed. Libraries Unlimited, 1996, $41 (0-8352-3458-4).

For many years, this book has been considered one of the basic titles in the field. Now in its third, updated edition, it continues to offer excellent material on selecting, preparing, and telling stories to and for children ages 3 to 13. Ideas are given for both beginning and experienced storytellers working in public and school library settings. The bibliographies of sources are also very helpful. From planning to performance, this manual is an invaluable aid.

899   Haven, Kendall. *Super Simple Storytelling: A Can-Do Guide for Every Classroom, Every Day.* Teacher Ideas Press/Libraries Unlimited, 2000, $25 (1-56308-681-6).

Although this manual for storytellers focuses on teachers using storytelling in the classroom, it also contains many tips of value to librarians. It offers excellent basic advice and gives 40 special storytelling exercises, a list of what an audience expects from storytelling, a simple step-by-step method of memorizing stories, ways to prevent storytelling disasters, a description of different types of stories with examples, and a chapter on how to teach students to be storytellers.

900   Kinghorn, Harriet R., and Mary Helen Pelton. *Every Child a Storyteller.* Teacher Ideas Press/Libraries Unlimited, 1991, pap., $25 (0-872878-68-6).

This manual shows how to turn students into expert storytellers. It demonstrates how various popular forms of literature—nursery rhymes, fables, how-and-why stories, tall tales, folktales, and fairy tales, for example—can be used in a variety of storytelling situations. As well as developing storytelling competencies in children, the authors show how to use crafts, pictures, reader's theater, and flannel boards in presentations. This clear, precise, school-oriented book is a basic work on training youngsters to tell stories effectively.

901   Leeming, David Adams. *Storytelling Encyclopedia: Historical, Cultural, and Multiethnic Approaches to Oral Traditions Around the World.* Oryx, 1997, $69.95 (1-57356-025-1).

A collection of more than 700 alphabetically arranged entries by various experts on the past and present status of the oral tradition around the world, this encyclopedia covers many topics: the Ancient World, creation myths, biographies of anthropologists and storytellers, stories from the great religions, important characters and themes, and landmark publications and authors. It has been criticized for its superficiality, but it is nevertheless a good starting point for basic information.

902   Lipman, Doug. *Improving Your Storytelling: Beyond the Basics for All Who Tell Stories in Work or Play.* August House, 1999, pap., $14.95 (0-8748-3530-5).

Written by a professional storyteller who has authored many books in this field, this work is aimed more at performing artists than at amateur storytellers. However, it offers many practical suggestions for perfecting one's art. Particularly interesting are the discussion of the meaning and structure of "story" and the outline of models for learning stories.

903   MacDonald, Margaret Read. *The Storyteller's Start-Up Book: Finding, Learning, Performing and Using Folktales Including 12 Tellable Tales.* August House, 1993, $26.95 (0-87483-304-3).

In 16 brief, well-organized chapters, the author covers such storytelling basics as selection, learning, performing, setting, and class performance. She enthusiastically conveys the value of storytelling and imparts confidence to beginning storytellers. In addition to numerous performance tips, this work gives extensive sources and a collection of 12 excellent tales to retell. There is an annotated bibliography at the end of each chapter.

904   MacDonald, Margaret Read, and Brian W. Sturm. *The Storyteller's Sourcebook: A Subject, Title, and Motif Index to Folklore Collections for Children, 1983–1999.* Gale, 2001, $150 (0-8103-5485-3).

This is a continuation of the earlier *Storyteller's Sourcebook, 1961–1982* (Gale, 1982, $150 [0-8103-0471-6]), which was named one of the outstanding reference sources of its publication year. It analyzes 210 collections of folktales and 790 picture books. The largest section is the Motif Index, where stories can be located under such headings as glass slipper, ogres, and the wise and the foolish (plus many subdivisions). Details of the story are also given. There are title, subject, and ethnic and geographic indexes. Lastly, there is a list of the collections and single volumes included in this book.

905   Pellowski, Anne. *The World of Storytelling: Expanded and Revised Edition.* H. W. Wilson, 1990, $60 (0-8242-0788-2).

Anne Pellowski is one of the world's foremost authorities on the storytelling tradition, and this fascinating volume gives a history of storytelling through the ages and reports on the current practices and content of storytelling throughout the world. The author also considers variations in style and format and how musical and pictorial aids are used to add to presentations. There is material on how storytellers are trained around the globe. This is an important work in the field.

906   Sawyer, Ruth. *Way of the Storyteller.* Penguin, 1998, $15 (0-1400-4436-1).

Although many books on storytelling have been published since this work originally appeared in 1942, none has achieved its scope or charm. This classic work combines literary history and criticism with an analysis of stories, personal anecdotes, and practical how-to instructions. The author examines storytelling as a folk art that is still alive and traces its development from early civilizations onward. Stories of unusual merit are highlighted and there are many tips on delivery. Two other classic manuals in the field are *Storytelling: Art and Technique* (Bowker, 1977, o.p.) by Augusta Baker and Ellin Greene (for a newer edition, see above under Greene) and Silvia Ziskind's *Telling Stories to Children* (H. W. Wilson, 1976, $45 [0-8242-0588-X]).

907   Sierra, Judy. *Storytellers' Research Guide.* Folkprint, 1996, $14.95 (0-9636089-4-0).

This excellent reference work for storytellers contains information on such topics as the definition of a folktale, copyright concerns, how to look for tellable tales and enhance a presentation, and how to find new folktales in the field and collect material on the cultural settings of stories. There are extensive lists of sources, including those on the Internet.

908   Sima, Judy, and Kevin Cori. ***Raising Voices: Creating Youth Storytelling Groups and Troupes.*** Libraries Unlimited, 2003, pap., $32.50 (1-56308-919-X).

This is a complete and essential handbook for anyone aiming to establish and sustain a successful group or troupe of storytellers in grades 4 through 12 (a troupe is defined as a group of young storytellers who are able to travel as performers). Although geared to a school setting, this manual is equally useful for community and public library groups and covers everything from the first meeting through the period of developing skills to the actual performance. Lists of resources are included along with reproducible forms.

909   Simpson, Martha Seif, and Lynne Perrigo. ***StoryCraft: 50 Theme-Based Programs Combining Storytelling, Activities and Crafts for Children in Grades 1–3.*** McFarland, 2001, pap., $38.50 (0-7864-0891-X).

A highly recommended collection of popular, child-tested programs on such subjects as cowboys and cowgirls, kites, dragons, and magic. Each unit includes suggestions for a bulletin board, music, an opener, stories, activities, a craft, and titles that can be booktalked. Each program is given a thorough step-by-step treatment and a section called "Helpful Hints." There are detailed instructions for each craft project.

910   Spaulding, Amy. ***The Wisdom of Storytelling in an Information Age: A Collection of Talks.*** Scarecrow, 2004, $35 (0-8108-5044-3).

This is a collection of "talks" about the status and importance of storytelling in the increasingly impersonal environment of the high-technology era. Spaulding points out ways in which the storyteller can be more effective than bare data and facts in inspiring and teaching young people. In short, her thesis is that "the word is mightier than the word processor."

911   Weissman, Annie. ***Do Tell! Storytelling for You and Your Students.*** Linworth, 2002, pap., $36.95 (1-58683-074-0).

A beginner's guide to storytelling at the elementary school level. The author, an experienced storyteller, gives step-by-step guidance in choosing a story, in developing preparation techniques, and in methods of presentation. She shows how stories can be integrated into the curriculum and includes special material on how students can be taught to tell stories. There is advice on running a storytelling festival in a school, complete with a timeline, strategies, and helpful hints. Another excellent book on training young storytellers is ***Children Tell Stories: A Teaching Guide*** (Richard Owen, 1990, $45 [0-9146-120-2]) by Martha Hamilton and Mitch Weiss.

912   Zipes, Jack. *Creative Storytelling: Building Community, Changing Lives.* Routledge, 1995, $55 (0-415-91271-7).

In this mix of the practical and the theoretical, the author advocates the creation of an active storytelling program involving teachers, administrators, librarians, community members, and a visiting storyteller. He suggests interesting ways of integrating stories into visual arts activities and creative dramatics, while also discussing structural functions and motifs in fairy and folk tales and supplying critical comments on the various genres. Traditional and modern versions of different tales are presented for classroom use with accompanying activities. This stimulating volume also discusses sexual stereotyping in many stories and decries the commercialization and watering-down of classic folk and fairy tales.

5. Storytimes and Read-Aloud Guides

913   Benton, Gail, and Trisha Waichulaitis. *Ready-to-Go Storytimes: Fingerplays, Scripts, Patterns, Music, and More.* Neal-Schuman, 2003, pap., $59.95 (1-55570-449-2).

This book and accompanying CD supply detailed information for librarians and teachers on presenting effective 30-minute storytimes for children aged 18 months to 5 years. Each takes advantage of a child's curiosity and encourages parent participation. Six chapters cover different themes—food, animals, deserts, colors, and clothes, for example—and each contains an outline, an interactive song, a read-aloud book suggestion, activities, and an activity sheet handout. A fine resource, particularly for beginning librarians.

914   *Books to Read Aloud with Children.* Bank Street College.

Sixty-four pages in length, this pamphlet contains an annotated list of almost 400 books suitable for reading aloud. They range from the classics to recent titles and are arranged by age and subject category. This list is available for $7.50 plus $2.50 shipping from Bank Street College, 612 W. 112th St., New York, NY 10025-1898.

915   Bradbury, Judy. *Children's Book Corner: A Read-Aloud Resource with Tips, Techniques, and Plans for Teachers, Librarians and Parents/Level Pre K–K.* Libraries Unlimited, 2003, $32 (1-59158-048-X).

The first in what will be four guides—arranged by grade level—to read-aloud resources, this volume covers the topic for toddlers, preschoolers, and kindergarten students. It provides recommended book titles, book selection tips, ideas concerning pre-reading discussion and presentation, and an assortment of activities. There are also useful parent pull-out pages for duplication.

916   Bromann, Jennifer. *Storytime Action! 2,000+ Ideas for Making 500 Picture Books Interactive.* Neal-Schuman, 2003, pap., $45 (1-55570-459-X).

After explaining her ten guiding principles for production of successful interactive storytimes, the author provides specific ideas for 500 recommended picture books. Each entry contains bibliographic information, a plot summary, and one or more activities, including crafts, playacting, discussion questions, and music. As well as these practical and entertaining activities, the author gives advice on program planning and on how to develop one's individual style. This is a recommended source for all those who conduct storytime programs.

917   Cullinan, Bernice E. *Read to Me: Raising Kids Who Love to Read.* Scholastic, 2000, pap., $6.95 (0-4390-8721-X).

This book is aimed at parents who want to help their children read and enjoy reading. It is an informative handbook that gives tips on how and when to read, and includes material on how to use the computer and television as aids to the reading process. This fine manual also contains a bibliography of sure-fire read-alouds suitable for preschoolers through teenagers.

918   Cullum, Carolyn N. *The Storytime Sourcebook: A Compendium of Ideas and Resources for Storytellers,* 2nd ed. Neal-Schuman, 1999, pap., $45 (1-55570-360-7).

This is an updated, expanded edition of the well-received 1990 book with the same title. The current volume contains material on about 150 individual storytime themes and subjects, with information on coordinating these with special events or holidays. Age group suitability is 3 through 7. For each topic, there are suggested books (usually 15 per entry), song cassettes and CDs, activities, crafts, videotapes, and other program ideas. This is a well-organized, well-researched source that will be of great value to anyone working with this age group.

919   Fox, Mem. *Reading Magic: Why Reading Aloud to Our Children Will Change Their Lives Forever.* Harvest Books, 2001, $12 (0-15-601076-3).

Fox, a best-selling picture book writer, extols the benefits of reading to preschoolers (even newborns) and makes suggestions for helping children to read by themselves. She stresses the need to read aloud to preschoolers every day and gives guidance on defining, choosing, and finding good books. Using case studies and inspiring advice, she closes with tips on dealing effectively with the challenges one faces when a child is learning to read.

920   McElmeel, Sharron L. *The Latest and Greatest Read-Alouds.* Libraries Unlimited, 1994, pap., $18.50 (1-56308-140-7).

The books discussed in this volume were all published between 1988 and 1994 and some may now be unavailable. They have a sound narrative appeal and are recommended for children ages 5 through 10—more than 50 picture books for children ages 5 through 7 and more than 100 read-alouds for grades K through 5. Each entry (arranged by author) includes a summary, reader's advisory information, and help in developing reading units. This is a useful but unfortunately dated resource.

921   Maddigan, Beth. *The Big Book of Stories, Songs, and Sing-Alongs: Programs for Babies, Toddlers, and Families.* Libraries Unlimited, 2003, pap., $32 (1-56308-975-0).

After a general introduction on programming in a public library for this age group and the accompanying challenges, the author presents a series of programs on various subjects. Each entry consists of a storytime involving three books, rhymes and songs, fingerplays, and a storytime souvenir.

922   Reid, Rob. *Cool Story Programs for the School-Age Crowd.* American Library Association, 2004, $32 (0-8389-0887-X).

Designed to help librarians and teachers serving students in grades K through 4, this work outlines 18 new, delightful, and offbeat programs sure to delight a young audience. Each plan includes an overview, then presentations that involve poetry, picture books, chapter book excerpts, and short stories. Suggested activities involve wordplay, reader's theater, dramatics, writing, music, sports, and crafts. Variations are also suggested for adapting these programs for young or older audiences. This is an entertaining resource by the author of *Family Storytime: 24 Creative Programs for All Ages* (American Library Association, 1999, $28 [0-8389-0751-2]), which outlines family-tested programs for young readers that run about 30 minutes each.

923   Richardson, Judy S. *Read It Aloud! Using Literature in the Secondary Content Classroom.* International Reading Association, 2000, $16.95 (0-87207-256-8).

Based on her column "Read It Aloud!" in the *Journal of Adolescent and Adult Literacy*, the author shows middle school and high school teachers how to use read-alouds from a variety of genres in the content areas of the curriculum. As well as the readings, there are suggested student activities, teaching ideas for special populations, and principles for selecting and using great read-alouds.

924   Russell, William F. *Classics to Read Aloud to Your Children.* Three Rivers Press, 1992, pap., $12 (0-51758-715-7).

Subtitled *Selections from Shakespeare, Twain, Dickens, O. Henry, London, Longfellow, Irving, Aesop, Homer, Cervantes, Hawthorne, and More Specially Arranged for Children Five to 12 by an Educational Expert,* this volume includes selections arranged according to age, with advice on delivery strategies. Two other anthologies of read-alouds by this author are *Classic Myths to Read Aloud: The Great Stories of Greek and Roman Mythology Specially Arranged for Children Five and Up by an Educational Expert* (Three Rivers Press, 1992, pap., $12 [0-51758-837-4]) and *More Classics to Read Aloud to Children* (Three Rivers Press, 1994, $12 [0-51758-227-2]).

925   Trelease, Jim. *The Read-Aloud Handbook,* 5th ed. Penguin, 2001, pap., $15 (0-14-100161-5).

Now more than a quarter of a century old, this manual has become the standard text on reading aloud to children. It not only gives wise advice on introducing children to books and tips for reading aloud successfully, but also contains an excellent annotated list of hundreds of books to which children will truly respond. This new edition shows readers how to use recent cultural and technological developments to motivate reading, exploring lessons learned from Oprah, Harry Potter, and the Internet. Important Web sites for children's literature and education are listed in an appendix.

C. GUIDES TO WRITING, ILLUSTRATING, AND PUBLISHING CHILDREN'S AND YOUNG ADULT LITERATURE

This is a selection of the many guides and manuals now available to those who wish to create and publish children's and young adult literature. Many titles— such as the books by Katherine Paterson, Joan Aiken, Uri Shulevitz, Ralph Fletcher, and Jane Yolen—are inspirational in nature; others are more practical manuals for would-be writers and illustrators. Many of the "inspirational" titles are also found in Chapter 1 of this book, under "Important Monographs and Critical Studies."

926   Aiken, Joan. *The Way to Write for Children.* St. Martin's, 1999, pap., $8.95 (0-312-20048-X).

927   Alphin, Elaine Marie. *Creating Characters Kids Will Love.* Writer's Digest, 2000, pap., $16.99 (0-89897-985-6).

928   Bicknell, Treld Pelkey, and Felicity Trotman. *How to Write and Illustrate Children's Books and Get Them Published.* Writer's Digest, 2000, pap., $19.95 (1-58297-013-0).

929   Bolton, Lesley. *The Everything Guide to Writing Children's Books: From Celebrating an Idea to Finding the Right Publishers: All You Need to Launch a Successful Career.* Adams Media, 2002, pap., $14.95 (1-58062-785-4).

930   *Children's Writer's and Illustrator's Market,* 14th ed. Writer's Digest, 2004, pap., $24.99 (1-58297-191-9).

931   Dils, Tracey E. *You Can Write Children's Books.* Writer's Digest, 1998, pap., $12.99 (0-89879-829-9).

932   Fletcher, Ralph. *A Writer's Notebook: Unlocking the Writer Within You.* HarperTrophy, 1996, pap., $5.99 (0-380-78430-0).

933   Henderson, Kathy. *The Market Guide for Young Writers,* 5th ed. Writer's Digest, 1996, $16.99 (0-89879-951-1) (this excellent manual is intended for writers ages 8 to 18).

934   Jones, Marcia Thornton, and Debbie Dadey. *Story Sparklers: A Creativity Guide for Children's Writers.* Writer's Digest, 2000, pap., $16.99 (1-58297-019-X).

935   Koehler-Pentacoff, Elizabeth. *The ABC's of Writing for Children: 114 Children's Authors and Illustrators Talk About the Art, the Business, the Craft and the Life of Writing Children's Literature.* Quill Driver, 2003, pap., $16.95 (1-884956-28-9).

936   Lamb, Nancy. *Writer's Guide to Crafting Stories for Children.* Writer's Digest, 20001, pap., $16.99 (1-58297-052-1).

937   Lee, Betsy B. *A Basic Guide to Writing, Selling, and Promoting Children's Books.* Learning Activities, 2000, pap., $4.95 (0-96588-533-X).

938   Mogilner, Alijanora. *Children's Writer's Word Book.* Writer's Digest, 1999, pap., $16.99 (0-89879-951-1).

939   Paterson, Katherine. *The Invisible Child: On Reading and Writing Books for Children.* Dutton, 2001, $24.99 (0-525-46482-4) (see also listing in Chapter 1).

940   Seuling, Barbara. *How to Write a Children's Book and Get It Published,* 3rd ed. Wiley, 2005, e-book, $15.95 (0-471-68574-7).

941   Shapiro, Ellen R. *Writer's and Illustrator's Guide to Children's Books Publishing and Agents: Who They Are! What They Want! And How To Win Them Over!* 2nd ed. Three Rivers Press, 2003, pap., $19.95 (0-76152-686-2).

942   Shepard, Aaron. *The Business of Writing for Children: An Award-Winning Author's Tips on Writing and Publishing Children's Books, or How to Write, Publish and Promote a Book for Kids.* Shepard, 2000, pap., $10 (0-93849-711-1).

943   Stein, Barbara, and Lucia Hansen. *Children's Media Market Place,* 4th ed. Neal-Schuman, 1995, o.p.

944   Underdown, Harold D. *Complete Idiot's Guide to Publishing Children's Books.* Alpha Books, 2001, pap., $16.95 (1-59257-143-3).

945   Wyndham, Lee, and Arnold Madison. *Writing for Children and Young Adults.* Writer's Digest, 1989, pap., $14.99 (0-415-94017-6).

946   Yolen, Jane. *Take Joy: A Book for Writers.* Writer, Inc., 2003, $16.95 (0-87116-194-X).

CHAPTER 8

BIOGRAPHIES OF AUTHORS AND ILLUSTRATORS

Note: Extensive Internet resources offering biographies of authors and illustrators can be found in Chapter 11.

A. GENERAL AND UNITED STATES SOURCES

947 *Authors and Artists for Young Adults.* Gale, various dates and ISBNs, $115 per volume.

This important set that now numbers about 65 volumes maintains the high level of other Gale publications. In essence, it bridges the gap between this publisher's *Something About the Author* (see below) and *Contemporary Authors.* The number of volumes published varies by year (in 2005, six volumes were added to the set). Each volume contains between 20 and 25 entries on writers, artists, film directors, graphic novelists, and other creative personalities of interest to young adults. The emphasis is on writers. Each entry contains a substantial biography that provides personal and professional information, a portrait, a bibliography of writings and adaptations, a secondary bibliography, and sources of additional material. The entries lean toward biography rather than criticism; they are well written, informative, and entertaining. Each volume contains a cumulative index. Although this is a costly reference tool, it is an important source of information about personalities associated with the arts and young adults.

948   Bingham, Jane M. *Writers for Children: Critical Studies of Major Authors Since the Seventeenth Century.* Scribner, 1988, o.p.

Although this book is now out of print, the information it contains is unique and still of value. It includes 84 lengthy essays (about six to eight pages each) on great writers of children's literature. Although all of the featured writers are deceased, their works are still read and respected. The articles are scholarly and written by authorities in the field. Each entry is accompanied by a bibliography of primary and secondary sources. The emphasis is on British and American authors, but luminaries from other countries include Andersen, the Brothers Grimm, de Brunhoff, Collodi, Perrault, and Spyri. A detailed index to the authors and their titles is provided. This is a well-researched reference work that could profitably be reissued.

949   Bloom, Harold. *Women Writers of Children's Literature.* Chelsea, 1998, $29.95 (0-7910-4486-6).

This reference work contains material on 12 women writers for children. Spanning several centuries and two continents, it includes entries on Alcott, Greenaway, Nesbit, Travers, and Wilder; more contemporary names are L'Engle, Le Guin, Paterson, and Fitzhugh. For each author, there is a two-page biographical sketch, a complete bibliography, and an eclectic group of critical extracts from books and journals. Some of the reviews go back to the 19th century and they often provide a new perspective on the classics.

950   *Contemporary Authors: A Bio-Bibliographical Guide to Current Writers in Fiction, General Nonfiction, Poetry, Journalism, Drama, Motion Pictures, Television, and Other Fields.* Gale, various dates and ISBNs, about $200 per volume.

This extensive set now numbers (as of 2005) 240 volumes. Each contains information on about a thousand contemporary writers. Entries include personal information, career history, writings, works in progress, biographical and critical sources, and author's comments. There is material on children's writers. Because the set is so large and expensive, it is found only in colleges, universities, and large public libraries. Related sets include *Contemporary Authors; First Revision Series, Contemporary Authors: New Revision Series, Contemporary Authors: Permanent Series, and Contemporary Authors: Autobiography Series.*

951 Cooper, John, and Jonathan Cooper. *Children's Fiction, 1900–1950.* Ashgate, 1998, $76.95 (1-85928-289-X).

Divided into five sections by decade, this volume covers the work of 206 American and British children's fiction authors. There are cross-references from pseudonyms to real names. Within each section, author and illustrator entries are arranged alphabetically and contain a short biography and a bibliography of works written and/or illustrated. The choice of entries is judicious, and there are cross-references for authors whose works span more than one decade. Unfortunately there is no index.

952 Copeland, Jeffrey S., and Vicky Copeland. *Speaking of Poets 2: Interviews with Poets Who Write for Children and Young Adults.* National Council of Teachers of English, 1995, pap., $15.95 (0-8141-4620-1).

This sequel to the authors' *Speaking of Poets* (NCTE, 1993, o.p.) contains an additional 20 interviews with celebrated poets, some new and some already established. Each interview covers the poet's background, inspiration, creative processes, and thoughts on sharing poetry with young people. Both adults and young poets from grades 5 through high school will find these interviews understandable, enlightening, and encouraging.

953 *Dictionary of Literary Biography.* Gale, various dates and ISBNs, $205 per volume.

There are now more than 300 volumes in this massive set that surveys both notable American and international authors and important literary topics. Collectively this series contains about 9,000 author entries and more than 800 topics. The set is available both in print and online. At present, four volumes are devoted to American writers of children's literature and four volumes to British writers (see the coverage on the United Kingdom below). The four volumes with American coverage are:

American Writers for Children Before 1900, Vol. 42. Gale, 1985, $205 (0-8103-1720-6). Among the 52 writers covered in this volume are Louisa May Alcott, Frances Hodgson Burnett, Mary Mapes Dodge, Howard Pyle, Kate Douglas Wiggin, and Joel Chandler Harris.

American Writers for Children, 1900–1960, Vol. 22. Gale, 1983, $205 (0-8103-1146-1). Forty-three scholarly entries cover such writers as L. Frank Baum, E. B. White, Esther Forbes, Lois Lenski, and Laura Ingalls Wilder.

American Writers for Children Since 1960: Fiction, Vol. 52. Gale, 1986, $205 (0-8103-1730-3). The coverage in this volume is now about 20 years old and should be updated. Some of the 44 subjects covered are Lloyd Alexander, Judy Blume, Beverly Cleary, Robert Cormier, Virginia Hamilton, Madeleine L'Engle, Lois Lowry, and Katherine Paterson.

American Writers for Children Since 1960: Poets, Illustrators, and Nonfiction Authors, Vol. 61. Gale, 1987, $205 (0-8103-1739-7). This work could also be updated. The 32 essays include coverage of Marcia Brown, Tomie dePaola, Dr. Seuss, Arnold Lobel, Milton Meltzer, Richard Scarry, Maurice Sendak, and William Steig.

954 *Dictionary of Literary Biography: Documentary Series: An Illustrated Chronicle.* Gale, various dates and ISBNs, $205 per volume.

This supplementary series to the publisher's *Dictionary of Literary Biography* (see above) now numbers about 20 volumes, only one of which deals with children's literature. It is Volume 14: *Four Women Writers for Children, 1868–1918* (Gale, 1996, $205 [0-8103-9365-4]). Louisa May Alcott, Frances Hodgson Burnett, L. M. Montgomery, and Gene Stratton Porter are the four novelists highlighted. For each, there is a bibliography of the author's works, a list of biographical works, locations of archival material, essays on their lives and works, facsimiles of manuscripts, letters, reproductions of book covers, reviews, and other archival documents. It is hoped that additional volumes in this series will be devoted to children's literature.

955 Drew, Bernard A. *The 100 Most Popular Young Adult Authors: Biographical Sketches and Bibliographies: Revised Edition.* Libraries Unlimited, 1997, $58 (1-56308-615-8).

Although this book focuses on writers of the 1990s, 12 of the biographies are of classic writers who appeal to teens. The audience range is from middle school (Betsy Byars, for example) to high school (V. C. Andrews). Each entry includes a brief biography, some critical comments, a statement by the writer about the creative process, and a bibliography of all the young adult fiction by the writer with short plot summaries. There are also bibliographies of other works by the author and suggestions for further reading. This handy reference for students and adults now has a companion volume by the same author, *100 More Popular Young Adult Authors: Biographical Sketches and Bibliographies* (Libraries Unlimited, 2002, $60 [0-56308-920-3]). This has a somewhat broader scope than the parent volume and features both lesser-known authors and more standard favorites such as Robert Louis Stevenson, Mary O'Hara, and Laura Ingalls Wilder. Coverage is the same, with a biography followed by short summaries and critiques of major works. Also similar in scope and treatment is the author's *100 Most Popular Genre Fiction Writers* (Libraries Unlimited, 2005, $50.50 [1-59158-129-5]). All three books are recommended.

956 *Favorite Children's Authors and Illustrators*, 6 vols. Child's World, 2002, $357 (schools and libraries, $249.90) (o.p.).

Designed to be used by upper-elementary and middle-grade readers, this is a collection of 222 biographical sketches and other material arranged in six volumes running alphabetically from Verna Aardema to Paul O. Zelinsky and including coverage on such celebrated authors as Avi, Virginia Hamilton, E. B. White, Julius Lester, and Gary Soto. In addition to biographical material, each entry includes a photograph of the subject, reproductions of book covers, quotations by and about the subject, interesting facts, sources of further information, and a selected bibliography through 2002. Great for both browsing and report writing.

957 Gallo, Donald R. *Speaking for Ourselves: Autobiographical Sketches by Notable Authors of Books for Young Adults.* National Council of Teachers of English, 1990, o.p.

This volume and its sequel *Speaking for Ourselves, Too* (NCTE, 1993, o.p.) contain 176 autobiographical sketches by noted young adult authors including Lloyd Alexander, M. E. Kerr, Walter Dean Myers, and Lois Lowry. Many describe their work and how they became writers. Each entry also contains a portrait and a selective bibliography. Although out of date and available only through used-book sources, these two volumes still contain valuable background material.

958 Hipple, Ted. *Writers for Young Adults*, 3 vols. Scribner/Gale, 1997, $295 (o.p.).

This three-volume set contains 129 informative essays, each about ten pages in length, on the best and most popular writers read by adolescents. The majority deal with young adult authors—Cormier, Crutcher, and Kerr, for example—but others cover writers studied in high schools, such as Hemingway and Steinbeck. Written in a conversational tone, each entry contains a biographical sketch, a photograph, plot summaries, critical analysis, interesting facts, and insights into writing techniques. The contributors are all young adult specialists and include Ted Hipple (the editor), Patty Campbell, Donald Gallo, and Cosette Kies. The articles are written for young adults but are also valuable for adult use. The index combines authors, titles, and subjects/themes in one alphabet. A companion volume also edited by Ted Hipple, *Writers for Young Adults, Supplement I* (Scribner/Gale, 2000, $80 [0-684-80618-5]), contains an additional 39 biographical entries, again young adult writers and others with young adult appeal such as Jane Austen and Stephen King. Coverage is similar to the main set. This work is highly recommended for both school and public libraries.

959   Hopkins, Lee Bennett. *Pauses: Autobiographical Reflections of 101 Creators of Children's Books.* HarperCollins, 1995, o.p.

The essays in this volume are one to three pages in length and contain statements (many autobiographical) on the lives and work of important writers for children. These often reveal hidden and fascinating aspects of the subjects' personal and professional lives. This is a companion to the author's earlier *Books Are by People* (Harper, 1969, o.p.) and *More Books by More People* (Harper, 1974, o.p.). All three volumes are available through used-book dealers and give valuable background information on many of the greatest names in the field of contemporary children's literature.

960   *Junior Authors and Illustrators Series.* H. W. Wilson, various dates and ISBNs.

One of the most used and respected series of books providing biographical information on children's authors and illustrators, this has now been running for more than 70 years. Each volume contains about 200 to 280 short (one- to two-page) entries with a photograph, first-person information from the subject, a biography, a list of selected works, and, frequently, suggested secondary sources. A total of about 2,000 profiles are included in the set. Writers of both fiction and nonfiction are included. New volumes appear approximately every five years. The series is available in print and in an electronic edition. In reverse chronological order, the nine volumes in the current series are:

Rockman, Connie C. *Ninth Book of Junior Authors and Illustrators,* 2005, $105 (0-8242-1043-3).

Rockman, Connie C. *Eighth Book of Junior Authors and Illustrators.* 2000, $90 (0-8242-0968-0).

Holtze, Sally Holmes. *Seventh Book of Junior Authors and Illustrators.* 1996, $75 (0-8242-0874-9).

Holtze, Sally Holmes. *Sixth Book of Junior Authors and Illustrators.* 1989, $75 (0-8242-0777-7).

Holtze, Sally Holmes. *Fifth Book of Junior Authors and Illustrators.* 1983, $75 (0-8242-0694-0).

De Montreville, Doris, and Elizabeth D. Crawford. *Fourth Book of Junior Authors and Illustrators.* 1978, $65 (0-8242-0568-5).

De Montreville, Doris, and Elizabeth D. Crawford. *Third Book of Junior Authors and Illustrators.* 1972, $60 (0-8242-0408-5).

Fuller, Muriel. *More Junior Authors.* 1963, $55 (0-8242-0036-5).

Kunitz, Stanley J., and Howard Haycraft. *Junior Book of Authors*, 2nd ed. 1951, $60 (0-8242-0028-4) (the first edition of the volume appeared in 1934).

961 Kutzer, M. Daphne. *Writers of Multicultural Fiction for Young Adults: A Bio-Critical Sourcebook.* Greenwood, 1996, $75 (0-313-29331-7).

After an introductory essay by Kutzer—"What Is Multicultural Literature?"—authorities in the field profile 51 writers of multicultural fiction, many of whom are writing about ethnic groups not their own. The subjects include Gary Soto, Laurence Yep, and Julius Lester as well as lesser-known or historically important writers such as Ann Nolan Clark and Florence Crannell Means. Each entry presents a biographical sketch, a section on criticism and themes, and a bibliography. This is an excellent work but now in need of an update.

962 *Lives and Works: Young Adult Authors 8 vols.* Grolier, 1999, $255 (0-7172-9227-4).

Profiles of more that 250 authors important to young adult readers—ranging from William Shakespeare to Francesca Lia Block—appear in this set. Entries are three or four pages in length and contain a portrait, a brief biography, concise critical comments on the author's major works, a list of selected works by and about the author, and, sometimes, Web addresses. Each volume contains a master author, title, and subject index for the entire set. Geared to middle school and junior high students, this attractive set will also be consulted by librarians and teachers.

963 McElmeel, Sharron L. *Children's Authors and Illustrators Too Good to Miss: Biographical Sketches and Bibliographies.* Libraries Unlimited, 2004, $48 (1-59158-027-7).

This book serves as an update and continuation of the two titles listed immediately below. Forty-five authors and illustrators are included, with an emphasis on new names in children's literature such as Laurie Halse Anderson, Toni Buzzeo, David Diaz, and Simms Taback. For each subject, there is an interesting biographical sketch, a photograph, a selected bibliography, and a list of further resources.

964   McElmeel, Sharron L. *100 Most Popular Children's Authors: Biographical Sketches and Bibliographies.* Libraries Unlimited, 1999, $50.50 (1-56308-646-8).

Using the same survey results that produced the companion volume on picture book creators (see entry below), the author identified the top children's authors popular in the middle grades and supplied background information on each. Material includes basic facts, a biographical essay, sometimes a picture, a bibliography—often with annotations, series notes, and sources of further information about the author. The genre index is thorough, with entries under such headings as "Mystery." There is also a general author/title index. McElmeel is also the author of *Bookpeople: A Multicultural Album* (Teacher Ideas Press, 1992, 0-87287-953-4) and *Bookpeople: A Second Album* (Teacher Ideas Press, 1992, o.p.).

965   McElmeel, Sharron L. *100 Most Popular Picture Book Authors and Illustrators: Biographical Sketches and Bibliographies.* Libraries Unlimited, 2000, $58 (1-56308-647-6).

Entries in this useful volume were chosen on the basis of a 1997 survey and are arranged alphabetically by the subject's last name. Each entry contains basic facts, a biography that also gives background information on the writer's books, information on specific books, a bibliography of published works arranged by genre, a list of material for further study including Web sites, and, in most cases, a photograph. In addition to a general author/title index there is one by genre and subject. This is an attractive resource for librarians and teachers.

966   *Major Authors and Illustrators for Children and Young Adults: A Selection of Sketches from Something About the Author,* 2nd ed., 8 vols. Gale, 2002, $485 (0-7876-1234-0).

This large set is designed for libraries that can't afford the much more extensive *Something About the Author* (see below). It supplies extensive updated information on the 950 authors and illustrators found in the first edition of this set (1993), plus material on 150 new authors and illustrators who have achieved more recent prominence. Organized by last name of the subject, each entry gives extensive biographical information (both personal and professional), a picture, a comprehensive list of their works, adaptations to other media, works in progress, secondary sources, and "Sidelights," which supply unusual factual data. Each entry is several oversized pages in length. Various genres are represented, including picture books, poetry, biographies, and general nonfiction. The set is thoroughly indexed. For owners of the original 1993 set, a supplement remains in print: *Major Authors and Illustrators for Chil-*

dren and Young Adults, 1st Supplement, Gale, 1999, $110 (0-7876-1904-0).

967   Marcus, Leonard. *Author Talk.* Simon and Schuster, 2000, $22 (0-689-81383-X).

Brief interviews with 15 well-known children's book authors, including Judy Blume, E. L. Konigsburg, Gary Paulsen, Laurence Yep, and Johanna Hurwitz, can be found here. The same questions were used in each interview and covered family, inspiration, and work habits. Two sample questions: "How do you write a book?" and "What do you do when you're not writing?" This work will be of interest to children in the middle school and junior high grades.

968   Murphy, Barbara Thrash. *Black Authors and Illustrators of Books for Children and Young Adults: A Biographical Dictionary.* Garland, 1999, $70 (0-8153-2004-3).

This is the third edition of the reference work once edited by Barbara Rollock. It contains more than 150 entries that are updated from previous editions and 121 new entries, making a total of 274 biographical sketches. Ranging in length from one paragraph to several pages, the entries cover a wide range of authors representing many countries (chiefly the United States) and cultures. Some of the authors wrote only for young readers; others wrote adult books popular with young readers. Some entries contain portraits. There are several appendixes, one on book awards and prizes, and author and title indexes.

969   Nakamura, Joyce. *Children's Authors and Illustrators: An Index to Biographical Dictionaries,* 5th ed. Gale, 1995, o.p.

For the serious children's literature researcher, this out-of-print and out-of-date work may be of some help in locating biographical material on specific authors and illustrators. More than 200,000 biographies of some 30,000 authors in 650 sources are listed. There are several omissions and inaccuracies but this work is still a monument to diligent index making.

970   Preller, James. *The Big Book of Picture Book Authors and Illustrators.* Scholastic, 2001, $16.95 (0-4392-0154-3).

The 75 short biographies included here are suitable for reading aloud to a younger audience to introduce favorite authors and illustrators and to help youngsters understand the writing process. Among the personalities included are Tomie de Paola, Cynthia Rylant, Aliki, Jerry Pinkney, and Leo Lionni. Each entry is two pages in length and contains a picture, an informal biography, activities, a book jacket illustration, personal anecdotes, and a sidebar of "Selected Titles." Some of this material appeared in the author's earlier work with Deborah Kovacs, *Meet the Authors and Illustrators, Vol. 1 (Grades 1–6)*, Scholastic, 1999, $21.95 (0-590-49097-4), which contains material on 60 authors divided into two sections: "Picture Book Authors" and "Intermediate Authors."

971   Schon, Isabel, and Lourdes Gavaldon de Barreto. *Contemporary Spanish-Speaking Writers and Illustrators for Children and Young Adults.* Greenwood, 1994, $49.95 (0-313-29027-X).

Now more than 10 years old, this bio-bibliography includes information on 249 Spanish-speaking authors and illustrators from North, South, and Central America as well as from Spain, the rest of Europe, and Morocco. Entries vary from a half page to five pages, and include personal data, career information, awards, a bibliography of the subject's works, and critical sources. This is still valuable for large Spanish-language collections.

972   *Something About the Author: Autobiographical Series.* Gale, various dates and ISBNs, $140 per volume.

The first volume in this set appeared in 1985. The set was discontinued in 1998 after volume 26. Each volume contains about 15 autobiographical essays by well-known writers and illustrators of books for young people. There are approximately 450 profiles in the entire set. Each essay is about 10,000 words long and is illustrated with photographs, dust jackets, and so forth. The tone of the entries ranges from the formal and fact-filled to the breezy and very personal, but all are well-written and interesting. Each entry ends with a bibliography of the author's full-length works and there is a cumulative index in each volume. The parent set, *Something About the Author*, continues the tradition of this set by occasionally publishing autobiographical entries by important authors and illustrators.

973   *Something About the Author: Facts and Pictures About the Authors and Illustrators of Books for Young People.* Gale, various dates and ISBNs, $139 per volume.

This outstanding reference source began was conceived by its founder and editor for many years, Anne Commire, to satisfy young readers who come to their librarian asking for "something about the author." As of 2005, the set consists of 160 volumes and covers more than 12,000 authors and illustrators ranging from established award winners and historically important personalities to authors and illustrators who are just beginning their careers. Entries are well researched and contain material collected directly from the subject usually through questionnaires and interviews. There are approximately 70 to 80 entries in each volume. The number of volumes published in a year varies. Each entry includes a biography that includes personal data, often from letters and diaries; a chronological bibliography of writings/illustrations; adaptations into other media; a list of works in progress; and a bibliography of material about the subject. Occasionally, earlier articles about prolific authors and illustrators are updated with a new entry. Illustrations include a photograph of the subject, important dust jackets, or representative pictures. Odd-numbered volumes contain a cumulative index for the entire set. This is a standard reference set that provides authoritative information. See entries above for information on *Major Authors and Illustrators for Children and Young Adults* (a selection of articles from *Something About the Author*) and on the companion set *Authors and Artists for Young Adults*.

974   *St. James Guide to Children's Writers*, 5th ed. St. James, 1999, $175 (1-55862-369-8).

This fifth edition (the previous ones were called *Twentieth-Century Children's Writers*) has entries on the most important English-language writers of fiction, poetry, and drama, and (for the first time) on selected authors of nonfiction. There are a total of 750 entries in this single volume, with more than 70 new to this edition. A panel of experts chose the authors to be included. Each entry contains a biography, a complete list of published works, and a critical essay written by a children's literature specialist. These critical essays are the most outstanding aspect of this work. Important 19th-century writers are covered in an appendix. Coverage is mainly of British and U.S. writers; however, there are some from Canada, Australia, New Zealand, and the Third World. This is the best one-volume source for information on children's authors.

975   *St. James Guide to Young Adult Writers*, 2nd ed. St. James, 1999, $175 (1-55862-368-X).

In its first edition (1995), this book was called *Twentieth-Century Young Adult Writers*. The present edition covers 450 well-known authors of fiction, poetry, and drama. The individual sketches include basic biographical facts, a list of publications, and a critical essay on the author written by a librarian or a young adult literature specialist. Entries in this oversize volume are usually two or three pages long. Coverage is mainly American, but there are entries for some Canadian, British, and Australian writers. This is an excellent one-volume source of accurate information, particularly valuable for the astute critical summaries.

976   Stanfield, John. *Writers of the American West: Multicultural Learning Encounters.* Libraries Unlimited, 2002, $32 (1-56308-801-0).

In this series of author profiles plus excerpts from autobiographies, the diverse peoples and the history of the North American West come alive. The entries concentrate on the childhood and youth of these writers. Each chapter introduces a different writer through profiles, personal narratives, a resource bibliography, and numerous suggested activities. An appendix lists 20 additional Western writers for further exploration.

977   Stevens, Jen. *The Undergraduate Companion to Children's Writers and Their Web Sites.* Libraries Unlimited, 2004, pap., $29.95 (1-59158-097-8).

An excellent source of information about children's (and some young adult) authors, this volume cites some general Web sites and print sources for biographical information and then highlights about 200 prominent authors arranged alphabetically from Alma Flor Ada to Charlotte Zolotow. Many writers of classics—Stevenson and Defoe, for example—are included along with contemporary figures such as Betsy Byars and Jerry Spinelli. Birth and death dates are given for each, followed (usually) by listings of Web sites, biographies and criticism, and bibliographies. Web sites are annotated and the date of last access is cited. The biographies and criticism sections average four or five entries, often listing such standard sources as *Something About the Author* and *Children's Literary Review*. If bibliographies of the author's works have been published separately, they are listed in the third section. This is a thorough, well-organized source of both print and nonprint resources.

978   Wyatt, Flora, et al. *Popular Nonfiction Authors for Children: A Biographical and Thematic Guide.* Libraries Unlimited, 1998, $37.50 (1-56308-408-2).

This volume features 68 modern authors who are known as writers of nonfiction for youngsters. Each entry includes a photograph of the author, basic facts, a short message to students written by the author, and an annotated bibliography of his or her works. The biographies are short—about two pages each—and usually contain information on the author's childhood and how they became writers. The annotations in the bibliographies are brief but accurate. There is an extensive subject index to the books listed.

B. AUSTRALIA

979   McVitty, Walter. *Authors and Illustrators of Australian Children's Books.* Hodder and Stoughton, 1989, £25 (o.p.).

About 140 important Australian writers and illustrators of children's books are covered here. Each entry is about one and a half pages long and contains a photograph, a short biography, comments by the author or illustrator, and a bibliography of his or her books. Black-and-white illustrations of dust jackets are often included.

980 *Who's Who of Australian Children's Writers*, 2nd ed. D. W. Thorpe, 1996, pap., $35 (1-875589-77-5).

This work is based on a national database created by sending question-naires to authors who have written at least one work for children. Entries are factual and basic, containing material on education, employment history, books, types of writing, recreational interests, memberships, and availability for guest appearances. Almost 1,100 writers are included. The number of abbreviations employed in the text makes this a rather difficult book to use.

C. CANADA

981 *The Canscaip Companion: A Biographical Record of Canadian Children's Authors, Illustrators, and Performers*, 2nd ed. Pembroke, Markham, Ont., 1994, $30 (1-55138-021-8).

Canscaip, the Canadian Society of Children's Authors, Illustrators, and Performers, was founded in 1977 and is headquartered in Toronto. This directory furnishes material on the members (346 at the time of print-ing), with each entry containing a picture, address, a 12- to 15-line biog-raphy, a list of published or recorded works, awards, and availability for workshops, etc. This material is kept up to date with the quarterly *Can-scaip News*, which contains more biographical information, news of the society's activities, and information about new members and their works.

982 Gertridge, Allison. *Meet Canadian Authors and Illustrators.* Scholastic, 1994, $10 (o.p.).

Written for children, this directory contains entries on 50 Canadian cre-ators of children's books. Each author is covered in two pages that con-tain an informal biography with interesting details of his or her inspiration and writing techniques, a portrait and reproductions of dust jackets, a list of "selected titles," and suggested activities relating to the books discussed. An appendix lists resources, such as magazine articles, for many of the authors.

983 Jones, Raymond E., and Jon C. Stott. *Canadian Children's Books: A Critical Guide to Authors and Illustrators*, 2nd ed. Oxford, 2001, pap., $32.95 (0-19-541222-2).

Available only in English, this guide covers English-language Canadian authors and illustrators and French-language authors whose works have been translated. The introduction gives a concise history of children's literature in Canada. There are 133 entries, most of them three to four pages in length, but longer in the case of very famous authors (Monica Hughes gets 12 pages). The authors state "Each entry provides an overview of the individual's career, an introduction to major themes, character types, and techniques, and a more detailed look at major works." Preceding each entry is a bibliography of the subject's books up to January 1999 with selected reviews from journals and additional bibliographic and critical sources. The appendix lists national English-language Canadian book awards and their winners.

984   *The Storymakers: Writing Children's Books; 83 Authors Talk About Their Work.* Pembroke, 2000, $24.95 (1-55138-108-7).

This is a collection of 83 interviews with Canadian authors of fiction and nonfiction, chosen by a panel of children's literature experts. Eleven of the authors are also illustrators. The alphabetically arranged entries are written by the authors themselves, who answer questions about birthplace, education, hobbies, childhood, "my first book (and how it happened)," "where my ideas come from," influences, favorite books, etc. The purpose is to have readers discover the authors' "passions, their secrets, their sources of inspiration, and their history." Bibliographies list books by the writers and secondary sources. A companion volume is *The Storymakers: Illustrating Children's Books: 72 Artists and Illustrators Talk About Their Work* (Pembroke, 1999, o.p.). It contains the same material plus a black-and-white reproduction of the artist's work. Some of the material in these two books appeared previously in *Writing Stories, Making Pictures: Biographies of 150 Canadian Children's Authors and Illustrators* (Canadian Book Centre, 1994, o.p.).

D. UNITED KINGDOM

985   *Author Zone Magazine.* Annual, Peters Books.

Intended for young readers, this colorful annual (the fourth was dated 2000) gives breezy information on about 50 authors per issue. The authors' answers to such questions as "Where do you do your writing?" and "What are your favorite TV shows?" are presented in an attractive format with lots of illustrations. There are also several special features (one issue included articles on Lemony Snicket, activities at the British Museum, and the popularity of storytelling). This publication is great fun.

986   Carter, James. *Talking Books: Children's Authors Talk About the Craft, Creativity, and Process of Writing.* Routledge, 1999, £12.99 (0-41519-417-2).

This work contains interviews with 13 famous British writers of children's books. Topics covered include how the subjects became writers, their writing routines and methods, the evolution of some of their titles, reflections on contacts with readers, and an exploration of issues relating to their work. The book is illustrated with manuscript pages, photographs of the authors, and so forth. Some of the featured writers are Gillian Cross, Helen Cresswell, Berlie Doherty, Neil Ardley, and Philip Pullman, who discusses the origins of the His Dark Materials trilogy. This is a very interesting collection of material on writers known on both sides of the Atlantic.

987   *Dictionary of Literary Biography.* Gale, various dates and ISBNs, $205 per volume.

Each of the many volumes in this massive scholarly set deals with a different theme or subject. Four cover various aspects of American literature for children (see entry earlier in this chapter) and four do the same for British children's literature. They are:

> *British Children's Writers, 1800–1880, Vol. 163.* Gale, 1996 (0-8103-9358-1). The 40 entries in this book cover such pioneers in children's literature as Randolph Caldecott, Lewis Carroll, Walter Crane, Charles Kingsley, and George MacDonald.

> *British Children's Writers, 1880–1914, Vol. 141.* Gale, 1994 (0-8103-5555-6). Among the 24 writers profiled here are J. M. Barrie, Kenneth Grahame, Kate Greenaway, Beatrix Potter, Arthur Rackham, and Robert Louis Stevenson.

> *British Children's Writers, 1914–1960, Vol. 160.* Gale, 1996 (0-8103-9355-7). The 37 entries in this volume include material on A. A. Milne, P. L. Travers, Mary Norton, J. R. R. Tolkien, and Enid Blyton.

> *British Children's Writers Since 1960: First Series.* Gale, 1996 (0-8103-9356-5). Joan Aiken, Susan Cooper, Helen Cresswell, Alan Garner, Leon Garfield, and Margery Sharp are among the 30 authors covered in this volume.

988   Nettell, Stephanie. *Meet the Authors and Illustrators: 60 Creators of Favourite Children's Books.* Scholastic, 1994, £9.99 (o.p.).

This book on contemporary British authors and illustrators is intended for use by children to round out an author visit or to add a new dimension to current readings. The coverage is informal and chatty with attractive page layouts that include a photograph of the subject and a select bibliography.

E. BIOGRAPHIES IN SERIES

989   *Author Studies Series.* David Fulton (distributed by Routledge), $23.95 per title.

This innovative series from England is designed to help primary teachers plan units about important British children's authors. Each book contains a wide range of activities plus biographical information, a review of the author's work, and a summary of major themes in the texts. Three titles currently available in this series are:

Bromley, Helen. *E. Nesbit.* 2003 (1-85346-933-5).

Elding, Sally. *David McKee.* 2003 (1-85346-934-3).

Wilkinson, Sally. *Michael Morpurgo.* 2003 (1-85346-927-0).

990   *Beech Tree's Stories Behind the Stories.* Beech Tree Books, various dates and ISBNs, $4.95 per title.

Beech Tree, a division of William Morrow, has reprinted five autobiographies of prominent children's and young adult writers. These books are intended for the young readers who would be reading the author's works (i.e., upper elementary through middle school). The books are informally written and give insight into the childhood of each subject and his or her path into writing for young people. The five titles are:

Byars, Betsy. *The Moon and I.* 1996 (0-688-13704-0).

Peck, Richard. *Anonymously Yours.* 1995 (0-688-13702-4).

Rylant, Cynthia. *But I'll Be Back Again.* 1996 (0-688-12653-7).

Uchida, Yoshida. *The Invisible Thread.* 1995 (0-688-13703-2).

Yep, Laurence. *The Lost Garden.* 1996 (0-688-13701-6).

991   *Introducing the Author and You Series.* Libraries Unlimited, $35 per title.

Designed to help both teachers and librarians, this series highlights reading strategies, activities, and lessons to foster a literature-based curriculum. Each book features the life and works of an author popular in grades K–6. Each book is either written by the author or in close collaboration with the author. Three titles currently available are:

Ada, Alma Flor. *Alma Flor and You.* 2005.

Buzzeo, Toni. *Toni Buzzeo and You.* 2005.

Stott, Jon C. *Gerald McDermott and You.* 2004.

992 *Meet the Author.* Richard C. Owen, various dates and ISBNs, $14.95 per title.

This is a set of appealing, easy-to-read autobiographies by well-known children's book writers. The books are intended for children in grades 2 through 5. Each is 32 pages long, hardcover, and illustrated with color photographs. This set supplies a fine introduction to the process of writing for very young readers. There are now about 30 titles in the series. Some of the contributing authors are Cynthia Rylant, Johanna Hurwitz, Paul Goble, Jane Yolen, Margaret Mahy, Laurence Pringle, Eve Bunting, and Lee Bennett Hopkins. For a complete list of authors and titles, contact the publishers at PO Box 585, Katonah, NY 10536, or visit www.RCOwen.com.

993 *Scarecrow Studies in Young Adult Literature.* Scarecrow, various prices.

This series, begun in 1998, is designed to present scholarly and provocative explorations of various aspects of contemporary young adult literature. The series is edited by Patty Campbell, a well-established authority in the field. Many of the titles supply probing and authoritative glimpses into the lives and work of leading young adult writers. Some that are currently available are:

Carroll, Pamela Sissi. *Caroline Cooney: Faith and Fiction.* 2001, $29.50 (0-8108-4068-5)

Hogan, Walter. *The Agony and the Eggplant: Daniel Pinkwater's Heroic Struggles in the Name of YA Literature.* 2001, $26.95 (0-8108-3994-6).

Jones, Patrick. *What's So Scary About R. L. Stine?* 1998, $32.50 (0-8108-3468-5).

McGlinn, Jeanne M. *Ann Rinaldi: Historian and Storyteller.* 2000, $23.50 (0-8108-2678-5).

Reed, Arthea J. S. *Norma Fox Mazer: A Writer's World.* 2000, $29.50 (0-8108-3814-1).

Reid, Suzanne Elizabeth. *Virginia Euwer Wolff.* 2003, $44 (0-8108-4858-9).

Stover, Lois Thomas. *Jacqueline Woodson: "The Real Thing."* 2003, $44 (0-8108-4857-0).

Tyson, Edith S. *Orson Scott Card: Writer of the Terrible Choice.* 2003, $44 (0-8108-47909-6).

994   *Who Wrote That?* Chelsea House, various dates and ISBNs, $35.57 per title.

Written for middle school and junior high grades, these attractive author biographies are 112 pages long. They are profusely illustrated, usually with color photographs. As well as the life story of the subject, each volume highlights the author's most important works and tells a little about each. There is an emphasis on the author's youth and the reasons why each felt compelled to write for children. The text also contains a chronology and a list of further readings. As of the beginning of 2005, there were 12 books in the series. Subsequent additions can be checked at www.chelseahouse.com. The in-print titles are:

Cammarano, Rita. *Betsy Byars.* 2002 (0-7910-6720-3).

Davenport, John. *C. S. Lewis.* 2004 (0-7910-7610-2).

Dean, Tanya. *Theodor Geisel (Dr. Seuss).* 2002 (0-7910-6724-6).

Lange, Brenda. *Edward L. Stratemeyer: Creator of the Hardy Boys and Nancy Drew.* 2004 (0-7910-7621-0).

Ludwig, Elisa. *Judy Blume.* 2004 (0-7910-7619-9).

Ludwig, Elisa. *Shel Silverstein.* 2004 (0-7910-7624-5).

Paterra, Elizabeth. *Gary Paulsen.* 2002 (0-7910-6723-8).

Peltak, Jennifer. *Edgar Allan Poe.* 2004 (0-7910-7622-9).

Shields, Charles J. *Mythmaker: The Story of J. K. Rowling.* 2002 (07910-6719-X).

Shields, Charles J. *Roald Dahl.* 2002 (0-7910-6722-X).

Silverthorne, Elizabeth. *Louisa May Alcott.* 2002 (0-7910-6721-1).

Wagner, Heather Lear. *Jane Austen.* 2004 (0-7910-7623-7).

995   *Young Adult Authors.* Twayne, various dates and ISBNs, $30 per title.

This series flourished during the mid-1990s and was edited by Patty Campbell, a specialist in young adult literature. As well as a summary of the life and art of the author, each book reveals extensive interviews with the subjects and an analysis of the author's work. A chronology, selected bibliography of secondary sources, photographs, and an index round out these books, which are accessible to both adults and teenage readers. Titles in the series are:

Bloom, Susan P., and Cathryn M. Mercier. *Presenting Avi.* 1997 (0-8057-4569-6).

Brown, Joanne. *Presenting Kathryn Lasky.* 1998 (0-8057-1677-7).

Crowe, Chris. *Presenting Mildred D. Taylor.* 1999 (0-8057-1687-4).

Davis, Terry. *Presenting Chris Crutcher.* 1997 (0-8057-8223-0).

Herringa, Donald R. *Presenting Madeleine L'Engle.* 1993 (0-8057-8222-2).

Johnson-Feelings, Dianne. *Presenting Laurence Yep.* 1995 (0-8057-8201-X).

Kies, Cosette. *Presenting Lois Duncan.* 1994 (0-8057-8221-4).

Krull, Kathleen. *Presenting Paula Danziger.* 1995 (0-8057-4153-4).

Monseau, Virginia R. *Presenting Ouida Sebestyen.* 1995 (0-8035-8224-9).

Nilsen, Alleen Pace. *Presenting M. E. Kerr.* 1997 (0-8035-9248-1).

Poe, Elizabeth A. *Presenting Barbara Wersba.* 1998 (0-8035-4154-2).

Reed, Arthea J. S. *Presenting Harry Mazer.* 1996 (0-8135-4512-2).

Reid, Suzanne Elizabeth. *Presenting Ursula K. Le Guin.* 1997 (0-8035-4609-9).

Salver, Gary M. *Presenting Gary Paulsen.* 1996 (0-8035-4150-X).

Stan, Susan. *Presenting Lynn Hall.* 1996 (0-8035-8218-4).

Stover, Lois Thomas. *Presenting Phyllis Reynolds Naylor.* 1997 (0-8035-78055-5).

F. SOME IMPORTANT RECENT MONOGRAPHS

Here are some briefly annotated recent biographies that deal with individual authors and illustrators of importance. For other studies on the works of specific authors, see Chapter 1.

996   Anderson, Brian. *Ezra Jack Keats: A Biography and Catalogue.* Pelican, 2002, $39.95 (1-56554-007-7).

This companion to *Ezra Jack Keats: Artist and Picture-Book Maker* (Pelican, 1994, o.p.) takes a look at all of Keats's work and includes 200 full-color illustrations.

997   Blake, Quentin. *Laureate's Progress.* Jonathan Cape, 2002, £14.99 (0-224-06481-9).

A lavishly illustrated autobiography of the famous illustrator of such picture books as *All Join In* and *The Enormous Crocodile.* A British publication.

998   Briggs, Raymond. *Blooming Books.* Jonathan Cape, 2002, £14.99 (0-224-06478-9).

The author/illustrator of such classics as *The Snowman* and *Father Christmas* talks about his life and work in this generously illustrated British publication.

999   *Dear Genius: The Letters of Ursula Nordstrom.* HarperCollins, 1998, $22.95 (0-06-023625-6).

Collected and edited by children's literature expert Leonard Marcus, letters to and from such luminaries as Margaret Wise Brown, Maurice Sendak, E. B. White, Garth Williams, and Louise Fitzhugh tell the story of the director of Harper's juvenile department from 1940 to 1973.

1000   Elleman, Barbara. *Tomie dePaola: His Art and His Stories.* Putnam, 1999, $35 (0-399-23129-3).

This is a handsome, oversized book that provides a critical survey and celebration of the subject's illustrious life and work.

1001   Elleman, Barbara. *Virginia Lee Burton: A Life in Art.* Houghton Mifflin, 2002, $20 (0-618-00342-8).

The creator of *Mike Mulligan and His Steam Shovel* (1939) and other excellent picture books is celebrated in this appreciative biography of an artist who played many other roles in her life, including those of dancer, teacher, and mother.

1002   Fensch, Thomas. *Of Sneetches and Whos and the Good Dr. Seuss: Essays on the Writings and Life of Theodor Geisel.* McFarland, 1997, $38.50 (0-7864-0388-8).

There are 26 selections in this collection of tributes to Dr. Seuss garnered from such sources as newspapers, magazines, and trade and professional journals.

1003   Hughes, Shirley. *A Life Drawing: Recollections of an Illustrator.* Bodley Head, 2002, £19.99 (0-370-32605-9).

In this British publication, the distinguished illustrator of many excellent children's books, including several concept books, discusses her life and her artwork.

1004   Kirk, Connie Ann. *J. K. Rowling: A Biography.* Greenwood, 2003, $27.50 (0-313-32205-8).

This study of the creator of Harry Potter looks at the life of the person behind the phenomenon and relates these facts to her work.

1005   Kushner, Tony. *The Art of Maurice Sendak: 1980 to the Present.* Abrams, 2003, $60 (0-8109-4448-0).

This "picture biography" by the noted playwright includes all of Sendak's recent work, particularly in the arenas of opera and the theater, with a recap of his accomplishments prior to 1980. This is a fine companion to Selma Lanes's *The Art of Maurice Sendak* (Abrams, 1984, o.p.).

1006   *Leonard Everett Fisher: A Life of Art.* University of Connecticut, 1999, $75 (0-917590-10-4).

Part biography and part autobiography, this is a handsomely designed testimonial to Fisher's life and work, with many excellent reproductions of his art stretching from the 1940s to the 1990s.

1007   Lorenz, Lee. *The World of William Steig.* Artisan, 1998, $60 (1-885183-97-6).

An attractive, well-illustrated overview of the artist's long career that discusses his childhood, his talented siblings, and how he earned his livelihood as an artist.

1008   Marciano, John Bemelmans. *Bemelmans: The Life and Art of Madeline's Creator.* Viking, 1999 (0-670-88460-X).

This thoroughly delightful biography, written by his adoring grandson, explores the life and works of this multifaceted genius.

1009   Schafer, Elizabeth. *Exploring Harry Potter: Beacham's Sourcebooks for Teaching Young Adult Fiction.* Beacham, 2000, $24.95 (0-933833-57-1).

An encyclopedic look at the first three Harry Potter books, with a wealth of information about the novels as well as the author. The "Teaching Harry" section contains interviews, chapter notes, discussion questions, and writing topics for each book. A timeline covers events both real and imaginary and there is brief coverage of the censorship problems these books have caused.

1010   Whalen, Sharla Scannell. *The Betsy-Tacy Companion: A Biography of Maud Hart Lovelace.* Portalington Press, 1995, $39.95 (0-9630783-0-5).

Whalen draws parallels between the life of this famous author of ten Betsy-Tacy novels (plus many others) and the characters, places, and events in her fiction in this generously illustrated biography.

CHAPTER 9

PROFESSIONAL ORGANIZATIONS, AGENCIES, PUBLISHERS, AND BOOKSELLERS

A. ORGANIZATIONS AND AGENCIES

1. United States

1011 *American Antiquarian Society.* 185 Salisbury St., Worcester, MA 01609-1634; (508) 755-5221; www.americanantiquarian.org.

Founded in 1812, this amazing institution holds (among many other treasures) a huge collection of historic children's books (see Chapter 10 for collection details).

1012 *American Association for the Advancement of Science.* 1200 New York Ave. N.W., Washington, DC 20005; (202) 789-0455; www.aaas.org.

Publications include *Science Books and Films,* one of the key reviewing journals of science materials for young people.

1013 *American Association of School Administrators.* 1801 North Quincy St., Arlington, VA 22209-9988; (703) 528-0700; www.aasa.org.

School Administrator, the organization's chief publication, appears 11 times a year and contains reviews of important professional publications.

1014 *American Association of School Librarians.* 50 E. Huron St., Chicago, IL 60611; (800) 545-2433 ext. 4382; www.ala.org/aasl.

Founded in 1951, this is the national professional organization for school librarians. The journal *Knowledge Quest* (formerly *School Library Media Quarterly*) appears five times a year.

1015 *American Booksellers Association.* 828 South Broadway, Tarrytown, NY 10591; (800) 637-0037; www.bookweb.org.

The American Booksellers Association publishes *The ABA Book Buyers Handbook,* which is regularly updated online, and produces and distributes materials for Banned Book Week. The monthly magazine *American Bookseller* ceased publication in 1998.

1016 *American Federation of Teachers.* 555 New Jersey Ave. N.W., Washington, DC 20001; (202) 879-4400; www.aft.org.

The two principal publications from this organization are the periodicals *American Teacher* and *American Educator.*

1017 *American Library Association.* 50 E. Huron St., Chicago, IL 60611; (800) 545-2433; www.ala.org.

ALA and its many divisions have active publishing programs. Included are the periodicals *American Libraries* and *Booklist.* Publishing services can be reached at extension 5416.

1018 *American Printing History Association.* Box 4922, Grand Central Station, New York, NY 10163; (212) 930-9220; http://printinghistory.org.

Founded in 1974, this association of about 800 members "works to record and preserve the heritage of printing and publishing." In addition to a quarterly newsletter, the association publishes *Printing History Journal* twice a year.

1019 *Assembly on Literature for Adolescents (ALAN) of the National Council of Teachers of English.* 1111 W. Kenyon Rd., Urbana, IL 61801; (877) 369-6283; www.ncte.org; www.alan-ya.org.

With membership in this Assembly comes a subscription to *The ALAN Review*, published three times a year.

1020 *Association for Childhood Education International.* 17904 Georgia Ave., Suite 215, Olney, MD 20832; (800) 423-3563; www.acei.org.

This association's principal periodical publication is *Childhood Education*, which includes reviews of professional and children's books.

1021 *Association for Library Service to Children.* 50 E. Huron St., Chicago, IL 60611; (800) 545-2433, ext. 2163; www.ala.org/alsc.

The official publication of this association is *Children and Libraries* (formerly *Journal of Youth Services in Libraries*).

1022 *Association of American Publishers.* 71 Fifth Ave., 2nd floor, New York, NY 10003-3004; (212) 255-0200; www.publishers.org.

This is the trade association of producers of all types of books in the United States. As well as acting as a clearinghouse on publishing, the association publishes a *Monthly Report*.

1023 *Association of Booksellers for Children.* 3900 Sumac Circle, Middleton, WI 53562; (608) 836-6050; www.abfc.com.

The membership of this organization, established in 1985, consists primarily of children's book retailers. The *Building Blocks* newsletter is distributed by email.

1024 *Association of Jewish Libraries.* c/o NFJC, 330 Seventh Ave., 21st floor, New York, NY 10001; (212) 725-5359; www.jewishlibraries.org.

This association works to advance Jewish libraries. It also promotes publications of Jewish interest. Among the many publications available from the association are many bibliographies and a periodical, *Judaica Librarianship*.

1025 *Books for Kids Foundation.* 129 W. 27th St., 6th floor, New York, NY 10001; (212) 252-9168; www.booksforkidsfoundation.org.

Through private funds and government grants, this organization promotes literacy among all children with an emphasis on the disadvantaged. It publishes *Books for Kids News*, a newsletter that appears twice a year.

1026   *Catholic Library Association.* 100 North St., Suite 224, Pittsfield, MA
01201-5109; (413) 443-2252; www.cathla.org.

This is an association of librarians, teachers, and booksellers concerned
with Catholic libraries. As well as sponsoring the Regina Medal (see
Chapter 6), the association publishes a quarterly, *Catholic Library World.*

1027   *Center for the Book in the Library of Congress.* Library of Congress,
101 Independence Ave. S.E., Washington, DC 20540-4920;
(202) 707-5221; www.loc.gov/cfbook.

This center uses the resources and the prestige of the Library of Congress
to stimulate interest in books, reading, literacy, and libraries. Much of its
activities are related to literature for children and young adults. The center also helps organize the annual National Book Festival.

1028   *Children's Book Council.* 12 W. 37th St., 2nd floor, New York, NY
10018-7480; (212) 966-1990; www.cbcbooks.org.

The members of this organization are primarily publishers of trade books
for children and young adults. The council maintains a Web site called
Awards and Prizes and publishes a valuable semiannual newsletter, *CBC
Features.*

1029   *Children's Literature Assembly of the National Council of Teachers of
English.* 1111 W. Kenyon Road, Urbana, IL 61801-1096; (800) 369-
3870; www.ncte.org; www.childrensliteratureassembly.org.

This affiliate of NCTE publishes its own twice-yearly periodical, *Journal
of Children's Literature,* and annually produces a list of *Notable Children's
Books in the English Language Arts,* which is posted and archived on the
Web site.

1030   *Children's Literature Association.* PO Box 138, Battle Creek, MI 49016;
(269) 965-8180; http://ebbs.english.vt.edu/chla/index.html.

Publications include the annual *Children's Literature* and the official journal of the organization, *Children's Literature Association Quarterly.*

1031   *Church and Synagogue Library Association.* PO Box 19357, Portland,
OR 97280-0357; (503) 244-6919; www.worldaccessnet.com/~csla.

The almost 2,000 members of this organization are devoted to promoting libraries in churches and synagogues. Among the CSLA's publications is the bimonthly *Church and Synagogue Libraries.*

1032   *Cooperative Children's Book Center.* 4290 Helen C. White Hall, School
of Education, University of Wisconsin-Madison, 600 N. Park St.,

Madison, WI 53706-1403; (608) 263-3720; www.education.wisc.edu/ccbc.

As well as maintaining an excellent non-circulating library of current and historical children's literature (see Chapter 11), this center sponsors and administers the annual Charlotte Zolotow Award (see Chapter 6) and is responsible for a number of excellent publications including the annual *CCBC Choices* (see Chapter 3), *The Multicolored Mirror: Cultural Substance in Literature for Children and Young Adults,* and the excellent bibliography *Multicultural Literature for Children and Young Adults* (see Chapter 5). The center also promotes literature for young people through activities such as book discussion groups, lectures, and workshops.

1033 *Education Resources Information Center.* ERIC Project, c/o Computer Sciences Corp., 4483-A Forbes Blvd., Lanham, MD 20706; (800) 538-3742; www.eric.ed.gov.

This massive bibliographic database on all aspects of education, including literature for children and young adults, is sponsored by the Institute of Education Sciences (IES) of the United States Department of Education. The bibliographic database currently (2005) contains more than 1.1 million citations dating back to 1966 and more than 107,000 full-text non-journal documents going back to 1993. These resources were once administered by a number of subject-specific clearinghouses. Many resources are now free, and the database is expected to grow.

1034 *Educational Paperback Association.* PO Box 1399, East Hampton, NY 11937; (212) 879-6850; www.edupaperback.org.

This is the trade organization of paperback book dealers and publishers. Founded in 1975, it offers many services to libraries.

1035 *Freedom to Read Foundation.* 50 E. Huron St., Chicago, IL 60611; (800) 545-2433, ext. 4226; www.ala.org/ala/ourassociation/othergroups/ftrf/freedomreadfoundation.htm.

This organization dedicated to supporting the freedom to read in the United States publishes a regular newsletter that is sent free to members.

1036 *International Reading Association.* 800 Barksdale Rd., PO Box 8139, Newark, DE 19714-8139; (302) 731-1600; www.reading.org.

Founded in 1956 to improve the quality of reading among young people, this organization of teachers, librarians, reading specialists, and child psychologists now has more than 90,000 members. It publishes many books and such periodicals as *The Reading Teacher.*

1037 *Jewish Book Council.* 15 E. 26th St., 10th floor, New York, NY 10010-1579; (212) 532-4949; www.jewishbookcouncil.org.

The Jewish Book Council works to promote the reading, writing, and publishing of high-quality English-language books with Jewish content. It sponsors the National Jewish Book Awards and Jewish Book Month and its publications include *Jewish Book Annual* and *Jewish Book World.*

1038 *Library of Congress.* 101 Independence Ave. S.E., Washington, DC 20540; (202) 707-5000; www.loc.gov.

The national library of the United States publishes many books and periodicals plus maintaining the national catalog. Publications include *Talking Book Topics,* which is available in regular and large-print editions and can be accessed on the Web at www.loc.gov/nls/tbt/index.html.

1039 *Modern Language Association; Division on Children's Literature.* 26 Broadway, 3rd floor, New York, NY 10004; (646) 576-5000; www.mla.org.

The membership of this organization is primarily college and university teachers of English. One of its important divisions is devoted to children's literature. This division co-edits with the Children's Literature Association the annual *Children's Literature.*

1040 *National Catholic Educational Association.* 1077 30th St. N.W., Suite 100, Washington, DC 20007-3852; (202) 337-6232; www.ncea.org.

This organization publishes numerous journals, books, and pamphlets.

1041 *National Center for Children's Illustrated Literature.* 102 Cedar, Abilene, TX 79601; (325) 673-4586; www.nccil.org.

Founded in 1997, this organization recognizes the artistic achievements of illustrators through gallery exhibits and educational programs.

1042 *National Coalition Against Censorship.* 275 Seventh Ave., New York, NY 10001; (212) 807-6222; www.ncac.org.

As well as maintaining a clearinghouse of litigation involving book censorship, this organization publishes the quarterly *Censorship News* and a regular newsletter for its members.

1043 *National Council for the Social Studies.* 8555 16th St., Silver Spring, MD 20910; www.ncss.org.

The periodical *Social Education,* for middle and high schools, is published seven times a years; there is a companion quarterly title for elementary schools, *Social Studies and the Young Learner.*

1044 *National Council of Teachers of English.* 1111 W. Kenyon Road, Urbana, IL 61801-1096; (877) 369-6283; www.ncte.org.

Publications include many monographs and important bibliographies of children's and young adult books. The organization's two principal periodicals are *Language Arts* for the elementary and middle school grades and *English Journal* for middle schools and junior and senior high schools. See also in this section *Assembly on Literature for Adolescents* and *Children's Literature Assembly*, both affiliates of NCTE.

1045 *National Council of Teachers of Mathematics.* 1906 Association Drive, Reston, VA 20191-1502; (800) 235-7566; www.nctm.org.

Among this association's publications are *Arithmetic Teacher*, for the elementary grades, and *Mathematics Teacher*, for grades 7 through 12.

1046 *National Education Association.* 1201 16th St. N.W., Washington, DC 20036; (202) 833-4000; www.nea.org.

Among the many publications issued by this large educational association is a monthly periodical, *Today's Education.*

1047 *National Science Teachers Association.* 1840 Wilson Blvd., Arlington, VA 22201; (703) 243-7100; www.nsta.org.

This is the official professional organization of the science teachers of America. Among its publications are three journals aimed at teachers: *Science and Children* (K–6), *Science Scope* (6–9), and *The Science Teacher* (9–12).

1048 *National Storytelling Network.* 132 Boone St., Suite 5, Jonesborough, TN 37659; (800) 523-4514; www.storynet.org.

This national organization and network is devoted to the development and spread of the art of storytelling in the United States. The official newsletter of this organization is *Storytelling Magazine.*

1049 *Reading Is Fundamental, Inc.* 1825 Connecticut Ave. N.W., Suite 400, Washington, DC 20009; (202) 673-0020; www.rif.org.

Founded in 1966 and funded by private and government funds, this national literacy program reaches 1.5 million children a year and distributes 16 million free books in about 25,000 sites. Booklists and other materials are available at the organization's Web site.

1050 *Society of Children's Book Writers and Illustrators.* 8271 Beverly Blvd., Los Angeles, CA 90048; (323) 782-1010; www.scbwi.org.

Established in 1968, this organization now has about 800 members. The society publishes a bimonthly newsletter, *SCBWI Bulletin*, and administers the Golden Kite awards (see Chapter 6).

1051   *Society of Illustrators.* 128 E. 63rd St., New York, NY 10021-7303; (212) 838-2560; www.societyillustrators.org.

This society of illustrators and art directors maintains the Museum of American Illustration and publishes the *Annual of American Illustration.*

1052   *United States Board on Books for Young People.* 800 Barksdale Road, PO Box 8139, Newark, DE 19714-8139; (302) 731-1600, ext. 274; www.usbby.org.

This is the United States Section of the International Board on Books for Young People (see "International" listings in this chapter). It publishes a semiannual newsletter and sponsors many conferences and other activities.

1053   *United States Holocaust Memorial Museum.* 100 Raoul Wallenburg Place S.W., Washington, DC 20024-2126; (202) 488-0400; www.ushmm.org.

This museum publishes a kit of materials on the Holocaust that is available to educators.

1054   *Young Adult Library Services Association.* 50 E. Huron St., Chicago, IL 60611; (800) 545-2433, ext. 4390; www.ala.org/ala/yalsa/yalsa.htm.

The official journal of this association is *Young Adult Library Services* (formerly *Journal of Youth Services in Libraries*), published twice a year.

2. International

1055   *Books for All.* Brunhildenstrasse 34, D-80639 Munich, Germany.

An international library project run jointly by the International Federation of Library Associations and Institutions and UNESCO to raise money to buy books for children in underdeveloped countries.

1056   *International Association of School Librarianship.* IASL Secretariat, PO Box 83, Zillmere, Queensland 4034, Australia; www.iasl-slo.org.

This organization is dedicated to promoting school librarianship worldwide and sharing library resources through the Internet.

1057 *International Board on Books for Young People.* Nonnenweg 12, Postfach, CH-4003 Basel, Switzerland; www.ibby.org; or USBBY Secretariat, 800 Barksdale Rd., Newark, DE 19714-8139; www.usbby.org.

This organization, founded in 1953, now has 61 national sections (see USBBY above) each devoted to promoting international understanding through children's books. Among other activities, IBBY sponsors the Hans Christian Andersen Award (see Chapter 6).

1058 *International Institute for Children's Literature, Osaka.* 10-6 Banpaku-Koen, Senri Suita-Shi, Osaka 565-0826, Japan; www.iiclo.or.jp/english/english.htm.

Founded in 1984, this institute offers research facilities, a large library, and many service programs. It also publishes *IICLO News* (eight pages per issue).

1059 *International Research Society for Children's Literature.* Anne de Vries, Pieter de Hoochlaan 7, 2343 CP Oegstgeest, Netherlands; www.irscl.ac.uk.

Established in 1971, this international organization considers serious cultural, social, and political questions in terms of children's literature, with particular attention to multiculturalism, gender questions, research, and historical studies.

3. Australia and New Zealand

1060 *Children's Book Council of Australia.* PO Box 765, Rozelle, NSW 2039, Australia; www.cbc.org.au.

The CBCA fosters children's literature in Australia through many activities, including sponsoring Children's Book Week, publishing the periodical *Reading Time*, and selecting its Book of the Year.

1061 *Children's Literature Foundation of New Zealand.* PO Box 96094, Balmoral, Auckland 1030, New Zealand; www.storylines.org.nz.

Formed by the amalgamation in 2000 of the New Zealand Children's Book Foundation and the Children's Literature Association of New Zealand, this organization serves as a clearinghouse for individuals and organizations in New Zealand involved in children's literature. It sponsors many activities and book prizes.

4. Canada

1062 *Association of Canadian Publishers.* 110 Eglinton Ave. W., Suite 401, Toronto, ON M4R 1A3; (416) 487-6116; www.publishers.ca.

This association has a membership of about 140 English-language book publishing companies in Canada. It publishes a newsletter.

1063 *Canadian Booksellers Association.* 789 Don Mills Rd., Suite 700, Toronto, ON M3C 1T5; (416) 467-7883; www.cbabook.org.

Members of this association are actively engaged in the retail sale of books in Canada. The organization publishes *Canadian Bookseller.*

1064 *Canadian Children's Book Centre.* 40 Orchard View Blvd., Suite 101, Toronto, ON M4R 1B9; (416) 975-0010; www.bookcentre.ca.

Noted for championing Canadian books for children and youth, the CCBC publishes the reviewing journal *Canadian Children's Book News* and the annual *Our Choice.*

1065 *Canadian Education Association.* 317 Adelaide St. W., Suite 300, Toronto, ON M5V 1P9; (416) 591-6300; www.cea-ace.ca.

Founded in 1891, this national bilingual organization promotes improvement in education in Canada and publishes the quarterly *Education Canada.*

1066 *Canadian Library Association.* 328 Frank St., Ottawa, ON K2P 0X8; (613) 232-9625; www.cla.ca.

This association of about 3,000 members is the Canadian equivalent of the American Library Association, with sections involving work with children and young adults. Among its publications is *School Libraries in Canada.*

1067 *Canadian Society of Children's Authors, Illustrators, and Performers.* 104-40 Orchard View Blvd., Toronto, ON M4R 1B9; (416) 515-1559; www.canscaip.org.

Founded in 1972, this is an organization of Canadian professionals in the field of children's culture. The quarterly newsletter is *Canscaip News.*

5. Ireland

1068 *Children's Books Ireland.* 17 North Great Georges St., 1st Floor, Dublin 1; www.childrensbooksireland.com.

This organization was formed in 1997 through a merger of the *Children's Literature Association of Ireland* with the *Irish Children's Book Trust.* It now sponsors a number of activities and publications relating to children's books in Ireland. It is responsible for the fall children's book festival, the attractive periodical *Inis*, and an annual bibliography of Irish children's books published during that year.

6. United Kingdom

1069 *Book Trust.* Book House, 45 East Hill, Wandsworth, London, SW18 2QZ, England; www.booktrust.org.uk.

This organization is a clearinghouse for information about books and reading in Britain. A subdivision is responsible for reading materials for young people. It publishes bibliographies, sponsors the National Children's Book Week, conducts many educational programs, and maintains a library/resource center at its headquarters in London.

1070 *Booksellers Association of the United Kingdom.* Minster House, 272 Vauxhall Bridge Rd., London SW1V 1BA, England; www.booksellers. org.uk.

The Booksellers Association represents more than 3,100 bookstores, from large chains to small independent booksellers. It publishes a magazine called *Bookselling Essentials.*

1071 *Centre for the Children's Book.* Unit 4 Terrace Level, St. Peter's Marina, Newcastle upon Tyne NE6 1TZ, England; www.childrensbook.org.uk.

This private/public institution is dedicated to establishing an institution that will contain a collection of important children's books, manuscripts, and original artwork connected with children's literature. It sponsors many exhibitions and other educational activities.

1072 *Chartered Institute of Library and Information Professionals.* 7 Ridgmount St., London WC1E 7AE, England; www.cilip.org.uk.

Formed in 2002 by a merger of the Library Association and the Institute of Information Scientists, this professional organization now has more than 32,000 members. There are two important divisions: the School Libraries Group and the Youth Libraries Group. This organization administers the Carnegie and Greenaway Awards (see Chapter 6).

1073 *Children's Book Circle.* c/o Rachel Wade, Hodder Children's Books, 338 Euston Rd., London NW1 3BH, England.

The Circle is open to anyone involved with children's books. It sponsors regular meetings in London with guest speakers and also administers the Eleanor Farjeon Award (see Chapter 6).

1074 *Children's Books History Society.* 66 Idmiston Square, Worcester Park, Surrey KT4 8SR, England.

This organization promotes and reports on the collecting and appreciation of children's books and the study of their history. Its newsletter contains articles about the history of children's books and reviews of books on the subject.

1075 *Federation of Children's Book Groups.* 2 Bridge Wood View, Horsforth, Leeds, West Yorkshire LS18 5PE, England; www.fcbg.org.uk.

This federation of children's literature book groups in the U.K. sponsors many activities and programs, including awards for the best work of fiction for children.

1076 *National Literacy Trust.* Swire House, 59 Buckingham Gate, London SW1E 6AJ, England; www.literacytrust.org.uk.

In addition to supporting and initiating projects relating to the nation's literacy, the trust coordinates the National Reading Campaign and Reading Is Fundamental, UK.

1077 *School Library Association.* Unit 2, Lotmead Business Village, Lotmead Farm, Wanborough, Swindon SN4 0UY, England; www.sla.org.uk.

Activities conducted by this organization that promotes libraries in schools include developing guidelines, sponsoring training courses, and publishing a quarterly journal.

1078 *Scottish Book Trust.* Sandeman House, Trunk's Close, 55 High St., Edinburgh EH1 1SR, Scotland; www.scottishbooktrust.com.

Like its equivalent in London, this agency conducts many in-service activities and maintains a collection of children's books, in this case with particular strength in Scottish authors and illustrators.

1079 *Scottish Youth Librarians Forum.* Glasgow City Libraries and Archives, The Mitchell Library, North Street, Glasgow G3 7DN, Scotland.

This group fosters cooperation among libraries in Scotland that serve young people.

1080 *Society for Storytelling.* PO Box 2344, Reading RG6 7FG, England; www.sfs.org.uk.

Founded in 1993, this society provides information and a network for anyone interested in storytelling.

1081 *United Kingdom Literacy Association.* Upton House, Baldock St., Royston, Herts SG8 5AY, England; www.ukla.org.

Formerly the United Kingdom Reading Association, this group represents all those teaching, learning, or developing literacy and language at all levels. It publishes a number of excellent books and periodicals, including *Literacy News*.

B. PROMINENT AMERICAN PUBLISHERS OF BOOKS ABOUT CHILDREN'S AND YOUNG ADULT LITERATURE

1082   *American Library Association.* 50 E. Huron St., Chicago, IL 60611; (800) 545-2433; www.ala.org.

1083   *August House.* PO Box 3223, Little Rock, AR 72203; www.augusthouse.com.

1084   *R. R. Bowker.* 630 Central Ave., New Providence, NJ 07974; (800) 526-9537; www.bowker.com.

1085   *Christopher-Gordon Publishers.* 1502 Providence Highway, Suite 12, Norwood, MA 02062; (800) 934-8322; www.christopher-gordon.com.

1086   *Facts on File.* 132 W. 31st St., 17th floor, New York, NY 10001; (800) 322-8755; www.factsonfile.com.

1087   *Gale Group.* 27500 Drake Rd., Farmington Hills, MI 48331-3535; (800) 877-4253; www.galegroup.com.

1088   *Garland Publishing.* 29 W. 35th St., New York, NY 10001; (917) 351-7118; www.tandf.co.uk/homepages/gphome.html.

1089   *Greenwood Publishing Group.* 88 Post Rd. W., Westport, CT 06881-5007; (203) 226-3571; www.greenwood.com.

1090   *Heinemann.* PO Box 6926, Portsmouth, NH 03802-6926; (800) 225-5800; www.heinemann.com.

1091   *Highsmith* (including *Alleyside* and *Upstart*). PO Box 800, Fort Atkinson, WI 53538-0800; (800) 558-2110; www.highsmith.com.

1092   *International Reading Association.* 800 Barksdale Rd., PO Box 8139, Newark, DE 19714-8139; (800) 336-7323; www.reading.org.

1093 *Libraries Unlimited* (also *Teacher Ideas Press*). 88 Post Rd. W., Westport, CT 06881-5007; (203) 226-3571; www.lu.com.

1094 *Linworth Publishing.* 480 E. Wilson Bridge Rd., Suite L, Worthington, OH 43085-2372; (800) 786-5017; www.linworth.com.

1095 *McFarland and Co.* Box 611, Jefferson, NC 28640; (336) 246-4460; www.mcfarlandpub.com.

1096 *National Council of Teachers of English.* 1111 W. Kenyon Rd., Urbana, IL 61801-1096; (877) 369-6283; www.ncte.org.

1097 *Neal-Schuman Publishers.* 100 William St., Suite 2004, New York, NY 10038; (212) 925-8650; www.neal-schuman.com.

1098 *Oryx Press.* 88 Post Rd W., Westport, CT 06881-5007; (203) 226-3571; www.greenwood.com.

1099 *Routledge.* 270 Madison Ave., New York, NY 10016-0602; (212) 216-7800; www.routledge-ny.com.

1100 *Scarecrow Press, Inc.* 4501 Forbes Blvd., Suite 200, Lanham, MD 20706; (301) 459-3366; www.scarecrowpress.com.

1101 *Shoe String Press.* 2 Linsley St., North Haven, CT 06473; (203) 239-2702; www.shoestringpress.com.

1102 *H. W. Wilson.* 950 University Ave., Bronx, NY 10452-4224; (800) 367-6770; www.hwwilson.com.

C. SOME ANTIQUARIAN BOOK DEALERS THAT SPECIALIZE IN CHILDREN'S AND YOUNG ADULT BOOKS

Although many antiquarian book dealers may have children's books in their stock, only a few actually specialize in "juvenilia" as a subcategory of antiquarian or rare books. Here are six leading dealers in the United States noted for children's books as their sole or main specialty.

1103 *Aleph-Bet Books.* 85 Old Mill River Rd., Pound Ridge, NY 10576 (by appointment only); (914) 764-7410; www.alephbet.com.

1104 *Books of Wonder.* 18 West 18th St., New York, NY 10011; (800) 207-6968; www.booksofwonder.com.

1105 *Garcia-Garst Booksellers.* 1516 N. Daubenberger Rd., Turlock, CA 95380 (by appointment only); (209) 632-5054; e-mail: ggbooks@jps.net.

1106 *Hobbyhorse Books.* PO Box 591, Ho Ho Kus, NJ 07423 (by appointment only); (201) 327-4717; www.hobbyhorsebooks.com.

1107 *Jo Ann Reisler Ltd.* 360 Glyndon St. N.E., Vienna, VA 22180 (by appointment only); (703) 938-2967; www.joannreisler.com.

1108 *Justin G. Schiller, Ltd.* 1270 Ave. of the Americas (Rockefeller Center), Suite 302, New York, NY 10020-1702, or PO Box 1667, FDR Station, New York, NY 10150-1667; (212) 332-7070; www.childlit.com.

In the United Kingdom, three dealers are known for their focus on juvenile literature.

1109 *The Canterbury Bookshop.* 23A Palace St., Canterbury, Kent CT1 2DZ, England; (0) 1227-464773.

1110 *Elizabeth Gant.* 8 Sandon Close, Esher, Surrey KT10 8JE, England; (0) 20-8398-0962; www.bookline.co.uk.

1111 *Marchpane Children's Books.* 16 Cecil Court, Charing Cross Rd., London WC2N 4HE, England; (0) 20-7836-8661.

Most dealers on both sides of the Atlantic issue catalogs, which sometimes become collectors' items in themselves. To be placed on a mailing list, write stating the nature and extent of your interest; recipients of the catalogs are rarely expected to pay for them.

Those seeking specific rare or out-of-print titles in children's literature now have many ways to search worldwide, thanks to the Internet. Out-of-print titles are often available through major outlets such as Amazon and Barnes and Noble. Throughout the United States and Canada, an ever-growing number of small and mid-sized book dealers now participate in the Advanced Book Exchange and often add newly acquired titles on a daily basis. The Exchange is not only free but also very user-friendly. Log on at www.abebooks.com and follow the clear instructions. One can search by title, author, or keyword. The keyword option often produces the most interesting results because the search engine examines millions of entries looking for a mention of the specified name or book descriptor. The corresponding search site in the United Kingdom is www.ukbookworld.com; there appears to be surprisingly little overlap between the two.

CHAPTER 10

SPECIAL COLLECTIONS AND RESOURCES

This chapter contains a very selective list of historical collections of children's literature found in the United States, Australia, New Zealand, Canada, Ireland, and the United Kingdom. If a collection bears a distinctive name (Kerlan Collection, for example) and it is the principal historical collection of children's books at the institution where it is housed, the entry is under the name of the collection. In other cases, the collection is listed under the institution where it is housed. For other lists of historical collections, consult the general children's literature Web sites in Chapter 11 and also use *Special Collections in Children's Literature* by Dolores Blythe Jones, listed below.

There are many books on book collecting. Two titles, both by Nicholas A. Basbanes and listed below, give entertaining and fascinating information about several of the collections mentioned in this chapter. And Rabinowitz and Kaplan's *A Passion for Books* is a collection of essays on books and their appreciation.

1112 Basbanes, Nicholas A. *A Gentle Madness*. Holt, 1995, $35 (0-8050-3653-9).

Subtitled *Bibliophiles, Bibliomanes, and the Eternal Passion for Books*, this work discusses such collectors as A. S. W. Rosenbach, Ruth Baldwin, and Betsy Beinecke Shirley.

1113 Basbanes, Nicholas A. *Patience and Fortitude*. HarperCollins, 2001, pap., $19.95 (0-06-051446-9).

Named after the two lions that guard the entrance to the New York Public Library on Fifth Avenue, New York City, this book's subtitle is *Wherein a Colorful Cast of Determined Book Collectors, Dealers, and Librarians Go About the Quixotic Task of Preserving a Legacy*. Children's book collectors including Lloyd E. Cotsen are highlighted.

1114 Jones, Dolores Blythe. *Special Collections in Children's Literature: An International Directory*, 3rd ed. American Library Association, 1995, o.p.

Sponsored by the Association for Library Service to Children, this publication contains hundreds of listing arranged geographically by country and then by state/province/county. Addresses are given for all entries, along with descriptive information about important collections and holdings. There is an extensive subject index and an index by the name of the specific collection. This still valuable resource is in need of an update.

1115 Rabinowitz, Harold, and Rob Kaplan, eds. *A Passion for Books*. Times Books, 1999, $19.95 (0-8129-3112-2).

This collection of short essays from writers ranging from John Milton to A. S. W. Rosenbach is subtitled *A Book Lover's Treasury of Stories, Essays, Humor, Lore, and Lists on Collecting, Reading, Borrowing, Lending, Caring for and Appreciating Books*.

A. IMPORTANT INTERNATIONAL COLLECTIONS

1116 *Center for Children's Literature (Center for Børnelitteratur)*, Danish University of Education, Emdrupvej 101, DK-2400 Copenhagen NV, Denmark; www.cfb.dk.

Founded in 1954, this center now holds one of the largest collections of children's literature in Europe. Although most of the 80,000 volumes in the collections are of Danish and Nordic children's literature, a sizable number of volumes are in other languages, including English. The center purchases all of the children's books published in Denmark.

1117 *CHILDE: Children's Historical Literature Disseminated Throughout Europe*; www.bookchilde.org.

This Web site was founded in 2000 as a result of a sizable grant from the European Commission on Cultural Projects to the Buckingham County Library Service in England. It is dedicated to preserving and promoting early children's book collections across Europe. There are now about seven founding partners representing collections in Great Britain, Ireland, Germany, the Netherlands, and Italy, with a number of other institutions with sizable collections already cooperating. A database is being created that will represent the holdings in these institutions of children's literature published before 1890. By creating these links among children's literature collections in Europe, it is hoped that preservation projects will be initiated and that these treasures will become available to a larger audience.

1118 *International Youth Library (Internationale Jugendbibliothek München)*. Schloss Blutenburg, D-81247 Munich, Germany; www.ijb.de.

The largest library for international children's and youth literature in the world, this magnificent institution was founded in 1948 by Jella Lepman, a World War II refugee who returned to Germany after the war. Lepman was also the founder (in 1953) of the International Board of Books for Young People (IBBY). She describes the early years of the library in her autobiographical *A Bridge to Children's Books*, first published in 1964 and now reissued by IBBY. Since 1983, the library has been housed in Blutenburg Castle, Munich, and is funded by German governmental agencies and a private foundation. Many valuable collections have been donated to the library and almost 1,000 publishers worldwide regularly send review copies of their publications to be added to the collection. About 9,000 volumes are added annually. At present there are almost 550,000 titles in the collection, representing 130 languages. Approximately 40,000 are books about youth literature. There is a circulating collection of 20,000 books in 15 languages, plus a sizable periodical collection, a large collection of nonprint media, and an active schedule of programs that include author readings and puppet shows. The library also sponsors a number of teaching and research programs, mounts many exhibits, and has a vigorous publishing program that includes the annual bibliography *The White Ravens*, a selection of the best international books for youth. Published in English, each issue contains approximately 250 choices (more information on this publication is in Chapter 1).

B. AUSTRALIA AND NEW ZEALAND

1119 *Centre for Children's Literature.* School of Professional Development, Christchurch College of Education, Christchurch 8030, New Zealand; www.cce.ac.nz.

An educational institution offering programs that lead to a certificate, a diploma, and a Master's of Education in children's literature, this school has a large collection in this subject area with a specialization in New Zealand imprints.

1120 *Children's Literature Research Collection.* State Library of South Australia, GPO Box 419, Adelaide 5001, South Australia; www.slsa. sa.gov.au.

Also referred to as *Treasures of the State Library of South Australia*, this is an impressive collection of historical and contemporary children's literature and other media from both Australia and overseas, with a concentration on Australian publications, There are currently about 70,000 books in the collection.

1121 *Dromkeen Children's Literature Collection.* 1012 Kilmore Rd., Riddells Creek, Vic. 3431, Australia; www.scholastic.com.au/common/dromkeen.

Often called "the home of Australian children's book illustration," this collection also focuses on Australian authors of the early 20th century such as Ivan Southall. As well as a large book collection, this resource contains a fine collection of original manuscripts and illustrations.

1122 *Lu Rees Archives of Australian Children's Literature.* University of Canberra, Canberra, ACT 2601, Australia; www.canberra.edu.au/lurees.

This library was founded in 1974, using as a foundation the collection of Lu Rees. The library now consists of about 14,000 titles including hundreds of foreign-language editions of Australian children's books. Since 1981, Australian publishers have been donating copies of their books, but the main importance of this collection is as a valuable historical record of the development of Australian children's literature.

1123 *National Library of New Zealand.* Molesworth St., Wellington, New Zealand; www.natlib.govt.nz.

Three separate collections of children's literature are housed in this institution. The first is the ever-growing National Children's Collection, which consists of books published in New Zealand plus about 50,000 volumes from other countries. The second is the Dorothy Neal White Collection of mainly Victorian and Edwardian titles; and the third is the Susan Price Collection, which—when it was donated in 1995—consisted of approximately 10,000 books mainly written and published in New Zealand.

1124 *State Library of Victoria.* 328 Swanston St., Melbourne, Vic., Australia; www.slv.vic.gov.au/collections/childrens_lit/index.html.

Beginning with *The Schoolmaster,* published in 1561, the children's literature collection at this state library totals about 84,000 volumes published between the 16th and 21st centuries. Founded in 1976, the collection contains both Australian titles and English-language books from other countries. In 1994, the library made a major acquisition, purchasing the Ken Pound collection of about 25,000 items of children's materials relating to Australia, including books, magazines, games, and ephemera.

C. CANADA

1125 *Arkley Collection of Historical Children's Literature.* University of British Columbia, Special Collections, 1956 Main Mall, Vancouver, BC V6T 1Z1; (604) 822-2521; www.library.ubc.ca/spcoll/.

A historical collection now totaling about 2,500 monographs, plus some manuscripts, this archive founded in 1963 received duplicates from the Free Library of Philadelphia. The "Alice" collection of R. D. Hilton Smith—on Lewis Carroll and *Alice in Wonderland*—was added, followed in 1996 by the Arkley family's gift of its historical collection of children's books. The collection spans the late 18th century to 1939. There are also historical collections of children's textbooks at UBC, taking the total in these collections to more than 6,000 items.

1126 *Canadian Children's Book Centre.* Suite 1000, 40 Orchard View Blvd., Toronto, ON M4R 1B9; www.bookcentre.ca.

The Canadian Children's Book Centre, also discussed in Chapter 9 under "Organizations," maintains a main collection of children's books at its headquarters in Toronto and also at four other centers across Canada.

1127 *Canadian Children's Literature Service. Library and Archives Canada.* 395 Wellington St., Ottawa, ON K1A 0N4; (613) 996-7774; www.collectionscanada.ca.

Since 1975, the children's and young adult collections in the National Library of Canada (now known as Library and Archives Canada) have been combined and maintained as a separate unit known as Children's Literature Service. Titles are in English, French, and other languages. In addition to all the children's books published in Canada, this collection seeks out books about Canada that are published elsewhere. At present, the collection contains about 150,000 items of fiction and nonfiction for ages 16 and under.

1128   *Osborne Collection of Early Children's Books.* 239 College St., Toronto, ON M5T 1R5; (416) 393-7753; www.tpl.toronto.on.ca/ uni_spe_osb_index.jsp.

The Osborne Collection consists of three separate parts: the Osborne Collection, the Lillian H. Smith Collection, and the Canadiana Collection. The first of these extends from a 14th-century manuscript of Aesop's fables through the centuries to 1910, the end of the Edwardian period. The collection totals some 5,600 items and is well documented in a two-volume catalog. The Lillian H. Smith Collection was established in 1936 and consists of picture books, fiction, fairy tales, and poetry published since 1910. The Canadiana Collection comprises children's books in English relating to Canada and published in the 19th and 20th centuries. This is one of the best-known and most valuable children's literature collections in existence.

1129   *University of Guelph: Special Collections Department.* Guelph, ON N1G 2W1; (519) 824-6931; www.lib.uoguelph.ca.

The Special Collections Department of the University of Guelph library maintains a diversified collection of historical children's books, including an extensive collection of Canadian juvenile literature. One of the gems of this collection is the L. M. Montgomery archive, which contains hundreds of editions of books by the author of *Anne of Green Gables* as well as the personal papers of the author.

D. IRELAND

1130   *National Library of Ireland.* Kildare St., Dublin 2; www.nli.ie.

Being a depository library, the National Library acquires all children's books published in Ireland in both English and Irish. It also has a fine collection of original manuscripts and illustrations, plus an interesting holding of 19th-century chapbooks. Nearby is the *Trinity College Library* (College St., Dublin 2, Ireland; www.tcd.ie). A copyright library since 1801, it has many 19th-century children's books and the Pollard Collection of about 600 schoolbooks published in the 18th and 19th centuries.

E. UNITED KINGDOM

1131 *Birmingham Library Services Central Library.* Chamberlain Square, Birmingham B3 3HQ, England; www.birmingham.gov.uk.

The Parker Collection of historical children's books is housed in the central public library in Birmingham. It consists of more than 12,000 titles dating from 1538 to the present day. Both fiction and nonfiction are included, and there is also a fascinating collection of 19th-century board games, jigsaw puzzles, and other recreational items.

1132 *Bodleian Library, University of Oxford.* Broad St., Oxford OX1 3BG, England; www.bodley.ox.ac.uk.

Because the Bodleian is a copyright library, it has amassed a great number of historical children's books in its regular collection. It also holds valuable historical collections that are housed separately. The most famous is the Opie Collection, acquired in 1988, which consists of 20,000 English children's books on all subjects, dating from the 17th century to the present and including some rare Victorian toy books. Peter and Iona Opie were scholars and researchers in the field of children's lore and literature. They were responsible for such classics as the *Oxford Dictionary of Nursery Rhymes.* The collection was purchased for £500,000 (the estimated worth is more than £1 million) and organized into 20 categories by children's author Gillian Avery and a group of volunteers. Catalogs of the collection, with extensive descriptive material on each item, are available in two sets (the first dealing with books before 1850 and the second dealing with books published after 1850) under the main title *The Opie Collection of Children's Literature: A Guide to the Microfiche Collection* (University of Michigan, Ann Arbor, Michigan). Two other important collections at the Bodleian are the Harding Chapbooks and the John Johnson Collection of children's books and ephemera.

1133 *Book Trust.* Book House, 45 East Hill, London SW18 2QZ, England; www.booktrust.org.uk.

Among its many programs, Book Trust maintains, at its headquarters, a library of current children's literature received mainly from publishers' gifts. The collection represents the children's books published in the last two years (discards are given to the National Centre for Research in Children's Literature at Roehampton—see below). There is also a general collection of books about children's literature and an international selection of magazines on children's literature. The collection totals about 10,000 items.

1134 *British Library.* 96 Euston St., London NW1 2DB, England;
www.bl.uk.

The *Cambridge Guide to Children's Books in English* describes the British
Library as "the best single collection in the United Kingdom, notwith-
standing its unsystematic acquisition of children's books before 1950.
Pre-1800 books . . . include the first edition of *The History of Little
Goody Two-Shoes (1744).* Special collections include chapbooks and a
collection of books by Isaac Taylor. The Department of Manuscripts
holds the works of many important writers: Lewis Carroll, Rudyard
Kipling, and Robert Louis Stevenson, among others."

1135 *Cambridge University Library.* West Road, Cambridge CB3 9DR,
England; www.lib.cam.ac.uk.

Another of the great British historical collections of children's literature,
this also profited by being a copyright library. It now exceeds 4 million
volumes. Particular strengths in the children's collection are chapbooks
(more than 2,500 items) and unique holdings in the Glaisher and
Munby collections.

1136 *Centre for the Children's Book (Sevenstories).* Unit 4, Terrace Level,
St. Peter's Marina, Newcastle-upon-Tyne NE6 1TZ, England;
www.centreforthechildrensbook.org.uk.

Dedicated to creating an institution that will preserve an important col-
lection of books, manuscripts, and original artwork, the founders of the
Centre (also known as the Centre for Children's Books) have turned an
old warehouse on a tributary of the River Tyne into a home for their collection. Named Sevenstories, it is scheduled to open officially in 2005.
The Centre has already bought the important collection of the publisher
Kaye Webb, and has been given manuscripts by writers including Philip
Pullman. In a tribute to this exciting development in British children's
literature, the celebrated author-illustrator Quentin Blake said, "Newcastle has taken the lead with the Centre for the Children's Book."

1137 *Hallward Library, University of Nottingham.* University Park,
Nottingham NG7 2RD, England; www.nottingham.ac.uk.

The main collection of interest here is the W. G. Briggs Collection of
Early Educational Literature. When it was given to the library by Mr.
Briggs in 1950, it consisted of a total of about 200 items including
school textbooks from 1600 to 1850 and many exercise books. It has
grown to about 2,000 items published prior to 1850—again, mainly
pedagogic texts.

1138 *Harrogate Library.* Victoria Ave., Harrogate, North Yorkshire HG1 1EG, England; www.harrogate.co.uk/library.

The Early Children's Books Collection at Harrogate Library consists of about 2,500 volumes, mainly English children's books of the Victorian era. There is particular emphasis on picture books that show the development of color in the printing process.

1139 *John Rylands University Library of Manchester.* Oxford Road, Manchester M13 9PP, England; www.rylibweb.man.ac.uk.

There are a number of important historical collections of children's books in this library. Among them are the Elfrida Vipont Collection, the Jack Cox Collection of material relating to the magazine *Boy's Own Paper,* and the Allison Uttley Collection of books and materials relating to this author and others including Arthur Rackham.

1140 *Leicester University Education Library.* 21 University Road, Leicester LE1 7RF, England; www.le.ac.uk/library.

The major historical collection in this library is the Winifred Higson Collection of about 2,600 books published from the 16th century to the 1920s. There is a supplementary collection of several hundred volumes published from 1930 on and a fine background reference collection.

1141 *Museum of Childhood at Bethnal Green.* Cambridge Heath Road, London E2 9PA, England; www.vam.ac.uk/vastatic/nmc/index.html.

This museum once housed the magnificent Renier Collection, which is now at the Victoria and Albert Museum (see National Art Library below). The museum currently has a small collection of reference books and special collections on children's literature, and retains a fascinating collection of toys, tracing the development of British playthings over more than 150 years. Also available are materials on the history of dolls' houses and their contents and exhibits that show how babies were cared for in the past.

1142 *National Art Library.* Victoria and Albert Museum, Cromwell Rd., London SW7 2RL, England; www.vam.ac.uk/nal/index.html.

The Victoria and Albert Museum is home to several of the most valuable children's literature collections in the world. First and foremost is the prestigious Renier Collection, the product of years of collecting by Fernand Gabriel Renier (1905–1988) and his wife, Anne. They began by collecting items including matchbox covers; in the 1930s, they started acquiring chapbooks and other early examples of children's literature. In

1970, this huge collection was given to the Victoria and Albert, and in 1989 was moved to the Museum of Childhood at Bethnal Green (see above). The toys and games have remained there, but the books are now back in the V and A. In 1989, the book collection totaled more than 80,000 books and each year grew by about 3,000 from the depository collection at Book Trust (see entry above), but now the collection is closed. In the main collection, all subjects are covered from all periods beginning with 1585 to 1988. Other collections in the National Art Library include the Guy Little Bequest, of 2,400 children's books acquired in 1961, the Queen Mary Gift of books formerly owned by members of the Royal Family, the Horton Collection of Soviet children's books acquired in 1981, the Harrod Bequest, of many children's books by artists of the 1860s, and the Beatrix Potter Collections. The latter consists of major collections of material related to Beatrix Potter and her books including three of the Linder collections. The museum also houses a collection of prints, drawings, and paintings, many of which are related to children's literature.

1143 *National Centre for Research in Children's Literature.* University of Surrey Roehampton, Digby Stuart College, Roehampton Lane, London SW15 5PH, England; www.ncrcl.ac.uk.

This fledgling organization is developing into one of the most important children's literature resources in the U.K. It houses various collections: a reference library of books and periodicals about children's literature, a collection of books of contemporary children's literature (the Book Trust gives them an annual donation of about 2,000 books—see entry above), a Teaching Practice Collection, and many books on education and teacher-related materials. The Centre has developed a Web site on European picture books and a database on research in children's literature.

1144 *National Library of Scotland.* George IV Bridge, Edinburgh EH1 1EW, Scotland; www.nls.uk.

The National Library of Scotland, a copyright library since 1710, contains a vast collection of about 5 million items, including a large historical collection of children's books. Among its special collections are the Eudo Mason Collection of about 3,600 volumes, the Lauriston Castle collection of 11,000 items, and the Hugh Sharp Collection of manuscripts and first editions by writers including Lewis Carroll and Edward Lear.

1145 *National Library of Wales.* Aberystwyth SY29 3BU, Ceredigion, Wales; www.llgc.org.uk.

In addition to a huge collection of children's books in the regular collection, this library holds many special collections: the D. J. Williams Collection of about 500 old children's books in Welsh; the Llanfyllin Collection, principally of religious and moral publications; and the C. J. Knight Collection of early 19th-century books.

Renier Collection see ***National Art Library, Victoria and Albert Museum.***

1146 ***University of Reading: The Library.*** Whiteknights, PO Box 217, Reading RG6 6AH, England; www.rdg.ac.uk.

Beginning with a collection of early 19th-century titles given to the library in 1950, this children's collection has now grown to more than 7,000 volumes covering literature primarily up to World War II and runs of periodicals. There are about 1,000 pre-1851 titles.

1147 ***Wandsworth Public Libraries.*** c/o Putney Library, Disraeli Road, London SW15 2DR, England; www.wandsworth.gov.uk/libraries.

The catalog of the Wandsworth Collection of Early Children's Books, originally published in 1972, lists about 4,000 titles, but the collection is now much larger. Although the earliest title is dated 1673, the bulk of the collection covers 1850 to 1959. Included in the collection are fiction, nonfiction, and chapbooks.

F. SELECTED MAJOR COLLECTIONS IN THE UNITED STATES

1148 ***American Antiquarian Society. American Juvenile Literature Collection.*** 185 Salisbury Ave., Worcester, MA 01609-1634; (508) 755-5221; www.americanantiquarian.org/children.htm.

This outstanding collection has been called "by far the largest and most interesting collection of (historical) children's books in the country." It includes about two thirds of all children's books published before 1821, or about 3,500 titles, plus a total of 17,000 books printed between 1700 and 1899 with major strengths in Louisa May Alcott, Samuel Goodrich (Peter Parley), and William Taylor Adams (Oliver Optic). The collection houses about 1,400 picture books from the archives of the New York publisher McLoughlin Bros. It also has extensive periodical holdings, including the first American children's periodical, *The Children's Magazine.*

1149 ***Arizona State University. University Libraries.*** Department of Archives and Manuscripts, PO Box 871006, Tempe, AZ 85287; www.asu.edu/lib.

This library houses a number of special collections relating to children's literature. The Contemporary Authors Manuscripts Collection contains archival material from many Arizona children's authors; the Child Drama Collection holds about 1,000 books on theater for young people; and the L. Frank Baum collection focuses on Oz books. The regular historical collection of children's books contains more than 1,000 titles. Former young adult literature professor Ken Donelson recently (2003) donated his 800-plus collection of books dating back to 1835, founding the Ken Donelson Special Collection of Juvenile Literature.

1150 *Baldwin Library of Historical Children's Books.* Department of Special Collections, PO Box 117007, Smathers Library, University of Florida, Gainesville, FL 32611; (352) 392-9075; http://web.uflib.ufl.edu/spec/baldwin/baldwin.html.

In 1977, Ruth Baldwin, an avid collector of children's books, gave her private collection of 35,000 volumes to the University of Florida. Under her direction, more than 50,000 volumes of 19th- and 20th-century titles were added over the next 12 years. At present, the library has about 93,000 titles, 800 of which were published before 1820, making this the second-largest collection of early American imprints in the United States (the American Antiquarian Society is number one). The collection contains about 3,000 editions of *Robinson Crusoe* and 100 editions of *Pilgrim's Progress*. Dr. Baldwin, who had a doctorate in library science, worked well into her 80s organizing and developing the collection. The Baldwin is the central research library for the Center for the Study of Children's Literature and Media.

1151 *Butler Library.* Rare Books and Manuscripts Library, Columbia University, 535 W. 114th St., New York, NY 10027; (212) 854-2231; www.columbia.edu/cu/lweb/indiv/butler.

The Butler Library at Columbia houses many valuable collections of children's literature, among them the Arthur Rackham Collection, which contains manuscripts, letters, first editions, and other publications relating to this beloved English writer; the L. Frank Baum Collection; the Walter Farley Papers; and the Tibor Gergely Papers. The main collection, the Historical Collection of Children's Literature, now numbers about 10,000 volumes and 450 periodicals. Frances Henne, who taught children's literature at Columbia for many years, also gave her extensive collection of 19th- and 20th-century imprints to the university. It now numbers more than 3,000 volumes.

1152 *Children's Literature Center of the Library of Congress.* 101 Independence Ave. S.E., Washington, DC 20540-4620; (202) 707-5535; http://lcweb.loc.gov/rr/child/.

After it became a copyright library in 1870, the Library of Congress increased its holdings in children's literature dramatically, and it now holds the largest collection of children's books in the United States with almost 200,000 items in the archives. Although this collection is not housed separately, help is available from the Children's Literature Center, which was founded in 1963 to help organizations and individuals who are studying, producing, or disseminating children's literature.

Children's Literature Research Collections. University of Minnesota see ***Kerlan Collection.***

1153 ***Cooperative Children's Book Center.*** 4290 Helen C. White Hall, 600 N. Park St., Madison, WI 53706; (608) 263-3720; www.education.wisc.edu/ccbc.

The Center, which was established in 1963 and is part of the School of Education at the University of Wisconsin at Madison, now has a collection of about 40,000 historical and contemporary titles with particular strengths in multicultural literature, publications from alternative presses, and Wisconsin authors and illustrators. The collection is also strong in material relating to Newbery winner Ellen Raskin.

1154 ***Cotsen Children's Library.*** Harvey S. Firestone Memorial Library, Princeton University, One Washington Road, Princeton, NJ 08544; (609) 258-1148; http://ccl.princeton.edu/.

The Cotsen collection has been described as "one of the great concentrations of primary source material (21,000 items) principally in the form of illustrated books, but including prints, drawings, manuscripts, games, puzzles, hornbooks, and toys, among a great many other objects." The story of the donor Lloyd E. Cotsen and how he assembled this huge collection is told in Nicholas A. Basbanes's *Patience and Fortitude* (see earlier in this chapter). The print material dates back to the 16th century and includes the only known copy of John Newbery's first publication for children, plus many alphabet books, chapbooks, illustrated classics, and folktales and fairy tales. This library conducts many programs for children, one of the few to do so.

1155 ***De Grummond Children's Literature Collection.*** McCain Library, Box 5148, University of Southern Mississippi, Hattiesburg, MS 39406; (601) 266-4349; www.lib.usm.edu/~degrum.

This is basically the collection of Dr. Lena de Grummond (1899–1989), who was Louisiana's state supervisor of school libraries for 15 years and later taught children's literature at Southern Mississippi for many years. A writer herself, she knew many writers and illustrators, and solicited books, manuscripts, and other materials from them. This collection alone represents the work of 1,200 individuals. The book collection is now more than 40,000 volumes (600 published before 1831) and 250 children's periodicals. It is considered one of North America's leading research centers in the field of children's literature and is the host to many conferences, exhibits, tours, and other programs. Among its great strengths are the Ezra Jack Keats holdings and titles by John Newbery and Kate Greenaway.

1156 *Elizabeth Nesbitt Room, University of Pittsburgh.* Room 305, Information Sciences Building, 135 N. Bellefield Ave., Pittsburgh, PA 15260; (412) 624-4710; www.library.pitt.edu/libraries/is/enroom.

This collection now numbers about 12,000 books and periodicals that date from 1695 through the 20th century. Included are chapbooks, picture books, series books, award winners, and works by Pennsylvania authors and illustrators. The collection also contains the complete videotape archives of "Mister Rogers' Neighborhood."

1157 *Eric Carle Museum of Picture Book Art.* 125 West Bay Road, Amherst, MA 01002; (413) 658-1100; www.picturebookart.org.

Opened in 2002, this is the first museum in the United States devoted entirely to the art of the picture book. It is a museum for everyone interested in this genre, with particular emphasis on the participation of parents and children. In addition to a general collection, the museum has as a focus on the work of Eric Carle. In 2004, the museum received a collection of more than 700 reference books relating to children's literature and illustration from Barbara Elleman, former editor of the American Library Association's *Book Links* magazine.

1158 *Free Library of Philadelphia, Special Children's Collections.* 1901 Vine St., Philadelphia, PA 19103; (215) 686-5370; www.library.phila.gov.

The non-circulating research collections of the Free Library of Philadelphia now total about 60,000 items on children's literature. Special collections include the A. B. Frost Collection, the Beatrix Potter Collection, the Arthur Rackham Collection, the Howard Pyle and his Students Collection, the Munro Leaf Collection, the Robert Lawson Collection, and the Kate Greenaway Collection. The 20,000-volume collection of the American Sunday School Union—the most prolific publisher of children's material in the 19th century—was donated to the library in 1962. Also of great importance is the A. S. W. Rosenbach Collection of Early American Children's Books, which now numbers about 13,000 volumes (the original gift consisted of 816 volumes that covered 1682 to 1836) (see also Rosenbach Museum and Library below).

1159 *Thomas Hughes Children's Library, Chicago Public Library.* 400 S. State
St., Chicago, IL 60605; (312) 747-4200; www.chipublib.org/001hwlc/
hwthc.html.

A retrospective collection from the library's depository collection of
10,000 children's books published between 1900 and 1950 formed the
basis of this library. To this has been added about 40,000 volumes from
the Illinois State Library's juvenile collection of books published between
1930 and 1970. There is a fine Newbery-Caldecott collection and many
holdings relating to Walt Disney.

1160 *Huntington Library.* 1151 Oxford Rd., San Marino, CA 91108;
(626) 405-2100; www.huntington.org/LibraryDiv/LibraryHome.html.

The Manuscripts Division of this magnificent library has materials relating to about 50 well-known artists and writers of children's books, and
the Rare Book Collection contains many treasures, including early
British and American textbooks, illustrated books, miniature books, and
a strong Lewis Carroll collection.

1161 *Jordan Collection, Boston Public Library.* Copley Square, Boston, MA
02117; (617) 536-5400; www.bpl.org/research/special/collections.htm#j.

Named after a founder of children's services at the Boston Public Library,
this collection now numbers more than 160,000 volumes of fiction,
nonfiction, and such genres as picture books and poetry, for children and
young adults. Founded in 1967, the collection was at first a representative selection of children's books from 1900 to 1970 (about 50,000
titles), but since the 1970s one copy of every title added to the circulating collection is also housed in the Jordan Collection.

1162 *Kerlan Collection, University of Minnesota.* 113 Andersen Library,
222 21st Ave. S., Minneapolis, MN 55455; (612) 624-4576;
http://special.lib.umn.edu/clrc/.

This wonderful collection was started by Dr. Irvin Kerlan (1912–1962)
after one of his patients gave him a children's book when he was ill in
1945. When the collection was donated to the University of Minnesota
in 1949, it contained 9,000 books and 180 manuscripts. This has grown
to more than 75,000 books, along with the original manuscripts and
illustrations for 10,000 of them. One of the largest donations was given
by Mildred L. Batchelder, who presented her huge collection of foreign
children's books in translation. The collection continues to expand, with
many authors donating manuscripts and books (Marguerite Henry's col-

lection was given in 1998, to name just one). In 1975, the Kerlan Award for excellence in creating children's literature was established (see Chapter 6). The Kerlan Collection is part of the Children's Literature Research Collections at the University of Minnesota, which also includes the Hess Collection of dime novels and Big Little Books, the Laura Jane Musser Oziana Collection about Oz and its creator, the Paul Bunyan Collection, and a National Council of Teachers of English library of award-winning books.

1163 *Lilly Library, Indiana University.* 1200 E. Seventh St., Bloomington, IN 47405; (812) 855-2452; www.indiana.edu/~liblilly/.

Of the 15,000 historical children's books found in this collection, the core (about 8,000 titles) comes from the Elizabeth W. Ball Collection of Historical Children's Materials, which was donated in 1983. Major strengths are ABC books, chapbooks (about 1,900 volumes), and examples from early English publishers such as Newbery (*The Little Pretty Pocket-Book* of 1744), Darton, and Harris. Another famous collection holds the works of George Cruikshank.

1164 *Los Angeles Public Library.* 630 W. Fifth St., Los Angeles, CA 90071; (213) 228-7272; www.lapl.org.

In addition to a fine general collection of children's literature, this main library houses some interesting special collections. These include the California Authors and Illustrators Collection (more than 2,000 titles from 1850 on by California writers), the California Collection of books with California settings, a special folktale and fairy tale collection of about 6,000 volumes, a Mother Goose collection, the Leo Politi Collection, and a collection of original art from picture books.

1165 *Mazza Museum.* University of Findlay, 1000 N. Main St., Findlay, OH 45846-3695; (800) 472-9502; www.mazzamuseum.org/.

Founded in 1982 by Dr. August C. Mazza and his late wife to help celebrate the 100th anniversary of the university, this collection of original art works now has several hundred pieces that represent the work of important contemporary American illustrators and some of the British and American greats from the past. The university also sponsors the Mazza Medallion, which is awarded every two years to an outstanding artist of children's books.

1166 *New York Public Library, Central Children's Room, Donnell Library Center.* 20 W. 53rd St., New York, NY 10019; (212) 245-5272; www.nypl.org/branc/central/dlc/dch.

The total number of volumes in this massive collection is now about 55,000, many of these being in the current circulating collection. In the non-circulating areas, there are thousands of titles reflecting the history of children's book publishing in this country, as well as the "Old Book Collection" of 2,000 English and American titles from the 18th and 19th centuries. In addition, there is an extensive reference book collection on all aspect of children's books. Many of the branches also contain interesting historical collections and the Main Reference Library, at 42nd Street and 5th Avenue, has many rare books and manuscripts in the Rare Books and Manuscripts Division.

1167 *Northeast Children's Literature Collections.* University of Connecticut, Archives and Special Collections, 405 Babbidge Rd., Unit 1205, Storrs, CT 06269-1205; (860) 485-4500; http://nclc.uconn.edu/.

With its aim "to preserve and make accessible historically and artistically significant works of children's literature," this collection now contains more than 14,000 children's books spanning the 19th and 20th centuries. It has a growing collection of manuscripts and artwork from such luminaries as Barbara Cooney, Eleanor Estes, Richard Scarry, and Leonard Everett Fisher. The library concentrates on writers and artists from the northeastern United States. One special archive is the "Black Beauty Collection" of 445 editions of the Anna Sewell classic plus related material.

1168 *Pierpont Morgan Library of Early Children's Books.* 28 E. 36th St., New York, NY 10016; (212) 685-0610; www.morganlibrary.org.

The Morgan Library contains about 10,000 children's books and related material from the 3rd century A.D. to the early 20th century. As well as the collection of the Morgans, there have been many other substantial bequests, including the 1965 Elisabeth Ball gift and the 1987 Gordon N. Ray gift of illustrated books. There are excellent holdings of material by and about Lewis Carroll, Beatrix Potter, Randolph Caldecott, and John Tenniel, plus such rarities as a Perrault's 1659 Mother Goose and Thackeray's original *The Rose and the Ring*.

1169 *Rosenbach Museum and Library.* 2010 Delancey Place, Philadelphia, PA 19103; (215) 732-1600; www.rosenbach.org.

Although most of the rare children's books collected by Dr. Rosenbach (1876–1952) were given to the Free Library of Philadelphia (see entry above), his main collection resides in this building. It includes such treasures as Lewis Carroll's own copy of the 1865 edition of *Alice in Wonderland* and original drawings by Sir John Tenniel. The great drawing card for children's literature enthusiasts here is the massive collection of more than 3,000 pieces of original artwork by Maurice Sendak, including his drawings for *Where the Wild Things Are* and 50 other works.

1170 *State University of New York at Albany.* University Library, Dept. of Special Collections and Archives, New Library Bldg., Room 354, 1400 Washington Ave., Albany, NY 12222; (518) 437-3935; http://library.albany.edu/speccoll/.

There are several special children's book collections at this institution, including the Clement Moore Collection of more than 200 items involving "A Visit from St. Nicholas," the papers of Marcia Brown, and the Maud and Miska Petersham papers. The largest holdings are in the Miriam Snow Mathes Historical Children's Literature Collection. Begun in the University's Library School in the late 1920s, the collection now contains about 10,000 children's books published from the 19th century through 1960.

1171 *University of California at Los Angeles.* Special Collections, Research Library, Box 951575, Los Angeles, CA 90095; (310) 825-4988; http://www2.library.ucla.edu/libraries/index.cfm.

Through the acquisition of several private collections, this library now holds a fine historical collection of children's books. Strengths include title issues by the John Newbery family, a large collection of chapbooks and toy books, and in-depth material on such early English children's writers as Edgeworth, Trimmer, and Sherwood.

1172 *University of South Florida.* Tampa Campus Library, Special Collections Department, 4202 E. Fowler Ave., Tampa, FL 33620; (813) 974-2731; http://web.lib.usf.edu/tampa/spccoll.

The main Historical Children's Literature Collection contains about 40,000 volumes plus masses of archival material. Holdings begin in the 18th century and extend to the present with an emphasis on dime novels, pre-Civil War schoolbooks, and popular juvenile fiction. Two special collections are the Everett Collection of more than 8,000 20th-century picture books and the Henry K. Hudson American Boy's Series Books, a 4,000-volume library that is complemented by a girls' series collection of 2,500 titles and by 500 anthropomorphic animal series books.

1173 *Wayne State University. Purdy/Kresge Library.* 106 Kresge Library, Wayne State University, Detroit, MI 48202; (313) 577-1825; www.lib.wayne.edu/resources/special_collections/index.php.

There are two special collections in this library. The first is the Eloise Ramsey Collection of Literature for Young People, about 14,000 items dating from 1601 to the present with strengths in ABC books, religious tracts, Isaac Watts, and Lewis Carroll. The second is an unusual collection, the Millicent A. Wills Collection of Urban Ethnic Materials for Young People, which contains children's books about urban centers and different ethnic groups.

G. PRIVATE COLLECTIONS

There are two private collections worth noting. The collection of Betsy Beinecke Shirley—about 6,000 items from the 18th century to the present—is particularly strong in early American imprints. This collection is gradually being given to Yale University in New Haven, Connecticut, through annual donations. The second is in Baltimore and is owned by Linda Lapides, a former young adult librarian at the Enoch Pratt Free Library. She and her husband Julian L. Lapides, a prominent attorney, collected books for more than four decades with a specialization in Baltimore publications.

H. OTHER IMPORTANT COLLECTIONS IN THE UNITED STATES

1174 *Connecticut Historical Society.* 1 Elizabeth St., Hartford, CT 06105; (860) 236-5621; www.chs.org.

Home of the Albert Carlos Bates Collection, the Caroline M. Hewins Collection, the Connecticut Imprints Collection, the Connecticut Printer Archive, and a general juvenile collection.

1175 *Detroit Public Library, Rare Book Collection.* 5201 Woodward Ave., Detroit, MI 48202; (313) 833-1400; www.detroit.lib.mi.us.

A large collection of rare children's books resides here, as well as the Kate Greenaway Collection and the Elsie Gordon Memorial Collection.

1176 *Illinois State University, Milner Library.* Normal, IL 61790-8900; (309) 438-2871; www.mlb.ilstu.edu.

There is a large historical collection plus the Circus Collection, the Historical Textbook Collection, the Lois Lenski Collection, and the Will Johnson Collection.

1177 *Long Island University, C. W. Post Library.* Northern Blvd., Brookville, NY 11548; (516) 299-2880; www.liu.edu/cwis/cwp/library/sc/sc.htm.

Home of the American Juvenile Collection of about 4,000 titles and the Christine B. Gilbert Historical Collection of Children's Literature.

1178 *Minneapolis Public Library.* 300 Nicollet Mall, Minneapolis, MN 55401; (612) 630-6000; www.mpls.lib.mn.us.

Minneapolis Public Library has a large historical collection, a Children's Folklore Collection, and a Children's Foreign Language Collection.

1179 *New York University, Fales Library.* 70 Washington Square S., New York, NY 10012; (212) 998-2596; www.nyu.edu/library/bobst/research/fales.

In addition to a rich collection of more than 15,000 volumes of and about children's literature, this library has the Alfred C. Berol Collection of Lewis Carroll (the world's largest collection on Carroll) and the Levy Dime Novel Archive.

1180 *Rutgers University, Archibald S. Alexander Library.* New Brunswick, NJ 08903; (908) 932-7006; www.libraries.rutgers.edu.

Rutgers's library holds a rich collection of the manuscripts of several contemporary children's writers, a Textbook Collection, and the Rutgers Collection of Children's Literature.

1181 *San Francisco State University, J. Paul Leonard Library.* 1630 Holloway Ave., San Francisco, CA 94132; (415) 338-1854; www.library.sfsu.edu.

Home of the Marguerite Archer Collection of Historic Children's Books, a collection of about 5,000 books and periodicals.

1182 *Simmons College Libraries, Archives Dept.* 300 The Fenway, Boston, MA 02115; (617) 521-2440; www.simmons.edu/libraries/archives/about.html.

In addition to the extensive Horn Book Magazine Archives, Simmons has a general collection and the Knapp Collection of historical materials. Simmons is also the home of the *Center for the Study of Children's Literature.*

1183 *University of Illinois, Education and Social Science Library.* 1408 W. Gregory Dr., Urbana, IL 61801; (217) 333-2305; www.library.uiuc.edu/edx.

This is a massive collection of children's literature that, when all the holdings are cataloged, will total more than 140,000 volumes, the second-largest (after the Library of Congress) collection of children's books in the United States. There is also a collection of curriculum material that now totals 57,000 items. The collection adds about 4,000 items a year.

1184 *University of North Carolina at Greensboro, Walter Clinton Jackson Library.* PO Box 26170, Greensboro, NC 27402; (336) 334-5304; http://library.uncg.edu/.

Lois Lenski donated her collection of more than 700 early children's books to this library in 1968, and the collection has since grown through other donations. There is also a valuable Manuscript Collection of Children's Books, and branches of the University at Chapel Hill and Durham have collections of rare children's books.

1185 *Yale University, Beinecke Rare Book and Manuscript Library.* PO Box 208240, New Haven, CT 06520; (203) 432-2972; www.library.yale. edu/beinecke.

In addition to thousands of items on children's literature in the rare books and manuscripts collection, this library has the unusual Gary Collection of Playing Cards and the ever-growing Betsy Beinecke Shirley Collection of American Children's Literature, now more than 2,000 volumes of children's literature from 1690 to the present.

CHAPTER 11

THE INTERNET AND OTHER
NONPRINT RESOURCES

There are literally thousands of Web sites devoted to various aspects of children's and young adult literature, and the number increases every day. Therefore, this chapter includes only those that appear to be the most useful and those that contain the most links to other Web sites. The importance of links cannot be overestimated as they greatly extend the range of information made available. Search engines such as Google and Yahoo can be extremely helpful. Use them to seek out individual author and illustrator sites and to search for specific genres and interests.

A. IMPORTANT WEB SITES

1. General and Miscellaneous

1186 American Library Association; www.ala.org.

The Web site of this national librarians' association and its many divisions supplies best books lists, details of prize-winning titles, and general information about authors and books.

1187 The Book Forum; www.thebookforum.com.

Supported by commissions received from the various stores that participate, this Web site is free and without fees for registration. Click on "Children's Fiction" in the "Bookshelves" section to get general news about children's literature and recent publications. In the "Children's Fiction" Forum, users voice comments and add reviews and opinions about books and authors. Individual topics are organized in threads, and each registered user is invited to create his or her own thread.

1188 Booktrusted.com; www.booktrusted.co.uk.

Operated by the Book Trust of London, this is a great resource for information on authors, organizations, events, prizes and awards, book recommendations, magazines and periodicals, and general news about children's literature. Though UK-oriented, it contains plenty of useful information for all English-speaking countries. There are links to 65 professional organizations and about 50 links for book prizes.

1189 Building Rainbows; www.buildingrainbows.com.

This is a book reviewing and discussion forum that contains more than 10,000 reviews of children's and young adult literature written by young readers. Reviews vary considerably in length (the shortest encountered was "It was awesome"), but most are a short paragraph or two. The home page provides many access points, including "Highest Rated Books." Unfortunately, the advertisements (the site is run in association with Amazon) can become intrusive.

1190 Canadian Children's Book Centre; www.bookcentre.ca.

This is a wonderful Web site to learn about Canadian literature for children. As well as news about book and author activities, this site gives online reviews, lists of professional resources, and an excellent listing of Canadian prizes and awards in the field of children's literature.

1191 Carol Hurst's Children's Literature Site; www.carolhurst.com.

This site has information about children's authors and illustrators, reviews of children's books, ideas on how to use children's literature in the classroom, and suggestions for book-related activities.

1192 Center for Children's Books; www.lis.uiuc.edu/~ccb/about_us.html.

This is the site of the Center for Children's Books at the University of Illinois at Urbana-Champaign. It contains several interesting sections. Click on Collection Development to find links in such areas as Reading Promotion Websites and Books Awards in Children's Literature (which covers more than 100 key awards). The Storytelling area includes bibliographies, resources, articles, important storytelling links, and a number of audio files. There is also a useful section on programming for young people.

1193 Children's Book Committee; www.bankstreet.edu/bookcom/index.html.

Valuable information about this committee, which operates out of the Bank Street College of Education in New York, can be found here, including descriptions of its activities, lists of prize winners, and general features about developments in children's literature.

1194 Children's Book News; www.achuka.co.uk.

Also known as Achuka, this British site gives lively information about children's and young adult books, authors, illustrators, and various genres written to appeal to young people.

1195 Children's Literature: A Guide to the Criticism; www.unm.edu/~lhendr/.

This is an online version of the book published in 1987 by G. K. Hall and written by Linnea Hendrickson. It is a critical study of books about children's and young adult literature, mostly from the 1970s and early 980s. Each item receives a three- or four-line annotation. In the first part, the books are listed by the author's last name and are given full treatment; in the second part, they are listed under subjects, themes, and series, using such headings as Adventure Stories and Africa. There are full indexes and an appendix on general resources in children's literature.

1196 Children's Literature Association; http://ebbs.english.vt.edu/chla/.

Devoted to the scholarly study of children's literature, this association provides on its home page information about the association and all kinds of links under such subjects as censorship, authors and illustrators, courses, and organizations.

1197 Children's Literature Comprehensive Database; www.childrenslit.com.

This extensive online database is available to individual subscribers for about $275 a year. Currently it consists of more than 1 million MARC records of children's and young adult books plus more than 200,000 book reviews, lists of awards and prizes, best book citations, and links to author and illustrator home pages. It is the most comprehensive children's literature resource available with access to reviewing sources in both the U.S. and other English-speaking countries. In 2003, the database added thousands of book jacket images that increase its visual appeal considerably.

1198 Children's Literature Web Guide; www.acs.ucalgary.ca/~dkbrown/index.html.

When seeking information about children's and young adult literature, one used to start with David K. Brown's famous Web site from the University of Calgary's Doucette Library of Teaching Resources. It was a veritable cornucopia of links and more links organized under such subjects as children's books awards, authors on the Web, stories on the Web, recommended book lists, resources for teachers, resources for parents, the year's best books, and children's bestsellers, to name just a few. Unfortunately, it has not been updated for several years and is therefore valuable only for retrospective information.

1199 Children's Picture Book Database at Miami University; www.lib.muohio.edu/pictbks/index2.php.

This database has bibliographic data and short summaries for more than 5,000 picture books suitable for grades PS–3. The database can be searched using 950 keywords or by author and title. The keyword approach makes this database particularly useful in developing literature-based thematic units.

1200 The Clearing House on Reading, English, and Communication; http://reading.indiana.edu/.

Formerly part of ERIC (the Educational Resources Information Center), this clearinghouse is located at the Indiana University School of Education. Publications relating to children's and young adult literature are indexed and there are links to online resources in these areas.

1201 Cooperative Children's Book Center; www.education.wisc.edu/ccbc.

In addition to organization news about the Cooperative Children's Book Center at the University of Wisconsin in Madison, this site has links to other children's literature sites, important organizations, exhibits, prizes and awards, and material on and interviews with authors and illustrators.

The center also operates a listserv—CCBC-Net—in which subscribers discuss a particular subject for one month.

1202 Cynthia Leitich Smith Children's Literature Resources; www.cynthia leitichsmith.com/index1.htm.

As well as original articles, this site contains almost 3,000 annotated links to home pages, interviews, bibliographies, publishing news, curriculum information, lesson plans, multicultural resources, and literary criticism. A major strength is the hundreds of links to home pages and other resources involving authors and artists. Recent award-winning books are listed and annotated along with pictures of dust jackets. For a substantial listing of awards state-by-state, plus a directory of national awards, click on "State and National Awards." Ms. Smith, of Austin, Texas, and her husband are both children's book writers.

1203 Digital Librarian; www.digital-librarian.com.

This is a fantastic resource founded by Margaret Vail Anderson, a librarian in Cortland, New York. Thousands of links to sites are arranged under about a hundred subjects, beginning with "Activism" and ending with "Yurts, Tipis & Tents." Clicking on "Children's Literature" gives access to hundreds of valuable sites on all facets of children's and young adult literature. Other related subjects to explore are "Book Collecting," "Librariana," "Literature," and "Reference."

1204 Educational Paperback Association Website; www.edupaperback.org/resources.cfm.

Links are provided to an excellent selection of sites. The area dealing with children's book awards is subdivided into sections on American Library Association awards, other awards, state and regional awards, Canadian children's book awards, and international awards. About 60 awards are discussed and links are given. The author and illustrator section links to Web sites of individuals from David Adler to Jane Yolen; a biography section provides information on and links to famous children's and YA authors and illustrators from Alma Flor Ada to Paul Zelinsky. There are list of authors who visit schools and sections on library resources that include journals, reference sources, and other useful links.

1205 Fairrosa Cyber Library of Children's Literature; www.fairrosa.info.

This site is organized and administered by Roxanne Hsu Feldman, the librarian at the Dalton School in New York City. It is divided into different compartments, the two most important being Reference Shelf and Reading Room. The Reference Shelf is subdivided into three parts: Authors and Illustrators provides links to hundreds of author and illustrator home pages and other biographical sites; the second part gives links to general literary sources and more specialized ones for writers, publishers, and booksellers; the third part, Articles and Reviews, gives access to reviewing and general journals in children's literature. In the Reading Room are links to digital versions of such classics as *Alice in Wonderland* and dozens of folk and fairy tales.

1206 High School Hub; www.highschoolhub.org.

Basically a homework helper for high school students, this site is organized by curriculum subject. In the English section, there are study guides to many of the novels that are read in high schools. Under Literature Guides, click on Literature CyberGuides to link to a treasure of lesson plans and activities for hundreds of important works in children's and young adult literature, organized under the following grade levels: K–3, 4–5, 6–8, and 9–12. These excellent guides were developed by SCORE (Schools of California On-line Resources for Education) and can be retrieved separately at www.sdcoe.k12.ca.us/score/cyberguide.html.

1207 Internet Public Library; www.ipl.org.

Hosted by the University of Michigan School of Information, this site has among its aims "finding, evaluating, selecting, organizing, describing, and creating information resources." Two of the most valuable areas are KidSpace and TeenSpace. Each is organized by subject area (math and science, art and music, for example). The children's Reading Zone offers many interesting areas to investigate, with information on and links to biographical material on famous authors and illustrators. There are also lists of children's magazines, picture books, comic strips, and so forth.

1208 Kathy Schrock's Guide for Educators; school.discovery.com/ schrockguide.

This is a useful site for educators particularly because of the many links relating to reading and children's literature. Particularly fine for enriching the curriculum and developing children's interests in learning.

1209 Librarian's Guide to the Internet; www.star-host.com/library.

Basic links to directories, guides, and other important reference sources are organized under such headings as "Exploring Digital Libraries," "Looking for People," and "Visiting Online Librarians." About three or four links are given under each subject. Nothing specific is given on children's literature but the sites listed give good background information.

1210 Librarians' Index to the Internet; http://lii.org.

Established by Berkeley Public Library, this site has now gained national importance and is maintained by librarians throughout California and administered by the state librarian. The home page lists a number of broad subjects. Under "Arts and Humanities," click on "Literature" and then on "Children's Literature." This page gives more than 100 links to important sites in the field. There are several other subjects under "Literature"—"Banned Books" and "Braille Books," for example—that will also be of value. Other large subject areas to explore are "Computers," and, for biographies, "People." This is an exciting site to browse.

1211 The Looking Glass: An Online Children's Literature Journal; www.the-looking-glass.net.

Begun in Toronto in 1997 and staffed by volunteers, mainly academics, this online journal features articles, essays, and news items about children's literature. It is free and has contributors from various countries including the United States, Canada, the United Kingdom, and Australia.

1212 National Center for Children's Illustrated Literature; www.nccil.org.

This center is also discussed in Chapter 9 under "Organizations," but its Web site is of particular interest because it supplies links to other sites involved in picture books, including those of famous illustrators such as Paul Zelinsky and Peter Sís.

1213 The Purple Crayon; www.underdown.org.

Maintained by Harold D. Underdown, this site supplies all kinds of advice from a pro on the writing, illustrating, and publishing of children's books. There are links to more than 60 practical articles, plus material on specific genres, literary agents, and submission of material. Particularly valuable is the introduction to 12 major literary awards and prizes with lists of recent winners.

1214 Reading About Children's Literature; http://io.uwinnipeg.ca/~nodelman/resources/allbib.htm.

This list of reading resources in children's literature was compiled by Perry Nodelman to accompany the third edition of his excellent *Pleasure of Children's Literature* (see Chapter 1). The bibliographies of books and articles are organized under topics including "Culture, Ideology and Children's Literature," "Contemporary Childhood," and "Critical Theory." This is a scholarly compilation of readings for the serious student of children's literature and is now primarily of historical importance.

1215 Resources for School Librarians (formerly School Libraries on the Web);
www.sldirectory.com.

Maintained by Linda Bertland, a retired Philadelphia school librarian, this
site contains a fantastic number of links and information relevant to literature and school libraries. The site is divided into six sections with access
in the table of contents to many subdivisions. The first section, "Learning and Teaching," covers topics including information skills, lesson
plans, and how to use primary sources. The section on program administration deals with annual reports, library promotion, standards, and so
forth. And a third section, "Information Access," covers such topics as
collection development, collection evaluation, services to Spanish-speaking students, and copyright. In this section's "Reading Room" there are
links to hundreds of Web sites organized under such headings as "Cool
Kid's Sites," "General Children's Literature Web Sites," "Books About
Children's Literature," "Journals and Research in Children's Literature,"
"Genre Lists," and "Young Adult Books." Lots of good resources here!

1216 School Libraries.net; www.school-libraries.net.

Originally sponsored by the Chico school district in California, this site
is now maintained by the School of Library and Information Science at
San Jose State University. It consists of links to hundreds of home pages
of school libraries in about 20 countries, with an emphasis on the United
States.

1217 School Library Associations on the Internet; www.iasl-slo.org/slibassoc.
html.

Hosted by the International Association of School Librarianship, this site
provides links to school library associations, arranged alphabetically by
country.

1218 School Library Resources; www.school-libraries.org/resources.

Divided into seven areas, this site provides links in areas including general school library resources, learning and teaching using the Web, information literacy and library skills, and professional associations and
organizations. A section called "Books, Book Reviews, and Reading
Resources" gives annotated links to about 50 journals and Web sites
involving children's and young adult literature. Unfortunately, as of summer 2005 this valuable site had not been updated in several years.

1219 School Library Resources; http://librarysupportstaff.com.

A fantastic compendium of information on school libraries and their
paraprofessional staff. The site, begun in 2000, is owned and maintained
by Mary Niederlander in Buffalo, New York. There are separate sections

for different staff positions, and a good deal of practical information like technical support and how to find a job. As well there are links involved to library-related reference sources and hundreds of journals, as well as abstracts of important articles.

1220 Secondary English; http://secondaryenglish.com.

This online periodical offers multimedia reviews, research, articles, and innovative activities for teaching language arts at the secondary level. It also provides useful links to many educational organizations.

1221 Selective Guide to Reference Books in Children's Literature (University of Illinois); www.library.uiuc.edu/edx/libsci.htm.

A compilation of hundreds of books and journals about children's and young adult literature. This has not been updated for several years and is now only of historical importance. This list is also available at www.library.uiuc.edu/lsx/child.htm.

1222 Tales of Wonder; www.darsie.net/talesofwonder.

This is a great resource, providing links to many of the most common folktales and fairy tales. There are many other sites on this topic; three are: SurLaLune Fairy Tale Pages (www.surlalunefairytales.com); Stories, Folklore, and Fairy Tales Theme Page (www.cln.org/themes/fairytales.html); and Folklore and Mythology Electronic Texts (www.pitt.edu/~dash/folktexts.html).

1223 Teaching Books; www.teachingbooks.net.

An amazing site for information about children's and young adult literature, this is available by subscription only. For a preview of the material available, visit the home page. The site is divided into different parts. Authors Up-Close gives in-studio movies of authors and illustrators. There is also a section of audio excerpts of readings of children's books, thus supplying opportunities to both see and hear authors talk about their works. Other sections include guides to thousands of children's and young adult titles, thematic book lists, material on book awards, and valuable links to other related sites. Lots of great material here. For subscription information, phone (608) 257-2919 or e-mail info@TeachingBooks.net.

1224 Teenreads; http://teenreads.com.

An attractive, newsy site, Teenreads gives information about young adult books and adult books suitable for young adults. There are reviews, links to reading guides, information about book clubs, and so forth. A companion site is Kidsreads (http://kidsreads.com).

1225 U.K. Children's Books; www.ukchildrensbooks.co.uk.

Coverage of authors and illustrators is a particular strength of this great British site that provides links to hundreds of home pages; although most are British, Americans including Jane Yolen and Jean Craighead George are represented.

1226 Vandergrift's Children's and Young Adult Literature Pages; www.scils. rutgers.edu/~kvander.

Kay Vandergrift's literature pages are the most outstanding reference sources on children's and young adult literature on the Internet. The site is divided into separate sections, each of them brimming with links and information. The Children's Literature Page provides links to reference sources on writing and publishing children's literature, many different bibliographies, material on how to evaluate children's books, a discussion of female stories, traditional literature, fairy tales, censorship, and many other subjects. As well as links, these pages give insightful material by the author, long associated with Rutgers University in New Jersey. The Young Adult Literature Page gives similar material for young adult literature. The History of Children's Literature incorporates a fantastic collection of facts, opinions, and links. And the Author Site surely must be among the most complete in existence. Arranged alphabetically by the last name of the author or illustrator, this is a superb collection of links. Each one of these pages is excellent; together they form an outstanding resource.

1227 Wheelock College Library; www.wheelock.edu/library/lilook/ lisubject_childlit.htm.

A fine example of a college library (Wheelock College is in Boston) supplying relevant links to help patrons interested in children's literature. The site provides the call numbers of major reference books, serials, and videocassettes in the Wheelock collection plus links to Web sites that cover organizations, databases, annual awards, and important book lists.

1228 YA Librarians' Homepage: The Virtual YA Index; http://yahelp.suffolk. lib.ny.us.

Sections of this site are "Comic and Graphic Novel Resources," "Journals," "Organizations and Associations," "Literature," "Online Resources," "Electronic Discussion Lists," "Publishers and Distributors." Each of these areas supplies links to numerous Web sites. For example, the organizations section leads to the home pages of many domestic and a few foreign associations involved with children and young adults, including associations in each of the 50 states.

2. Author and Illustrator Biographies

Many of the sources listed above contain extensive links to author and illustrator biographies. Of particular use are Children's Literature Comprehensive Database (see also the special entry below), Children's Literature Web Guide, Cynthia Leitich Smith's Literature Resources, Fairrosa Cyber Library, and Vandergrift's Children's and Young Adult Literature Pages (click on Author Sites). A valuable print directory is *The Undergraduate's Companion to Children's Writers and Their Web Sites* by Jen Stevens (Libraries Unlimited, 2004, $29.95 [1-59158-097-8]). See Chapter 8 for more information on this book and other print sources.

1229 Authors4Teens; www.Authors4Teens.com.

This subscription-based site is managed by Greenwood Electronic Media but the content is controlled by noted author and young adult literature expert Donald Gallo. In early 2005, the file contained lengthy interviews with 47 prominent young adult authors including Chris Crutcher, Jerry Spinelli, and Chris Lynch. As well as the interview, each entry provides links to sound files, pictures, video, e-books, and related Web sites. The material is updated periodically and includes information on reviews, speaking engagements, and personal recollections. The price is $75, $100, or $125 a year depending on the identity of the subscriber (college/university, public library, school library, or individual).

1230 Autobiographies of Children's Authors and Illustrators; www.suffolk.lib. ny.us/youth/bibauthillus.html.

This list of print autobiographies by children's authors and illustrators was created at the Suffolk Library System on Long Island. From Verna Aardema to Paul Zindel, it is a rich, unique bibliography. Another valuable resource from this system is "Professional Resources," which gives links to a wide variety of sources including important professional associations.

1231 Children's Literature Comprehensive Database; www.childrenslit.com.

General information about this important database is given earlier in this chapter. Most of its contents are available only by subscription, but access to the author/illustrator area is free. Select "Features" and then "Meet the Authors and Illustrators." This provides links to more author/illustrator home pages than any other source on the Internet.

1232 Philip Nel's Authors and Illustrators Page; www.ksu.edu/english/nelp/weblinks/literary/childrens.html.

This is a great site for links to information on about 200 authors and illustrators. In addition to home pages, these links include other resources, including publisher's material. Two or three links are provided for most entries.

1233 Puffin Books; www.puffin.co.uk.

Click on the Author Area of this child-friendly site operated by Puffin Books, U.K. publisher of hundreds of paperback titles for children and young adults. The numerous author links (to British and international writers) often provide informal information and interesting asides on the subject's life and works.

1234 The Scoop; http://friend.ly.net/users/jorban/main.html.

Divided into sections including "Activities" and "Interviews," this site supplies useful and interesting links. The section on "Authors" connects to about 40 prominent authors and about 30 illustrators. Some of these links are to home pages; others are to original biographical material and publishers' bios. Also of interest is a link to "How to arrange an author visit to your school, library, or bookstore."

1235 The Virtual Sharyn November, 6.0: Authors and Illustrators; www.sharyn.org/authors.html.

This wonderful resource is updated regularly and contains links to home pages and other material for hundreds of authors, old and new. Though this site originates in the U.K., there is a fair representation of authors from other English-speaking countries. The lists are extensive (the C listing alone numbers about 70 names). In addition to author links, this site also lists Web sites of publishers of children's books and supplies links to other related resources.

ADDITIONAL AUTHOR AND ILLUSTRATOR LINKS

Many publishers maintain pages that provide information about their authors and illustrators. Publisher sites can be located by using a standard search engine; the author areas are usually featured prominently on the site's home page. Here are a few samples of these sites:

> HarperCollins Children's Author Pages
> www.harperchildrens.com/hch/author/
>
> Houghton Mifflin
> www.eduplace.com/author/
>
> Random House Children's Books Author Pages
> www.randomhouse.com/author/author_search.html
>
> Simon & Schuster
> www.simonsays.com

In addition, many of the search engine directories have compiled links to children's authors and illustrators. One of the best is Yahooligans (http://yahooligans.yahoo.com), which provides access to about 350 authors and illustrators and to other sites relating to children's literature.

3. Awards and Prizes

Note: Many of the Web sites discussed at the beginning of this chapter under "General and Miscellaneous" have substantial information about awards and prizes. For example, consult Children's Literature Web Guide, Cynthia Leitich Smith Children's Literature Resources, Internet School Library Media Center, and Vandergrift's Children's and Young Adult Literature Pages. Also consult Chapter 6, where you will find Web sites for individual awards and prizes.

1236 Awards and Prizes Online; http://awardsandprizes.cbcbooks.org.

The Children's Book Council maintains this fee-based site that features winners of almost 300 literary awards, from the beginning of each award to the present. This now involves about 7,000 books by about 5,000 authors. The awards are grouped under four headings: Adult-Selected Awards; Young-Reader-Selected or Children's Choice Awards; Australian, Canadian, New Zealand, and United Kingdom Awards; and International Awards. Discontinued awards are included. One can search by various access points, including award title, authors' and illustrators' names, book titles, year, age group, and keyword. The site is updated on a regular basis; subscriptions cost $150 a year. This is the most up-to-date and complete source currently available.

1237 Children's Literature Awards/Prizes; www.nolanet.org/award.htm.

Part of the NOLA Regional Library System's Web site, this page contains annotated links to about 20 American awards, with basic material on their origins, purposes, and criteria. A similar list can be found at www.norweld.lib.oh.us/ys/awards.htm.

1238 Children's Literature Book Award Information; www.tarleton.edu/~cwilterding/awards.htm.

Maintained by Catherine Jewel Wilterding, this site links to dozens of awards (mostly American) in alphabetical order. For each, a foundation date is given and selection criteria are outlined.

1239 Children's Literature Comprehensive Database; www.childrenslit.com.

This comprehensive, subscription-based database is discussed earlier in this chapter. It is possible to access links concerning awards and prizes without being a subscriber. Click on "Awards" on the homepage to find links to hundreds of awards arranged alphabetically. A fantastic free resource on the subject.

1240   Database of Award-Winning Children's Literature; www.dawcl.com.

Under various names, this excellent resource has been in existence for several years. It was founded and is maintained by Lisa R. Bartle, now a librarian at California State University at San Bernardino. It covers 57 awards. Background information, including selection criteria, and a link to each award's home page are given under "Explanation of Awards." The "Instructions" section explains each of the search choices—age of reader, genre, and setting, for example. In the "Search the Database" mode, one can search by a number of access points including those mentioned above, plus format, setting/period, gender of protagonist, etc. Individual title entries contain bibliographic information and a two-line annotation. There are now about 5,000 records from six English-speaking countries contained in this amazing site.

4. Digital Texts and Electronic Books

E-texts and e-books, once considered a thing of the future, have become a reality. The full texts of many classic books that are in the public domain can be found on the Web and accessed without special software. E-books (electronic books) usually require dedicated software, often called "Readers" and often available without charge. There are also services such as Questia and NetLibrary that make digital texts available on a subscription basis. As an example of how this phenomenon is growing, Google, the Internet search service, announced in December 2004 that some of the nation's leading research libraries—including Harvard, Stanford, and the New York Public Library, along with Britain's Oxford University Library—have agreed to a project by which some or all of their holdings will be converted into digital files that will be freely searchable over the Web. The following sites direct users to children's and young adult literature in e-texts and e-books.

1241   Children's Literature Center: Library of Congress; www.loc.gov/rr/child.

This site allows for access to all of the children's materials dispersed throughout the Library of Congress—more than 200,000 children's books and related items. It also gives hints on what areas, in addition to the main collection, where items of interest may be found (for example, rare books and books for the blind). Access to the complete online catalog is available from this site.

1242 Digital Book Index; www.digitalbookindex.org.

This site provide links to more than 100,000 digital title records from more than 1,800 commercial and noncommercial publishers, universities, and various private sites. About 66,000 of these books, texts, and documents are available free; many others are available at very modest cost. About 3,500 are contemporary or classic children's books. One can search the catalog by author, title, keyword, subject, and publisher. The catalog listings repeat this information and also give the format, price (if any), and the location of the text.

1243 East of the Web; http://eastoftheweb.com/ebooks.

A commercial producer and distributor of e-books, East of the Web offers a user-friendly site with a large collection of short stories, many of them classic stories that can be accessed without charge. There is also interesting background information on electronic book publishing.

1244 Electronic Text Center: University of Virginia; http://etext.lib.virginia.edu.

About 70,000 texts and 35,000 related images reside on this amazing site. Click on "Collections" then "English" and then "Young Readers" (http://etext.lib.virginia.edu/subjects/Young-Readers.html) to find the full text of several hundred classics, organized by author and accessible without any additional software. One of the great treats here is the Beatrix Potter books with their illustrations!

1245 Fairrosa Cyber Library of Children's Literature; www.fairrosa.info.

The Fairrosa Cyber Library, described in more detail above, offers links to the full text of about 40 children's classics in its Reading Room. Titles such as *Little Women, Alice in Wonderland,* and *The Secret Garden* are available.

1246 International Children's Digital Library; www.icdlbooks.org.

This is one of the most exciting current developments in the field of electronic children's books. Begun in 2002 and sponsored by the Human-Computer Interaction Laboratory at the University of Maryland and the Internet Archive in San Francisco, this agency hopes to make a library of international children's literature available free across the globe via the Internet. At present about 400 books are available in about 20 languages (about half are in English). It is hoped that by 2010 there will be 10,000 volumes available. Many of the present holdings have been taken from established historical collections such as the Baldwin Library at the University of Florida and the Library of Congress. The site is attractive and easy to search and use (it was designed to be used independently by children).

1247   Library of Congress's American Memory Web Site; http://memory.loc.gov.

Although this is not geared to children's literature, it is an outstanding collection of about 100 digitized collections of primary sources that represent more than 7.5 million documents. Click on "Literature" as a subject and you will find important authors and titles in the history of American children's literature, such as Louisa May Alcott.

1248   The On-Line Books Page; http://onlinebooks.library.upenn.edu/.

This site provides access to more than 20,000 books that can be read on-screen. Founded by John Mark Ockerbloom in 1993, the Books Page features both adult and children's classics. Only books that are in the public domain and in English have been digitized. The site can be browsed by author, title, or subject. In 1998, this site started indexing major serials archives. Also included are links to other directories and archives of online texts and special subject lists, e.g., Newbery Award Books Online.

1249   Project Gutenberg; www.gutenberg.org.

This is an online database that contains full-text electronic versions of more than 15,000 books, all of which can be read without charge. Most of the works were published before 1923. It was founded by Michael Hart and contains such favorites as *A Christmas Carol, Red Badge of Courage*, and *The War of the Worlds*.

B. LISTSERVS

1250   CHILD_LIT; www.rci.rutgers.edu/~mjoseph/childlit/about.html.

The purpose of this listserv, or online discussion group, is to examine "the theory and criticism of literature for children and young adults." Founded by Michael Joseph of Rutgers University, it has many professors as members as well as other professionals interested in these topics.

1251   KIDLIT-L.

This is an interesting online discussion group or listserv dealing with children's literature. Founded by Prude Stelling at Binghamton University in New York State, it site can be reached by e-mail at listserv@ bingvmb.cc.binghamton.edu.

1252   LM_NET; www.eduref.org/lm_net.

A very active discussion group for school library media specialists worldwide. Its archive can be searched back to 1994.

1253 PUBYAC; www.pubyac.org.

A discussion group in which librarians discuss practical solutions to problems involved in working with children and young adults in public libraries.

C. OTHER NONPRINT RESOURCES

1. Audiobooks

The only up-to-date print directory that lists children's audiobooks is the large two-volume directory (formerly called *Words on Cassette*) ***Books Out Loud: Bowker's Guide to Audiobooks*** (Bowker, 2004, $225 [0-8352-4611-6]). This annual directory includes both adult and juvenile audiobooks and is arranged by title with many different indexes, including author and reader. The comparable title for videocassettes and DVDs is the four-volume ***Bowker Complete Video Directory*** (Bowker, 2004, $380 [0-8352-4622-1]).

The following is a short list of companies that produce and sell audiobooks of children's and young adult literature. The list is by no means complete but it does supply the names of the companies that produce the largest number of titles annually. For each, an address is given and either a Web site or telephone number or both.

1254 Audio Book Contractors, Box 40115, Washington, DC 20016. (202) 363-3429.

1255 Audio Bookshelf, 44 Ocean View Dr., Middletown, RI 02842. (800) 234-1713; www.audiobookshelf.com.

1256 Blackstone Audio Books, Box 969, Ashland, OR 97520. (800) 729-2665; www.blackstoneaudio.com.

1257 Bolinda Audio Books, Shelton Pointe, 2 Trap Falls Rd., Suite 113, Shelton, CT 06484. (888) 235-2019; www.bolinda.com.

Books on Tape *see* Listening Library.

1258 Brilliance Audio, 1704 Eaton Dr., PO Box 887, Grand Haven, MI 49417. (800) 648-2312; www.brillianceaudio.com.

1259 Chivers Audiobooks, 1 Lafayette Rd., Box 1450, Hampton, NH 03843. (800) 621-0182.

1260   Full Cast Audio, 618 Westcott Ave., Syracuse, NY 13210.
(800) 871-6809; www.fullcastaudio.com.

1261   HarperAudio, HarperCollins, 10 E. 53rd St., New York, NY 10022;
(212) 207 7491; www.harpercollins.com (choose the Audio channel).

1262   High Windy Audio, PO Box 553, Fairview, NC 28730.
(800) 637-8679; www.highwindy.com.

1263   HighBridge Audio, 33 S. Sixth St., CC-2205, Minneapolis, MN 55402.
(800) 755-8532; www.highbridgeaudio.com.

1264   Houghton Mifflin, 181 Ballardville St., Wilmington, MA 01887.
(800) 225-3362; www.houghtonmifflinbooks.com.

1265   Library of Congress, 101 Independence Ave. S.E., Washington, DC
20540; (202) 707-5000; www.loc.gov (publications include *Talking
Book Topics* and *Braille Book Review*).

1266   Listen and Live Audio, PO Box 817, Roseland, NJ 07068;
(800) 653-9400; www.listenandlive.com.

1267   Listening Library, 400 Hahn Rd., Westminster, MD 21157;
(800) 541-5525; www.listeninglibrary.com.

Little, Brown *see* Time Warner Bookmark.

1268   Penguin Audiobooks, 375 Hudson St., New York, NY 10014;
(800) 788-6262; www.penguinputnam.com.

1269   Random House Audio Publishing Group, 1540 Broadway, New York,
NY 10036; (800) 733-3000; www.randomhouse.com.

1270   Recorded Books, 270 Skipjack Rd., Prince Frederick, MD 20678;
(800) 638-1304; www.recordedbooks.com.

1271   Simon and Schuster Audio, 1230 Ave. of the Americas, New York, NY
10020; (212) 698 7664; www.simonsaysaudio.com.

1272 Spoken Arts, 195 South White Rock Road, Holmes, NY   12531; (800) 326-4090; www.spokenartsmedia.com.

1273 Time Warner Bookmark, 1271 Ave. of the Americas, New York, NY 10020; (800) 759-0190; www.twbookmark.com/audiobooks/index.html.

1274 Weston Woods (Scholastic), 12 Oakwood Ave., Norwalk, CT 06850; (800) 290 7531; www.scholastic.com/westonwoods.

2. Online Bookstores

There are hundreds of online booksellers in addition to the well-known Amazon (www.amazon.com) and Barnes and Noble (www.bn.com). To search for booksellers by category—general, antiquarian, children's and so forth—use Bowker's Bookwire service (www.bookwire.com/bookwire/booksellers.html). For rare books, the following two sites are good starting places:

1275 Alibris; www.alibris.com.

Alibris is also one of the world's largest sources of rare, used, and hard-to-find books.

1276 Rare Books on the Web; www.geocities.com/albertmasters/ rarebooksontheweb.html.

Compiled by Albert Masters, this page provides links to libraries, special collections, book dealers, book collectors, digitized reproductions of texts, and general sites about rare books.

NAME INDEX

Names of authors, editors, organizations, collections, awards and prizes, publishers, and book dealers can be found in the Name Index. Titles of books, periodicals, annuals, and Web sites are listed in the Title Index. References are to entry numbers, not page numbers. Authors are listed by last name; awards and other entries are usually listed by first name.

I

J

L

M

S

University of Illinois, Education and Social Science Library, 1183

University of North Carolina at Greensboro, Walter Clinton Jackson Library, 1184

University of Reading: The Library, 1146

University of South Florida, 1172

University of Southern Mississippi's de Grummond Award, 740

V

Vaillancourt, Renee J. *Bare Bones Young Adult Services,* 864

Vandergrift, Kay E., ed. *Mosaics of Meaning,* 185

Ways of Knowing, 186

Van Meter, Vandelia L. *America in Historical Fiction,* 403

Van Orden, Phyllis J. *The Collection Program in Schools,* 286

Selecting Books for the Elementary School Library Media Center, 285

Viguers, Ruth Hill. *Margin for Surprise,* 127

Virginia State Reading Association Young Readers Award, 786

Volunteer State Book Award, 787

Volz, Bridget Dealy. *Junior Genreflecting,* 375

von Franz, Marie-Louise. *The Interpretation of Fairy Tales,* 115

W

W. H. Smith Book Awards, 687

Wade, Barrie. *A Guide to Children's Poetry for Teachers and Librarians,* 413

Wadham, Rachel L. *Bringing Fantasy Alive for Children and Young Adults,* 388

Wadham, Tim. *Bringing Fantasy Alive for Children and Young Adults,* 388

Programming with Latino Children's Materials, 583

Wagner, Heather Lear. *Jane Austen,* 994

Waichulaitis, Trisha. *Ready-to-Go Storytimes,* 913

Walker, Barbara J. *Developing Christian Fiction Collections for Children and Adults,* 500

Walter, Virginia. *Children and Libraries,* 817

Teens and Libraries, 865

Wandsworth Public Libraries, 1147

Ward, Marilyn. *Voice from the Margins,* 363

Warner, Marina. *From the Beast to the Blonde,* 187

No Go the Bogeyman, 188

Washington Post Children's Book Guild Nonfiction Award, 741

Waterson, Elizabeth. *Children's Literature in Canada,* 85

Watson, Victor. *The Cambridge Guide to Children's Books in English,* 76

Talking Pictures, 109

Wayne State University. Purdy/Kresge Library, 1173

Webber, Desiree. *The Kid's Book Club,* 826

Travel the Globe, 567

Webster, Joan Parker. *Teaching Through Culture,* 584

Weiner, Stephen. *The 101 Best Graphic Novels,* 393

Weiss, Jaqueline Shachter. *Profiles in Children's Literature,* 77

Weiss, Mitch. *Children Tell Stories,* 911

Weissman, Annie. *Do Tell! Storytelling for You and Your Students,* 911

West, Mark I. *A Children's Literature Tour of Great Britain,* 102

Everyone's Guide to Children's Literature, 78

Psychoanalytic Responses to Children's Literature, 171

Trust Your Children, 891

Western Australia Young Readers Book Award, 646

Westfahl, Gary. *Science Fiction, Children's Literature, and Popular Culture,* 389

Weston Woods (Scholastic), 1274

Whalen, Sharla Scannell. *The Betsy-Tacy Companion,* 1010

Whitbread Children's Book of the Year Award, 688

White, Donna R. *A Century of Welsh Myth in Children's Literature,* 103

White, Kerry. *Australian Children's Fiction,* 263

Y

Z

TITLE INDEX

Titles of books, periodicals, annuals, and Web sites are listed in the Title Index. Names of authors, editors, organizations, collections, awards and prizes, publishers, and book dealers can be found in the Name Index. References are to entry numbers, not page numbers.

A

G

H

O

S

Subject Index

Names of authors, editors, organizations, collections, awards and prizes, publishers, and book dealers can be found in the Name Index. Titles of books, periodicals, annuals, and Web sites are listed in the Title Index. The use of the term "General" in a subject heading indicates that the book is suitable for more than one age group (e.g., both children and young adults) or that it covers several aspects of the subject. References are to entry numbers, not page numbers.

R

About the Author

JOHN T. GILLESPIE is former Dean and Instructor of Library Science at Long Island University, New York. He has authored numerous books in areas of library management, school libraries, and children's and young adult literature.